Connections:

Memoirs of an American Historian in the Communist East Bloc

Claude R. Foster

Edited by Brenda L Gaydosh

Alpha
Academic
Press

Published in the United States of America

COPYRIGHT DISCLAIMER

Connections: Memoirs of an American Historian in the Communist East Bloc

First Edition: October 2019
Alpha Academic Press
Paperback ISBN-13: 978-1-948210-09-6

Book Cover Photograph by Allan Hailstone

Table of Contents

Terms and Abbreviations

Betreurerin	Chaperones
BRD (FRG)	Bundesrepublik Deutschland (Federal Republic of Germany) – West Germany
CDU	Christian Democratic Union, political party in both East and West Germany, continuing after reunification
Comecon	Council for Mutual Economic Assistance (1949-1991); an economic organization of the countries of the East Bloc, led by the Soviet Union
DDR (GDR)	Deutsche Demokratische Republik (German Democratic Republic) – East Germany
Gymnasium	Most advanced of the German secondary schools; term originates from Greek
Intershop	Government-run stores in the DDR where with Western currency, one could buy high-quality goods
Losungen	Published booklet of daily Scripture readings; literal translation mean "watchwords"
Konditorei	Confectionary Shop
Prague Spring	Short period of political reform in Czechoslovakia (1968) under the leadership of Alexander Dubček
Stasi	Staatssicherheitsdienst (State Security in the DDR)
SED	Sozialistische Einheitspartei Deutschlands (Socialist Unity Party of Germany) – governing Marxist-Leninist Party of the DDR
Christliches Hospiz	Christian Hospice (Christian lodging for travelers)
Volkskammer	Unicameral legislature of the DDR
Willkommen	Welcome

MAP - Bundesrepublik Deutschland / Deutsche Demokratische Republik

MAP – Czechoslovakia / Poland

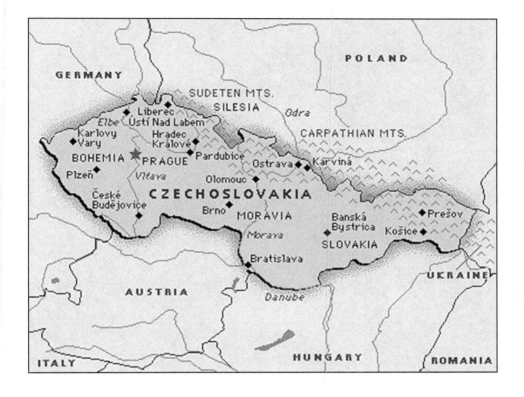

PREFACE

The first time I saw Dr. Claude Foster was fall 1996, when I enrolled in his colleague's "The Holocaust" graduate course. I was embarking on a second career, away from mathematics and toward history. Dr. Irene Shur had invited Dr. Foster to speak to her class. Immediately I was impressed with his wit, passion for teaching, and interests (common with mine). From an early age growing up Catholic in the 1960s, I had developed an affinity for martyrs. Here was a professor who had recently published a biography of a Christian martyr of the Nazi era – Paul Schneider. I wanted to know more about Dr. Foster's research and I wanted to take his courses – "The Reformation" and "History of Germany" – which I did in the next two years. In that time, I realized what I wanted to do with the next years of my life. I finished my MA in History at West Chester University and earned a PhD in History from American University, writing my dissertation about Father Bernhard Lichtenberg (suggested by Claude), a Roman Catholic priest and martyr of the Nazi era. In that time, Claude and I became friends and then colleagues, as I taught as an adjunct at West Chester University.

My comradery with Claude seemed to bring me full circle back to the day when Sister asked us Sunday school pupils, "What would you do if the communists came to America and told you that you could no longer believe in God?" If I could find Sister now, I would thank her for scaring me to death at that time. She indicated that the communists would kill us if we held to our faith. From that point, although I might not have known the word "martyr," I knew that the concept would never leave me. Thus, when I met Dr. Foster, I felt a "connection."

Claude traveled to East Germany (DDR) for the first time in 1964. He continued to visit the DDR and ultimately other parts of the Communist East Bloc for the next twenty-five years. There, he developed connections with people - on benches, on trains, in the cafes, in the streets, in academic settings – and he connected his newfound friends with others. In the Communist East Bloc, he developed lifelong friendships, and European scholars welcomed his input (and translations) at conferences. In the following pages (Memoirs), Claude writes about his experiences with the people of the Communist East Bloc. He does not simply show us how the people lived and what they thought about their lives, but he helps us feel their joy, pain, struggles, and frustrations. In addition to the stories and history, you will experience Claude's poetic gift, not only in poems he records here, but also in the manner that he writes.

As an associate professor of history, I realize the significance of Claude's memoirs as primary sources and it is my hope that many students, who have not yet grasped the essence of the Cold War, will reflect on the lives of the people in these pages. From Claude Foster's memoirs, we acquire a true understanding of life under Communism during the Cold War.

Brenda Gaydosh

Author, *Bernhard Lichtenberg: Roman Catholic Priest and Martyr of the Nazi Regime* (2017)

PROLOGUE

How I came to write my memoirs

On July 22, 2002, in the beautiful Weimar City Hall, I was invited by Weimar's mayor to place my signature in the Golden Book of the City. Mayor Volkhardt Germer had read the Paul Schneider biography I published in 1995, *The Buchenwald Apostle: A Sourcebook on the German Church Struggle*, and he was impressed by the effort that I had made to tell the story of a brave Protestant pastor to my countrymen. Pastor Paul Schneider, a member of the Confessing Church, was murdered at Buchenwald (outside of Weimar) on July 18, 1939. The Hänssler Verlag published a German language translation of the biography in 2001, selling all ten thousand copies of the book. Brigitte Otterpohl, who had translated the biography into the German language, also had informed Mayor Germer of my efforts each summer to bring support from the United States to churches and individual families during the DDR days. The Weimar mayor read the biography and considered it, "a significant contribution to German historiography." Weimar residents, especially the clergy, informed the mayor of the benefits they had received during the DDR period from the American tourists led by Professor Foster. No doubt, it was the letter from Manfred and Brigitte that set the matter in motion.

I only learned of the recommendations after having received the letter from Weimar's mayor, Dr. Volkhardt Germer on June 3, 2002:

> Very Honorable Professor Foster:
>
> The Day for honoring you—for your promotion of German/American contacts and for your indefatigable engagement on behalf of Weimar—draws closer and I do not want to miss the opportunity of personally inviting you to Weimar.
>
> At a reception on July 22, 2002, in the main chamber of the Weimar City Hall, you are invited to place your signature in the Golden Book of the City of Weimar and thereby preserve the memory of this event for posterity.
>
> It will be a great joy for me to welcome you in Weimar on this date.
>
> With friendly greetings, Dr. Volkhardt Germer

On July 22, as I sat at the table on which the Golden Book lay in the beautiful Renaissance Chamber of the Weimar City Hall, I was curious as to who else might have signed the book. I turned back some blank pages until I came to the signature Vladimir Putin. On June 5, 2009, the media reported that President Barack Obama, during his visit to Buchenwald, also had signed the Golden Book of the City of Weimar. I found it amusing that an unknown American historian should be sandwiched between Putin and Obama.

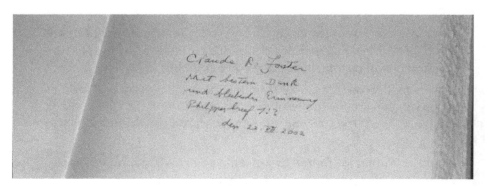

A champagne reception followed with about one hundred of my German friends and acquaintances in attendance, as well as friends from Poland and the United States. Why was such a high honor bestowed upon me? Beginning in the early 1970s, each summer I guided groups of my countrymen to the German Reformation sites. We resided in Weimar where I had made many friends. Most of the people who accompanied me came from Christian congregations. I told my countrymen about the needs of the churches in the DDR. Each person took a money gift from his or her congregation. At that time, the dollar was very strong in the East Bloc. The money transfer to congregations in the DDR had to be made in secret. Each member of our group also took gifts of clothing that we distributed in the families that we visited.

On the evening of the same day on which I had inscribed my name into the Golden Book of the City of Weimar, I was invited to address the Weimar Goethe Society. The theme I selected was "An American in Communist East Germany." In my address, I employed many anecdotes of my experiences in East Germany derived from the many summers I had resided in that state. The audience responded to my remarks with great appreciation and urged me to publish the presentation. Thus, I wrote my memoirs...

INTRODUCTION

Before embarking on the narrative describing my experiences in the Communist East Bloc in general and my experience in Communist East Germany in particular, I describe my introduction to the Federal Republic of Germany and to my encounter with Europe.

Upon the recommendation of my two major professors at the University of Delaware in Newark, Delaware, where I received my Master of Arts Degree in history in June 1955, I was granted a Fulbright Scholarship at the University of Freiburg for the academic year 1955-1956. During the year of preparation, I studied intensively the German language. From the public library, I checked out volumes of German language records and spent part of each day listening to them. I reached a point where I could recite the recordings from memory. I also took some lessons at the Berlitz Language School in Wilmington. I had been admitted to graduate study for a Ph.D. at the University of Pennsylvania, but I decided to defer my study there until after my Fulbright year in Germany. The Fulbright Grantees, destined for Germany, set sail from New York on the "Italia" in August 1955. In order to wave farewell to my wife, Lois, and me at dockside, Lois' parents and my parents traveled with us to New York City.

One of the highlights of our 4-week orientation in Bad Hönef was the meeting with Chancellor Konrad Adenauer in his rose garden that marked the entrance to his home in Rhöndorf. In 1949, at age 73, Adenauer had been elected chancellor (by one vote—his own) of the new state of the Federal Republic of Germany. On a crisp September morning, before he was chauffeured to his office in nearby Bonn, the Fulbright Grantees were invited to meet with the Chancellor in his garden. Our orientation supervisor suggested that we present the Chancellor with a bouquet of select roses. As the roses were presented to the Chancellor (a rose connoisseur), he smiled and said, "If you give me roses, you may visit me every day."

At the end of orientation, the Fulbright Grantees set out for their respective universities. About ten of us were bound for Freiburg in Breisgau. The circa 4-hour train ride brought us into the heart of the Black Forest. After the train pulled out of the Karlsruhe station, we noticed that the landscape gradually ascended and it was forested with evergreens. Through the *Experiment in International Living*, the first month's housing in Freiburg had been arranged with German families. Lois and I were assigned to the Rosenstihl family. The Rosenstihl residence was very specious and was located on the outskirts of Freiburg in the precinct of Littenweiler. In the rear of the house was a riding school and stalls, which housed the horses. The elderly matriarch of the family, Frau Ida Schaller Rosenstihl, had three daughters who resided with her. Lois and I were given a very large room on the second floor. There was running water in the room, but the bath and toilette were outside the room at the end of the corridor. Chairs, a table, and a double bed constituted the furniture.

We matriculated at the university. I enrolled for courses in history and for courses of instruction in the German language. Although I had a sufficient vocabulary in German to understand lectures on historical subjects, I wanted to become fluent in the language. Lois also enrolled in the German language courses. At the end of the month, rather than seek new accommodations, Lois and I asked the Rosenstihl family members if we might continue to reside with them for the duration of our stay in Freiburg. The family seemed happy to comply with our request. Therefore, for the remainder of our sojourn in Freiburg, we resided at the Rosenstihl Riding School and took breakfast and the evening meal with the family. Living with a German family, where the German language only was spoken, was an excellent supplement to our German language courses at the university.

During the spring vacation in 1956, we joined a 3-week student itinerary to Greece. For a person raised in modest circumstances and the only one in his family, up to that point, to have received a university education, the privilege to study in Germany and to travel to Greece was overwhelming. We departed Freiburg for Italy, April 4, on the 5:08 a.m. train and arrived in Brindisi at 10:00 a.m. on April 5. There were twenty-four people in our group. The total cost for the package tour, exclusive of ship passage, was 455 Marks per person. Our guide was Peter Butz, an assistant at the Freiburg University Zoological Department. Ever thrifty, and convinced that the weather now was mild enough, I booked deck class passage on the ship, the Angelica, from Brindisi to Piraeus. I assumed that we would be furnished deck chairs and blankets. When we arrived in Brindisi, it became clear that deck class literally meant deck class. When we noticed farmers and shepherds boarding the ship with foul and livestock, and occupying most of the space designated for deck class passengers, we quickly changed our accommodations to economy cabin class, a cabin that we shared with other passengers.

The ship docked at Corfu where some passengers got off but the number of farmers and shepherds, with foul and livestock traveling deck class, increased. Sailing through the Corinthian Canal was an exciting experience. We could almost touch the sides of the canal from either side of the deck, and the high earthen walls extended far above the top of our ship. It was as if we were in a roofless tunnel. In Piraeus, Athen's port, we left the ship and traveled the short distance to Greece's capital. This spring visit to Greece took us to Delphi, Sparta, Olympia, Mycenae, Corinth and many other sites associated with classical antiquity. On the Acropolis and the Areopagus, standing on these hills from which much of our western culture was engendered, we sensed that we were walking in the footsteps of Draco, Solon, Cleisthenes, Thucydides, Socrates, Plato, Aristotle, and the Apostle Paul.

On the return trip, the train from Brindisi was crowded. We had reserved seats, but many native Italians had to stand in the corridors. Just outside our compartment door stood a young mother, cradling an infant in her arms. I offered the young woman my seat. She was very grateful and soon she and her child were asleep. Hours later, I felt a tug at my elbow. I had dozed while standing in the corridor. The train had stopped in Bari. Many passengers got off the train to make purchases on the railroad platform, and then they returned to the train. The woman had brought me a cup of espresso. Without thinking that I had had nothing to eat for many hours, I drank the espresso. Soon I was wide awake! The young woman thanked me before getting off the train in Bari. I returned to my seat.

My major professor at Freiburg University was Dr. Gerhard Ritter. Professor Ritter's lectures on the Reformation were held in the Aula, the largest auditorium at the university, which could seat several hundred auditors. At a reception, I had opportunity to speak with Professor Ritter. When he learned of my interest in Reformation studies and that I planned to complete my dissertation at the University of Pennsylvania, he invited me to visit him in his home on Mozart Strasse, near the Freiburg City Park. At that meeting, in his study, Professor Ritter introduced me to many sources for my study of the Reformation.

In the summer of 1956, Lois and I returned to the United States. I began my doctoral curriculum at the University of Pennsylvania. Because most graduate courses were offered in the late afternoon or in the evening, I could accept invitations to substitute teach in the Wilmington Public Schools. Fortunately for me, shortly before I began my graduate studies, Professor Otakar Odložilík, via London University and Columbia University, also had arrived at the University of Pennsylvania from the Charles University in Prague. At the establishment of the Communist regime in Czechoslovakia, Professor Odložilík, in 1948, emigrated. After one year of graduate study at the University of Pennsylvania (1956-1957), and having decided to write my dissertation on Johannes Bünderlin, an almost unknown reformer of the sixteenth century, I chose to accept the invitation offered to me by the Baden/Württemberg Superintendent of Education, Dr. Kaspar, to teach the English language at the Johannes Kepler Gymnasium in Freiburg, beginning in the autumn of 1957. I had met Superintendent Kaspar during my study at the University of Freiburg. Residing for an extended period again in Germany, and in a position in which I could financially sustain myself, I believed that I could locate the universities or archives where Bünderlin's four books [published in Strasbourg in 1529-1530], were to be found. Finding these books and writing a commentary on them would be a major part of my dissertation. Lois returned to Chattanooga, Tennessee to reside with her parents during my absence. Early in 1958, Lois' mother broke both wrists in a nasty fall. It was most fortunate that Lois could care for her mother during the recuperation period. I sailed on the Maasdam in the late summer of 1957 and arrived in Freiburg in early September.

I reported to the Johannes Kepler Gymnasium and received my teaching schedule. I was pleased to note that I had no Friday or Saturday classes. The four-day schedule gave me desirable weekend flexibility. At first, I resided in a hotel near the gymnasium, but I realized that such accommodations over time would be too expensive. Each afternoon, after class, I searched for a residence. Because Freiburg had an expanding university population, finding a room was very difficult. One day, after classes, Dr. Gerhard Fisch, a colleague at Kepler, and I drove in Dr. Fisch's car to have lunch in a nearby restaurant. As we proceeded along Hermann Straße, I noticed a plaque on one of the buildings which read "Evangelisches Stift: Carl Mez Lehrling Heim" (Carl Mez Internat for Apprentices). Dr. Fisch parked the car and I went into the building. After entering the lobby, immediately to the right was the office. The door was open. A man sat at a desk. I introduced myself and explained that I was seeking a long-term accommodation. The man to whom I spoke, Heinrich Lindenberg, was the director of the Heim. Herr Lindenberg was short of stature, with a military bearing, and with no wasted words in his communication. I would learn that he was the Napoleon of his domain. In my introduction, I told Herr Lindenberg that I was a US citizen, but not that I was a teacher at the Kepler Gymnasium. He inquired concerning my age. I told him that I was twenty-nine years old. Herr Lindenberg then said that I was too old for accommodation in the apprentice home. I replied that it seemed odd to me that age would be a factor in gaining admission, for surely there were apprentices older than I was. It was 1:00 p.m. Herr Lindenberg instructed me to return at 4:00 p.m. His afternoon siesta was about to begin. As I walked out of the office into the lobby, Herr Lindenberg followed me. At a prominent position on the lobby wall was a plaque that read, "This house, destroyed during the war, was rebuilt through the generosity of Christians in the United States." Knowing that Herr Lindenberg was behind me and observing my position, I stood for a long time regarding the plaque, and then, without glancing back, I exited the lobby.

When I returned to the Carl Mez Heim at 4:00 p.m., Herr Lindenberg offered me two possibilities—a room on the ground floor that I would share with another person [in the Heim, two persons shared a large room with two bunks and two desks], or a single accommodation in a very small room on the fourth floor, which Herr Lindenberg described as a "broom closet." Because I preferred to live alone and because I liked to read until late at night, a practice that could prove disturbing to a roommate, I chose the "broom closet."

The meal schedule included Breakfast, 6:00 to 8:00; Midday meal,

12:00 to 2:00; Supper, 6:00 to 7:00. The main meal was the midday meal. Ersatz coffee was the beverage at breakfast. At midday and supper, hot tea was available. Soup was served at the midday meal with the exception of Saturday when Eintoph (a thick stew), a stew made up of the week's leftovers was served. We usually sat eight at a table in the large dining hall. I sat at the first table with Herr Lindenberg and Frau Grete Lindenberg. Herr Lindenberg sat at the head of the front table from where he had a commanding view of all tables and diners. Frau Lindenberg sat next to her husband and I usually sat next to her. I noticed that the residents were hesitant to take the seat next to Frau Lindenberg; therefore, that seat fell to me by default. Opposite me sat Ernst Hermann Hützen who was to become a life-long friend.

Although, after learning that I was a teacher at the Johannes Kepler Gymnasium caused Herr Lindenberg to become friendlier, it was an event in mid-October that raised my stock dramatically. When the daily mail arrived for the circa 50 residents of the Carl Mez Heim, Herr Lindenberg placed the mail on the wide window shelf. Each day, upon entering the lobby, the first thing we did was to check to see if we had mail. I knew that Professor Karl Barth at the Basel University conducted an evening seminar. Basel, Switzerland is only a one-hour train ride from Freiburg. Because I very much wanted to participate in that seminar, I had written Professor Barth requesting permission to attend. Via a postcard, Professor Barth then responded to my request. On Thursday, October 17, when I returned to the Carl Mez Heim from the Kepler Gymnasium, Herr Lindenberg excitedly approached me and exclaimed, "Herr Foster, you have post from Professor Karl Barth!!! You are permitted to participate in his seminar!!!" Of course, the only way that Herr Lindenberg could have known of the permission was by reading my post.

Professor Barth, the main author of the Barmen Confession (May 1934), the apologia that guided the Confessing Church in its resistance to Adolf Hitler and the national church headed by Hitler's sycophant, Ludwig Müller, was the most esteemed Protestant theologian in Europe. Herr Lindenberg was quite overwhelmed that one of his residents—the almost rejected resident—was invited to participate in Professor Barth's seminar.

On Tuesday, November 12, 1957, the US Secretary of State, John Foster Dulles, announced plans to deploy medium range missiles in Western Europe. This announcement set off a huge debate in Germany. In the Kepler Gymnasium teachers' lounge, I was caught in the middle of this debate. Some of my colleagues agreed with the secretary that medium range missiles in Western Europe, and specifically in West Germany, would act as a deterrent against Soviet ambitions to expand westwards, but other colleagues pointed out that deploying missiles in Western Europe would provoke the Soviet Union and could lead to hostilities. "In any such European conflict between the United States and the Soviet Union, Germany would be the battleground," they argued. Finally, on Saturday, February 1, 1958, the US Jupiter rocket carried the satellite "Explorer I" into orbit and the United States had entered the space race with the Soviet Union. Wernher von Braun, Hitler's V2 rocket expert, now having changed employers, warned, however, that the Soviet Union was at least five years ahead of the United States in rocket and space technology.

One day at the end of one class and in the interval before the next class was scheduled to begin, I went to the teachers' lounge. When I returned to the classroom, I discovered in the open textbook, which I had left on the lectern, a postcard-size photograph of Adolf Hitler. Among the thirty-five pupils in the room, there was absolute silence as the audience anxiously waited to see my reaction. Knowing that the pupils expected me to become incensed and to react in anger and to demand that the culprit who had placed the photograph in my text identify himself, I deliberately waited for a long time, fixing my gaze on the photo, refusing to show any sign of shock or anger. After a long pause, I lifted the photograph from the textbook and displayed it so all could see it. In so doing, I said, "I don't know who placed this photograph in my book, but whoever it was, I wish to thank him. I've always wanted such a photograph." At this remark, the disappointment registered on the faces of the pupils told me that I had ruined their fun.

After Herr Lindenberg had read the postcard that Professor Karl Barth had written to me, I was accepted into the inner circle. Herr Lindenberg, Hermann Hützen, [an engineer residing in the Carl Mez Heim with whom I became friends and with whom I remain in friendship at this 2012 writing], and I occasionally would walk the short distance to the Black Forest Inn just around the corner from the Carl Mez Heim. Because there was an evening Stammtisch (a favorite table at which one or a group prefers to sit) in one corner of the Black Forest Inn where a group of men met on a regular basis, and from which table the volume of noise frequently drowned out conversation, Herr Lindenberg, Hermann Hützen and I selected a table on the opposite side of the inn from where the Stammtisch stood. One evening as we sat drinking the excellent, local Ganter beer, Herr Lindenberg related his adventure at the end of the war, "My battalion surrendered in Austria to the Soviet Army. There were thousands of prisoners being herded into barbwire enclosures. There was no place to house us and no food to feed us. There were many trucks and jeeps coming and going. Pandemonium prevailed. Before our unit was herded toward the enclosure, I seized the opportunity to slip into the bushes. I waited until darkness fell and then by moonlight, I started to walk westwards. Sleeping in the forest by day and walking by night, eating whatever I could find, berries and occasionally a morsel given to me by a compassionate farmer, I gradually made my way from the Soviet-controlled region into areas under British command. My wife, son and daughters, having had no news from me, were astonished when, one day, disheveled and malnourished, I stood at their door in Hamburg. That our family could be reunited after my escape from the Red Army captivity and my long, tedious trek from Austria to Hamburg, and in Hamburg to find my family in a city which, on July 24, 1943, had been fifty percent destroyed by a British air raid, in Operation Gomorrah, and in which raid 30,000 people, including 5,500 children had been killed—under these conditions to be reunited with my family was like a miracle for us." Herr Lindenberg continued, "As I regarded the massive destruction in Hamburg, I remembered the destruction our Luftwaffe earlier had inflicted on Warsaw, Rotterdam, and Coventry, and the words of our Lord were confirmed in my conviction: 'He who takes the sword, perishes with the sword.' With our bare hands, as survivors in every major German city did, we carried the debris to an open area where, out of the rubble, we created mountains. Today, children play on these mountains, and in winter, the Rubble Mountains become ski and sled slopes."

Herr Lindenberg ruled the Carl Mez Heim in strict discipline. Only residents above a certain age received a house key. All others had to be in house by 10:00 p.m. or be locked out and wait and hope that a resident with a key might come along. Before breakfast, on Sunday morning, at 8:00 o'clock, the residents assembled in the large lobby and sang a hymn before entering the dining hall. Those residents who preferred to remain in bed received no breakfast. Each resident [two to a room] was responsible for keeping his room tidy. Workshops in the basement afforded opportunity of exercising craft skills. The office was equipped with bookshelves, which contained a limited number of volumes, mostly historical novels, biographies, church history and atlases. Various daily newspapers and magazines also were available.

After the Sunday morning breakfast, a few of us residents accompanied Herr Lindenberg to the nearby Lutheran Church for the morning worship service. Each Sunday, exactly ten minutes before the service began, Professor Gerhard Ritter entered the sanctuary and took his seat, always in the same pew. In connection with Sunday worship, I found somewhat disconcerting the sign at the head of a narrow thoroughfare that led through a quiet, residential neighborhood. Apparently, this avenue was used as a shortcut by motorists seeking to avoid a longer, and more circuitous artery leading to the Autobahn. In order to preserve their Sunday rest, the neighborhood residents had persuaded the City Council to pass an ordinance banning auto traffic through their neighborhood on Sunday.

Occasionally, Herr Lindenberg arranged day trips for us, usually on a Saturday when we were free from our work schedule. One such trip made a deep impression on me – a visit to Verdun and to the World War I battlefields in the Vosges Mountains. Early one Saturday morning, a large bus parked before our residence. The bus driver had been briefed by Herr Lindenberg concerning our itinerary. We traveled to Hartmannsweilerkopf, a Vosges mountaintop, bitterly contested in World War I. Though still recognizable, rusted barbwire and concrete machine gun and artillery bunkers, the ugly scars of war, gradually were being healed by time's recuperative power and nature's encroaching foliage. Out of powdery cement crevices that once housed instruments of death, green vines and polychromatic flowers joyfully proclaimed life. On this high plateau, we saw a military cemetery. French and German soldiers, who fell on this terrain, were buried in fraternal ranks under the very sod for which they once had contended.

I have pleasant memories of my residence in the Carl Mez Heim. While residing there, I enjoyed my teaching tenure at the Kepler and at the Saint Ursula Gymnasia, respectively. The Carl Mez Heim, located behind the beautiful gothic cathedral, only a fifteen-minute walk from my residence, afforded me convenient access to the Freiburg University, where I continued to do research in the history seminar library. It was while I resided in the Heim that my friend, Hermann Hützen became engaged to Ingeborg Röber, the beautiful young woman who supervised the kitchen staff for both the Carl Mez Heim and the Martha Heim [the residence for female apprentices, located next to the Carl Mez Heim]. Occasionally on their hikes in the Black Forest, Hermann and Inge invited me to accompany them. One of our favorite trails led through the Black Forest to the Münster Valley and to the Benedictine chapel built by the Irish/Scottish monk Trupert in 604. Another favorite goal for a hike from Freiburg was to the village of Staufen and to the inn in which, according to legend, the devil claimed the soul of Professor Faustus. We usually walked through the forest to Staufen, a five- to six-hour walk. After a glass of the famous Badische wine in the inn, we returned to Freiburg on the local train. Hermann and Inge married on August 26, 1961. On subsequent visits to Freiburg, I visited them in their home. They had two children, Stefan and Claudia. Inge died of cancer on May 21, 1981. In 1987, Hermann married Rosi Toussaint, who taught the French language in a Freiburg Gymnasium. Hermann and Rosi visited us in the US in 1987 and in 2009. Whenever I return to Germany, I stop for a visit with Hermann and Rosi in their home in Kirchzarten in the Black Forest.

In July of 1958, I returned to the United States and once again took up my graduate study at the University of Pennsylvania. Each summer I returned to Freiburg to study and to continue to search for sources related to the subject of my dissertation, Johannes Bünderlin. Because, during those summer months, I was completely absorbed in preparing my dissertation, Lois preferred to spend that period with her parents in Chattanooga. My friendship with Herr Lindenberg having been consolidated, whenever I returned to Freiburg, the "broom closet" was reserved for me.

In Freiburg, I had become friends with my language teacher, Dr. Otto Stefan Wehrle. Apart from the language classes that I took with Dr. Wehrle, we also met on Saturday mornings on the cathedral square where, from one of the outside tables of the konditorei, we could observe the bustling marketplace and admire the red sandstone cathedral that, after a rain, appeared refreshed as if after a bath. Dr. Wehrle had a marvelous command of his native language (he also spoke Swedish, French and English). Speaking German with Dr. Wehrle every Saturday for two hours was a wonderful language instruction for me. Dr. Wehrle had many fond memories of the Fulbright students in his class in 1955-1956. "Do you remember," he asked, "the evening I was invited to dinner by the American couple who had rented a flat in suburban Freiburg? You and your wife also were invited that evening. Mrs. Smith, our hostess, was beautiful and charming. The table was attractively set. Mrs. Smith indicated that I should sit next to her. All the dishes were on the table, but there was a certain hesitation. Each one waited for the other to begin. Finally, Mrs. Smith turned to me and said, 'Please, Dr. Wehrle, greifen Sie an.' Her husband laughed. I could feel my face flush at her request, 'please, Dr. Wehrle, attack.' Of course, what she meant to say was 'greifen Sie zu,' which means 'help yourself.' But, after all, at that point, Mrs. Smith had had only a few weeks of instruction in the German language."

During the teaching tenure at the Kepler Gymnasium, I became friends with many colleagues. Some of the friendships last until today. Bernhard Hermann, who taught various subjects at a neighboring school, befriended me. Bernhard invited me to meet his family, Hildegard, his wife, and their 2 sons. Bernhard loved to hike in the Black Forest. We usually started in the morning. Hildegard would drive us to our starting point. Bernhard pointed out the trail we would take and estimated the time Hildegard could pick us up at the end of the trail, in late afternoon or early evening. We took sandwiches and a canteen of water, but usually the trail, at some point, would meander through a village where we could turn in at a Gasthaus for food and drink. The hikes with Bernhard in the beautiful Black Forest are among my fondest memories. Bernhard is jovial and Hildegard, with her easy-going Baden personality, his perfect complement.

One evening after dinner in the Hermann's Littenweiler residence, Bernhard, Hildegard and I sat sharing a bottle of Kaiserstuhl wine. The Kaiserstuhl (the Emperor's Throne, an area of volcanic earth west of Freiburg, near Old Breisach on the Rhine River) has the reputation of being the warmest area of Germany. The ancient Romans saw the region as the perfect vineyard. I had asked Bernhard how the war had impacted him. "Near the end of the war," Bernhard said, "I was among the troops assigned to defend Berlin from the approaching Red Army. At that point, even children, old men and women were conscripted to defend the city. Street to street, we fought in the rubble of Berlin as the Red Army pressed ever closer and shells exploded all around us. There hardly was a building that was not totally or partially destroyed. On naked walls, however, still could be read the fanatical slogans of allegiance: 'Führer befehl; wir folgen' (Leader, command, we follow) and 'Unsere Mauer möge zerbrechen, unsere Herzen nie' (Our walls may collapse, never our hearts)."

Bernhard continued, "One of the more disturbing and heart-wrenching scenes was the sight of Wehrmacht soldiers hanging from lampposts. Because they had decided to surrender, the soldiers were hanged by troops of the fanatical SS units. I was captured by a Red Army unit. Although I held my hands high over my head, I could tell by the actions of my captors that they did not intend to take me prisoner. They threw me up against a wall, raised their weapons and took aim. I uttered a fervent prayer and prepared to die. Just then, a loud voice pierced the air. A Red Army officer, coming upon the scene, ordered the soldiers to lower their weapons. At that time, I did not understand the Russian language. The urgency of the command, however, and the result, which followed, was my first lesson in the Russian language. That my life did not end in the ruins of Berlin against that bullet-pocked wall, I owe to that officer who happened to appear at the right instant. Perhaps in gratitude to him, I later took up the study of Russian and now I am quite proficient in the language."

Each summer (with the exception of 1961 when our son, Stephen, was born), I traveled to Freiburg to continue my studies and to begin the writing of my dissertation. My professor, Otakar Odložilík, noticed that I was registered for only one graduate course. "Mr. Foster," he said, "you'll never complete your curriculum at this rate, and I will be retired before you can submit a dissertation." I told Professor Odložilík that I could not afford to register for more than one class. "We'll have to remedy that situation," he said. Thereupon, Professor Odložilík wrote a recommendation requesting a scholarship for me. The University of Pennsylvania granted me a George Leib Harrison Scholarship, which covered all tuition fees and granted me fifty dollars a month pocket money. In subsequent years, upon Professor Odložilík's recommendation, I was granted university scholarships so that I was able to complete the Ph.D. program with no personal financial cost. Even after I had received the Ph.D. degree, the university granted me a postdoctoral grant, which enabled me to register for graduate courses both in religious studies and in German literature.

In the early morning hours of Sunday, August 13, 1961, the East German government sealed the borders between East and West Germany. Nine days later, the East German state began the erection of the Berlin Wall, a wall that would divide the city until November 9, 1989. From September 1949 to August 1961, almost three million East Germans had "voted with their feet," and had left the Soviet-sponsored DDR to emigrate to the western-sponsored BRD. In June 1961, the rumor that the DDR might seal its borders with the West led to an exodus of 30,000 people. In order to stave off the stampede, Walter Ulbricht gave an international press conference in Leipzig on June 15. A question, probably a "planted" question, was raised concerning the possibility of the DDR sealing its borders with the BRD. Ulbricht responded, "I understand your question to mean that in the BRD there are people who wish that we would mobilize the workers of the capital of the DDR to construct a wall. I know of no such plans. The workers of our city are occupied primarily with constructing housing, and their entire energies are devoted to the task of building. No one has the intention of erecting a wall."

On June 26, 1963, five months before his assassination, President John F. Kennedy visited Berlin. At 9:50 a.m., the presidential plane landed at the Köln/Bonn airport. The Chancellor, Konrad Adenauer, greeted the president, "Your visit, Mr. President, is a political achievement." President Kennedy responded, "Your security is our security; your freedom is our freedom; every attack on your nation is an attack on our nation." President Kennedy told his BRD admirers, "In the long bow from Berlin to Saigon, the United States will defend freedom. We regard this task not only as our duty, but as our prerogative." The president also told the mesmerized masses, "In order to insure the security of your cities, we risk the security of our cities." At 11:35 a.m. on June 26, 1963, President Kennedy stood at the Berlin Wall and looked across the wall at the Brandenburg Gate from which hung huge drapes, blocking his view into East Berlin. Later he presented his famous "I am a Berliner" speech to 400,000 people assembled on the square before the West Berlin City Hall. Referring to the wall that had incarcerated 17,000,000 people living in East Germany, President Kennedy said, "There are those who say that the future belongs to Communism; they should come to Berlin." The president was unable to respond to the question held up on large posters, "When will the wall fall?" Later, on June 29, when Nikita Khrushchev visited East Berlin, he said, "I have read that the American president regarded the wall with great disdain. He doesn't like it. But I love it; I love it very much."

On Tuesday, December 17, 1963, a ray of light flickered in the Berlin darkness. The authorities in East and West Berlin signed an agreement, which, for the first time since August 13, 1961, would permit citizens of West Berlin to visit relatives in East Berlin during the Christmas/New Year period from December 20, 1963 to January 5, 1964. Because I entertained the fond hope of visiting East Germany, I followed these events with great interest. I realized that what occurred on the international stage of world events determined what the individual could and could not do.

My First Visit to the DDR

"We strongly urge you to abandon your plans to travel into the so-called German Democratic Republic" (Communist East Germany). In the summer of 1964, while residing in Freiburg in the Federal Republic of Germany (West Germany), I received this message from the United States Consulate in Stuttgart. The letter from the Consulate was a response to my letter in which I had announced my intention to travel to the German Democratic Republic. In the event of any difficulty I might experience in that state, I wanted the United States Consulate to be aware of my intention and itinerary. The Consulate reinforced its admonition with the dissuasion that I not embark on my journey: "The United States Government has no diplomatic relations with the so-called German Democratic Republic. If you should encounter difficulties while traveling in that region, you are on your own."

In my letter to the Consulate, I had explained that, as a student of the Reformation, I wanted to visit the sites associated with Martin Luther and the German Reformation. Most of those sites are situated on the territory of what, from October 7, 1949 to October 3, 1990, was called the German Democratic Republic. For instance, Luther was born in Eisleben on November 10, 1483 and died in that city on February 18, 1546. When Luther was a youth, his family resided in Mansfeld. As a youth, Luther attended school in Magdeburg in 1497. At age fifteen, Luther was sent to Eisenach as a pupil in the Saint George's Latin School, which he attended from 1498 to 1501. The rebuilt and purported residence of the pupil Martin Luther became a major tourist attraction. In 1501, Luther matriculated at Erfurt University, where he received the Bachelor and Master of Arts Degrees on September 29, 1502 and January 7, 1505, respectively. It was in Stotternheim on July 2, 1505 that Luther experienced the thunderstorm and the lightning strike that provoked his panicked cry, "Saint Anna, help me! I will become a monk." On July 17, 1505, Luther entered the Erfurt Augustinian Friary. He was ordained a priest in Erfurt in 1507, and he celebrated his primiz on May 2, 1507 in the Augustinian Friary Church. Luther earned his doctorate at Wittenberg and became a professor at that university in 1512. It was at Wittenberg that the Ninety-Five Theses were composed and promulgated in 1517. From July 4-14 of 1519, the famous debate with his theological opponent, Johannes Eck, took place in Leipzig. From May 4, 1521 to March 1, 1522, Luther was in seclusion at the Wartburg castle near Eisenach, not far from his paternal ancestral home of Möhra. During this Wartburg residence, Luther translated the New Testament from the Greek language into the German language. Other important German Reformation sites include Weimar, Mühlhausen, Frankenhausen and Schmalkalden, all located on the territory of what was, from 1949 to 1990, the German Democratic Republic.

The political situation in the summer of 1964 was particularly acute. The Cold War provoked crisis after crisis on the world political stage. In the aftermath of World War II and the defeat of Nazi Germany and Japan, the wartime alliance of capitalism and communism was ruptured by the sharp ideological contradiction between the former allies. It was with great disappointment that I read the letter from the consulate. I very much wanted to visit the German Reformation sites, but, at the same time, I did not want to risk being detained by an alien state that had no diplomatic relations with the United States. I had a wife and a 3-year-old son to consider. On the other hand, my correspondence with scholars in the DDR had been congenial, had demonstrated a generous willingness to help me in my research and even expressed pleasure at my indication that I would like to visit. Weighing the grave warning from the US consulate not to risk traveling to East Germany, and being somewhat intimidated by the ominous language, I recovered my composure with the aid of an observation by Emily Dickinson: "If your nerve deny you, go above your nerve," and the German proverb, "To see the sites is worth ten times reading or hearing about them."

On the threshold of making, which at that time appeared to be such a daring decision, I thought of some bold adventures in history far greater than the wager that I was about to assume and I received a new resolve from the challenge stated by Lion Feuchtwanger:

> What good are thoughts
> if they remain only action's seed?
> Sterile the idea never translated into the deed.
> Concept remains a moribund banality
> When never engendered into vitality.

The fact that on Tuesday, March 4, 1964, Soviet interceptors had shot down a US air force plane over Thuringia, Soviet air space, increased tension between the two blocs. The three American pilots bailed out and were taken captive. The Soviets insisted that they were spies. The United States maintained that the plane's penetration into Soviet air space was the result of a navigational error. By March 27, the pilots were released to the West, but the propaganda drums continued to beat. On Wednesday, May 13, 1964, the first major step in erecting the Aswan Dam in Egypt had demonstrated the communist/capitalist rivalry. The Egyptian President, Gamal Abd el-Nasser, welcomed the leaders of Iraq and Yemen, respectively, but the special guest of honor was Nikita Khrushchev, the Soviet Union being the chief financier of the project. The generous Soviet aid to Egypt made the US even more wary of the Soviet Union's attempt to export the revolution. In the summer of 1964, both the capitalist and communist camps sought to exploit the political instability in the Congo for their respective goals. The fact that President Lyndon B. Johnson signed into law civil rights legislation on Thursday, July 2, 1964, was, at least in part, according to the East Bloc Communist propaganda, a result of the pressure felt from communist accusations concerning US capitalist exploitation of and discrimination against black people. Despite the passage of the Civil Rights Bill, race riots in New York, Philadelphia and Chicago broke out. The communist press crowed, "In contrast to major cities in the US, our cities are islands of tranquility." The propaganda war between East and West was intense and the ideological nationalism that sharply segregated the two blocs created irreconcilable antipathy. Was this a good time for a citizen of the United States to travel into the East Bloc? The petition of Hildegard Nies challenged me, "God, when we go forth, do not permit us to confine ourselves to the known paths, and to shake familiar hands only. Give us the courage to meet the stranger and to engage the unknown." Conjuring up in my mind one of my favorite quotes from Johann Wolfgang von Goethe ("Learning and art are native to the world and confronted by them, all nationalistic barriers collapse.") and remembering a grassroots adage expressing the idea that human beings, wherever they might reside, have common concerns and interests, namely, "Everywhere in the world people cook with water," I decided to take the risk.

I traveled by train from Freiburg im Breisgau to Frankfurt/Main where I transferred to a train that would transport me to my first stop in the DDR. I checked and re-checked my documents: my US passport and documents from the DDR travel bureau in East Berlin, stamped and signed by state officials. My itinerary was firmly fixed. The DDR state authority admonished me to adhere strictly to this schedule. No alterations! From Frankfurt, the train passed through Fulda. Fulda, Germany's Monte Cassino, was founded March 12, 744 as a monastery on an abandoned Irish/Scottish friary site by the monk Sturm, a disciple of Saint Boniface. From a window on the left side of the train, I could see the basilica on the hill in which was located the tomb of Saint Boniface, the eighth-century Anglo/Saxon missionary to the Germanic tribes. I remember reading about this Anglo/Saxon monk from England whose zealous Christian missionary activity established the Christian faith among pagan Germanic tribes and earned him the title, "The Apostle to the Germans" and "The Patron of Thuringia." Ordained in 722 by Pope Gregory II, Winfred, to whom the pope gave the name "Bonifatius-Benefactor," established churches in regions now known as Thuringia, Fresia, Hesse, Württemberg, Westphalia and Bavaria. One of the acts attributed to Boniface was the felling of the oak dedicated to the war god, Thor, located in the contemporary Hessian village of Geismar. This act became a favorite theme for artists. It also earned Boniface the enmity of those Germanic tribes that resisted conquest and conversion. Boniface's missionary activity corresponded with the Franks' "Drang nach Osten" (push to the East) and made him an important agent in the Merovingian, Carolingian, and Papal design to conquer and to convert those Germanic tribes still outside Frank hegemony and papal tutelage. If Charlemagne may be considered "Pater Europae" (Father of Europe), then this Anglo/Saxon monk from Wessex, England may be described as "Fundator Europae" (Founder of Europe).

After the stop in Fulda, the train traveled a short distance to Bebra, the last station in the Federal Republic of Germany for express trains before entering the German Democratic Republic. From Bebra, only passengers traveling into the DDR remained on the train. During the short trip from Bebra to the border checkpoint at Gerstungen, a strange silence and atmosphere pervaded the car. The passengers became like robots staring into space. Hardly a word was spoken. The faces of the people, who earlier had been engaged in relaxed conversation, now reflected apprehension and stress. Soon I was to learn the reason for this remarkable transition. As the train pulled into the Gerstungen station, I could see custom officials lining the platform. On the crosswalk above the tracks and in a tower on a hill overlooking the station, I saw heavily armed guards. The train came to a stop. From loudspeakers mounted over the platform came the announcement: "Welcome to the German Democratic Republic." Giant-lettered slogans lined the platform, so boldly and plainly posted: "For public benefit and the honor of the Republic." "Socialism is building the world of tomorrow." "The Republic needs everyone; everyone needs the Republic." I had to get off the train with my luggage in Gerstungen in order to present my passport, to receive my visa and to have my luggage inspected. On subsequent trips to the DDR, foreign visitors were permitted to remain on the train; luggage was checked on the train and passports were stamped by custom officials walking through the train. This procedure was a much more convenient and time-saving technique. In the little office where I received the necessary visa stamps and my Einreisegenehmigung and Ausreisegenehmigung (permission to enter and exit cards), there was a large picture of Walter Ulbricht. Everywhere, during my visits to the DDR, I encountered the portrait of Walter Ulbricht, and later, that of his successor, Erich Honecker. The custom declaration that had been sent to me by the travel bureau, I had completed en route. I was not transporting coffee, cigarettes, or any goods that were required to be itemized on the declaration. The official who checked my passport and the documents sent to me from Berlin, smiled and said, "Willkommen in der DDR" (Welcome to the DDR). As far as I could surmise, I was the only US citizen among the travelers. When I got back on the train, the West German newspaper and the news magazine from the US that I had left on my seat had been removed. It was strictly forbidden to carry printed news matter from the West into the DDR. Since I already had paid for my accommodations, I did not need to exchange money at the official rate of exchange that was one dollar for four east marks. But, because I wanted cash in pocket for whatever purchases I might want to make, I changed money with the "bank lady" who came through the train for that purpose. Upon my exit from the DDR, the exit card would be collected.

After a long delay at the Gerstungen station, the train began to move. Looking out the window, I saw the sad and frustrated faces of those passengers who were detained at the station for a more thorough luggage and, perhaps, body search. Next stop, Eisenach. The train entered the Thuringian Forest. Before I began my journey, my friends told me that once the train had entered the Thuringian Forest, "The Green Heart of Germany," I should move to the right side of the train. From that vantage point, when there was a break in the stand of trees that crowned the hill on which the Wartburg stood, I would be able to see the castle perched on its rock pinnacle. Sure enough, a few kilometers before the train entered the Eisenach station, the Wartburg came into view.

Although my accommodations were for two nights in the Erfurter Hof Hotel in Erfurt, I detrained in Eisenach in order to visit the Wartburg. Since it was early afternoon and Erfurt was only a one-hour train journey from Eisenach, I reasoned that I could see the Wartburg and then continue my itinerary. I also had indicated this intent in my visa application. I checked my luggage in the baggage checkroom in the main hall of the station, exited the station and, on the street, inquired of the first person I encountered, "Wie komme ich auf die Wartburg?" (How do I get to the Wartburg?) The gentleman whom I asked smiled. From my question, he knew that I was not a resident of Eisenach or Thuringia, because no Thuringian would have to ask such a question. The man pointed down the main street on which we stood immediately in front of the rail station. He responded, "Go straight down this street until you reach the Nicholas Gate. Just before the gate, turn left into Wartburg Allee, and this street will bring you to the street that leads to the Wartburg. You can't miss it."

I thanked the Eisenach native for his directions and I set off at a brisk pace in the direction of the Nicholas Gate that I could see from where I walked and which was not very far from the station. Just one block from the rail station, I came upon a bakery. The aroma coming through the open door was irresistible, and I was hungry. I went in. In the glass display cases were all manner of delicious looking pies, cakes, tarts, cookies and donuts. The round, sugar-coated, jelly-filled pastry, about palm size, caught my attention. The card description before this pastry in the display case read, "Berliner." This description of a jelly donut called to mind the humorous boo-boo by President John F. Kennedy in his Wednesday, June 26, 1963 Berlin speech. Seeking to reassure the West Berlin residents that the US never would desert them, President Kennedy identified himself with the West Berliners, "Ich bin ein Berliner," which is ambiguous (one translation: "I am a jelly doughnut.") The president should have said, "Ich bin Berliner" (I am a Berliner). A second piece of pastry, a round, palm-sized cake covered with vanilla icing, was marked, "Amerikaner." As a symbol of my first pilgrimage into the DDR, I purchased one Berliner and one Amerikaner. As I approached the Nicholas Gate, I ate both pastries.

Turning into the Wartburg Allee, the street ascended ever higher in the direction of the hill on which the Wartburg stood. I passed a promontory (the Pflugensberg) on my left with an imposing building overlooking the street that I later learned housed the administration of the Protestant Church in Thuringia. After about a twenty-minute walk, I saw on the left side of the street a museum for classic automobiles. A short distance from the museum, I came to the base of the hill on whose summit the Wartburg had been erected. There were two approaches to the Wartburg. One could walk up the steep street that accommodated auto traffic and that broke off from the right side of the Wartburg Allee, or one could take the pedestrian path that led up the hill through the forest. I decided to take the path. On my right, at the very beginning of my climb, I noticed the Richard Wagner/Fritz Reuter museum, two men, though not Thuringian natives, who had had a significant association with the region. The Wartburg was the setting for Richard Wagner's "Tannhäuser." Fritz Reuter, the Mecklenburg author and master of the Low German dialect, lived his last days in Eisenach and is buried there.

It was a beautiful summer day and the climb to the Wartburg became ever steeper, but I did not mind because I imagined myself walking this path with Saint Elizabeth, Luther, Goethe, and other famous people who had at one time resided here and must have walked this same path that connected castle and city. At a clearing in the forest, I came upon the Esel Station (donkey station). For a fee, a weary hiker could be carried by a donkey the last and most steep stretch to the top of the hill. Observing the sure-footedness of these docile creatures transporting their heavy human cargo to its destination, I thought of the proverb that ascribes, in one respect at least, superior intelligence to these beasts. While we humans repeatedly make the same mistakes, it is said that a donkey never stumbles more than once at the same spot. I did not want to burden a burro with my one hundred and ninety pounds, and, as I could see from a donkey train already in ascent, my gait was faster.

Luther had described the Wartburg Castle and the Coburg Castle, both of which had been his residence for a period as being located in the realm of the birds. As I made my way up the forest path toward the crest of the hill on which the Wartburg was pinnacled, I could hear and observe the posterity of those jackdaws and crows to which Luther referred in his Wartburg epistles. In a letter dated May 12, 1521, Luther wrote to his colleague, Philip Melanchthon, "from the realm of the birds." From the Wartburg on September 13, 1777, Goethe wrote to Charlotte von Stein in Weimar,

> Here I now reside, my Dearest.... Oh, up here!—if only I could transmit to you the view that now enraptures me. This place is the most glorious residence that I have ever experienced, so elevated and enchanting that one must consider oneself here to be a guest only, otherwise one could perish from the height and happiness.

At the end of September 1777, Goethe wrote again to Charlotte, "I reside on Luther's Patmos and I am as entranced with this place as he was. I consider myself the most blessed of people." Finally, I stood on the outer courtyard, thirteen hundred feet above sea level, in the northwestern hills of the Thuringian Forest. From this spot, one has a panoramic view of the city of Eisenach and the Hörsel Mountain, situated across the deep valley. The Hörsel Mountain is the locale for the opening scene of Wagner's Tannhäuser. In that scene, Heinrich, the protagonist, by singing the name "Mary," liberates himself from the conjugal fetters with which Venus, in her Hörsel Mount erotic lair, had bound him. As the two women, Venus and Mary, embody respectively carnal and spiritual love, the Hörsel Mount and the Wartburg represent respectively the sensual and the spiritual. Having been delivered from the siren Venus' indulgent couch on the Hörsel Mount, Heinrich, as a noble knight, pledges his fealty to the chaste and saintly Elizabeth of the Wartburg. As the opening scene of Tannhäuser depicts degradation on the Hörsel Mount, the final scene on the Wartburg declares salvation to the penitent Heinrich when he views the soul of his patroness, Elizabeth, as a stellar epiphany, ascend into heaven.

In earlier centuries, cannon on this Wartburg courtyard would have been able to command the most accessible approach to the castle. The Burschenschaften Denkmal (Student Fraternity Monument) stands on a hill on the opposite side of a valley that cuts through part of the city. From my reading of history, I knew that 450 students (one out of every twenty) representing fraternities from Jena, Berlin, Leipzig, Rostock, Kiel, Heidelberg, Erlangen, Giessen, Würzburg, and other university centers, carrying their black, gold and red banner, assembled at the Wartburg in October 1817. The student fraternities, opposed to the old order of German territorial particularization espoused by the Congress of Vienna after the defeat of Napoleon, met at the Wartburg on the 300th anniversary of the posting of Luther's Ninety-Five Theses. Because Luther, with his translation of the New Testament into the German language, which he had completed at the Wartburg, linguistically had united the Germans, the students saw in Luther and the Reformation the precursor to German national political union. Therefore, the rallying cry for the students became "Einheit" (unity) and "Freiheit" (liberty)—that is, the merger of thirty-five territorial states into one united nation, governed by parliamentary democracy. In 1534, Luther's German language translation of the entire scriptures, including Old and New Testaments, was published. This Luther (German) translation of the Bible became the national pedagogue and the cultural concord that yoked the Germanic peoples together and by which generations of Germans were educated, much as the 1611 King James English language translation of the Bible served as a bond and mentor for the English-speaking world.

I crossed the drawbridge stretched over a deep and wide rock-faced crevasse. Once inside the castle keep, I proceeded to the office where I could purchase a ticket to tour the castle. Documents reveal that the Wartburg was erected in the eleventh century. In the course of the centuries, new construction and renovation have altered the original blueprint. According to popular Thuringian legend, the Margrave, Ludwig the Springer, one day came across the crest of this hill. Impressed by the view of the Thuringian Forest available from this peak, Ludwig is reported to have exalted, "Wart Berg, Du sollst mir eine Burg tragen" (Wait mountain, one day you will carry a castle for me.). The first documented mention of the Wartburg is from 1080. I listened to the guide. She said that the original castle was periodically expanded. Carbon fourteen examination of the timber beams that support the ceiling of the dining hall reveal that the oak trees from which the buttresses were selected were felled in 1168. In the Middle Ages, the castle was a center for troubadour and minnesänger competition. In the pre-Reformation period, the most famous resident of the Wartburg was Elizabeth of Thuringia (1207-1231). Elizabeth, born in 1207, was the daughter of King Andreas II of Hungary and his queen, Gertrud von Andechs. At age four, Elizabeth was engaged to the Landgrave of the Thuringian court who later ruled as Ludwig IV. The engagement of the children, Elizabeth and Ludwig, is a prime example of the importance that the Middle Ages placed upon dynastic unions. In 1221, the fourteen-year-old Elizabeth and the twenty-one-year old Ludwig were married. Elizabeth bore her husband three children, Hermann in 1222, Sophie in 1224 and Gertrud in 1227. Because Landgrave Ludwig IV died in the crusading army of the emperor Frederick II in Otranto (Apulia) on September 11, 1227, Gertrud never knew her father. As the 20-year-old Elizabeth received the news concerning her husband's death, she wandered the Wartburg corridors, wringing her hands in anguish and crying out, "Dead for me are all earthly joys and honors. Now my only comfort is in Him who consoles and who promises never to abandon widows and orphans." Following the example of her spiritual champion, Francis of Assisi (1182-1226), Elizabeth dedicated her life to ministering to the poor and to the ill. Regarding his wife's charity, Ludwig is reputed to have remarked with humor, "Just so she does not give away the Wartburg, I'll be content."

After Ludwig's death, his brother Heinrich became Landgrave of Thuringia. He presented Elizabeth with the ultimatum, "Either conform to court life or leave the Wartburg." The poor on the forest path that led from citadel to city, waiting for Elizabeth to appear, was vexatious for the castle aristocracy who resented, in their forest frolics and hilarious hunts, the sight of the poor and the ill patiently waiting for their benefactress. Elizabeth left the Wartburg and went to Marburg. With the assistance of her confessor, Konrad of Marburg, the twenty-year-old widow established a hospital for the poor and named it after Saint Francis of Assisi. Elizabeth became a Franciscan Tertiary. She died on November 17, 1231 at twenty-four years of age. On November 19, 1231, she was buried in the Franciscan hospital in Marburg. In 1235, Pope Gregory IX canonized her and her remains were transferred to the Marburg Cathedral. Reading the description of Elizabeth's residence at the Wartburg and listening to the guide's recitation, I concluded with Elizabeth's biographer, the Cistercian monk, Caesarius von Heisterbach: "Elizabeth, most worthy of esteem and precious to God, was born of nobility, shone like a morning star in the midst of our dark world." Her Cistercian biographer associated Elizabeth's person with brilliant spiritual illumination much like Dante Allighieri, Italy's greatest poet, had written concerning Elizabeth's example, Saint Francis of Assisi: "Like a sunrise, he dawned upon the world." One historian has noted, "It may be said that, apart from the Virgin Mary, no other woman has a broader reverence in the world than Saint Elizabeth of the Wartburg." In the year 2007, the citizens of Thuringia marked the 800th anniversary of Saint Elizabeth's birth and they named the year 2007 the Saint Elizabeth year.

In the Saint Elizabeth chamber, with its Byzantine glass mosaics by the artist August Oetken, designed from 1902 to 1906, the life of the Wartburg mistress is depicted. The first mosaic shows the astrologer-magician, Klingsor, reading the stars and discovering the revelation of Elizabeth's birth. The second mosaic portrays messengers from the Thuringian Landgrave, Hermann I, visiting King Andreas and Queen Gertrud of Hungary, the parents of Elizabeth, and requesting them to engage the four-year-old Elizabeth to the eleven-year-old Ludwig. The betrothal is represented by showing the two children together in a cradle. The third mosaic pictures Elizabeth placing her crown before an altar, thus signifying her humility before the cross of Christ. The fourth mosaic reveals Elizabeth with her female companions at the spinning wheel. In this mosaic one also sees a crusader's ship, indicating that her husband, Landgrave Ludwig IV, was about to embark on a crusade in the army of Emperor Frederick II.

The Elizabeth salon was supplemented by the Elizabeth gallery, a series of paintings by Moritz von Schwindt in 1855. The paintings depict, respectively, the 4-year-old Elizabeth arriving at the Wartburg in 1211, her farewell to her husband as he departed on a crusade, her charitable acts, visiting the sick, feeding the hungry, comforting the dying, and hosting the homeless (Matthew 25:34-40). Over the main portal of the gallery, Schwindt painted the "miracle of the roses." One day her husband, returning from the hunt, intercepted Elizabeth on the path. He noticed that she carried something beneath her cape. Resenting what he considered to be her extravagant charity and, determined, now that he had apprehended her in the deed, to put an end to her mission of mercy, Ludwig demanded, "What are you carrying beneath your cape, Elizabeth?" "Roses," she responded. "Let me see," he ordered. At the command of her husband, Elizabeth opened her cape and behold the rolls that she had taken from the Wartburg kitchen had been transformed into roses.

The small chapel in the Wartburg castle was built in 1320. The original chapel, probably on the western side of the structure, had been destroyed by fire. The crucifix, positioned at the central spot in the chapel, dates from 1230. The fresco on one of the chapel walls is very old and faded. It depicts six apostles who, with the exception of Peter, no longer can be identified. Because he holds keys in his hand, Peter can be identified (Matthew 16:17-19).

Standing in the Sängerkrieg Hall (Troubadour Hall), where medieval minnesängers, playing their harps, lutes and lyres and singing their compositions, had competed for prizes, I imagined that I could hear Heinrich von Veldecke, Wolfram von Eschenbach and Walter von der Vogelweide. Wolfram wrote part of his "Parcival" at the Wartburg and Walter von der Vogelweide wrote poems there in honor of his host, Hermann I.

Finally, I stood in the atelier that was my primary goal at the Wartburg, the cell that had served as Luther's scriptorium from May 4, 1521 until March 1, 1522. In this retreat, from late December 1521 until

March 1522, Luther translated the second edition of the Greek New Testament that had been edited by Erasmus of Rotterdam and had been published in 1516. I felt a sacred awe in this room that had hosted the great Reformer. This castle cloister had shut out the chaos and noise of the world and had shut in the tranquility and solitude that such a masterpiece, created in ten weeks, demanded. Although four centuries separated me from that grand event, in my imagination I could picture the 38-year-old Augustinian monk at the desk, quill in hand, exalting over every Greek phrase that he translated into his beloved German. The secret of the success of his magnificent achievement Luther himself describes, "One must translate in conformity with the language spoken by the people. One should not ask Latin letters (Vulgata Bible translation that was Jerome's (347-420) Latin Bible translation employed by the medieval Roman Church) how one should speak German."

The story of Luther, in the midst of his translating the New Testament, being assaulted by the devil, the devil who of course desired at all costs to prevent the Word of God from being made available to the common people in their native tongue, has Luther, to repulse the enemy, hurling an inkpot at the satanic foe. Commenting on this tale, some critics queried whether at this point Luther suffered from hallucination or insanity. Carl Gustav Jochmann answered the defamers:

> Because he threw an inkpot at the devil, they thought Luther insane. But Luther knew well what he did; and an inkpot also today is the proper weapon against evil, particularly when the splattered ink spots leave indelible traces, which Luther's manifold writings do.

Standing there and observing the place on the wall where the inkpot was supposed to have shattered, I thought of Napoleon Bonaparte's aphorism, and given the career of the "little corporal," it was a prophecy to which credibility could be ascribed.

> In the course of human affairs, there are only two supreme weapons, the sword and the pen, and the ultimate victory will belong to the pen.

Luther's letters from the Wartburg, especially regarding his New Testament translation, reveal that he compared his Wartburg seclusion to the exile of the first-century scribe, John, who penned the Book of Revelation. Luther referred to the Wartburg as "my Patmos," and, in a letter to Johannes Lang on December 18, 1521, "my solitude." For Goethe and for Luther, inspiration was enhanced in this "realm of the birds" in "the green heart of Germany," as an ancient sage had observed, "Solitude is the best Revelation."

I studied the exhibitions in the Wartburg museum. What a wealth of information I was able to assimilate on this first visit, and this visit, over the years, would transfer into many visits. I exited the Wartburg and returned to the city on the same path that had led me to this symbol of the German Reformation, indeed a symbol for the history of the German nation—as one description has it, "All German history meets itself at the Wartburg."

Not many days after my Wartburg visit, another significant historical event associated with the Wartburg took place. Walter Ulbricht, the SED Party Secretary, and the Thuringian Bishop, Moritz Mitzenheim, met on Tuesday, August 18, 1964 at the Wartburg. Only later, after I had spent part of each summer in the DDR and when I had the privilege of personally meeting and conversing with Bishop Mitzenheim, would the significance of that Ulbricht/Mitzenheim meeting become clear to me.

The many other sites in Eisenach associated with Luther I would have to see during some future visit. It was late afternoon, and, in the evening, I was expected in Erfurt. After claiming my luggage, I took the train to Erfurt. The journey required only about one hour. I detrained at the Erfurt station and immediately could discern that Erfurt was a much larger city than Eisenach. From my guidebook, I had learned that Erfurt was the regional capital of Thuringia. Erfurt is a city of spires. More spires can be seen over this city than in any other city in Thuringia. Because an International Garden Exhibit is held in Erfurt, the city is referred to as "The Flower City." Fortunately, the old city had not been completely destroyed during the war. According to the correspondence from the DDR travel bureau, the Erfurter Hof, where the bureau had made a reservation for me, was across the street from the train station.

Excellent directions! I walked out of the station and could see across the street at about the third floor level a large sign: ERFURTER HOF. I crossed the street, entered the hotel lobby and presented my travel documents at the reception desk. The clerk said, "Good evening, Dr. Foster. We've been expecting you. Here is your key and room number. The elevator is just there in the corridor."

My room was on the second floor not far from a balcony that looked out on the large square in front of the railroad station. The Erfurter Hof and this view from the balcony later would be conjured up in my memory when, on Thursday, March 19, 1970, from that same balcony on which I stood in July 1964, Willy Brandt, the chancellor of the BRD and Willi Stoph, the minister president of the DDR, in the first meeting between BRD and DDR heads of state, greeted a mass of people chanting, "Willy, Willy, Willy." It was not difficult to discern which Willy the masses wished to greet. After retiring to his room next to the balcony, Willy Brandt was informed by his aide that the chants of "Willy am Fenster" ("Willy to the window") persisted. Thereupon the chancellor opened the window of his room facing onto the square and received the boisterous greeting of the DDR citizenry. The fears of the Politbüro hard liners, who had opposed inviting the BRD Chancellor to the DDR, were confirmed in the enthusiastic homage with which Willy Brandt was received by the masses.

I ate dinner in the hotel dining hall and went early to bed. I wanted to be rested for the next day and my tour of the Erfurt historical sites. After an early breakfast, I started my tour. The reminder that I was in an East Bloc state loomed before me in a street sign: "Juri Gargarin Ring." The major traffic artery that circled the old city now was named after the Russian cosmonaut.

The first mention of Erfurt is in a letter from Boniface (671-754) to Pope Zacharias II, dated 742, in which Boniface wrote, "A bishopric should be established in 'Erphesfurt' because of its good, strategic location." Boniface also wrote, "Erphesfurt, for a long time, had been the site of a pagan settlement." Archaeological artifacts indicate that Aryan Christians, for a period (circa fifth century) before the resurgence of the Germanic religions, lived on the geography. After what came to be known as the region of Thuringia was conquered by the Franks, and the populace was converted by Boniface and his disciples, the territory came under the ecclesiastical authority of Rome.

I visited the Erfurt Cathedral, founded circa the mid-eighth century, and the Severi Church standing opposite each other on Cathedral Hill and overlooking the old city. I studied the beautiful gothic art in the cathedral and the exquisitely sculptured wooden choir benches. As the population of Erfurt increased, work on expanding the cathedral continued over centuries. After the founding of the university in 1392, the second oldest university after Köln on German soil, there developed a close relationship between academic and clerical professions in Erfurt. Standing at the end of the long center aisle, I noticed that the far end of the aisle did not meet the center of the altar area but was somewhat skewed from the center. Turning to one of the guides shepherding tourists through the cathedral, I called his attention to this peculiarity. The guide smiled and said wryly, "Sir, medieval architects were not necessarily committed to a straight line." Reflecting that generations of architects, artisans and laborers had toiled to construct this magnificent edifice, a skewed center aisle did not seem important. As I exited the cathedral, the eleven and one-half ton bronze bell, "Maria Gloriosa," the most famous bell in all Thuringia, tolled the hour. This marvelous "Maria Gloriosa" has been tolling the hours for Erfurt's inhabitants since 1497.

After taking my leave of the cathedral and Saint Severi, I proceeded to the Krämer Bridge, the commercial center of medieval Erfurt. The bridge is built over the Gera River. As the Vecchio Bridge in Florence over the Arno River and the Rialto Bridge in Venice over the Grand Canal were the centers of medieval commercial life, so also around and on Erfurt's Krämer Bridge were clustered the guilds and markets. Medieval Erfurt was an important commercial, educational and political center. The waid plant, from which a blue dye was extracted, and an important textile industry made Erfurt one of Europe's earliest capitalist hubs.

Proceeding along the Gera River, I came to the site where Saint George's Borse (Beer Pocket) once stood—the student residence in which Martin Luther once had resided. After Luther's July 2, 1505 experience in Stotternheim— a village just outside Erfurt, where a lightning bolt striking near him wrung from the panic-stricken 22-year-old student the spontaneous cry, "Saint Anna, help me! I will become a monk"—Luther changed his vocation and his residence. On July 17, 1505, the Erfurt University student walked the short distance from the "Beer Pocket" to the Augustinian monastery. Passing through the friary gate, the life of boisterous student conviviality was replaced by monastic asceticism and silence.

I entered the Augustinum. First, I walked about the sanctuary of the gothic church. I stood at the large white stone located in the center of the chancel area between the choir benches that lined each side of the presbytery. Beneath this stone, upon which the Erfurt Augustinians prostrated themselves to assume their monastic vows of poverty, chastity and obedience, lies interred Johannes Zecharie an inquisitor of Jan Hus at the Council of Constance (1414-1417), the council that condemned the popular Bohemian priest to the stake on July 6, 1415. On the tomb of Jan Hus' inquisitor and prosecutor, Martin Luther, in 1506, took his monastic vows. In 1519, in the Leipzig debate, Johannes Eck would accuse Luther of being a Hussite. After Eck accused him of espousing ideas for which Jan Hus, one hundred and fourteen years earlier, had been burned at the stake, Luther immersed himself in Hus' writings. Later Luther would announce to his followers, "We were all Hussites without knowing it." That the father of the Protestant Reformation was ordained an Augustinian monk on the grave of the Augustinian inquisitor who condemned Jan Hus to the stake made me reflect on the lines from William Cullen Bryant:

> Truth crushed to earth will rise again—
> The eternal years of God are hers;
> But error, wounded, writhes with pain,
> And dies among his worshippers.

Luther's consecration as an Augustinian monk on the tomb of Hus' prosecutor began what was to lead to the fulfillment of the prophetic words ascribed to Hus, addressed to his executioners, as they fettered him to the stake on July 6, 1415: "Today, you burn a goose (the word Hus in the Czech language means 'goose'), but there is coming a nightingale that you will not be able to burn."

Although the sanctuary of the Augustinian Church could accommodate hundreds, the custodian told me that no more than forty or fifty people attended Sunday services. Services during the winter months were conducted in the "Chapter Chapel" that was much smaller than the sanctuary and which could be heated, I was told. The "Chapter Chapel" had received its name from the medieval early morning worship conducted there, after Matins and Lauds, by the monks, during which worship, chapters from the Bible and from the works of Saint Augustine were read.

After regarding the beautiful stained glass windows, some of which dated from the Middle Ages and which, during Wolrd War II, had been dismantled and shipped into areas of safe deposit, I left the sanctuary and entered the friary quadrangle. There, under a carpet of green grass, lie the mortal remains of the friars who had spent their lives in the monastery and who, true to their vows, had sought, by ora et labora (prayer and work), to make their contribution to the Kingdom of God. I climbed the stairs to an upper level of what once had been a dormitory. Now the rooms are filled with exhibits depicting the history of the Reformation in Erfurt. Off one of the large exhibit rooms are cells that once had housed the friars. In such a cell, before departing for Wittenberg, the young Martin Luther, from 1505 until 1511, had resided. There were not many tourists in the building and I was able to proceed from exhibit to exhibit in a relaxed manner. I was attracted to the exhibit displaying Luther's Seal: a black cross on a red heart nestled in the bosom of a white rose, surrounded by a blue field and encircled by a gold ring. In a letter of July 8, 1530, Luther described the symbols, "The cross must come first, black and within a heart which has its natural color, so that I can be reminded that it is our faith in Christ crucified that makes us blessed and happy. Such a heart should be placed in the center of a white rose, to grant my faith joy, comfort and peace. This is why the rose must be white and not red, as white is the color of all spirits, souls and angels. Such a rose in turn is in the middle of a sky-colored field symbolizing heaven; my joy in faith is the beginning and my heavenly bliss is the future. The golden ring around the field is a symbol of my eternal happiness in heaven, a bliss that is greater than all joy and possessions. It is gold as gold is the most precious and exquisite ore." Around the rim of the seal, one reads the word "Vivit"—He lives.

On my way back to the Erfurter Hof, I passed a large bronze statue of Martin Luther that commands a prominent place in the center of Erfurt. I thought to myself, "In this state that espouses atheistic materialism, there stands the great Reformer with an open Bible in his hands and incised in the base of the statue the words from Psalm 118:17"—"I shall not die, but live and proclaim the works of the Lord."

After dinner in the Erfurter Hotel, which, for a first-class hotel, was not very good, I walked to the center of the city to observe the nightlife. I soon discovered that in Erfurt, a city of over 200,000, there was not much to do. There were four or five movie houses showing only films approved by the state. The telephone book, whose pages were in a much smaller format than I was used to, contained 120 pages. In Freiburg, BRD, a city of 150,000 in 1964, the telephone book contained 208 pages. Later, after becoming acquainted with DDR citizens, I was told that, except for Party functionaries and physicians or people with special clearance, there was a 17-year waiting period to procure a telephone. In the center of Erfurt, the news flashes were electronically recorded in bold, illuminated letters on the top of a tall building: "The US seeks to force South American states to sever relations with Cuba;" "Russia has just produced a new 'Wonder' tractor;'" "Another BRD soldier dies as a result of brutal training methods." I returned to my hotel room and took a shower. I then lay in bed and read the literature that I had collected on my Erfurt Reformation trek. Early the next morning, I took the train for the one-half-hour trip to Weimar. Seated on the left side of the train, just before the train arrived in Weimar, the large monument, erected after World War II on the upper slope of the Ettersberg (Buchenwald), came into view. During my visit in Weimar, I planned to visit the former labor camp that now is a large museum.

Instructions from the DDR travel bureau informed me that the Hotel Elephant, in which my reservation had been booked, was about one mile from the railroad station and that a taxi stand was located outside the station's main entrance. Later, during my many residences in Weimar, I would discover how historic the Hotel Elephant is. I read an account by Nicholas Karamsin from July 1789 in which he wrote, with enthused anticipation, as he entered Weimar, "Is Wieland here? Is Herder here? Is Goethe here? I ordered the coachman to stop at the Elephant Inn." I got off the train and descended the steps that led down to the station's main concourse. In the large hall, a banner strung high in the air announced, with bold letters, local patriotism: "Welcome to the Poets' City of Weimar." I thought, "That is certainly true, for without its best known residents, Goethe, Schiller, Wieland and Herder, Weimar would have remained an unknown provincial town." I proceeded to the taxi stand and saw approximately fifteen people in line, but no taxi. I inquired of one of the would-be passengers how long one should expect to wait for a taxi. The instructions from the travel bureau did not mention that one must be prepared to wait for a long time for a taxi. The gentleman smiled and said, "If you want to ride in a taxi, you must have much time at your disposal." I explained that I had a reservation at the Hotel Elephant. With my luggage, I could not walk to the hotel, but neither did I wish to waste the morning waiting for a taxi. The gentleman replied, "You can take the bus to the Hotel Elephant. The bus runs every half hour. Get off at Steuben Straße, just before Wieland Platz. From there, you can walk to the hotel, only a few blocks. Go to Wieland Platz, turn left into the Frauenplan. On your right, you will see Goethe's house, now a museum. Go past Goethe's House. Ahead of you, you will see the market square. Turn right at the square and only a few steps on your right, next to the 'Black Bear' restaurant, you will come to Hotel Elephant."

I thanked the gentleman for his advice and directions, and, as we concluded our conversation, a bus arrived. "Take this bus," my adviser said, "to Steuben Straße, the stop just before Wieland Platz." I thanked my guide again, got on the bus and requested the driver to inform me when we arrived at Steuben Straße, Wieland Platz bus stop. The trolley bus was powered by electricity. A long arm from the top of the bus made contact with a cable stretched above the bus route. I placed my luggage in the luggage storage area located in the center of the bus and took a window seat. At the mid-morning hour, seats were available. I soon was to learn, however, that at the peak traffic time, early morning and late afternoon, all public transportation vehicles were packed with riders and that squeezing onto the bus had become an exercise in which Weimar residents were well trained and innovative.

FRAU GIESE

As the bus proceeded through the heart of Weimar, I studied the pedestrians and the buildings. In Eisenach and in Erfurt, I had noticed the distinction in attire between East and West Germans. While most DDR citizens whom I encountered were neatly dressed, the quality of the clothing was inferior to what I had seen in the BRD. That which captured my attention was the condition of the buildings. Most of the buildings were in a sad state of disrepair. In some cases, the stucco had fallen from walls, revealing bare timber, which, subject to the elements, had begun to disintegrate. Shingles were missing from roofs and most of the buildings were in desperate need of fresh paint. By 1964, almost twenty years after the war had ended, the BRD had recovered from the worst signs of devastation, but in the DDR the evidence of decay, neglect and lack of maintenance was obvious. Weimar had suffered an air raid on February 9, 1945 that destroyed many buildings in the inner city, including classical and historic edifices. The question naturally was raised, as it would be repeated concerning the bombing of Dresden on February 13, 1945, "Why bomb these non-military targets when the war almost was over?"

At the Goethe Platz, Weimar's central public transportation hub, I was fascinated by the large building of early twentieth-century architecture on my right. It housed the post office. Looking out the bus window on my left, I could see a park and a small frame shack with a broad open counter. People were queued at the counter looking up expectantly to a man in a white jacket who stood at a grill on which the famous Thuringian sausages were simmering. With huge tongs, the cook clasped a sausage, placed it inside a roll and handed the roll to the first person in the queue. The customer placed his money on the counter and then moved on to permit the next patron to be served. Even at mid-morning, the chef was doing a thriving business.

After a fifteen-minute bus ride, the driver turned to me and said, "Steuben Straße stop." I collected my luggage and got off the bus. From where I stood on the sidewalk, immediately ahead, I could see the Wieland Platz. I walked the short distance to the square. There he stood, Christoph Martin Wieland, the large bronze statue of one of Weimar's great writers. Benches on the small square around the statue made this place an attractive location from which to observe the activity on the Frauenplan. From the Wieland Platz, I turned left into the Frauenplan, as the man at the railroad station had instructed. After a few steps, I observed the Goethe House Museum on my right, a large stately building whose façade commanded the small park and street located immediately in front of the museum. "Frauenplan," I mused, "Women's Quarter," probably thus named because there had been a convent on this site in the earliest days of settlement in this area." I continued walking for about one block, passing on my left the Schiller Esplanade, the shopping center of Weimar. A few steps beyond the Schiller Esplanade, I came upon the market square. Turning right onto the square, I saw first the large, sculptured Black Bear over the main portal of the restaurant and immediately beyond the bear, over the main hotel entrance, loomed the figure of an elephant, just as my adviser at the railroad station had described. Later, I was to discover that the beautiful Renaissance city hall on the market square had a lion in the ancient coat of arms, and opposite the city hall, across the broad market, the house in which Lucas Cranach resided from September 26, 1552 until his death on October 16, 1553, bore the artist's coat of arms, a winged serpent. "Bear, Elephant, Lion and Winged Serpent," all were represented on the Weimar market square. I later would conclude, "Each figure and building, like ancient apocalyptic allegories, with which the respective symbols were associated, possessed a history of its own."

I entered the hotel and went to the reception desk. "Yes, Dr. Foster," the man at the reception responded to my introduction of myself. "We have been expecting you. Our Berlin bureau booked your reservation some weeks ago." The façade and lobby of the Hotel Elephant, in marked contrast to the buildings that I had seen on my journey from the rail station, were elegant and well maintained. The Hotel Elephant, which is the setting for Thomas Mann's novel, "Lotte in Weimar," attracted guests from around the world and, therefore, special effort was made to make the hotel most appealing to tourists.

After checking in, I took the elevator to the third floor where I was pleased to discover that my room faced the market square. From my room, I could see the beautiful Renaissance City Hall on the one side of the market and the Lucas Cranach residence on the opposite side. On a prominent spot stood a large Neptune Fountain. I also could observe the colorful and bustling activity on the square and, with open window, hear the sounds of communal conviviality and smell the aroma of sizzling Thuringian sausages. The market magnet drew young and old from every corner of the city, and the bazaar on the quad became a city in miniature. The lines from Goethe's Faust came to mind:

> I hear the sounds of the congregated people—
> A vibrant village leaven.
> Here they are happy; here indeed is their true heaven.
> The proud and the humble
> celebrate together in convivial glee.
> Here I feel humanity's common bond.
> Here I desire to be!

It was morning and as soon as I had stored my luggage in my room, I launched out on my sight- seeing tour of "Germany's Athens." The first objective in my culture quest was Goethe's Garden House, situated in the park and on the banks of the Ilm stream. At the reception desk, I learned that the park was located just a short walk from the hotel. I exited the lobby, turned right, and walked past the Park Hotel, immediately adjacent to the Hotel Elephant, but not in the same deluxe category as the Hotel Elephant. I then walked past the Franz Liszt Music University and crossed the Ackerwand Straße where I saw a path descending to the Ilm Stream. Just before I entered the park, I noticed the bronze bust of Alexander Sergeevich Pushkin (1799-1837). "Appropriate," I thought, "that this Russian writer, whose works synthesized the classical with the romantic and demonstrated a literary kinship with Goethe, should have a memorial in Weimar." I walked down the wide path that gradually descends toward a small timbered bridge over the Ilm. I paused in the middle of the bridge to look down at the Ilm channel, which, at that point, from bank to bank, is about twenty yards wide. From the bridge, I could see the Garden House on the far side of a broad meadow. Having crossed the bridge, I noticed that one path leads in the direction of the Garden House while another path parallels the Ilm current. At the end of the bridge where the two paths meet, there is a large area in which was situated two benches. On one of the benches, a petite, elderly woman sat. I took the path that leads to the Garden House, situated circa one hundred and fifty yards from the bridge. The Garden House is well named for it is surrounded by a beautiful garden with many flowers and plants. The Garden House is nestled into the lower slope of a hill. The garden, primarily behind the house, ascends the scarp to its highest level. From the crest of the incline, one looks down over the garden to the Garden House and to the park beyond, an inspiring panorama of nature. In a large rock, immediately above the Garden House, one of Goethe's poems is incised -

SELECT STONE

The suitor at this tranquil place, seeking in memory the beloved's face, said,

Oh, Thou stone my witness be.
You need not rise to be sworn—
Your companions also succor me.
Memorials of my devotion,
Each stone and tree;
symbols of nature's grace,
which I, with deep emotion,
singularly and gratefully embrace.

But you, stone alone,
be spokesman of my bliss,
as once from the multitudes
the muse her advocate selected
with an endowing kiss.

The Garden House was in the process of being renovated. No admission! In "Weimar Information," a guide for tourists, I could read about the history of the house. It is a two-storied structure. Goethe resided here from 1776 until he moved into the larger house on the Frauenplan in 1782. Throughout his life, however, the Garden House, just a twenty-minute walk from his city residence, remained a favorite retreat for the poet. In the brochure, I could see sketches from Goethe's own hand that were deposited in the Garden House. There was even a picture of the cot   that accompanied Goethe on his many journeys. The cot could be folded and packed with the large trunk, also on display, on the rear of Goethe's carriage. Surely, in this environment the muse frequently visited the poet. Looking out on the park and on the paths that provide the pedestrian with a pleasant, ambulatory respite, I thought of Goethe's poem that describes his first encounter with Christiane Vulpius—a meeting which, according to the story, took place on this very commons on July 12, 1788, and which ultimately led to the union between Christiane, a plebeian, and Johann Wolfgang von Goethe, a patrician:

FOUND

I went to the greenwood,
That's all I meant.
To search for nothing was my intent.

In the shade bloomed a flower bright;
As stars shining,
As tender eyes in the night.

I desired to pick it,
But it softly said,
Should I be broken, withered and dead?

Roots and all, I dug it up from
Its native earth.
In my garden I planted it,
Where it goes on blooming in beautiful rebirth.

"Yes," I thought, "Goethe was correct to capture romance's initial attraction in this place where the roses bloom best and the honeysuckle aroma perfumes the air. Christiane and Goethe, as many lovers after them, were drawn to each other in this beautiful greenwood." Soon after this meeting, Christiane became Goethe's housekeeper and paramour, and, in December 1789, the mother of his only son.

I departed the garden and retraced my steps on the path that leads to the bridge. When I came to the area where the two paths meet at the edge of the bridge, I noticed that the petite, elderly woman, whom I earlier had seen, still was seated on the bench. My next goal was the Goethe/Schiller tomb in the Weimar cemetery. From the hotel lobby, I had a brochure that depicted the locations of Weimar's cultural and historical sites. From my location in the park, however, I was not certain of the orientation needed to expedite my walk to the cemetery. "Simplest thing to do is to ask for directions," I thought. "This woman certainly is a native of Weimar." I, therefore, invoked the proverb, "Better to ask twice than to err once." "Pardon me," I said. "Can you please tell me how I can get to the Goethe/Schiller tomb from here?"

The woman looked up and said, "The cemetery is not far from here, but the way there is rather circuitous. Perhaps it would be better if I guided you." I replied, "I don't want to take your time. If you describe the way, I'm certain that I will be able to find the tomb." This petite, elderly woman then stared me full in the face. I could not escape her gaze. She had beautiful blue eyes, but there was a look of fatigue and sadness in her eyes that provoked pity in me. Then I noticed how shabby her clothes were. "Young man," I heard her say, "I don't have a thing to do." I could tell by the expression on her face and the tone of her voice that she was imploring me to permit her to do me a favor. I thought of Emily Dickinson's observation: "How charming the magnanimity which conferring a favor on others, by some mirage of valor, considers itself receiving one! Of such is the kingdom of knights." "And of ladies also," I thought. I responded to the offer, "In that case, Madam, please accompany me." And so it began, one of the more beautiful friendships of my life.

On our way to the cemetery, my guide suggested that we go by way of the Römer House that she wanted me to see. "The Römer House, built here in the park," she said, "was especially ideal for those evenings of polite society when Goethe and Schiller would read their works to an admiring Weimar populace." Inscribed in the rock cliff, at the foot of the ascent that leads from the lower park level to an upper level where the Römer House stands, is another poetic meditation by Goethe:

SOLITUDE

Oh you salutary nymphs
which dwell in cliffs and trees,
grant to each passive petitioner
that which his heart doth please.

To the sorrowful grant comfort,
to the despairing, a future more bright,
and permit that the lover's pining passion
find compensatory respite.

For the gods bequeathed to you
what they to humans denied;
that each who trusts in you
may in your consolation and concord abide.

As we walked from the park toward the cemetery, my newfound guide leading the way, introduced herself. "I'm Elisabeth Giese. My friends call me Elsbeth." I introduced myself and explained that I had come to the DDR to see those sites associated with the German Reformation, and, being an admirer of Goethe and Schiller, I also wanted to visit Weimar.

"You mean that you came all the way from the United States to visit cultural sites in the DDR?" She asked with a voice that reflected her astonishment. "Well, each summer I reside and sometimes teach in the BRD," I explained. "Therefore, the journey from Freiburg to Weimar is not out of the question, at least from the point of view of distance. Cutting through the red tape and overcoming political obstacles that discourage such an itinerary is much more difficult than the kilometer challenge." I could see that Frau Giese was impressed by the fact that a United States citizen, traveling alone in the DDR, had persevered until all obstructions that would have prevented his journey had been overcome. Several times, still awe-struck, in a soft voice, Frau Giese repeated to herself, "all the way from the United States!" Frau Giese added, "I have lived in Weimar since 1935. I was born and educated in Mecklenburg. I studied nursing and worked in that profession for many years. And you are a teacher?" she queried. "Yes," I replied. "I teach history and the German language in a secondary private school in Wilmington, Delaware on the East coast of the United States." "Where's Wilmington, Delaware, more exactly?" Frau Giese asked. I answered, "Wilmington is south of New York and north of Washington D.C." Frau Giese nodded, "Ah, then I know about where your home is."

We arrived at one of the main entrances to the cemetery. Immediately in front of us, at about one hundred yards distance, at the top of a slightly ascending path, stands the building that houses the Goethe/Schiller tomb. Before we began the ascent, Frau Giese pointed out a grave to the right of the path. A small metal box was mounted on a steel post above the grave. The box had a door with a latch. Frau Giese turned the key and opened the door. There inside still legible was the epitaph:

> Here rests in God Karl Bernhard Buchholz, Landscape Painter,
> Born in the Vippach Castle on February 23, 1849, Died May 28,
> 1889 in Upper Weimar. Peace To His Ashes.

After reading the epitaph, Frau Giese closed the small steel panel and, turning the key in the latch, she resealed the brief biography in its metal crypt. My guide then drew me off to a side path. As we walked this path, Frau Giese stopped in front of a large white marker with the incised silhouette of a lovely female face. The marker was erected at eye level and faced the path—the name on the marker—Charlotte von Stein (1742-1827). I knew that Charlotte von Stein had been, for some time, Goethe's purported paramour. I remember having read a letter that Goethe addressed to his aunt, Johanna Fahlmer, on February 14, 1776, four months after he had arrived in Weimar. Goethe had written the following:

> Frau von Stein is a glorious soul to whom I want to say
> that I am bonded and "genistet"—(nested.)

Charlotte was seven years older than Goethe was. She had been married for eleven years when Goethe came to Weimar in 1775, and she had borne seven children to her husband, the stable master for the ducal family. Scholars are divided in their opinion concerning the relationship between Goethe and Charlotte. Was it platonic love or were they lovers? Between 1775 and 1826, Goethe addressed 1,650 letters to Charlotte. She apparently recovered her letters to him and destroyed them. Goethe's Italian itinerary in 1786 seems to have provoked resentment in Charlotte. Soon after he returned to Weimar, in July 1788, Goethe met Christiane Vulpius. As we stood at the gravesite, Frau Giese said, "Later I will show you Frau von Stein's house. I live next door to her house."

Continuing along this side path as it ascends toward the Goethe/Schiller tomb, Frau Giese stopped at the grave of Johannes Daniel Falk (1768-1826). In the cemetery wall, before which the Falk family grave is situated between two linden trees, there is incised the prayer:

> Under these green linden trees lies Johannes Falk
> liberated by Christ from sin.
> Children from German towns, who approach this site,
> should fervently pray for him.
> Eternal Father, the soul of our father,
> whose remains rest in this shadowy grave,
> we commend to Thee.
> Because he cared for children, permit him, as Thy child,
> to join Thy heavenly family.

Next to the epitaph for Johannes Falk, I read the inscription on his wife's marker:

> Here rests in God, next to her youngest sixteen-year-old son, Bernhard,
> Caroline Falk, born February 14, 1778, died September 21, 1841.
> Because God took seven of her own children, she became a mother
> for orphaned children. God will wipe away all tears from her eyes.

Frau Giese explained, "Johannes Falk was a great benefactor for orphans. He and his wife took in orphans to rear and to train them in a vocation so that the orphans ultimately could support themselves. He was born in Danzig on the Baltic Sea. His father was a wig maker and the family lived in very modest circumstances. With little regard for education, the father put Johannes to work in the shop. Because the father disapproved of worldly literature, a prayer book, a Bible and a hymnal were the only books permitted in the home. Johannes had to save his allowance to purchase the writings of authors he wished to read. Since he could not risk reading the books in his home, Johannes read them at night by the light of a street lantern. At age thirteen, Johannes wrote in his diary,

> Oh, if only I could go to school! That is my great desire.
> But father will not hear of it.
> My mother would approve, but she is unable to have her will.
> What's the use?

"Confined to his father's shop month after month, the boy Johannes looked out on the Baltic Sea and sensed a deep yearning to experience the wider world. He wrote,

> Year after year, I observe the birds traversing the Baltic Sea,
> but not one of them on such a broad journey
> ever has invited me.

"A teacher, who admired the boy's thirst for knowledge, with the help of the pastor of Saint Peter's Church in Danzig, the Reverend Majewski, finally persuaded the father to permit Johannes to attend the secondary school. Upon completing the secondary school, the Danzig city counselors, noting the industry with which the young Johannes pursued his studies, provided a stipend that enabled him to matriculate at Halle University. Before Johannes departed for Halle, the counselors charged him:

> You are in our debt, Johannes.
> If, in the future, poor children
> knock on your door, they will represent us,
> the Danzig counselors.
> Don't turn them away."

Frau Giese continued, "Because he could speak the French language fluently, Falk was employed as a translator by Napoleon's troops occupying Thuringia. In this capacity, he was able to alleviate the burdens that his countrymen were called to bear. The population gave him the nickname, 'The Compassionate Counselor.' In 1814, four of his children died of the plague. Falk suffered a nervous breakdown. He desired to die. But, God had a mission for him. He wrote,

'Because God knows that you have a heart full of love for your fellow humans, He preserved your life. Now you should direct this love toward poor orphan children.' Falk established The Lutheran Court, a home for orphaned children. By 1819, Falk and his wife had lost six of their own children. Despite the overwhelming grief that Falk and his wife experienced, he still could write,

> Only a continuing sanctification insured by active love
> which we have for others, not merely for our egotistical
> personal hope of heaven, can make us genuine disciples.
> Woe to him who forgets that the same God Who gave us the Bible
> also gave us eyes, ears, hands and feet."

Frau Giese and I lingered long at the Falk family grave as I listened with great empathy to her narrative about one of Germany's earliest Christian philanthropists who sought to translate the admonition of Jesus concerning the Christian's responsibility for the poor into concrete action. We then walked the few steps from Falk's gravesite to the building that houses the tomb of Goethe and Schiller. Inside the mausoleum, we descended the steps that led to the lower level where two highly polished wooden coffins, separated from each other by only a few feet, rested on concrete block foundations. The foundations in turn rested on a red brick floor. Although it was a warm summer day, the temperature in the basement vault, located much lower than the ground level, was very cool, almost cold. As we stood facing the caskets, I noticed that Schiller's coffin (Friedrich Schiller 1759-1805) was on my left and the sarcophagus that contained Goethe's mortal remains (Johann Wolfgang von Goethe 1749-1832) was on my right; that is, Schiller lies on Goethe's right. Later I would notice that the large bronze statue of the poet pair before the Weimar National Theater has Goethe on Schiller's right. After some moments of meditation before the shrine, Frau Giese and I ascended the steps. As we walked from the building containing the mortal remains of Goethe and Schiller, Frau Giese said, "It is fitting that these two friends should rest next to each other. After they became friends and Schiller moved to Weimar in 1799 from Jena, they were in contact with each other almost on a daily basis, either by personal visit or in correspondence. When Schiller died on May 9, 1805, Goethe wrote a beautiful tribute to his friend:

He belonged to us.
May that proud word
our profound pain suppress.
After life's wild storms,
he was content in our haven to find tranquility and rest.
In the meantime, in the transcendent
of Truth, Goodness and Beauty,
his spirit strode mightily onward apace.
And behind him lay in empty apparition
that which confines us all—the commonplace."

Frau Giese continued, "In his play, Die Jungfrau von Orleans (The Maid of Orleans), Schiller placed in the mouth of the martyr, Joan of Arc, the words for whose realization all people in the East Bloc, and for all those who must live under the yoke of tyranny, yearn:

Do you see the sun sinking in the West?
So certain as she in all her glory will announce a new dawn;
So inevitably must the day of truth be born."

Recently (2008), DNA research determined that they are not Schiller's remains buried in the Goethe/Schiller crypt. Upon his death in 1805, Schiller was buried in a sepulcher, apparently in which other corpses also were interred, in the Saint James cemetery. Later, in 1827, after the Princes' mausoleum in the Weimar cemetery had been constructed, what was believed to be Schiller's remains were transported to the new tomb. The current research maintains that the skeletal remains, thought to be Schiller's, selected from the Saint James' crypt, are in reality those of an unknown person. DNA samples derived from two of Schiller's sisters and two of his sons do not match the DNA samples taken from the Schiller sarcophagus in the Weimar cemetery. If this research is accurate, the remains lying next to Goethe in the Princes' crypt remain unidentified, and the skeletal remains of Schiller still must be entombed in the original burial place. It is reputed (perhaps an apocryphal account) that in selecting what was thought to be Schiller's remains to be transported from the St. James' cemetery crypt to the Princes' Mausoleum, the Weimar mayor, being informed that Schiller was tall of stature, selected the remains that he considered to be the tallest skeleton.

Frau Giese led me to the rear of the building containing the Goethe/Schiller crypt. There we discovered a Russian Orthodox Chapel. Frau Giese explained to me, "This chapel was built for Maria Pawlowna, the daughter of Czar Paul I of Russia. She was married to the Grand Duke of Saxon-Weimar-Eisenach, Karl Friedrich. To alleviate her homesickness, Maria had wagons of earth transported from Russia to Weimar. This chapel is built on Russian earth. In the center of the chapel, there is a large iron grate in the floor through which one can see into the subterranean burial chamber that contains Maria's sarcophagus. The grate and burial chamber are so constructed that the rays from the midday sun, shining through a chapel window, illuminate grate and burial chamber."

Leaving the chapel, Frau Giese guided me along a path that led deeper into the vast campo santo. At the place where a fountain stands, we came to a fork in the path. Behind the fountain is a metal stand. Buckets, to provide visitors the means to carry water to the flowers that adorn the graves, are suspended on hooks from the metal frame. Frau

Giese led the way to the left fork. She stopped at the entrance to the path and pointed to a large erect-standing grave marker. I read the epitaph:

> You blessed eyes—
> what you have seen,
> be it as it may have been,
> it was indeed beautiful.

I recognized the quote from the tower watchman in Goethe's Faust II. A husband and wife lie buried under this marker. I then noticed the dates of their respective life spans. Both had lived through two world wars. I thought, "Despite the terrible suffering and deprivation that those wars caused, the love of this couple remained triumphant." Standing at this grave marker with such a moving epitaph, the words of the poet, Heinrich Heine, came to me: "Each individual constitutes a world that with each one is born and that with each one dies. Under every tombstone lies a world history."

We continued along the path. About one hundred yards from the fountain we came to a gravesite on the right of the path. From Frau Giese's demeanor, I knew that this grave had special significance for her. I read the name incised in the stone grave marker, "Oskar Rommeis, died October 2, 1944." The name of a woman, Alice, died 1929, also was incised on the marker. To the right of the grave stood two tall evergreen trees. The broad leaves of ferns nodded over the marker. "This is the grave of my dear Oskar," Frau Giese said. "Each time I come to the cemetery, I come here. Oskar was my husband." My face must have registered an inquiry because Frau Giese hastened to add, "It may seem a riddle that my husband's name was Rommeis and my name is Giese. I'll explain the riddle later."

I had been so immersed in sightseeing and in listening to Frau Giese's commentaries that I had forgotten about lunch. "Would you like to see some sites in the city?" Frau Giese asked. "Yes, I would," I responded. From the cemetery, we walked a few blocks into the center of Weimar. I saw an attractive café and invited Frau Giese. We selected a table at a large window from which we could observe the activity on the square. We both had coffee and a piece of pastry and discussed what we should do for the remainder of the afternoon. "It's only mid-afternoon," Frau Giese said. "We still have time to visit the Goethe House Museum." We spent about two hours going from room to room in Goethe's large home on the Frauenplan in the center of Weimar—the home in which he lived from 1782 until his death in 1832. We entered the home and were greeted by the Latin word "SALVE" (welcome) and the verse:

> Why do you stand outside?
> Are not open gate and door?
> Come confidently inside,
> where you will be welcomed all the more.

Frau Giese added commentary to what we were observing. "I have visited Goethe's birth house in Frankfurt/Main," I told Frau Giese. "According to what I learned there, Goethe was born into a patrician family on August 28, 1749. He enjoyed a privileged childhood and youth, completing his university studies in Strasbourg in 1772." "Yes," Frau Giese nodded assent. Then I thought, "Why am I telling Frau Giese a story she knows far better than I do?" Frau Giese must have read my thoughts for she smiled and added, "Goethe came to Weimar on November 7, 1775 when he was twenty-six years old. He died here on March 22, 1832 at the age of eighty-three. That means that, despite his many travels and his cosmopolitan reputation, he was pleased to call this cozy, provincial town of Weimar his home for more than five decades. By the time of Goethe's death, this little remote Thuringian nest had gained world renown through her most famous son and later would receive the accolade: 'Germany's Athens.'"

As we stood on the Wieland Square, looking up at the large bronze statue of the famous poet and tutor for the ducal family, Frau Giese said, "Wieland not only was a great poet and pedagogue, he also was a man of very practical wisdom. For instance, ascribed to him is the adage: 'Because of the multitude of trees, he was unable to see the forest.' Also, the prophecy of Christoph Martin Wieland (1753-1813), tutor of the crown prince, Karl August, in Wieland's letter of November 10, 1775 to Friedrich Heinrich Jacobi, was fulfilled. Wieland wrote, 'If it is possible that anything of significance occurs in Weimar, it will be because of his (Goethe's) presence.'" Goethe later would write of his chosen residence:

> Oh Weimar, Thou hast a special fate,
> Like Bethlehem in Judea, small and great—
> Europe's muse because of Thy spirit and imagination,
> complemented also by Thy jovial salutation.
> The quiet sage searches and rapidly surmises
> how two extremes in Thee do nest—
> Thou who art peculiarly given to good,
> reveal the ardor of Thy breast.

Because Weimar became the center of Germany's cultural life, hosting great figures in Germany's humanistic tradition such as Goethe, Schiller, Herder, Wieland and Liszt, in the year 2000, it was given the honorary title of "Kulturstadt Europas" (Europe's Cultural City). In one of the exhibits, Frau Giese pointed to a quote from Goethe's writings:

> I have the unique advantage to have been born in a time when the greatest cosmopolitan events took place and impacted on the period in which I lived my life. For instance, the Seven Years War (1756-1763), the independence of the American Colonies (1776-1783), the French Revolution (1789-1799), the Napoleonic era and the defeat of Napoleon (1799-1815). To all of these significant events, I was contemporary. I can come to very different conclusions than those who now are being born and who must derive their knowledge of those events from books.

Frau Giese and I walked about in the small garden behind the Goethe House. Goethe's library also held fascination for us: hundreds of volumes representing every discipline known to the nineteenth century. The fossil, rock and mineral collection also arrested our attention. Finally, we visited the room in which Goethe, at midday on March 22, 1832, died. According to his secretary Johann Peter Eckermann (1792-1854), Goethe raised himself up in the chair in which he lounged and, pointing to the blinds that had been drawn to keep out the rays of the brilliant March sun, he entreated, "Mehr Licht" (more light). Of course, such a petition coming from the expiring poet whose whole life was a quest for greater illumination, took on transcendent, allegorical significance.

From the Goethe House, Frau Giese and I walked the two blocks of the Schiller Esplanade to the National Theater, stopping on the way for a brief tour of Schiller's House. A large bronze statue of Goethe and Schiller stands on the square in front of the theater. In the foundation upon which the statue stands is a plaque that reads, "Dem Dichterpaar, Das Vaterland," (To the poet pair from the Fatherland). The statue, sculptured by Ernst Rietschel, has stood on the theater square since 1857. Later, in 1989, in the month leading up to the fall of the Berlin Wall (November 9, 1989), when thousands of DDR citizens were escaping to the BRD through the open Hungarian border with Austria, and by seeking asylum in BRD embassies in Czechoslovakia and other East Bloc states, I remember seeing a sign draped over the shoulders of the Goethe/Schiller statue on the Weimar Theater Square. The sign read, "Wir bleiben hier," "We stay here." On that occasion, I thought to myself, "Given the ponderous weight of the bronze figures, anchored in a massive concrete foundation, and the fact that the poet pair had occupied this location since 1857, it is proper that they remain where they are." I had read the history of the Weimar Republic, how it was born out of Germany's defeat in World War I, but to see the Theater, in which the delegates convened to create the first democratic German republic, was exciting. Anxious to divorce themselves from Prussian militarism ("Los von Berlin—get away from Berlin"), centered in Berlin, the political leaders of the new Germany selected Weimar, Germany's humanistic and cultural capital, as the birthplace of the new nation. Friedrich Ebert (1871-1925), the Weimar Republic's first president wrote, "The whole world will welcome the fact when the spirit of Weimar is united with the founding of a new German State." The constitution, without mention of kings or emperors, was adopted in July 1919 on the spot on which Frau Giese and I stood. There were many large placards erected on the theater square bearing a quote from Goethe.

One such placard read,

> Many glorious things in the world
> are destroyed by war.
> Whoever protects and preserves,
> he deserves the greatest score.

"We are not far from Saint James' Church," Frau Giese said. "I would like to show you the grave sites of Lucas Cranach, the elder, the famous Reformation artist, and also the grave of Christiane Vulpius, Goethe's wife." We walked the short distance to the church. Surrounding the church was a small cemetery (Gottesacker—God's acre). First, Frau Giese showed me the sacristy in which Goethe and Christiane had been married in 1806. "There's an interesting, popular commentary on Goethe and Christiane's marriage," Frau Giese said. "From the time he met her in the park, in July 1788, and up until October 1806, Christiane was Goethe's housekeeper and paramour. On October 14, 1806, when Napoleon's troops occupied Weimar, the looting of shops and homes took place. Goethe's patrician home in the center of Weimar was an irresistible temptation for the pillagers. French officers, intent on enriching themselves with valuable booty, stormed through the main portal of the home. Christiane stood in the corridor, blocking the officers' advance and demanded, 'Who are you?' Startled by this bold defiance from a defenseless female blocking their path to booty, the officers responded, 'We are French officers of his Excellency Napoleon.' Whereupon Christiane snapped, 'Then conduct yourselves as such.' Disarmed by such a challenge flung at them by this temerarious housekeeper, the officers, before whom whole armies had fled in panic, retreated from the home, their chivalric self-esteem dealt a humiliating blow when rebuked by a petite woman armed only with words. This act by Christiane in saving his home from the vandals Goethe rewarded by legitimatizing their cohabitation in the union of marriage. Johann Heinrich Koes, residing in Weimar at the time, recorded in his diary: 'October 19, 1806: Heute wurde Goethe mit der Mamsel Vulpius in der Stadtkirche oeffentlich getraut (Today, in the city church, Goethe and Miss Vulpius were married in a public ceremony'). The plebeian had saved the property of the patrician from being looted, and the patrician was willing to acknowledge the plebeian's superior courage. Of course, at some point, Goethe ultimately may have overcome the social bias against plebeian/patrician marriage, but the defense of his home by Christiane, according to popular commentary, was the tour de force which decided the matter."

In the sanctuary, Frau Giese pointed out a plaque on the wall with a text in the English language: "You can see from this obituary," she said, "that Weimar was and continues to be a magnet for people everywhere who are attracted to German classical culture. The story is that this British lady died here in Weimar while on her pilgrimage to meet Goethe and Schiller." I read the text on the plaque:

Elizabeth M. Gore (1754-1802)

Eliza to untimely fate a prey,
a foreign grave receives thy lifeless clay.
No sculptured woes, no pomp of mourning here
with proud inscriptions mark thy modest bier.
But hither oft by silent sorrow led
memory retires the real tear to shed.
Our hearts thy dearest monument shall be
until our last relics rest in peace with thee.

Monument to Elizabeth M. Gore, daughter of Charles Gore, Esq.,
erected by Hannah Countess Cowper and Emily Gore.

Cranach's grave (1472-1553) is immediately next to the exterior sanctuary wall, and it is covered under a thick blanket of ivy. Then we walked to Christiane's grave in the center of the cemetery. Appropriately enough, a rose bush at the gravesite put forth beautiful blossoms. Incised in the flat stone marker, over which the rose bush spread its aromatic canopy, was Christiane's name, the dates of her life (1765-1816) and Goethe's tribute to this flower that he had discovered not far from his Garden House in the Ilm Park.

Vainly, O sun, do you seek to penetrate the clouds' thick veil;
The entire meaning of my life is her loss to bewail.

On our way back toward the market square from Saint James' Church, we passed the City Church of Saints Peter and Paul. Because it was in this church in which The Reverend Superintendent Johann Gottfried Herder conducted his ministry from 1776 until 1803, the church, among Weimar's inhabitants, is known as the Herder Church. The church greets the visitor with the incised words: Domine, Dirige Me in Verbo Tuo, (Guide me, O Lord, according to Thy word). In the chancel of the church, we admired the magnificent crucifixion scene painted by Lucas Cranach. We then walked to the narthex of the church where we discovered the marker of Herder's grave (August 25, 1744-December 18, 1803). "Herder is buried here beneath this bronze plaque," Frau Giese said. "A most appropriate place for the burial of the great clergyman." Sculptured in the bronze tablet that marks Herder's grave are the words: "Licht, Leben, Liebe" (Light, Life, Love). Outside on the church square stands a large bronze statue of Herder. Although heavily damaged in an air raid on Friday, February 9, 1945, the church had been restored.

It had become early evening. Despite an afternoon packed with activity and much walking, Frau Giese did not appear tired. On the contrary, in contrast to the woman whom I had seen on the park bench who appeared elderly, weary and lethargic, bearing the boredom of time that marked off her days, Frau Giese had become a vibrant and loquacious tutor. She bubbled over with energy and delight in teaching me about her country and her culture. The sad mien on the face and in the eyes of the woman in the park had been transformed into a smiling countenance and sparkling eyes. Frequently, Frau Giese would break forth into a gleeful giggle at my reaction, surprise, and appreciation to her instruction. "After such a strenuous afternoon, you must be hungry," I said. "Not particularly," she replied. Frau Giese was petite and frail and I could surmise, because of her obvious poverty, that she had disciplined herself in regard to her diet. I also was aware that our afternoon together had brought her such joy, that she nourished her spirit through encounter with a kindred spirit who desired to learn from her. "I have nourishment of which you are unaware," (John 4:32), flashed into my mind. "A testimony to Weimar's cultural cosmopolitanism," Frau Giese said, "is that last April, on the 400th anniversary of his birth, excellent productions of William Shakespeare's works were performed in our Weimar Theater. Shakespeare's statue has occupied an honored place in our city park since 1904. I have read," Frau Giese continued, "that, with the exception of his native land, no country in the world esteems Goethe as much as England does. And just as much as Goethe also belongs to the English, Shakespeare belongs to the Germans."

"It is 6:00 p.m." I said. "The museums are closed. I suggest we go to dinner. I would like to shower and change clothes. Your residence, I note, is on Ackerwand Straße across from the park. That's only a ten-minute walk to the Hotel Elephant. Please return at 7:30 p.m. and meet me in the lobby. We can have dinner in the hotel." Frau Giese looked shocked at my suggestion. Her happy face took on a sober and sad expression. "I can't go to the Hotel Elephant," she said. "It's for elegant society only. I have nothing to wear." Then Frau Giese's face reflected a nostalgic look as she added, "My dear Oskar and I, after having attended the theater, frequently dined there. But those days are gone and I no longer have the splendid dresses I once possessed." "Frau Giese," I interrupted. "I'm a guest in this hotel and you're my guest. I'm very hungry. I'll wait for you in the hotel lobby at 7:30 p.m. Please don't disappoint me. We must make plans for tomorrow." With those parting words, I entered the hotel, but, before I went to my room, my curiosity piqued. I asked the receptionist if I might look at the telephone book that was on his desk behind the counter. He handed me the book, a small format. There were eleven pages in the book. I knew that Weimar's population was 65,000. My curiosity satisfied, I returned the book and went to my room, showered and changed clothes. I returned to the lobby shortly before 7:30 p.m. I waited. At 7:30, Frau Giese didn't appear. I sat in a corner of the lobby where I had a commanding view of the hotel entrance. Finally, at 7:35 p.m., a petite figure entered the lobby. It was Frau Giese. I was greatly relieved to see her. Frau Giese had changed dresses, but she was painfully conscious that her dress, in contrast to the patrician attire of the women entering the dining hall, appeared plebeian.

The headwaiter seated us. From our table we could look through the wide open doors onto the hotel veranda where other guests were seated. The dining area was very spacious and, on this balmy summer evening, the open doors to the patio greatly increased the dining area. The Hotel Elephant is situated close to the Franz Liszt Music School and one of the attractions in summer dining at the hotel is the privilege of listening to the students as they practice. From the open windows of the music school, a rich combination and sometimes a cacophony of sounds waft over the diners. As we took our seats at the table, I could see that Frau Giese was in a nostalgic mood. "How often Oskar and I used to sit here," she said, "but that was more than a quarter of a century ago." She continued, "As I told you in the cemetery, Oskar was my husband. Let me explain the history of the grave marker where you read the name 'Oskar Rommeis'"

The waiter stood at the table prepared to take our order. "What can you recommend?" I asked Frau Giese. "Well," she replied, "many years ago the veal cutlet was the specialty of the house; but it's expensive." "Bring us two orders of the veal cutlet," I said to the waiter. Addressing Frau Giese, I inquired, "do you prefer red wine or white wine?" "You decide," Frau Giese answered. The wine selection constituted wines from Bulgaria and Hungary, but there were a few Rhine wines and a limited number of wines from Italy and France. "Ah, here's a Rhine wine from Bacharach," I said. "That's bound to be good." "But the wines from the BRD, France and Italy are much more expensive than the wines from our Comecon (commercial union of the East Bloc states) neighbors," Frau Giese said. "Waiter," I instructed, "bring us this Bacharach white wine." The waiter thanked me, gave a slight bow and set off on his mission. "Now, Frau Giese," I said, "we can return to the mystery of the cemetery marker." "It's a long story," Frau Giese responded. "We've all evening," I replied.

"All right," Frau Giese said, as she, like an athlete poised for the start of a marathon, took in a deep breath. "Despite the economic crisis in Germany caused by the collapse of major financial institutions, my half-sister, Valisha (born, after my mother's death, in my father's second marriage), and I, living very frugally, were able to spend a brief vacation on the Baltic Sea. It was fortuitous that we took our vacation in June because in July 1931 there was a general collapse of the national economy. Chancellor Heinrich Brüning and Foreign Minister Julius Curtius, residing in London from June 5 to 9, petitioned the British government to adjust the reparation payments that Germany, in accordance with the Versailles Treaty, was obligated to pay. It was your president, Herbert Hoover, who suggested that a general moratorium on war debts be invoked for the period from July 1, 1931 until June 30, 1932. In July 1931, because of financial instability, the banks were stormed by people trying to withdraw their savings. Almost four million people were unemployed. In July 1931, my sister and I would not have been able to take a Baltic vacation. Therefore, the providential event that occurred on the Baltic Sea had to occur when it did. It was Sunday, June 7, 1931 at 4:30 p.m. I shall never forget that day on the Poel Island in the Baltic Sea. I was caught in the surf's undertow and was being pulled out to sea when a gentleman walking the beach heard my panicked cries and raced into the waves and pulled me to safety out of the tide that had enveloped me and was drawing me into the deep. That gentleman was Oskar Rommeis.

"Valisha and I learned that Herr Rommeis resided in the same hotel where we had our accommodations. We agreed to meet for dinner. In the course of our dinner conversation, I repeatedly thanked Herr Rommeis for risking his life to save me, for the undertow was very strong and could have engulfed him as it had enveloped me. Valisha and I learned that Herr Rommeis was a widower with no children and that he was a bank president in Weimar. Herr Rommeis was very congenial, and Valisha and I found his company most pleasant."

In the course of Frau Giese's narrative, the waiter had brought our food and wine. The waiter opened the wine at our table and poured a small portion into my glass so that I could test the wine's quality. After I had nodded assent, the waiter filled Frau Giese's glass and then mine. As we ate, Frau Giese continued her story.

"We exchanged addresses," Frau Giese said. "Did the exchange of addresses actually lead to correspondence?" I asked. "Indeed it did," she responded. "When it was time to depart, Oskar accompanied us to the rail station, put our luggage on the train and stood on the platform waving goodbye with a huge white handkerchief. We didn't have to wait long for Oskar's first letter. While the letter was written to both Valisha and me, the epistle primarily was addressed to me. Even during our developing association at the Baltic Sea, it was clear that Oskar's attention was directed more toward me than toward my younger sister.

Fortunately, Valisha was not jealous. The correspondence between Schwerin in Mecklenburg and Weimar in Thuringia steadily increased. Valisha and I shared an apartment. I was employed as a nurse in the local hospital. Valisha was a secretary for a business firm.

After many months of correspondence with Oskar, one day he sent us an invitation to visit Weimar. "After all," he wrote, "Weimar is Germany's Athens, the cultural center of our nation. Every educated German must have visited Weimar." Valisha and I were excited about the invitation. Oskar wanted us to come in the spring of 1932. We arrived in Weimar in May. Oskar met us on the railroad platform. He resided in a beautiful house on the border of the park, not far from Goethe's Garden House, where we met today. Oskar apologized, 'I've been a widower since 1929 and the house certainly isn't in the immaculate condition in which Alice maintained it.' Valisha and I felt very comfortable in this spacious house in such a beautiful location. We shared a large bedroom whose windows opened onto the park. Oskar's housekeeper, Frau Edith Braun, came each day to perform the domestic chores. Oskar explained, 'As a banker, I don't have time to clean and maintain this large house, and, as a man, I can't do this work with the same skill and expertise as Frau Braun. Fortunately, Frau Braun lives with her family only a short walk from here. Frau Braun also is an excellent cook and prepares the midday meal for me.'

"When Valisha and I arrived in Weimar in May 1932, Germany still was reeling from the presidential election of April 10th. Paul von Hindenburg, commander of the Reichswehr in the Great War and now a paternal figure for the German nation, had defeated Adolf Hitler for the office of president. Oskar pointed out to Valisha and me that Hitler, though defeated, had won 36.8 percent of the vote, which made him and his National Socialist Party a political force to be reckoned with in the increasing anarchical politics of the Weimar Republic. Although Hindenburg had defeated Hitler in the campaign for the presidency of the Weimar Republic, the Nazi Party made great gains in regional elections. In Prussia, for instance, the Nazi Party went from having 2.9 percent of the vote to gaining 36.3 percent of the vote, from having 9 delegates in the Prussian Parliament to having 162 delegates in the parliament.

"Oskar was the perfect host. During our visit, he had arranged to be free from his duties at the bank. After a casual breakfast, we, with Oskar as our expert guide, set out to see the city. Each day of our 10-day visit was filled with activity. Some of the same sites to which I introduced you today, Valisha and I saw for the first time with Oskar. Because the famous Franz Liszt Music School is in Weimar, we attended a concert almost every evening. Per population quota, Weimar probably has more musical talent than any other city in Germany. After the concerts, we usually ended the day in this very dining hall. Oh, what memories this Hotel Elephant conjures up in me!"

We had finished eating our dinner. The waiter cleared the table, and Frau Giese, as we began to sip our second glass of wine, continued her narrative. "One beautiful spring day Oskar took Valisha and me on a picnic to the Ettersberg. We walked the three or four miles from Oskar's residence. Most of the way, we walked a forest path that led up to the vast Ettersberg plateau. From there we had a wonderful panorama of the countryside. Oskar explained that Anna Amalia spent many summers here, and that she established an open-air theater on the Ettersberg. He also said that Goethe and his secretary, Johann Peter Eckermann, used to walk to the Ettersberg tableland. As we stood in the shade of a giant oak tree (we noticed that most of the trees on the Ettersberg were beech trees), Oskar explained that legend reports that it was while seated at the base of this giant oak tree that Goethe wrote the insightful aphorism,

> Let man be noble,
> helpful and good;
> for that alone distinguishes him
> from all creatures which we know.

"Seated there in pleasant company, in this idyllic natural setting with stately trees offering shade from the warm May sun and the awe-inspiring panorama, and with Goethe's maxim to admonish us, it would have been incomprehensible had it been related to us that soon this pacific plateau would get a new name, Buchenwald (Beech Forest)." After pronouncing the word "Buchenwald," Frau Giese paused as if reflecting on the contradiction between the Ettersberg to which Oskar had introduced her and the Himmler-mandated labor camp that in the summer of 1937 began the violation of this pastoral setting, transforming it from Elysian tranquility into a site of brutality, suffering and death.

Frau Giese resumed, "One of the sites that Oskar showed us was the residence where Friedrich Nietzsche (1844-1900) spent the last three years of his life—the Villa Silberblick, at 36 Humboldt Straße, not far from Oskar's residence on the rim of the park. During the last years of his life, Nietzsche, who resided with his sister, Elisabeth Foerster-Nietzsche, suffered from a mental illness. After Nietzsche's death on August 25, 1900, his sister transformed the Villa Silberblick into a shrine. Thomas Mann, Hugo von Hofmannstahl, Stefan Georg, Gerhart Hauptmann, Richard Demel, Oswald Spengler and Martin Heidegger all made pilgrimages to this shrine. On January 31, 1932, Adolf Hitler visited the Villa. Elisabeth Foerster-Nietzsche was so delighted by his visit that she exalted, 'When one knows him as well as I do, one must love this great and glorious man.' She presented Hitler with her brother's walking cane. Elisabeth Foerster-Nietzsche died on November 8, 1935. Since she was such an admirer of Mussolini and Hitler, and DDR officials consider Nietzsche to be an ideological trailblazer for National Socialism, Nietzsche's shrine now is closed. It is rumored that taxi drivers must report to the Stasi (DDR secret police) passengers who request to be driven to 36 Humboldt Straße."

Frau Giese continued, "When our Weimar vacation ended, Oskar accompanied us to the rail station. He gave Valisha and me a parting hug. We thanked him for his generous hospitality. He made us promise that we would visit him again. 'There still is much more to see,' he said. Although there were no overt exchanges of affectionate gestures or expressions, Oskar and I sensed a strong attraction for each other. We continued to correspond. Valisha and I accepted Oskar's invitation to visit him in the summer of 1933 and 1934, respectively. Much had occurred in Germany during this period. Oskar's prediction of May 1932 concerning the growing strength of the National Socialist Party proved, to his and to our chagrin, to be correct. On January 30, 1933, Hitler became chancellor of the Weimar Republic. By the summer of 1933, Germany was a one-party state. Under Hitler's rule, the economic situation improved; the unemployment figures declined. By the recognition of the Locarno Treaty of 1925 (whereby Germany recognized as inviolate the borders of her western neighbors) and the friendship treaty with Poland in January 1934, it appeared that Hitler's government was willing to guarantee peace in Europe. On the anniversary of Hitler's first year in office, the British newspaper, the Daily Telegraph, reported,

> A year ago it was doubtful whether Hitler really had the makeup of true greatness. But today it must be admitted that not only does a powerful and decisive rider sit in the German saddle, but also that that rider, who now holds the reins, is so certain of his path that he gives the impression that he already has ridden the course."

Frau Giese and I each had drunk two glasses of the delicious Bacharach wine. Because the evening was young and Frau Giese still had much to tell me, it was time to order a second bottle.

Frau Giese picked up the story: "During the summer 1934 visit that Valisha and I enjoyed in Weimar, Oskar and I realized that we were in love with each other. We planned to marry in the fall of 1935. At the end of our 1934 visit, Valisha and I returned to Mecklenburg. I had many details to care for before permanently moving to Weimar. Finally, the day came and Valisha and I again traveled to Weimar for an autumn wedding. Oskar and I went to the city hall to get a marriage license. After the enactment of the Nuremberg Laws of September 1935, each German citizen had to provide proof of his/her Aryan ancestry and a family health history. The civic authorities suspected that my maternal grandfather had been ethnically Jewish. In nineteenth-century Germany, there was a great number of Jewish/Gentile marriages. Even though my grandfather fought in the Prussian Army for the unification of Germany in the 1870 Franco/Prussian War, and was a life-long member of the Lutheran Church, for the Nazis that meant nothing. The fact that, later in life, he suffered from manic-depression also proved to be a detriment in seeking to acquire a marriage license. The Nazis considered manic-depression a genetically transmittable disease. After the war I learned that, beginning in July 1933, an estimated 360,000 people who had been diagnosed with schizophrenia, epilepsy, or manic-depression and what was described as 'idiocy,' were sterilized. According to the Law for the Protection of the Hereditary Health of the

German People, I possibly could carry the gene of an hereditary disease, and, the fact that it would have been transmitted by a Jewish grandfather made it all the more impossible for Oskar and me to acquire a marriage license."

As Frau Giese related this story to me, I thought about the rupture in the German/Jewish community over the Zionist Question that prevailed in the late nineteenth and early twentieth centuries. German Jews, who were assimilated into the German nation, rejected the Zionist demand that Jews should seek a homeland in Palestine. Frau Giese's grandfather, no doubt, would have subscribed to Hermann Cohen's (1842-1918) apologia for the assimilated German Jewish population:

> We love our Germanness, Deutschtum, not only because we love our homeland as a bird loves its nest, but because we have drawn our intellectual culture from the treasures and mines of the German spirit—the spirit of classical humanity and of true cosmopolitanism. What other people has a Kant? And what people has this spiritual unity of poetic heroes such as have enlivened our spiritual history through Lessing and Herder, through Schiller and Goethe? What people has ever had this unity of classical poetry and philosophy?! The German intellectuals are all prophets of humanity. It is really natural that we German   Jews feel ourselves integrated as Jews and as Germans. I read Faust not only as a beautiful poem, but my love goes out to it as to a German epiphany. I feel the same way about Luther, Mozart and Beethoven, and Freiherr von Stein and Bismarck.

Frau Giese continued her tale. "What to do now? I had given up my position in Mecklenburg, had closed all of my accounts and had arranged for my personal belongings to be transported to Weimar. Oskar and I faced a dilemma. We spoke with Oskar's pastor. It was decided that we would take our marriage vows in the privacy of the parsonage. Valisha would be the single witness. Oskar's pastor belonged to the Confessing Church, that group of Protestant clergy who resisted the National German Church led by Hitler's handpicked bishop, Ludwig Müller. Established in Barmen in May 1934 by Karl Barth, Martin Niemöller, and many other pastors, the Confessing Church, together with some Roman Catholic leaders, was the major defiant voice in National Socialist Germany. In March 1935, more than five hundred Confessing Church pastors briefly had been arrested for defying state directives. Oskar's pastor told us that when the state legislates unjust laws, no one is obligated to obey such laws. In such a case, the state has abandoned its ordained purpose of maintaining order and justice and has forfeited its claim to obedience from its citizens. 'Before God, you are married,' the pastor assured us. 'But you must keep your marriage a secret.' Oskar and I accepted this solution. I moved into Oskar's residence as Fräulein Elsbeth Giese, the bank president's housekeeper.

"Now you understand the mystery of the grave marker. Oskar died on Monday, October 2, 1944. When I became the official housekeeper, Frau Braun did not lose her position. She and I maintained the bank president's home. Of course, Frau Braun knew that Oskar and I resided together as husband and wife, but her loyalty to Oskar sealed her lips. In fact, among Oskar's friends, our relationship was known. At social events, Oskar introduced me as his wife. Weimar is a small city and Oskar was well known. It must have seemed strange to some that the widowed bank president chose for his social companion his housekeeper with whom he attended theater and concerts, and with whom he frequently dined in this hotel. Whether or not the civic officials ever suspected that Oskar and I secretly had married without state license, I do not know. As long as I officially was Fräulein Elsbeth Giese, the civic officials did not concern themselves."

I listened to Frau Giese's story with great interest. Darkness, gradually encroaching upon the long summer twilight, made the candlelight coming from the veranda tables glow in enhanced illumination. As the evening advanced, the sounds of music coming from the Franz Liszt Music School faded. Frau Giese continued her story. "Since Oskar had no children, he bequeathed his property to me. I therefore remained in the house until after the war." "And then?" I inquired. Frau Giese said, "The inhabitants of Thuringia were greatly relieved when, on Thursday, April 12, 1945, the same day on which your president, Franklin Delano Roosevelt, died, US troops occupied Weimar. On the preceding day, US troops had liberated Buchenwald. After the liberation of the camp, the physical evidence of what had taken place there horrified many of us. General Eisenhower ordered that leading public officials as well as people in the general population be forced to walk through the camp in order to witness what the Nazis had done to thousands of innocent people. We later learned that 56,000 people from many different nations had died at Buchenwald. Buchenwald's surviving inmates took an oath on April 19, 1945. I can recite the oath:

And so, on this assembly yard, which has seen the horrors of fascism,
we swear to all humanity that our fight will never be over
until the people of the world have called each and every one of these
criminals to justice!
Our quest is to tear out the Nazi evil by its roots.
Our goal is a new world of peace and freedom.

"Only later did we learn that Churchill, Stalin and Roosevelt, at the Yalta Conference in February 1945, had agreed to partition Germany into zones of occupation. We were shocked and dismayed to watch US forces, in conformity with the Yalta agreement, withdraw from Thuringia, and to learn that our state fell into the Soviet orbit. There are some very sad stories concerning the American exit from and the Soviet entrance into Thuringia. On Tuesday, July 3, 1945, during the night, the US forces executed their withdrawal. This night withdrawal, of course, was designed to keep the general populace ignorant of what was occurring. Such a mass exodus of military personnel and equipment, however, could neither be done in silence nor kept secret. There are heart-rending stories of how Thuringian inhabitants followed the US forces to the zonal border that separated the US zone from the Soviet zone. The desperate people in their efforts to follow the US forces into the US zone were beaten back by US military police. Our liberators had become our jailers, forcing the pursuing Germans back into the Soviet zone. The military police did not arbitrarily conduct such action. We learned that the Yalta agreement divided Germany into zones and that the accord stipulated that each zone, with its population, be assigned to its respective occupying power. The US military police were under orders to prevent Germans from fleeing the Soviet zone into the US zone. I was not among those seeking to flee. By the time I discovered that Thuringia was inside the Soviet zone, it was too late for flight, and besides Weimar is a great distance from the US/Soviet zonal border."

As we sipped our wine, Frau Giese, noting my rapt attention, continued, "The Red Army occupation of Thuringia and Weimar began. Because they brought with them German Marxists who had spent the war years in the Soviet Union under Stalin's tutelage, the Soviets were well prepared to administer their zone. On Sunday, April 29, the day before Adolf Hitler committed suicide, the so-called 'Gruppe Ulbricht' landed in East Berlin. They were a group of German Marxists who had spent the war years in the Soviet Union under the leadership of Walter Ulbricht, the current First Secretary of the SED. Not many days after the withdrawal of the US forces and a provisional city government here in Weimar of German Marxists was in place, I received a visit from some of the new officials. They were accompanied by Red Army soldiers and several army trucks. I was told that, in the name of the people, the ill-gotten goods and property that had come to me through the exploitation of the proletariat by capitalist bankers now was being expropriated in the name of the people of the new socialist society. I was given my new address, 23 Ackerwand Straβe, and the key to one small room on the ground floor of a building that contained several flats. The soldiers entered the house and began collecting furniture, silverware, rugs and paintings. The residence that Oskar had built and that over many years he had tastefully furnished, and in which I was permitted to share with him the last nine years of his life, was gutted. I was in shock. My pleas fell on deaf ears. The Germans, who supervised the confiscation, were heartless. They remained unmoved by my tears.

As I stood watching and weeping, one of the young Russian soldiers was touched by my grief. Even though he could not express his empathy, I could read in his countenance and eyes the anguish he felt for me. For the new masters of our society, I was a capitalist. In their view, capitalists not only had supported Adolf Hitler, but capitalists always had been the sworn enemy of the proletariat. I would be permitted to work in a local clinic and to reside in my one room. At age sixty-two, in 1955, I was permitted to retire and was granted a minimum pension. The amount of the pension, as we Germans say, is not enough to sustain life, but sufficient to keep one from dying. Later, because of serious health problems, I was given 'handicapped status' that affords me discounts on transportation fees and tickets for concerts, museums and theater. Of course, at retirement, state officials would have been happy to grant me an exit visa to the BRD. In that manner, the DDR would not have to pay my pension and a room would become available to ease the critical housing shortage. But I have no family or friends in the BRD. Weimar has become my home and the grave of my dear Oskar is here. I am now over seventy years old and I am not well. I also have made arrangements to be buried next to Oskar and his first wife, Alice. Thus for the rest of my life I shall seek to recall our proverb: Poverty and Hope are respectively Mother and Daughter. While one converses with the Daughter, one forgets the Mother."

I listened to Frau Giese's narrative with great empathy. It had become late. Frau Giese and I were the only guests still seated in the dining hall. The wine bottle and the glasses were empty. I asked for the check. Frau Giese and I walked to the lobby. It was after 11:00 p.m. "I'll accompany you to your residence," I said. "That's not necessary," Frau Giese responded. "My room isn't far from here." "I insist, Frau Giese. It's late. You should not walk alone so late at night." Frau Giese nodded assent but added with a smile, "Our government reminds us every day in the media that the DDR, unlike the capitalist states, is practically free of violent crime."

We exited the hotel, turned right, walked past the Park Hotel and onto the broad square before the Franz Liszt Music School. The equestrian statue of Karl August, Goethe's patron, created by the sculptor Adam Donndorf, and erected in 1875, dominates the square. Within ten minutes, we stood at the entrance of Frau Giese's residence, just across from the park and next to the large three-story Charlotte von Stein House that Frau Giese pointed out. "Regard the lighted candles in the upper story windows," Frau Giese said. "According to popular legend, Charlotte lit these candles in the evening as a welcome sign for Goethe in his nocturnal strolls."

"I have another full day in Weimar," I said. "Please meet me for breakfast in the lobby at 8:00 a.m. and we can plan our day." Frau Giese smiled and declared, "I'll meet you in the lobby after you have had breakfast," and then she added, "Thank you for a most wonderful day."

I replied, "I must thank you. With your help, I was able to see so much in Weimar. Until tomorrow. Good night." We shook hands and I returned to the Hotel Elephant. Lying in bed, I reviewed the events of the day, the sites I had seen and what I had learned from Frau Giese. Meeting her in the park certainly was a most fortuitous event.

That evening at our second dinner in the Hotel Elephant, Frau Giese was subdued. Of course, I thought after two days of extensive touring and explanation, she must be exhausted. But the subdued mood was provoked more by the thought that our time together in Weimar was coming to an end. I escorted Frau Giese to her flat. She thanked me for the meals. "I have not had such meals since Oskar and I dined at the Hotel Elephant," she said. "I would like to go to the train station with you in the morning," she requested. "Certainly," I responded. "Come to the hotel at 9:00 a.m." We shook hands and I returned to my room.

The next morning, we took the bus to the station. We stood on the platform waiting for the train to Leipzig. Those few minutes before departure were remarkable. We both realized that we had found in each other a kindred spirit. The soon to be thirty-six-year-old teacher and the seventy-year-old petite widow had, in a short span of two days, become bonded together in a beautiful friendship. Years later, I would read a letter by Georg Förster addressed to Friedrich Ludwig Meyer. The letter, dated September 1785, described Förster's visit with Goethe, Herder and Bertuch. How applicable are the words from 1785 to my experience in the summer of 1964! Förster wrote, "Two of the more happy days of my life, I have experienced here." As the train from Eisenach to Leipzig pulled into the station, tears glimmered in Frau Giese's eyes. I gave her a big hug, pressed dollars into her palm and, upon her plea to return, I promised I would. I stood at the train window and waved as the train pulled out of the station. Frau Giese waved a large white handkerchief in response. I stood at the window until her petite figure vanished from my sight.

My journey in the DDR continues, Summer of 1964

Emerging from the rail station, I noticed Goethe's tribute to Leipzig in giant letters on the top of a tall building: Mein Leipzig lob' ich mir ("I praise my Leipzig"). The subsequent lines of this accolade immediately flashed into mind: Es ist ein klein Paris und bildet seine Leute (It is a modest Paris and it educates its citizens). In Leipzig, my accommodations were in the Park Hotel, opposite the railroad station and across the broad avenue. After checking in, I decided to take a nap. The two days in Weimar had been strenuous, and I sensed that I had an allergic congestion. After being refreshed, I walked into the center of Leipzig. I was anxious to see Auerbach's Cellar where one of the famous scenes in Goethe's Faust takes place. At the top of the steps, leading down into the basement level, stood large bronze figures of the Auerbach's Cellar characters. Opposite the building in which Auerbach's Cellar is located, I saw a restaurant. I ordered a bowl of Solianka, a meaty soup topped with sour cream. Very tasty! A short distance from Auerbach's Cellar, on the Market Square, I admired the Renaissance City Hall, constructed in 1556 within nine months by the architect, Hieronymus Lotter, and I saw the building in which Martin Luther and Johann Eck are reputed to have conducted their famous debate in July 1519. A short streetcar ride took me to the Battle of the Nations memorial at the center of a huge campus on Leipzig's outskirts. After a 15-year construction period, the monument was dedicated in October 1913. This memorial marks the victory of Russia, Prussia, Austria and Sweden over Napoleon on October 18, 1813. From the top of the huge monument, 500 steps to the observation platform, a view of the 1813 battlefield can be seen. In the nearby Russian Orthodox Church, also built to commemorate the battle and to serve as a memorial to the 22,000 Russian soldiers who fell in the battle, I discovered a display of the colors of various Russian divisions. Leipzig is a big city, and I did not meet anyone with whom I could strike up a conversation. I saw the Karl Marx Square bordered by the buildings that house, respectively, the Gewandhaus Orchestra, the city hall and the skyscraper (466 feet tall) Karl Marx University, its architectural design suggesting an open book— a most appropriate concept for a university, and especially in the city, which is the home of the German Library that collects copies of all publications in the German language. At present, the acquisitions exceed six million. Also, in front of the university named for him was a huge bronze relief of the head of Karl Marx. Surrounding the head were the figures of masses of people, but sculptured on a much smaller scale so that from a distance the head only of Marx was recognizable, while the masses remained indistinguishable. It was only by approaching the head of Marx that the masses (proletariat and farmers) became recognizable. The artist's pedagogical purpose was obvious. The proletariat, according to Marx, the subject of history, fulfills its predestined calling under the tutelage of Karl Marx.

I stood in reverent silence at the grave of Johann Sebastian Bach in the chancel of the Saint Thomas Church (originally built in the early thirteenth century), and listened to the voices of the boys' choir, the Thomaner, founded in 1212. A large bronze statue of Bach stands on the square outside the main church entrance. Having visited his birthplace in Eisenach, and the church, Saint George, in which he had been baptized on March 23, 1685, I reflected on this life of Protestantism's musical genius (whose sacred music some say is the transposition into music of Luther's theology, and that the composer himself testified was composed, SOLA DEO GLORIA) come full circle in the Leipzig Saint Thomas Church in 1750. It is worth noting what Bach himself wrote concerning meditative music: "In reverent music, God is at all times graciously present."

I sat in the park opposite my hotel and read the news electronically spelled out across the top of the building. I made a comment concerning the news to a man also seated on the bench. He waved his hand dismissively at the bold headlines and said, "I never bother with that." After a construction period of fifteen years, the Leipzig rail station, one of the larger rail hubs in Europe, was completed in 1915. The station has 26 roofed platforms and 5 tracks outside the main concourse. Rail traffic in Germany started with the Leipzig to Dresden line in 1839. Today more than 500 trains a day utilize the Leipzig station.

The next day I traveled to Dresden. The distance between Leipzig and Dresden is not that great, but the rail transportation in 1964 was like a snail's pace. Fellow DDR passengers, chafing at our "slow motion" transit, joked, "Imagine the progress we have achieved in our socialist

DDR. Train transportation from Leipzig to Dresden used to take a full sixty minutes; now it takes only three hours!" The city of Dresden still showed signs of the devastation of Tuesday, February 13, 1945 when the city was destroyed by an Anglo/American air raid. Thirty-five thousand people were killed in the raid. With the war almost over, many have questioned the reason for this attack. I saw the Semper Opera House, visited the Zwinger Art Gallery and the Green Chamber, housing thousands of precious gems. I stood for a long time at the ruins of the Frauenkirche that had been, before February 13, 1945, one of the more beautiful churches of Europe. In the huge mound of toppled stone, I saw lying a large bronze statue of Martin Luther that once had stood before the church. "Will this Dresden landmark ever be restored?" I asked myself. At the writing of these memoirs, I am happy to record that, through international contributions, the Frauenkirche has been rebuilt and was consecrated on Reformation Day, October 31, 2005, and the statue of Martin Luther once again stands before the church. I took a short boat ride on the Elbe in one of the paddleboats of the White Fleet. As the ship returned from the mountainous region that the natives call the Saxon Switzerland, the view of Dresden is inspiring, and because of the attractive location of the city it has been described as "Florence on the Elbe."

While in Dresden, I finally was able to accept the invitation that Dr. Helmut Deckert had extended to me on August 8, 1961, to visit the Saxon Regional Library. Dr. Deckert greeted me with warm hospitality. I thanked him for the great assistance in helping me procure documents needed for my dissertation. As a token of my gratitude, I presented to him the volume that he earlier had requested, "The Qumran Library," by Frank Cross, published in 1961. Dr. Deckert was very pleased with the book. He said, "Because our DDR currency has practically no value in the West, we cannot afford to purchase western publications. Therefore, these book gifts are exceptionally valuable for us."

From Dresden, I traveled to Wittenberg. North of Leipzig, at the Merseburg rail station, a refined looking, pregnant young woman boarded the train. Every seat was occupied. The young woman stood patiently in the aisle while three young men sat comfortably engaged in conversation. The DDR boasted that complete gender equality had been achieved. Several years later, while traveling on a train near Prague, the train passed a siding where I observed women working in a railroad track crew, lifting heavy steel rails and wrestling with wheelbarrows filled with gravel. "Yes," I thought, "women have achieved full equality, even the right to lift heavy steel rails into place, to struggle with ponderous weights and the right for pregnant women to stand while the men remain seated." When it became obvious that no one was going to offer the young woman a seat, I offered her mine. It was a very hot day and there were no air-conditioned trains in the DDR.

In Wittenberg, I walked from the station into the city. As I was about to cross the intersection where the remains of the old city wall still can be seen, I noticed a stone marker at the base of an oak tree. The incised message on the marker read, "In Memory of the Deed of Dr. Martin Luther, December 10, 1520." The deed to which the marker referred was when, at 9:00 a.m. on that date, summoned by Philip Melanchthon, Luther's colleague, the Wittenberg University Student body convened to watch the reformer (Martin Luther) burn the papal bull, Exsurge Domine (Psalm 74:22), that threatened Luther with excommunication. A short distance from the Luther oak, I came to the former Augustinian friary, now a Lutheran Theological Seminary. I checked into the Wittenberg Hotel, next to the seminary. Pushing open one of the heavy wide doors, the main portal to the quad, I found myself in a courtyard. There were benches and a fountain. On the far side of the courtyard was the large building that once had housed the monks, and, after the Reformation had begun, had become the Luther family residence. Now it is home to the Lutheran Museum. I entered the reception area, purchased an admission ticket and then proceeded to follow the arrows that directed the visitor from room to room. In the exhibits, under glass-topped tables, many of Luther's original manuscripts, as well as the Protestant Reformation, are presented in chronological order. From the posting of the Ninety-Five Theses on October 31, 1517 to Luther's death on February 18, 1546, the exhibits present a synthesis of the great watershed in history, which marked the transformation from the medieval to the modern world, and because the Reformation took place at the time of European exploration and colonization, it shaped the religious contours of North and South America.

After leaving the museum, I turned left into Collegien Straße, the main street, and came to the public square. There, immediately before the old city hall, stand two large bronze statues, one of Martin Luther and the other of Philip Melanchthon. As I stood on that broad square and reflected on the Reformation heritage, it was difficult to imagine how that tradition could have been so exploited as when in September 1933, the delegates of the National German Christian Church that had been created by Adolf Hitler, stood on that square, right arm raised in the Nazi salute, and sang Luther's great hymn, "Ein feste Burg ist unser Gott" (A Mighty Fortress is our God"). I continued down Collegien Straße toward my goal, the Castle Church, whose spire can be seen from one end of Collegien Straße to the other. Around the peak of the spire in large letters are the words, "Ein feste Burg ist unser Gott." The Castle Church had been severely damaged in wars that had been waged in the seventeenth and eighteenth centuries. The church was completely renovated in the late nineteenth century. The wooden door, on which it is reputed that Luther had posted his ninety-five theses, had long since disappeared. In the renovated church, the theses are poured in the large bronze door. I entered the sanctuary and proceeded to the transept where Luther's grave is located, immediately in front of and beneath the elevated pulpit. The dates of his life are recorded on the grave marker (November 10, 1483-February 18, 1546). On the opposite side of the transept, just inside the theses door, is the grave of Philip Melanchthon. His dates also are recorded (February 16, 1497-April 19, 1560). As I stood for a long time in meditation before the graves of the great reformers, I reflected on how their respective ministries had transformed the European world, and how their translation and interpretation of the biblical word still inspires millions of people. The bronze grave plates of the Saxon dukes who protected Luther stand in silent witness in the presbytery, their bold motto proclaimed for posterity: "Verbum Dei manet in aeternam" (The Word of God Will Endure in Eternity). As I left the apse of the church to return to the center aisle, I noticed the columns that lined both walls of the sanctuary. On top of each column stood the figure of a duke, count or baron, with his coat of arms, who had been converted to Luther's teaching and who had provided support for the Reformation.

After exiting the church, I sat on a bench in the park that is adjacent to the Castle Church. In this arboreal setting, I was able to review the impressions that such close contact with the past provokes. Gazing across the street from the bench on which I sat, the twentieth century suddenly intruded into my preoccupation with the sixteenth century. There on a slightly elevated knoll, stood a Russian tank, a reminder that Wittenberg, in early 1945, had fallen to the Red Army. Only a short distance separated Luther's 95 Theses, poured in bronze in the Castle Church door, the symbol of the Protestant Reformation, from the steel red-starred Soviet tank, an iconic descendant of the Bolshevik Revolution. "Which effigy, theses door or red star, would prevail in the contest for the heart of the nation?" I returned to the public square. On a stately house on the square, I noticed a plaque, which instructed that this house had been the residence of Lucas Cranach the Elder. Then, through a small alley between the buildings that rimmed the square, I came to the City Church. It was in this church that Luther most frequently preached. In the choir, one sees Lucas Cranach's famous "Last Supper" triptych. The artist took the liberty to paint Luther, Melanchthon, and other reformers, as well as himself, at the table with Christ. Returning to Collegien Straße, I saw Melanchthon's three-storied house. I entered and went through each room, noticing particularly the reformer's study and the rooms rented to students, who also could be tutored on the premises or in the small, but pleasant, garden at the rear of the house.

From Wittenberg, I took the train to Berlin. As the train passed through Jüterbog, a short distance north of Wittenberg, I could see far and wide many Red Army tanks maneuvering on their sandy, flat exercise ground. It was from this base, and others like it, that on Wednesday, June 17, 1953, when the Berlin proletariat had risen in revolt against their Communist government, that Soviet tanks were deployed to supplement the Berlin Red Army arsenal and to quash the uprising. On Thursday, May 28, 1953, the DDR authorities arbitrarily had increased the production quota for the workers by ten percent. This act provoked rebellion. Ten thousand workers appeared before the SED party headquarters and demanded an interview with Walter Ulbricht and Otto Grotewohl. The political leaders did not respond to the proletariat's demand. On June 17, the workers took their protest onto the streets. The revolt spread to other cities. There was a call for the resignation of the government and for democratic elections. The Soviets were forced to intervene. The Soviet commander proclaimed martial law and a curfew from 9:00 p.m. until 6:00 a.m. Soviet tanks were dispatched. Finally, by June 19, the protest had been crushed.

The Marxist playwright, Bertolt Brecht, residing in East Berlin, witnessed the brutal suppression of the proletariat (21 killed, 187 injured, 1,200 arrested) by the state that claimed to be the champion of the proletariat. Outraged, Brecht fired off a telegram of caustic sarcasm to Walter Ulbricht: "Inasmuch as the population of the DDR has demonstrated its unworthiness to be citizens of the DDR, I suggest that we dissolve the population and elect a new one." As I stood at the grave of Bertolt Brecht (February 10, 1898-August 14, 1956) at the Dorothean Cemetery in the center of East Berlin, I could not help but recall these words of the famous playwright. Obviously, Brecht's concept of a proletarian socialist republic differed greatly from the Ulbricht and the SED Politbüro's ideal. A short distance from Brecht's grave, I came upon the grave of Johannes Becher (May 22, 1891-October 11, 1958), the first DDR minister of culture. Standing at the gravesites of Brecht and Becher, I reflected, "If the events of June 17, 1953 had shocked these sensitive Marxist visionaries, how would the events of August 13, 1961 have impacted them? Mercifully they did not have to witness the demise of their idealistic ideology." Not far from the graves of Brecht and Becher are the graves, side by side, of Johann Gottlieb Fichte (1762-1814) and Georg Wilhelm Friedrich Hegel (1770-1831), two champions of the school of German idealism that posited the progressive course of human freedom. "Contradictory," I thought, "that these two advocates of liberty should be resting in East Berlin, in a geography which, at least for the present, was dominated by a creed alien to their testament." "A strange dialectic dominated DDR political propaganda," I thought. "While invoking the great German idealistic thinkers and even the playwright Brecht to buttress their party's credo, in practice the DDR politicians pursued policies in stark contradiction to what they claimed as their peculiar and exclusive cultural heritage. This deceptive dialectic called to mind the observation of the French diplomat, Charles Maurice, Duke of Tallyrand (1754-1838): 'Language is given to man in order that he may cloak his thoughts.'"

During the year in which I held a Fulbright Scholarship at the Freiburg University, the Fulbright Grantees in Germany made a trip to Berlin in March 1956. In February 1956, Khrushchev had delivered his "de-Stalinization speech." In 1956, the main boulevard in East Berlin still was named Stalin Allee, but now in 1964 the boulevard was named Karl Marx Allee. After the "de-Stalinization speech," removing Stalin's name from buildings and street signs began apace throughout the entire East Bloc. In his speech, Khrushchev claimed that Stalin was guilty of liquidating many loyal Communist Party members. Khrushchev said, "Anyone who Stalin considered to be a possible rival or who, in any way, disagreed with his policies, Stalin labeled, 'An Enemy of the People.' Under this accusation, thousands of comrades were tried in kangaroo courts and executed." Some years later, when I enrolled in the Weimar Summer Course for the German Language and Literature, a Russian colleague commenting on Khrushchev's "de-Stalinization speech," provided a humorous insight. The colleague said, "In 1956, at the Twentieth Party Congress of the Soviet Communist Party, thousands of delegates from all over the Soviet Union took their seats in the vast auditorium. The delegates were in a state of shock as Khrushchev delivered the speech that labeled Stalin a traitor to the Marxist/Leninist principles." My Russian colleague said to me, "Khrushchev wanted to be certain that Stalin was dead before he gave such a speech. That is why he waited three years before he presented his accusations. The speech concluded, a voice from the vast multitude of delegates cried out, 'Why didn't you say those things while Stalin still lived?' Khrushchev looked up from the podium and demanded, 'Who said that?' There was no response from the delegates. Once again, Khrushchev demanded, 'Whoever said that, stand up!' Again, absolute silence. Khrushchev then smiled wryly and said, 'That's why.'"

Accommodations had been reserved for me in Hotel Unter den Linden, in proximity to the Brandenburg Gate, the Wilhelm von Humboldt University, the German Opera House, the Pergamum Museum, Alexander Square and Saint Hedwig's Cathedral—all within easy walking distance from the hotel. I visited the Pergamum Museum where I once again (first time, March 1956) could marvel at the rich culture from antiquity housed in this museum. I found of particular interest, the ancient Ishtar Gate that stood at the end of the glazed brick corridor through which the inhabitants of Judah were led into the Babylonian Captivity under Nebuchadnezzar in 587 B.C. From the museum, I walked along one of the channel arms of the Spree River that flows through Berlin and returned to Unter den Linden Boulevard. Turning left onto the boulevard, I proceeded to Alexander Square. On my left, I saw the imposing Cathedral that, like the Wartburg, had been the center of many significant events in German history. High up on the pinnacle of the Cathedral, I could see the scripture verse that had impressed Pastor Paul Schneider during his tenure (November 1923 to July 1924) as a missionary in Berlin: "Faith is the victory that overcomes the world." It would be Pastor Schneider's confidence in these words that armed him with the courage to resist National Socialism and provided him the stamina to persevere in his Christian witness at Buchenwald. The next object on my tour was the historic Saint Mary's Church, where in March 1956, I had heard Bishop Otto Dibelius (May 15, 1880-January 31, 1967) preach.

On my way back to the hotel, I stopped at Saint Hedwig's Cathedral. There I visited the grave of Father Bernhard Lichtenberg (December 3, 1875-November 5, 1943). Father Lichtenberg had served the Saint Hedwig's parish from 1932 to 1943. Because of his criticism, even before Hitler came to power, of Nazi Party ideology and because of Goebbels' personal animosity toward him, Father Lichtenberg was a marked man. Following Kristallnacht (November 9, 1938), when the shop windows of Jewish merchants were broken, and synagogues were torched by the Gestapo and the SA, Father Lichtenberg offered prayers for the persecuted Jews and non-Aryan Christians from his pulpit in the cathedral. Infuriated by Father Lichtenberg's compassion for the Jews, the Gestapo searched for means to incarcerate him. His public protest on August 28, 1941 against the state policy of "euthanasia" led to a search of his office on October 23, 1941. He was arrested. It did not help Father Lichtenberg's case when the Gestapo discovered a copy of Mein Kampf in his residence with very critical remarks that he had written on the page margins. Father Lichtenberg was held in the Tegel prison in Berlin from 1942 until 1943. The quote associated with Father Lichtenberg is, "Even if in chains, a priest remains a priest." On Friday, November 5, 1943, Father Lichtenberg, along with other inmates, was on a train transport to Dachau. The train stopped in Hof. For a period, the prisoners were placed in a local prison. Because he earlier had been so brutally beaten and was in such a bad condition, Father Lichtenberg was transported to the Lutheran hospital. The staff desperately sought to rescue him from impending death. A priest was summoned and Father Lichtenberg was given the last rites. As the hospital staff kept vigil about his bed, he murmured, "What kind people you are!" Then he expired.

From Saint Hedwig's Cathedral, I walked down Unter den Linden past my hotel and, after about a four-block walk, came to the Brandenburg Gate. Looking through the gate, I could see the wall marking the perimeter that since August 13, 1961, segregated the East from the West. Heavily armed guards patrolled the area. I stood for a long time regarding this grim, gray- concrete girdle that stretched for miles through the city, and that held East Berlin and the city's inhabitants in a rigid, cement straightjacket.

The time fixed on my visa was about to expire. I had to return to the BRD. Before exiting East Berlin at the Friedrich Straße rail station, I entered a café to have a cup of coffee and some pastry. It was rare to find a table for oneself alone. I noticed a free place at a table where a young woman sat. Approaching the empty chair, I addressed the young woman, "May I sit here?" She nodded consent and said, "Bitte schön." We came into conversation. She noticed my luggage that I placed next to the table and also my camera that I had placed on the table. "Are you an American," she asked. "Yes," I responded. "I am now about to return to the BRD." She sighed, "With your passport, you can walk through that checkpoint into the West, but I can't. The wall separates Germany from Germany and has caused much heartbreak. My husband is in the BRD and I am here with our little daughter. He cannot come to us and we cannot go to him." "How did that happen?" I asked. The young woman was attractive, but her face and eyes revealed a certain sad resignation. She answered, "When the borders were sealed on August 13, 1961, my husband was playing in a dance band in West Berlin. He realized that if he came back to East Berlin he probably never would be able to perform in the West again. A certain period of grace was given for DDR citizens in the BRD to return to the DDR. My husband, hoping to be able to arrange for the emigration of his wife and daughter to West Berlin, remained in West Berlin to work for our emigration. The grace period for his return expired and his efforts to acquire emigration for his family failed. Now he is in West Berlin and his wife and daughter are in East Berlin, and a high wall and armed guards seal our segregation. Of course, we are in contact by mail, but that is no substitute for the personal presence of a husband and a father. Because I have no telephone, and anyway there is no telephone connection between East and West Berlin, our little daughter doesn't even get to hear her daddy's voice." I interjected, "You mean that you have not seen your husband or your daughter her father since August 1961?" The young woman responded, "We meet for three weeks of vacation each summer on the Black Sea in Romania. My husband now has a BRD passport. At the end of those three weeks, it is very difficult for us to part, for it means almost an entire year without any personal contact. The separation is particularly difficult for our little girl."

The young wife and mother continued, "Of course, we keep hoping that our petition to reunite our family will move our civic authorities to have pity on us, but there are too many people, despite the sealed borders, who manage to escape to the West. In our country, there is a shortage of personnel at every job. The yearning to be liberated from this walled-in existence expresses itself even in humor:

> Two Communist idealists were discussing political ideology. Karl asked Fritz, 'Fritz, suppose there was no wall, no barbed wire, no guards, dogs or mine fields. Suppose that the border was open and everyone could move East or West. Would you go to the West?' Fritz answered, 'Yes.' Greatly agitated, Karl replied, 'You are not the Marxist I thought you were if you would go West as soon as the restrictions were removed.' Fritz replied, 'But what would I do here all by myself?!'"

I laughed. My table companion was glad that her humorous tale had pleased me, and, despite her deep melancholic yearning, she smiled. "Permit me to give you one more DDR joke before you return to West Berlin," she said. "Our propaganda relates that in the capitalist world those who don't work possess the wealth and those who work possess nothing. With us in our socialist society, it is just the opposite.

In the capitalist world, our propaganda maintains, man is exploited by man; with us in the socialist society, it is just the opposite." We both laughed heartily.

The young woman continued, "Of course the wall, we are told, protects us from imperialist, capitalist aggression from the West. It protects us from the siren calls to material debauchery to which, from 1945 to 1961, three million of our fellow citizens fell victim, and our population was reduced to about seventeen million. There's the story of the Communist Party Congress in Moscow where Khrushchev asked Mao Tse-tung, 'How many of your fellow Chinese do you estimate resist your government?' Mao Tse-tung answered, 'About seventeen million.' Then Khrushchev asked Ulbricht the same question, 'How many in the DDR resist your government?' Ulbricht replied, 'It would be about the same number.'" We laughed again. I had finished drinking my coffee and the time for me to leave East Berlin had arrived. I shook hands with the young woman and wished her well. She gave me a slight smile, but the sadness in her eyes would haunt me for a long time. With my passport, I would pass through checkpoint Friedrich Straße ("Checkpoint Charlie") with no difficulty, and this young woman, for lack of a simple piece of paper, was kept from union with the one she loved. I knew that she envied me, and I wished with all my heart that I could have taken her and her daughter with me to West Berlin to reunite this family, but the plight of the common people is not a priority on the agenda of international politics or in the consideration of the politically powerful. I handed the DDR custom official my exit card. He examined my passport and visa and smiled with the remark, "In order." As simple as that I crossed from East Berlin into West Berlin. I thought, "As I move freely, from East to West, without any danger, others are dying at the wall they try to scale."

I returned to the Carl Mez Heim in Freiburg. Soon a letter from Frau Giese arrived.

Weimar, Tuesday, July 28, 1964,
Ackerwand Straße 23, parterre, DDR

Very Esteemed Doctor!
The beautiful Weimar hours have passed and now remain the memories. Despite very trying and complicated times, may these memories elevate us above the mundane. May these memories provide reflections for you in your future and tranquil meditation for me in my life's twilight. Our companionship was most beautiful and in parting we can say:

All mankind becomes brothers (Friedrich Schiller, Ode to Joy)
Let man be noble, helpful and good (Goethe, The Devine)

All that is beautiful in Weimar, in the classical sites, we were permitted to behold and our spirits were refreshed. How glorious is God's creation! I have inquired about the Buchenwald slides. I am sending them registered mail to you…. Included is a guide to the Buchenwald museum. In response to your request, I inquired at the bank…. It is permitted to send dollars in the normal post, but there is the risk that the post may be lost. It is recommended to transfer the money to my account, number 245, Savings Bank, Weimar, Am Graben, account of Elsbeth Giese, handicapped status, Ackerwand 23. It was a great pleasure for me to guide you in Weimar. No thanks are necessary. I thank you for the stimulating and interesting conversations, for the coffee hour and for the wonderful evening in Hotel Elephant. I send best greetings with the request that you also greet your wife, the little man and your homeland from me. I wish you all the best and a safe journey home.

I commend you to God, Your elderly Frau Giese

As I concluded the reading of Frau Giese's letter that conjured up memory of the beautiful hours we had spent together, I thought of Oscar Wilde's comment: "Memory is the diary to which we daily have access." Frau Giese continued to write to me, sending me a package one day before she died.

On Wednesday, September 9, 1964, there was a major act to overcome the rigid segregation of families in the BRD and the DDR. The DDR authorities announced that for retired citizens an annual visit to relatives in the BRD up to four weeks would be permitted. In the case of a relative's death or serious illness, visits to the BRD also would be permitted. For West Berliners wishing to visit relatives in East Berlin, visas would be granted for the time periods of October 30 to November 14, 1964; from December 19, 1964 to January 3, 1965; at Easter and at Pentecost (1965), West Berliners could visit relatives in East Berlin for a fourteen-day period. We now know that the Wartburg meeting between Ulbricht and Bishop Moritz Mitzenheim prepared the way for this breakthrough. It was Bishop Mitzenheim who suggested this alleviation and who was successful in gaining Ulbricht's consent. No sooner was this good news announced than the world was reminded what the Berlin Wall really meant for the majority of DDR citizens. A twenty-year-old man was shot by East Berlin border guards as he tried to scale the wall from East to West. West Berlin border guards returned fire and in the midst of the confusion, an American soldier pulled the seriously wounded young man into the western zone.

On Monday, October 5, 1964, the world was startled to learn of the stamina, courage and perseverance of fifty-seven East Berlin inhabitants. After months of hard and secret labor, they escaped through a tunnel under the Berlin Wall. I remembered my conversation with the young woman in the Friedrich Straβe café and wondered if perhaps she might have been among those who fled.

Professor Richter and "Vitamin 'B'"

During the spring and early summer of 1965, I was given an interim assignment (to replace a teacher who had become ill) to teach the English language at the Kepler Gymnasium. It was pleasant to serve once again on the faculty on which I had taught from 1957 to 1958, and to renew old acquaintances. Each morning, after the breakfast ersatz coffee in the Carl Mez Heim, I stopped at the Grossbrückhaus Konditerei (coffee shop) on my way to the gymnasium to enjoy a cup of genuine coffee. At that early hour, the konditerei had few patrons. I sat in a corner, drank my coffee and read the daily press, newspapers conveniently made accessible to customers. Each morning in an opposite corner sat a young man, his attention immersed in a notebook. Finally, one morning I greeted him. We came into conversation. It was then that I discovered that he also taught at Kepler gymnasium and that he employed this early morning hour to review his notes. He was a "Referendar," a teacher in training, providing instruction under the guidance of an experienced mentor. We introduced ourselves to each other. "I'm Manfred Otterpohl," he said. "I just began my referendar training this spring at Kepler Gymnasium. My wife, Brigitte, teaches at the Saint Ursula Girls' Gymnasium on Bahnhof Straße, just a few blocks from here. After I drive my wife to her school, I stop here for a cup of coffee and a little preparation and review time." This conversation and acquaintanceship led to a friendship that is vital until this day (2012).

My wife Lois, son Stephen, and five pupils from the Tatnall School (a private school in Wilmington Delaware, where I taught) accompanied me to Freiburg. We resided in the Carl Mez Heim. Because my classes at Kepler Gymnasium were scheduled in the early morning, I was able to spend the remainder of the day guiding Lois, Stephen, and the pupils to places of recreation and interest in the Black Forest. We were invited several times on hikes by Manfred and Brigitte. One pleasant day's excursion was to the Zähringer Castle on the outskirts of Freiburg.

On the same day on which I received a letter from Frau Giese, President Lyndon B. Johnson authorized US military forces in Vietnam, who up to this time had been described as "advisors," to take offensive action against the Vietcong. By July 28, it was announced by the media,

US military personnel in Vietnam would number 125,000. The friction between East and West became ever more abrasive. Was it wise, as a US citizen, to travel to the DDR in whose media the US government was described as criminal? But if I did not make the journey, I would lose the opportunity to continue to educate myself concerning the German Reformation sites. I also knew that Frau Giese would be bitterly disappointed. We had looked forward to our reunion for an entire year. In contrast to the feat of Major Edward White on June 3, floating for twenty minutes in the alien realm of space, secured to his spacecraft by a slender lifeline only, I considered my venture into the hostile political environment of the DDR, albeit without a lifeline, a modest risk.

After seeing my wife, son and the pupils off for the US, I traveled to the DDR. There were many elderly DDR residents on the train, returning from visits to relatives in the BRD, visits made possible based on the agreement signed between BRD and DDR authorities on September 9, 1964. Ever since the 1964 travel permission for DDR retired and elderly, the trains from Bebra into the DDR were full. The strong coffee aroma in each car indicated that DDR citizens returning to their home, after having visited the BRD, had stocked up on coffee. As we approached the border checkpoint, Gerstungen, people, who earlier had been engaged in relaxed conversation, now showed signs of tension and apprehension. As the train pulled into the Gerstungen station, the scene, as I remembered it from the previous year, was repeated. Over the loudspeakers came the "Welcome to the DDR." The custom officials came through the train. I had nothing to declare. My travel documents were in order and I was quickly cleared. An elderly DDR couple, seated a few rows in front of me, became very nervous when the custom official requested them to open their luggage. One suitcase contained far in excess the amount of coffee per person permitted to be imported. To make matters worse, the couple had written on their declaration that they had nothing to declare. The elderly man and his wife were visibly shaken when the custom official informed them that they must detrain with their luggage for a more thorough inspection. Finally, after more than an hour of checking documents and inspecting luggage, the train was permitted to depart. On the platform, however, were many travelers who had been required to get off the train for closer scrutiny, or because their travel documents were not in order, or because of a violation of custom regulations. The elderly couple did not reappear before departure. As the train pulled out of the station, the large bold-lettered signs along the platform, "Welcome to the DDR," seemed in sharp contrast to a long line of cowed, nervous, frustrated and disappointed people who had aspired to bring a few extra pounds of coffee over the border or had hoped that the currency that they had concealed on their person would go undetected. I could see two lines, one for men and one for women. The lines filed into two separate rooms. I later learned that body searches were conducted in these rooms. Those travelers, seeking to import into the DDR undeclared BRD currency or DDR currency that had been purchased for them by family or friends at a favorable exchange rate in BRD banks, would be severely punished.

I learned that some of the more affluent DDR citizens, who were eligible for travel to the West, in order not to be a moocher on relatives and friends, took large amounts of their DDR currency with them. The export of DDR currency was forbidden. One of my friends (Reise-Mündig = "Journey mature" as the DDR citizens described it, people of retirement age) devised a scheme, however, whereby she was able to transport her DDR currency across the border. After boarding the train in Weimar, she remained in her seat until just before the train arrived in Eisenach, the last DDR station before the border checkpoint at Gerstungen. She went to the toilet. In the train toilets there were wastebaskets, about knee-high, inside wall brackets. She pulled the wastebasket up out of its bracket and taped the envelope with her DDR currency to the bottom of the basket. She then replaced the basket to its place inside the wall bracket. The envelope, taped securely to the bottom of the basket, was not visible. If the envelope should be detected, there would be no way for the custom officials to know who had concealed the envelope. Of course, the lady ran the risk of losing the money, but that was to be preferred to going to prison. After the train departed Gerstungen, the lady returned to the toilet and retrieved her money. This friend told me that, employing this technique, she had transported money into the BRD at least six times without loss.

Between Gerstungen and Eisenach, I once again sat on the right side of the train in order to catch a glimpse of the Wartburg when, at the break in the tall stand of trees commanding the summit of the Thuringian Forest, it came into view. As the train pulled into the Weimar station, I caught a glimpse of Frau Giese through the train window. There she stood on the station platform, her petite figure dwarfed by the large space surrounding her. Frau Giese looked up and down the platform, anxiously seeking the guest for whom she had waited for one year. I got off the train and placed my luggage on the platform just in time to have my arms free as she rushed into my embrace. Her beautiful blue eyes sparkled with joy. We both bubbled over with enthusiasm. The long awaited reunion at last had occurred.

Frau Giese and I spent three glorious days together. We retraced our steps from summer 1964. We traveled to the beautiful Tiefurt Park, to Belvedere, to the Saint Stephen's Church in Schöndorf, built as a memorial for those who had died in the nearby Buchenwald labor camp. Each day, we reserved time to walk in the park and to sit on our bench, where we first had met. There was never a lull in our conversation. When I was not asking questions, Frau Giese was providing background information to the many sites we visited. At lunch, at dinner and at an afternoon coffee break, our conversations continued. The seventy-one-year-old petite German woman and the thirty-six-year-old American, delighting in each other's company and engaging in vivacious conversation, must have seemed an odd couple indeed to the Weimar inhabitants. "You're spoiling me," Frau Giese said. "I've not eaten such good food since my dear Oskar and I used to dine in Weimar's best restaurants. Usually I have very simple and Spartan meals in my flat. After you depart Weimar, I must return to my modest diet."

The next morning after breakfast, I walked into the lobby of the Hotel Elephant. In a large chair, which appeared to swallow her petite form, sat Frau Giese. Because of her poverty and attire, Frau Giese felt very uncomfortable in the environment of wealth and luxury. After we greeted each other, she said excitely, "I've an idea. Currently in Weimar the International Summer School for German Language and Literature is in session. Some of the lectures are opened to the public. This morning there's a scheduled lecture on Goethe's Faust. I thought you might like to hear that lecture." I was very pleased to hear this suggestion. "Faust is one of my favorite dramas," I said. "I read Faust with my advanced students. After I received my Ph.D. from the University of Pennsylvania in 1963, I was awarded a post-doctoral scholarship that permitted me, tuition free, to take courses in the graduate division. One of the courses I selected was a seminar on Goethe's Faust taught by a famous German scholar." Frau Giese responded, "This lecture will be of special interest for you."

The building in which the summer courses were conducted was only a short distance from the hotel. Frau Giese and I entered the building. In the lobby, located immediately at the entrance to the lecture hall, many people were assembled and engaged in conversation. There was still some time before the scheduled start of the lecture. Frau Giese pointed to a tall, bald-headed gentleman, wearing thick-lensed spectacles, standing on the opposite side of the lobby and engaged in conversation with several people. Since Frau Giese frequently attended the lectures open to the public, she knew the gentleman. "I want to introduce you to Professor Hans Richter," she said. "He's the director of the Friedrich Schiller University International Summer School."

Frau Giese and I approached Professor Richter. After his conversational partners moved on and Professor Richter stood alone, Frau Giese seized the opportunity. "Professor Richter," she said, "may I introduce to you Dr. Claude Foster, a tourist from the US. Dr. Foster is here in Weimar for a few days. I told him about the summer school curriculum and the public lectures. Dr. Foster especially is interested in attending this morning's lecture on Faust." Professor Richter extended his hand. We shook hands. Behind the thick lenses, I perceived friendly eyes and on his face a congenial smile, as he said, "Delighted to meet you. Welcome to Weimar." I thanked Professor Richter and requested permission to attend the Faust lecture. Professor Richter smiled again and said that I was most welcome to attend the lecture. "After the lecture," Professor Richter added, "there will be a coffee break here in the lobby. You're most welcome to remain." "So far, so good," I thought. Despite the very caustic media assaults on the US government and its policies, as a private US citizen, this media animosity was not transferred to me. In all my encounters with DDR citizens and officials thus far, I had been treated politely.

After a very thought-provoking lecture on Faust, in which the professor for German literature from the Karl Marx University in Leipzig portrayed Faust as a proletarian precursor for the current DDR socialist society, the audience returned to the lobby for a coffee break. In the meantime, I had had opportunity to peruse a copy of the summer school catalogue that Frau Giese picked up for me in the lobby. I noticed that the Summer School for the German Language and Literature was sponsored by the Friedrich Schiller University in Jena. There were two three-week summer sessions of the school.

Professor Richter asked me if I had enjoyed the lecture. "Yes," I said, "but it is the first time that I've heard the interpretation that Faust was a precursor of the modern proletariat." Professor Richter blushed. I could see that that part of the lecture was embarrassing for him. "Well," he said, "that's an interpretation that some of my colleagues have developed." An understanding smile played on Frau Giese's face. "You're welcome to attend other lectures in our program," Professor Richter invited. "Unfortunately, I must leave on Monday for Leipzig to continue my itinerary," I responded. "Had I known that I could have access to some of the lectures in the summer school course, I would have planned to stay longer in Weimar." "There's always next summer," Professor Richter offered. At that suggestion, I became very inquisitive. "Would I, as a US citizen, be permitted to enroll in such a course?" I asked. "Certainly," Professor Richter responded. "If you will write directly to me at the beginning of the New Year, I will reserve a place for you. I'm chairman of the Department for the German Language and Literature at the Friedrich Schiller University in Jena, not far from here. Since this is a summer course, we prefer to conduct it in Weimar because, after all, Weimar has an international reputation. Most of the students who register for our international course come from eastern European states and are seeing Weimar for the first time. Take the course catalogue with you. My address is in the catalogue. I hope that you can join us next summer."

Frau Giese beamed at the invitation. I thanked Professor Richter and told him that, barring unforeseen obstacles, I hoped to register for the course in the summer of 1966. "Until next summer then," Professor Richter said, extending his hand. We shook hands and said "aufwiedersehen." Having direct contact with the director of the course who received me with such warm hospitality, was my first lesson in what DDR citizens called vitamin "B,"—Beziehungen—Connections; the most necessary vitamin for survival in the DDR.

Buchenwald Concentration Camp

Earlier I had indicated to Frau Giese that I wanted to visit Buchenwald. "Let's walk to the Goethe Square," she said. "From there we can take the bus to Buchenwald." The bus came promptly. After about a twenty-five-minute journey, we arrived at our destination. The drive to Buchenwald provoked a somber mood in me. I had read much about the labor camps, but I had never seen one. The bus traveled west out of the city and began the long ascent toward the peak of the Ettersberg. On both sides of Ettersberg Straße were concentrated the buildings that made up the enclave of the Soviet forces stationed in Weimar. Frau Giese pointed out the school for officers' children and a theater. Apparently, the Russian officers were permitted to have their families reside with them in Weimar, a privilege not extended to the common soldier. After passing through the Soviet enclave, the road to Buchenwald branched off to the left from the main road at a point where an obelisk monument provided the first indication that we were approaching the site. The very rough road now had a steeper incline and was lined by forests on both sides. At one point on the left, a high bell tower was to be seen, constructed as part of the Buchenwald Memorial when the camp was opened as a museum on Sunday, September 14, 1958. Finally, after the circa four-mile journey from the center of Weimar, the bus came to a halt on a large parking lot. Bordering the parking lot were buildings that housed the museum administration.

Frau Giese and I got off the bus and walked toward the camp entrance. Before approaching the main gate, we entered an auditorium where a film on the history of the camp was shown. The film prepared us for the grim physical evidence that we were about to see exhibited. In the capital of the heavy iron entrance gate was wrought the old Prussian motto of justice, "Jedem das Seine" (To each his due). The clock in the tower above the gate pointed to three-fifteen, indicating the hour of liberation at 3:15 p.m. on Wednesday, April 11, 1945. Extending from each side of the main gate was a one-storied long wing. The left side housed the solitary confinement cells. Frau Giese and I entered the left wing. The first room on the right had been occupied by the SS guard in charge of the solitary confinement block. We proceeded down the long, narrow corridor, bordered on both sides by cells with heavy steel doors. Each door had a small opening at eye level so that the guard, without opening the door, could observe each prisoner in his cell. Some of the doors were open, affording full view of the cells. A wooden frame, attached by chains to the wall, was the bunk. As we proceeded along the corridor, Frau Giese pointed out to me a cell on the right side, where the door was open, cell number 23, only a few steps from the quarters of the SS guard. There was a photograph in this cell and a flower wreath at the base of a large candle. The elevated barred window looked out onto the assembly yard. "This was Pastor Paul Schneider's cell," Frau Giese said. "He was inmate number 2491. He was a Buchenwald inmate from Saturday, November 27, 1937, until Tuesday, July 18, 1939, on which date he was murdered with a lethal injection by the camp physician. Because Pastor Schneider refused to doff his beret in honor of Hitler's birthday on April 20, 1938, from that date on he was confined to this cell until he was murdered. According to the inmates who survived Buchenwald, Pastor Schneider preached brief sermons from his cell window to the inmates on the assembly yard. Of course, each time he was detected offering such solace to his fellow inmates, he was flogged both in his cell and sometimes before the entire cowed assembly. Pastor Schneider, nevertheless, persisted in his ministry that earned him the title, 'The Preacher of Buchenwald.' His widow, Margarete Schneider, who later visited the Buchenwald museum, wrote a book about her husband's resistance to National Socialism and how her husband's challenge to National Socialism, based on his Christian faith, ultimately led to his incarceration."

Frau Giese and I stood for a long time in reverent silence before the cell door of this Christian martyr who, for fifteen months in solitary confinement, was subjected to every diabolic torture his SS jailer, Martin Sommer, could devise. At that moment in the summer of 1965, I could not have imagined that fourteen years later, on the evening of Wednesday, July 18, 1979, the fortieth anniversary of Pastor Schneider's martyrdom, I would hear Margarete Schneider speak in Weimar's Herder Church. That speech by Pastor Schneider's widow would inspire me to begin an odyssey with her that would reach its destination in the autumn of 1995. But that story comes later.

A few cell blocks removed from Pastor Schneider's cell, on the same side of the corridor, Frau Giese pointed out the cell of the Austrian priest, Father Otto Neururer, inmate number 4757 (1882-1940). Frau Giese said, "Because Father Neururer baptized an inmate, Martin Sommer, the SS block warden, hanged Father Neururer by his ankles in his cell until he died on May 30, 1940. The witness to the baptism, Father Matthias Spanlang, inmate number 1667 (1887-1940), was subjected to the same method of execution on June 5, 1940."

Frau Giese and I walked about the vast plateau on which the many barracks once had stood, and that had housed thousands of inmates from thirty-five different nations. After the liberation, and because of the fear of contagion, the barracks were demolished. The area that once contained block on block, crammed together in tight proximity, now was a wide open space. A large building that once had served as a storage area still stood at the far end of the camp. This building had been converted into a museum. Frau Giese and I walked from exhibit to exhibit. Man's inhumanity to man especially was accentuated in the exhibits that depicted what had occurred daily in this camp. After departing the museum, we were silent, each one alone with his thoughts about what had transpired here and numbed by the scenes that had stamped themselves indelibly on our minds. It was only a few steps from the museum to the stump of the Goethe oak tree. The tree had been destroyed by an allied air raid. "Under the oak tree that once stood here," Frau Giese said, "it is reputed that Goethe penned the words:

> Let man be noble,
> Helpful and good,
> For that alone distinguishes him
> From all creatures which we know."

I thought to myself, "What a diabolic contradiction between the Buchenwald camp and the Goethe oak around which the camp had been built." Once again, Frau Giese and I read the statistics: From 1937 to 1945 more than 250,000 people from thirty-five different nations, at one time or another, had been incarcerated at Buchenwald. Circa fifty-six thousand of those inmates (shot, beaten, hanged, tortured, exhausted or by lethal injection) had died here.

Frau Giese pointed out the execution site of Ernst Thälmann, the German Communist leader. "He was shot on this spot on August 18, 1944," Frau Giese said. "Soon will be the twentieth-first anniversary of Thälmann's death, and there will be special ceremonies to mark the event. School children will be bussed here to participate." From that site, we entered the crematorium. We also viewed the place where eight thousand Russian prisoners of war were executed. According to what we read in the literature, 450,000 people visited Buchenwald annually. "In preparation for their 'Jugendweihe' (youth dedication to the DDR Socialist State of Workers and Farmers), 65,000 fourteen-year-olds annually are brought to Buchenwald to have them reflect on what took place here and to promote the assurance that under their DDR government no such infamous place would be possible." As the crimes against humanity committed in the concentration camps would be revealed at the end of the war, the statement in Josef Goebbels' diary would prove prophetic: "Should we lose the war, the labor camps will prove to be a boil out of which will ooze a corruption that will poison life in Germany for many years."

Frau Giese continued, "After Oskar and I married, we continued to come here for picnics. It is distressing indeed to realize that our favorite pastoral setting became the site of man's brutal inhumanity to man. I remember well July of 1937. Oskar and I packed a picnic lunch and as usual took the forest path leading to the Ettersberg. We took our German shepherd dog with us. Near the top of the path, just before it emerged from the forest onto the Ettersberg tableland, we encountered several men cutting lumber in the forest. The men were as startled to see us, as we were to see them. With ravenous gaze, they stared at our picnic basket. We could see that they were desperately hungry. Our dog, Schutz, sensing a possible danger for his masters, became agitated. Oskar commanded Schutz to sit and then Oskar placed the basket at the disposal of the starved strangers with the invitation, 'Help yourselves.' The men pounced upon the food and in seconds devoured the entire lunch, including two thermos containers of tea. Just as the last morsel of food had been gulped down, two men in black uniforms appeared. We recognized their SS emblems and uniform. They also were as surprised to see us, as we were surprised to see them. 'What are you doing here?' they barked at us. The aggressive tone directed at his masters caused Schutz's fur to bristle. He bared his teeth and sounded a warning growl. The guards pulled back. Then in a milder tone, they said, 'The Ettersberg now is off limits to the civilian population.' Oskar protested, 'But Weimar citizens always have come here for picnics.' One of the officers responded, 'That is no longer possible. A government project, closed to the public, is to be erected here. You'll have to find another recreation area.' The guards obviously were afraid of Schutz because they sought to assume a tone and attitude toward us that did not provoke Schutz's instinct to protect his masters. Oskar and I, however, had no choice but to retrace our steps to Weimar. It was only much later that Oskar and I realized that on that summer day in 1937 we had witnessed the initial stages of what was to become the Buchenwald labor camp."

Frau Giese and I walked to the bell tower that we had passed on our way to the main campsite. Before the tower on a broad sloping terrain were large concrete markers, each marker incised with the name of a nation from which inmates at Buchenwald had come. Immediately in front of the tower were the impressive bronze figures of Fritz Cremer (1906-1993) which, from 1954 to 1958, the gifted sculptor had sculpted. From the heights of the Ettersberg, the figures look out over a vast panorama into a broad and unfettered landscape, in sharp contrast to the fate of those inmates, crammed into row upon row of frame barracks. The expression of anguish, yearning, but also of determination, depicted in the faces of the figures, provokes empathy and admiration in the observer.

While at Buchenwald, Frau Giese and I came into conversation with a man, who now was a guide at Buchenwald and who had once been an inmate during the Nazi administration of the camp. Of course, the guide never mentioned the Soviet administration of Buchenwald in the postwar period, 1945-1950, and we were wise enough not to broach the topic. Such a daring inquiry could have led to unpleasant circumstances, especially for Frau Giese, but also for me. Frau Giese said, "There is a sequel to the Nazi-administered Buchenwald camp that no one is permitted to mention. After the Americans withdrew from

Thuringia in July 1945, the Soviet occupying force retained the camp to incarcerate former Nazis and anyone suspected of having supported or sympathized with the Third Reich. Property owners and those regarded as capitalists were especially subject to incarceration under conditions comparable to those the Nazis had imposed. I am certain that had my dear Oskar been alive, although he had opposed the Nazi Party, he would have been sent to Buchenwald. Rumor has it that at least 7,100 inmates died here under the Soviet administration. Many innocent people died, people who may have joined the National Socialist Party in the early years in order to promote their careers or at a time when Hitler was in good standing with European political leaders, and even a treaty partner with Josef Stalin."

Many years later, when I became friends with a man, who as a child had emigrated from Thuringia to the US with his mother and two brothers, this sequel concerning Buchenwald under Soviet administration, flashed into my mind. My friend told me that his father was not a member of the National Socialist Party, but that he did own a modest business enterprise. My friend said, "My father was arrested and taken to Buchenwald. An inmate, who was released from the camp, told my mother that father was very ill. We never heard another word. After years of waiting for some information and, before the border between the BRD and the DDR was sealed, my mother, my two brothers, and I emigrated to the BRD, and from there to the US."

Frau Giese and I took the bus back to the center of Weimar. There still was time to visit the Wittum Palais, home of Anna Amalia, the mother of Duke Karl August, Goethe's patron. Anna Amalia's promotion of the arts was imitated by her son who, at the urging of Karl Ludwig Knebel, prevailed upon the twenty-six-year-old Goethe, the author of the very popular Storm and Stress literary achievement, The Sufferings of the Young Werther, to take up residence in Weimar. The time arrived for my departure. I invited Frau Giese for dinner in the Hotel Elephant as I had done a year earlier. Once again, after a good dinner and stimulating conversation, we were the last guests in the dining hall. I walked with Frau Giese to her flat. "Tomorrow we will go to the station together," she said. She sighed and added, "Then we must wait another year before you return to Weimar, but next year you will be able to remain longer if you participate in the summer school course." I promised that I would return. The next morning, just before boarding the train, I pressed a large amount of dollars into Frau Giese's palm. "Use the money as you need it over the coming year," I said. "I'll also send you packages from home." We hugged each other and I boarded the train headed for Dresden. As she had done the previous year, Frau Giese stood on the platform and waved a large white handkerchief. Her petite figure gradually faded from sight. I sat looking out the window at the summer Thuringian landscape, alone with my thoughts.

A Connection in Dresden

After walking about Dresden, I decided to have a late lunch in a cozy restaurant that I noticed facing the Elbe River. The restaurant is named "The Italian Village." Because there were only a few free places available at the tables, I approached a table where a young man sat alone and requested, "May I sit here?" The young man replied, "Bitte schön." I took my seat, picked up the menu and searched for my lunch selection. I introduced myself to my table companion, and we came into conversation. He introduced himself as Rainer Schulze. Rainer was in vocational training to become a waiter. This day on which we met happened to be his day off. I told Rainer that I had only a superficial knowledge of Dresden, having spent only one day in the city in the summer of 1964. Rainer offered to be my guide. We walked about the city, Rainer explaining each site visited. In 1965, many buildings in the center of Dresden were still rubble from the air raid of the night of Tuesday, February 13, and the early morning and midday raid of February 14, 1945. In those attacks, the Anglo/American squadrons dropped more than 22,000 tons of bombs on a city crowded with 500,000 refugees fleeing from the advancing Red Army. For four days fire raged over a twenty-kilometer-square district. Dresden was transformed into a giant crematorium. At least 35,000 people died in the raids. Since many bodies of refugees who had no one to inquire concerning them were cremated, the death toll probably was much higher than 35,000.

The destruction of Dresden, coming just nine days after the Big Three Yalta conference, in which Roosevelt, Stalin and Churchill agreed on allied occupation zones of a defeated Germany, raised the question of "why!" Now that the war was almost over, why destroy the "Florence on the Elbe" with such a horrendous loss of life among non-belligerents? Many were convinced that the Dresden raid was made out of revenge for the Luftwaffe's destruction of Coventry, England on Thursday, November 14, 1940. Die Frauen Kirche, one of the more beautiful churches in Christendom and a landmark of the city of Dresden, lay in ruins. (Note: On Reformation Sunday, October 30, 2005, on the 488th anniversary of the presentation of Luther's Ninety-Five Theses, October 31, 1517, and after generous international contributions to restore the church, the Frauen Kirche was reopened in a sacred worship dedication service).

After a full afternoon of sightseeing, Rainer invited me to his flat that he shared with his widowed mother in suburban Dresden. Frau Schulze was very gracious. "Where were you with your little Rainer on the evening of February 13, 1945?" I asked her. "Fortunately for us," Frau Schulze replied, "at that time, we lived outside of Dresden, in the direction of the Saxon Switzerland. From our modest residence, we could see the city engulfed in a sea of flames. The fires burned for days. Many of our friends and acquaintances were cremated in the inferno."

Frau Schulze had a modest pension, and in order to supplement her pension since Rainer had not yet completed his training to be a waiter, she continued to work as a guide at the Bismarck Tower, not far from their flat. From the Bismarck Tower, one had a splendid view of the city. "I dread the winters at the tower," Frau Schulze said. "There's no possibility of heating the tower. I wear layers of clothes and stay away from the door because each time the door is opened, there is a blast of cold air. How I rejoice at the coming of spring and summer!"

I invited Frau Schulze and Rainer for dinner. "You must suggest where we should have dinner," I said. Rainer smiled and replied, "Not far from here is one of the last private restaurants in Dresden. The proprietor is a friend of ours. Somehow he is able to acquire the supplies he needs to keep his restaurant in business. He believes that the authorities, knowing how bad the food and how boring the menus are at the state-owned restaurants, tolerate and even are pleased that a few private restaurants still exist." We went to the restaurant. The proprietor welcomed Rainer and Frau Schulze with a hearty handshake. I was introduced. The proprietor seemed especially pleased that a US citizen had found his way to his restaurant, tucked away as it was in a remote corner of suburban Dresden. The restaurant was completely occupied. For his friends, however, with their foreign guest, the proprietor found a table. We enjoyed a delicious dinner.

Rainer and Frau Schulze put me on the late streetcar that would transport me back to the city center and to the immediate location of my Inter City Hotel, Astoria. We exchanged addresses and promised to write to each other. I was scheduled to depart Dresden on the next day, and soon thereafter to return to the United States.

On Sunday, September 5, 1965, Dr. Albert Schweitzer (January 14, 1875-September 5, 1965) died in his clinic in Lambarene. I decided to prepare a lecture on the life of Dr. Schweitzer to present to my pupils and colleagues on the ninety-first anniversary of Dr. Schweitzer's birth on January 14, 1966. I had read enough concerning the life and mission of Dr. Schweitzer to know that, as a young pastor and professor in Strasbourg, he decided to transform the call he felt to minister to the people in Africa into the deed. The words of Leon Feuchtwanger came to mind:

> What good are thoughts if they contain only action's seeds.
> Useless the idea never translated into the deed.
> Concept remains an empty banality
> When never engendered into vitality.

The news that Erich Appel, DDR economic minister, had committed suicide in his office was very troubling because even among the most loyal SED members, doubts concerning whether or not he really committed suicide persisted. It was known in Party circles that Appel opposed subjugating the DDR economy to Soviet needs. Was it suicide or murder? One could not resist thinking about Jan Masaryk, Czechoslovakia's Foreign Minister, whose body, on March 10, 1948, had been found in the courtyard below his office. Masaryk had opposed the Soviet Union's helot, Klement Gottwald, in his attempt to bring Czechoslovakia into total submission to the Soviet Union. The official state-controlled media reported that Masaryk suffered from depression and had committed suicide. In my many later visits to Czechoslovakia, I never encountered anyone who believed the official report. In order to parry the suspicion that Erich Appel had been murdered, Walter Ulbricht announced to the Party Assembly that Appel suffered from depression. In a publication of 2009, Christa Wolf, who in 1965 was an SED Party member, wrote,

> Walter Ulbricht said to his Party members that Erich Appel suffered depression.
>
> Whoever wishes may read Erich Appel's diary.

Not one Party member requested to see Appel's diary. Such a request would have revealed that the Party member doubted the official Politbüro pronouncement of suicide. After the collapse of the DDR, Erich Appel's widow told Christa Wolf that Appel never had kept a diary.

On Thursday, March 24, 1966, I received a card from Frau Schulze:

Dear Dr. Foster and Family,

With this post, I wish to thank you again for the wonderful surprise at Christmas. The package arrived. As you write, dear Dr. Foster, you plan to return to the DDR in the summer. We anticipate your visit with great joy. It is possible that Rainer may not be at home. He probably will have to report for military service. We will wait and see what happens. I rejoice at the thought of your visit. Naturally, it would be more interesting for you if Rainer should still be at home.

Yesterday, Rainer attended the funeral of his mentor who last summer served us so well in the Dresden Main Station Restaurant. He died of a stroke at sixty years of age. A few weeks before his death, Rainer's teacher celebrated with us Rainer's completion of his waiter apprenticeship.

My health is somewhat improved. The weather could be better and warmer. That is our news for today. We wish you and your family a blessed Easter and good health. We look forward to a happy Wiedersehen. From far away, we greet you with all best wishes.

Frau Schulze and Rainer

Summer School in the DDR, 1966

After residing for a brief period in the Freiburg Carl Mez Heim and enjoying a reunion with director Lindenberg, Hermann Hützen, Manfred and Brigitte Otterpohl, Bernhard and Hildegard Hermann, Dr. Otto Stefan Wehrle, Professor Eugene and Dr. Maria Wölfle and other friends, I once again took the train to the DDR. At Gerstungen, the DDR border checkpoint, the experience of the summers of 1964 and of 1965, respectively, was repeated. As the train approached the border, conversation ceased. Travelers became silent, apprehensive and even fearful. Once again, a strong coffee aroma filled the train as DDR pensioners, returning from a visit in the BRD, had packed in their luggage the allowable allotment of coffee and, as the custom inspection would reveal, in some cases, much more than the permitted quota. The painful scenes of 1964 and of 1965 were replayed when, detected with more than their restricted allotment of certain items and when certain items, required to be listed, had not been entered on the custom form, people were ordered off the train so that a more thorough search of their luggage and of their person could be conducted. As I had done in 1964 and in 1965, after the train departed from Gerstungen, I looked out the windows on the right side of the train in order to catch a glimpse of the Wartburg when, the castle, perched high in the Thuringian forest, for an instant appeared in a clearing of the otherwise thick stand of trees.

I detrained in Eisenach on Friday, July 1, 1966. According to instructions sent to me from Professor Hans Richter, the director of the summer school and Mrs. Elfriede Böttner, the secretary for the summer school, I reported to the summer school administrative headquarters in Haus der Intelligenz on Johann Sebastian Bach Straße. Since there were no taxis at the Eisenach railroad station and a long queue was in place at the taxi stand, I decided to walk with my luggage (circa three quarters of a mile) to the Haus der Intelligenz. Later, I would discover that I could have taken a bus to within a block of the center. As I had done in 1964, I walked from the station to the Wartburg Allee, up the Allee, passed the Pflugensberg to where the Johann Sebastian Bach Straße intersected with the Wartburg Allee. On my right, I saw the Christliches Hospiz and, per instructions, I turned left into the Johann

Sebastian Bach Straße and walked circa two blocks to the Haus der Intelligenz on the left side of the street. I was somewhat startled and amused at the large banner with bold letters stretched over the main entrance of the Haus der Intelligenz. The bold letters spelled the word, INTERKURS. The banner announced to all arriving participants that the International Course for the German Language and Literature had its headquarters in this building. This building was not, as participants from the West at first were tempted to think, a center for procreative activity. I entered the building and recognized Professor Hans Richter whom I had met in Weimar in 1965. Professor Richter was seated at a table in the lobby. He rose immediately to greet me. He seemed genuinely glad to see me. He then introduced me to the lady seated next to him at the table, Frau Elfriede Böttner, secretary for the summer school course and Professor Richter's assistant. During the many subsequent summers in which I was to enroll in the summer school course, I learned to esteem Frau Böttner. She combined expert efficiency with a pleasant and affable personality, always ready and willing to help each participant of the course. Her patience, to me, seemed inexhaustible. Frau Böttner was partially lame in one leg and walked with a distinct limp. We all assumed that the lameness was the result of a childhood illness.

"You are the first participant to arrive," Professor Richter said. "On Sunday at 12:00 noon is the scheduled convocation and the official beginning of the course. All participants will meet in the main chamber of the city hall on the market square. Now I will take you to your host family where you will reside during the period of the course. Meals for all course members will be served in the Eisenach City Hotel, which is just a short walk from here."

Insisting on carrying the heavier one of my two suitcases, Professor Richter led me to my host family. The Rückert family resided at 2 Dittenberger Straße, about four blocks from the Haus der Intelligenz. Professor Richter and I walked the steep incline that led up from the Johann Sebastian Bach Straße to Dittenberger Straße. We came to a large house on the corner. Professor Richter rang the bell. An attractive blond woman, Frau Rückert, opened the door and bade us enter. Professor Richter already was acquainted with Director and Frau Rückert because they met when Professor Richter had visited them and requested them to host an American guest attending the summer school course. I was introduced. Frau Rückert escorted Professor Richter and me to a spacious room on the second floor which, in addition to a window looking out upon the garden, also had a large ceiling window. She also showed us the bath just opposite the room. We deposited my luggage in the room and returned to the living room for a brief conversation. Frau Rückert explained that her husband was taking his afternoon nap. I learned from the conversation that Director Rückert had been director of the Eisenach Theater, but that he now had been retired for several years. Frau Rückert then conducted Professor Richter and me to the garden behind the house. There, at the garden table, she treated us to coffee and cake. From where I was seated, I was delighted to note that one had a perfect, full view of the Wartburg, sentineled over the city of Eisenach. "What an inspiring scene," I thought. "Here from one's private garden, daily one could regard an historic symbol of the German nation; one could be reminded of Saint Elizabeth, of Tannhäuser and of the Minnesänger, of Martin Luther, of the Burschenschaften and of Johann Wolfgang von Goethe, and of the unique role the Wartburg had played in association with the main personalities and events in German history."

After reminding me to come to the city hall at 12:00 noon on Sunday, Professor Richter took his leave. "You must be tired," Frau Rückert said to me. "If you like, you may take a shower and rest. I will call you for Abendbrot (supper) when my husband also will appear." I thanked Frau Rückert and started to climb the stairs to my room. "Oh, I almost forgot," Frau Rückert said. Taking a key from a hook on the vestibule wall, she handed it to me with the remark, "Here's a house key. We are home most of the time and we retire late at night, but, in the event that we are not here, you'll need a key." I thanked Frau Rückert, went to my room, unpacked, took a shower and sank into a large, comfortable bed. Through the ceiling window, I looked out at the blue, Thuringian summer sky. I fell asleep.

After I had slept for a couple of hours, I was awakened by a soft knock at the door of my room and I heard Frau Rückert's voice: "Dr. Foster, we invite you to join us in the garden for Abendbrot." I answered, "Thank you. I'll be there in a few minutes." I got dressed and proceeded to the garden. There I met Director Richard Rückert (February 7, 1893-June 2, 1973) and Director and Mrs. Rückert's daughter, Rosi, and her husband, Carstans. The young couple, with their two little daughters resided in a third floor apartment of the large house. Frau Rückert introduced me. I learned that Carstans was an engineer in a local factory and that Rosi was on the administrative staff of the Eisenach hospital. The two little girls already had eaten their dinner and were playing in a corner of the garden. In the course of the dinner conversation, I learned that Director Rückert was scheduled to attend an orientation meeting for host families. "We will meet in the Haus der Intelligenz at 8:00 p.m. Would you like to accompany me?" he asked. I accepted the invitation and, after a good dinner and congenial conversation concerning my interest in the DDR and the summer school course, Director Rückert and I walked to the Haus der Intelligenz.

Frau Rückert, Richard Rückert, Claude

I realized that the privilege to participate in the Friedrich Schiller Summer School course in Eisenach, an urban community that Luther described as his "beloved city," was rare, indeed, and I was determined that, for the next three weeks, I would absorb as much as I possibly could. I agreed with the adage, "Concentration is the chisel of memory." In the large room, where I earlier had met Professor Richter, chairs were set up to accommodate the families who had agreed to host participants in the summer school. Director Rückert and I took seats near the rear of the room. At 8:00 p.m., a local party member, who, of course, with the exception of me, was known to the audience, introduced the official who had come from Berlin to present a pep talk. Since I had arrived a day earlier than the convocation for the summer school participants, the Berlin functionary did not know that a summer school applicant was in the audience, let alone a guest from the US, a nation that, in the DDR media, was accused of waging a dirty war of aggression in Vietnam. The speaker spent most of his time repeating the party line on major political events and then he reminded the families that hosting students from foreign countries provided a unique opportunity to present the DDR in a positive light. The agent said, "Those of you who will be hosting guests from capitalist states like France, Great Britain, Denmark, Belgium, Norway, Sweden and the Netherlands should exploit every opportunity to present our DDR homeland in the most positive fashion. Those of you who will host students from our allied socialist countries should seek to strengthen the bonds of fraternity and friendship we have with our socialist treaty partners and with the international proletariat."

I told the Rückert family that I planned to attend the 9:00 a.m. worship service in the Saint George's Protestant Church on the market square, just opposite the city hall. While the family slept late on Sunday morning, Frau Rückert provided me breakfast. I walked the circa one mile from the Rückert residence to the Saint George's Church. As I entered the church, I noticed the bronze tablet on the narthex wall that read, "Johann Sebastian Bach was baptized in this church on March 23, 1685." At least one-half hour before the scheduled service, I entered the sanctuary. I wanted time to look about the sanctuary that also served as a museum. In the many alcoves off the side aisles, there was depicted on placards, in chronological order, the major events in the history of the Thuringian Christian Church. A few minutes before 9:00 a.m., I took a seat on the center aisle about in the middle of the large sanctuary. There were many empty pews. I noticed, however, that just before the service was to begin, two or three women at a time and in short intervals, entered the sanctuary through the transept door of the church, located in the front of the church in the chancel area. Two, three, or four women at a time and in brief intervals also entered the church through the main door and walked down the center aisle to the front of the sanctuary. I noticed that these women apparently were acquainted with one another, for when the women who had entered the church through the main front portal saw the women who had entered through the transept door, and when the women who had entered the church in the chancel area saw the women approaching from the main front door, their faces registered recognition and surprise. Later I was to learn from Maria Urbaitiene from Kaunas, Lithuania the reason for this puzzling scene. As the organ music filled the sanctuary with the great hymns of the Christian faith, I noticed that many of the women, who had entered the church in such a shy, hesitant and secretive manner, wept. I also took note that most of the women had red, blue, purple and even orange-dyed hair. Why so many dyed-haired feminine heads? Soon I discovered that most of the women with the dyed hair were in the Soviet delegation. Even at a great distance, I was able to identify the female members of the Soviet delegation by their polychromatic heads.

After the service, I went out onto the square. It was a beautiful summer day, a blue sky and large cumulus clouds slowly drifted across the heavens. As the women who so cautiously had entered the sanctuary exited the church, I heard their conversation. They were speaking the Russian language. Since the service had lasted only about one hour, there still was time for sightseeing before the scheduled convocation at 12:00 noon. I walked to the Luther House Museum, just a short distance from the church. A gentleman, short of stature and very eager to tell me the story of the house, led me from exhibit to exhibit. Herr Quadron I soon perceived was an expert on the history of the Reformation in Eisenach and Thuringia. Herr Quadron said, "We believe that it was a house on this site and in this construction (of course, this house has gone through many renovations) in which the youth Martin Luther resided from his fifteenth until his eighteenth year, from 1498 to 1501." Herr Quadron obviously delighted in guiding a foreigner through his realm, a domain with which throughout many years of residence (he resided in a flat on the third floor of the building; the first and second floors being devoted to museum space) he had grown familiar, knowing each nook and cranny and each squeaking timber in the stairs which led to the second floor. "The youth, Luther," he explained, "for his care of the Cotta children, received lodging in this house from the Cotta family. During his residence in Eisenach, the boy Martin also attended the Saint George Latin School that prepared him for study on a university level, Latin being the language of academia in the sixteenth century. Martin also was a 'Partekenhengst,' a member of a boys' choir (Kurrende) who sang before the houses of Eisenach citizens for bread and cake morsels. The morsels were called 'Parteken,' derived from the Latin word 'pars,' meaning fragments or parts." Large paintings were mounted on the wall. One painting depicted the boy Luther singing for Frau Cotta; another painting portrayed the monk Luther being interrogated by his superior, Cardinal Cajetan, in October 1518, in Augsburg. This painting called to mind the dispute that developed in that interview between the German Augustinian priest and the Italian Cardinal. In his writings, Luther had challenged Rome's teaching concerning the Treasury of Merit, a dogma based on the 1343 Bull, Unigenitus, of Pope Clement VI. The Bull claimed that a Treasury of Merit exists, a deposit of all the merits of Christ and the saints, and that the Vicar of Christ had been empowered to draw merits from that treasury and extend them as an indulgence to sinners in need of satisfying the temporal penalty (poena) for their sins. Such a doctrine, of course, greatly enhanced the sale of indulgences, especially in the early sixteenth century when Pope Leo X was seeking to build Saint Peter's Basilica. Cajetan insisted that Unigenitus claimed that, by His sacrifice, Christ's merits are a treasury. Luther replied, "If the Bull so states, I will surrender the point." Cardinal Cajetan then turned to that section of Unigenitus where it reads, "Christ by his sacrifice acquired a treasure." Then in an instruction which revealed the German resentment to what the Germans considered Italian intellectual snobbery vis à vis Germans, and which the Cardinal could regard only as patronizing, this Augustinian, rebellious monk remarked, "To be and to acquire do not mean the same thing. You need not think we Germans are ignorant of grammar." After this exchange, Luther, to avoid probable arrest, had to flee Augsburg.

Another large painting reproduced the scene of Luther entering the Wartburg on May 4, 1521. A collection box, which the Eisenach partekenhengst employed to collect donations from their benefactors, lay under a glass-topped table. "We can assume," director Quadron said, "that this box often was handled by the boy Luther himself." Copies of the Bible in Latin and German lay under glass-topped tables. One of the Bibles from the fifteenth century contained vibrant watercolor scenes. "The colors have not been refurbished," Herr Quadron said. In large letters stenciled on one of the walls was the verse from Isaiah 30:15: "In quietness and confidence shall be your strength." On another wall, the words from Isaiah 7:9 were to be seen: "If you do not stand firm in faith, you will not stand at all." "These, of course, were key verses for Luther in his ministry, especially at the Diet of Worms on April 18, 1521, where the great Reformer responded to the imperial and papal demand that he recant, 'Here I stand. I can do nought else. God help me. Amen,'" the director commented.

After the tour with Herr Quadron, it was time to report to the city hall. I gave Herr Quadron a handsome tip in dollars. When he saw the dollars, a broad smile crossed his face. "Intershop Currency," he said. He meant by that remark that he would be able to purchase western goods in the special shops (called Intershops) administered by the DDR government, but in which shops western currency only was accepted. "Come again!" Herr Quadron said. I had told Herr Quadron that I was a participant in the summer school course and expected to be in Eisenach for about three weeks.

About seventy people filed into the large chamber at the city hall. As conversations were conducted, various languages were heard. I soon noticed that the few individuals from western capitalist states had traveled independently to Eisenach, as I did. The participants from the East Bloc states, however, had traveled in a delegation, the largest one being from the Soviet Union. I learned that the applicants from all the East Bloc delegations had been selected for the course by a university and by a state committee, respectively. Selection apparently had been made on the basis of academic promise to the school or university where the individual taught and political loyalty to the party. In subsequent conversations with some of my East Bloc colleagues, I was to learn that the canon for political loyalty was not always reliable in selecting people for study abroad.

We took our seats. Professor Hans Richter introduced the Eisenach mayor who had a few words of greeting. The mayor then introduced a party functionary from Berlin who welcomed us in the name of the DDR regime. This gentleman was not the agent from Berlin who had addressed the host families on Friday evening. I was almost tempted to think that it was the same representative of Friday evening because, apart from words of greeting to the summer school participants and the omission of references meant for host families only, the speech delivered was word for word what I had heard on Friday evening. I was amused. I thought, "two different functionaries, but the same speech." It was clear that the person, both on Friday evening and at Sunday noon, merely was reading a text that had been prepared by some anonymous party bureaucrat; "a one size fits all," approach.

After the speech, Professor Richter and Frau Elfriede Böttner invited us into another large chamber where a buffet lunch awaited us. We also could pick up supplemental information that listed the times and locations of the various courses and lectures, the meal schedule and the planned excursions. I noted immediately the day on which an excursion to Weimar was scheduled. I wanted to alert Frau Giese. Along with the majority of the DDR population, Frau Giese had no telephone. I wrote a postcard informing her of our expected arrival and assured her that I could leave the tour in order to spend that day with her. During the buffet lunch, I came into conversation with teachers and professors from Poland, the socialist Republic of Czechoslovakia, the USSR, Lithuania, Latvia, Estonia, Hungary and Bulgaria. There were only a few participants from Western Europe. I was the only US citizen in attendance.

Professor Richter inquired concerning my accommodations. "Yes, I am most satisfied," I said. "The Rückert family is very affable and I feel at home. The opportunity to gaze daily at the Wartburg from the Rückert garden is a great benefaction that I had not anticipated." I wrote the postcard to Frau Giese and walked through the center of Eisenach. Appropriately, in the heart of the city, there is a large bronze statue of Martin Luther with an opened Bible. I returned to my residence in time to have afternoon refreshments (coffee and cherry tart) with the Rückert family. When I told the family that the speech that I had heard at the convocation was the same speech that Herr Rückert and I had heard on Friday evening, my hosts heartily laughed. Frau Rückert exclaimed, "Well, Dr. Foster, this was your initiation into the mysteries of DDR politics and propaganda." Director Rückert added, "We have an adage that reflects your first experience with our highly placed political officials: 'Political officials are like books in a library; the least useful are placed on the highest shelves.'" We all laughed at Director Rückert's observation.

After dinner, Rosi, Carstans and the children retired to their apartment. Director and Frau Rückert and I sat in the living room sipping wine, engaged in animated conversation until 1:00 a.m. This would be the pattern of every evening during my residence with the family. From those conversations, I learned a great deal about life in the DDR. After we had become better acquainted and the family became satisfied that my interest for German culture and for the German Reformation was sincere, Director and Frau Rückert spoke openly about their concerns and criticisms regarding their society—expressing to a foreigner in the privacy of their living room opinions that they would not have expressed to their neighbors or in a public place.

Monday morning, I was up early and made my way to the Eisenach Hotel, near the Haus der Intelligenz. At about 8:00 a.m., most summer school participants were there. At breakfast, I sat at table with teachers and professors from various East Bloc states. The largest delegation was the Soviet one. The members of the delegations, however, came from different schools and universities and, before meeting to travel to Eisenach, had had no contact with one another. On that first day at breakfast, I noticed that the conversation was cautious. Perhaps the circumspection was because a US citizen sat at table with them, but also, I believe, because there were a few teachers and professors from the satellite Baltic States. In addition, there were "Betreuer" (guides) assigned to each class. The "Betreuer" were student assistants in the German Language and Literature Department at the Friedrich Schiller

University. Most of the "Betreuer" were affable aides with no propaganda agenda, but some were very zealous apologists for SED policies. These latter "Betreuer," not only guided, assisting foreign students to adjust to life in the DDR, but they also echoed the propaganda that SED party members presented almost every evening in the cultural programs. As one Polish participant remarked, "The student Betreuers remind me of the proverb, 'As the old birds sing, so chirp the young ones.'" These "young chirping birds," most of us were convinced, reported our conversational themes to party functionaries. Therefore, in the presence of certain "Betreuer," circumspection was advisable. After breakfast, we assembled at the Haus der Intelligenz and, depending upon the level of instruction for which we had matriculated, we were assigned to the proper group. Apart from language classes, there were lectures on German literature and history that were open to the entire student body. Most of these lectures were in the evening. After each evening lecture, there was opportunity for refreshments and fraternization.

After our morning classes, we returned to the hotel for Mittagessen (midday meal). After a midday break, classes resumed at 3:00 p.m. Abendbrot (supper) was served at 7:00 p.m., and from 8:00 p.m. until later in the evening, we were in the Haus der Intelligenz for lectures and fraternization. Each evening, at about 10:00 p.m., I began the fifteen-minute uphill walk to Dittenberger Straße. Each evening when I arrived at my residence, Director and Frau Rückert were seated in the living room. They invited me for a glass of wine and conversation. Each evening we sat together in interesting exchange until about 1:00 a.m.

Gradually, I became acquainted with my colleagues from the East Bloc. The conversations became less stolid and less pro forma, and we even permitted ourselves to tell selected political jokes. One lady who sat at table with me, Maria Urbaitiene, was from Kaunas, Lithuania. I noticed that she was polite, but very formal, in her conversation with Russian colleagues. As we became better acquainted, and on occasions when we were alone at table, I learned the reason for her polite, but cool attitude. "The Soviet Union occupies our country," she said. "Lithuanians are a very patriotic people. We resent having to live under

Soviet hegemony." I remembered that Maria was one of the women whom I had seen on that first Sunday morning in the sanctuary of the Saint George's Church. She was not one of those women with the dyed hair. Maria had beautiful dark eyes and natural black hair. The women from the various East Bloc delegations had entered the church three and four at a time. They seemed surprised to see one another. Maria explained, "The Communist government policy is to erode the influence of Christianity and ultimately to destroy the Christian faith. In Kaunas, for example, where I am a language instructor and my husband, a professor of chemistry, neither of us would dare to attend Catholic worship services in the beautiful Kaunas Cathedral where all of our ancestors worshipped. The university is a state university. The official party ideology is atheism. The Party teaches that religion is an opiate, a drug employed by capitalism to enervate the masses and keep them in subjugation to the captains of industry. If my husband or I were seen in a worship service in the church, we would be branded enemies of the proletariat and probably would be suspended from our university positions. We remain clandestine Christians. About one Sunday a month, we take an early train to a city where we are unknown. In a distant city, we can risk attending church. In order to be selected to attend this summer school, the candidates had to be nominated by their faculty and approved by local party functionaries. If the bureaucrats in Kaunas had known that my first act in Eisenach would be to attend a Christian worship service, I never would have been selected. I am in the Soviet delegation and came to church that morning with a colleague from Latvia and one from Estonia. We trust one another. In the sanctuary, we were as astounded to see colleagues from the Soviet Union as they were astonished to see us. It must have been a puzzling scene for you as a US citizen to see people slipping into the church, hoping that no one had seen them enter, and then to see the startled faces of these members of the Soviet delegation as they discovered one another in a Christian worship service. Of course, if the leader of the Soviet delegation had not slept late that morning and had decided to come early to the market square, we would have had to have had an explanation for our conduct. If needed, we had an explanation. We were there to see the museum exhibits. Because our overseer was absent, the old Russian proverb was applicable: 'Heaven is high and the

Tzar far distant.' I believe you Americans say, 'When the cat's away, the mice will play.'" We both laughed. Maria continued, "There also were members of the Polish, Czechoslovakian, Hungarian and Bulgarian delegations in the church. In fact, there were more foreigners in the church than there were native Germans. This need to be in the sanctuary on Sunday morning reflects the spiritual hunger on the part of people who cannot risk expressing their faith in their native environment. As the organ played the great hymns of the Christian faith, I could not help but weep. Did you notice that most of the members of our delegation also wept?" "Yes, I noticed," I replied. "I know, of course, of the persecution directed at the Christian Church by the several Communist governments, but, if what I witnessed in the Saint George's Church was any indication, persecution merely has driven the Christian witness underground." Maria nodded and said, "That's exactly the case. Despite all the party-sponsored discrimination, the vast majority of my countrymen still profess the Christian faith. We who are in public life must recite the party line, attend political rallies and carry propaganda banners. As teachers of the youth, we are expected to be enthusiastic disciples of Marx and Lenin. In order to secure our position, we must not do anything that would cast doubt on our loyal support of the government or on our ardor for the ultimate proletarian victory over capitalism. Publicly, my husband and I conform to the party line and directives. Christians and patriots in the Baltic States, in fact, in the entire East Bloc, subjugated under the tyrannical Red Army, in order to survive, invoke the proverb, 'Outward conformity is the security of the weak.' In our situation, to follow our conscience would result in dismissal and loss of livelihood. We imitate Joseph of Arimathea, the secret disciple, and Nicodemus, who sought Jesus out under the cover of darkness. But, remember, it was these secret disciples who, after the crucifixion, buried the body of Jesus while the twelve, having abandoned their Master, were nowhere to be found." Maria smiled and added, "After the space walk of the Soviet Cosmonaut Alexej Leonow in March 1965, it was proclaimed, 'The Soviets are on their way to the moon!' One of our farmers hopefully asked the question, 'All of them?'"

The curriculum in the summer school was varied and interesting. Apart from the systematic drills in German grammar, each evening, lectures on the German classical period were presented. Of course, there was as well a dominant accent on contemporary DDR authors and the Bitterfeld literary phenomenon. The Bitterfeld Movement, under the slogan, "Pick up a pen, buddy," sought to transform factory workers into literary artists. Since the proletariat is the subject of history and the future belongs to the working class, the socialist society, in preparation for the advent of world socialism, should begin now to enlist the industrial worker to glorify his vocation and to prophesy his messianic mission. In the political lectures, there were strong doses of party line propaganda. It was pointed out frequently that it had been in the Eisenach Golden Lion Inn (According to Eisenach documents, there has been an inn on this site since 1266. The inn was first named "Colorful Lion." Sometime in 1731, the name "Golden Lion" appeared in the documents. The inn now serves as a museum for the history of social democracy in Germany.) that Wilhelm Liebknecht (1826-1900) and August Bebel (1840-1913) had founded the German Socialist Party on August 7, 1869. The purpose of this congress was the foundation of a general German democratically regulated united labor party. The so-called "Eisenacher Program" demanded among others the abolition of class power, a modern right to vote, free education in primary schools, independent courts, therefore, the formation of a "free people's state." The programatic struggle between the followers of Bebel and the General German Labor Association resulted in a continuation of the Congress the following day, but without the GGLA. Then, the actual foundation of the Social Democratic Labor Party of Germany took place at the hotel "Zum Mohren" in Eisenach on August 8, 1869. The Hotel Zum Mohren does not exist anymore today.

One evening, a functionary from Berlin emphasized the need for dialogue between East and West. At the conclusion of the lecture, questions and comments were entertained. I asked, "Why not have an unimpeded media exchange between East and West? I personally have a free subscription to Neues Deutschland, the official SED daily publication. Dialogue could be enhanced if there were access to all ideas." The speaker's response to my suggestion was that printed matter from capitalist countries was too expensive for import into the DDR. I responded, "In exchange for the free subscription to Neues Deutschland, which I have received since 1964, I would like to provide to a DDR colleague a free subscription to a newspaper published in the US." There was a long pause and a dead silence in the room as the lecturer sought to formulate an answer to my suggestion. Of course, everyone knew that the reason why western publications were not to be seen in the East Bloc was not because those publications were expensive. The speaker then offered the rationale that the proletariat had to be protected from strident capitalist propaganda. The functionary's clever riposte was so transparent and, knowing that the auditors were accustomed to such explanations, I did not pursue the issue. We all knew that we were being told the big lie by a party bureaucrat. It was a painful experience for both the lecturer and the audience. When the party representative gave his answer, I noticed that Professor Richter's bald pate turned red and that Frau Böttner wore an embarrassed expression on her face. Out of deference for Professor Richter and Frau Böttner, for whom I had developed a great fondness, and also because I did not want to gain the reputation as an antagonist (I wanted to be able to visit the DDR each summer), I determined, in the future, not to ask provocative questions.

After the presentation by the Politbüro functionary, and, as the course participants spent some time in convivial conversation, a Polish colleague said to me, "That's an interesting idea that you presented about an exchange of newspapers between East and West. Our media reports only that which is published in the Soviet newspapers, Izvestia and Pravda. We say, 'Izvestiya means information and pravda means truth, but as we all know, in Izvestia there is no truth and in Pravda, there is no information.'" The resolve not to ask provocative questions was severely tested when, on one evening, a representative of the SED, quoting a line from Karl Kautsky's writings from 1892, "In the long run capitalist civilization cannot be sustained. Either it will move forward toward socialism or revert to barbarism," said that the political leadership of the US had demonstrated the veracity of Kautsky's observation, which Rosa Luxemburg had reduced to the apothegm, "Socialism or Barbarism." To illustrate his point, the speaker gave the example of the atomic bomb attacks on Hiroshima and Nagasaki on August 6 and August 9, 1945, respectively. He said, "This is an example of the barbarism of which Karl Kautsky and Rosa Luxemburg warned. The US employed atomic weapons not only to end the war, as was announced, but also to intimidate the Soviet Union. World War II was not over before the US began to prepare for World War III. The new enemies would be socialism and those societies that wished to recognize in the Soviet Union the paradigm for a socialist world order. The political leadership of the US did not hesitate to kill thousands of innocent people in these barbarous acts. As Karl Kautsky predicted, capitalism indeed had become barbarism. The noted scientist, Carl Friedrich Weizsäcker, on hearing the news of the atomic attacks, said, 'It is horrible that the Americans have done this. I regard it as insanity.' And one of the fathers of the atom bomb, Albert Einstein, in questioning the argument presented for employing an atomic weapon—namely that it would bring an early end to the war—wrote, 'No goal, no matter how high, can justify the use of illegitimate means to achieve it'" Even if one entertains grave reservations concerning the use of atomic weapons, the premise that the weapons were used to bully the Soviet Union and as a prelude to Capitalism's war against Communism strains credulity. I ached to respond to this presumption, but realizing that my earlier observations had placed the lecturer in a painful position and that I was the only course participant who raised "awkward" questions, I decided, because I wished to be able to visit the DDR in subsequent summers, not to make myself a persona non grata in the DDR. In the camaraderie among us that followed the presentation, a professor from Bratislava approached me and said, "Dear colleague, in my country we have a proverb that you may apply as you like to your exchange with the SED bureaucrat: 'A dictatorship is a regime in which all fear one and one fears all.'" With a wry smile, which spoke volumes, he thus introduced me to Moravian and Slovakian grassroots wisdom.

Early one evening, when no lecture was scheduled, I sat with Director and Frau Rückert and listened to the news broadcast on a BRD television network. The doorbell rang. Director Rückert walked to the television set and turned the channel to the East Berlin station. Then he went to the door. Dr. Sommer, the family physician, entered the living room. I was introduced. I learned from the conversation that Director Rückert was taking medicine for a cold and Dr. Sommer, on his way home, stopped to discover if Director Rückert had had any negative reaction to the medication. Dr. Sommer stayed only a brief period.

Upon his guest's departure, after Director Rückert had closed and locked the door, he went to the television set and switched the channel back to the West German station. Frau Rückert smiled at her husband's action and said in a somewhat chiding voice, "Richard, Dr. Foster will regard your action as hypocrisy." Director Rückert gave his wife an affectionate smile and said, "It may be hypocrisy, my dear, but you must admit it's much more comfortable."

Throughout my many years of summer residence in the DDR and in candid conversations with friends, colleagues, and even SED party members—of course in an environment where we could not be overheard—similar scenes to what I had experienced in the Rückert living room in July 1966 were repeated. These scenes suggested Will Rogers' humorous comment: "A family is well-ordered if it can sell its parrot without misgivings." A DDR parrot joke that parallels Will Rogers' wit relates that a parrot of a DDR citizen escaped from its cage. The owner hurried to the police station and breathlessly exclaimed, "My parrot escaped; my parrot escaped!" The police responded, "We're not responsible for retrieving escaped parrots!" The owner then said, "But in case you recapture him before I do, I want you to know that I do not share his political opinions."

DDR citizens were discouraged from watching western programs, but the ether knows no boundary and, despite state-sponsored intimidation, satellite dishes were positioned to receive BRD programs. Parents impressed upon their children not to discuss in school what the family watched on television. Each evening, before the daily news, a clock appeared on the television screen. The clock for DDR television had roman numerals; the clock for western television had Arabic numerals. Some elementary school teachers, who were political zealots, and who desired to penetrate family secrets, asked their pupils, "Does your television clock have numbers like this or like this?" The teacher then would write an example on the chalkboard, and the little children, anxious to answer, thereby would reveal the television channel the family watched.

One evening, Frau Rückert showed me a handsome pair of lady's boots. "These boots have an interesting history," she said. Director Rückert laughed at his wife's story introduction. "They are very attractive boots," I said. Frau Rückert continued, "My sister in the BRD sent them to me as a Christmas present. Of course, I had to pay a rather high custom duty. Here is the absurdity in the story of the boots. These boots are manufactured not far from here in the DDR. These boots are made for export only. They are nowhere to be seen in our shops. These boots, made in the DDR, are exported to the BRD. They were purchased in the BRD by my sister and sent to me, and although I reside not far from the DDR factory where the boots are manufactured, I must pay a custom duty to receive them. Our government receives payment in hard currency from the BRD. DDR citizens have DDR currency only. The last thing our government desires is payment in its own currency. The story of the boots reflects a capitalist practice in what is supposed to be a socialist state."

"My wife's boot tale," Director Rückert added, "illustrates how far the East Bloc Marxist states have departed from Marx's ideology. In the quest for wealth, those states imitate the capitalist rivals. Marx's criticism of capitalism now is applicable to us. Marx wrote,

> Money determines the value of all things. It has robbed the entire world, humanity and nature of their respective, intrinsic worth. Money alienates man from his essence and from his work; and this foreign agent dominates him, and he worships it."

After Director and Frau Rückert and I became very comfortable in conversation with one another, Director Rückert seemed to feel obligated to explain his political biography. "In the early 1930s," he began, "there was only one effective way of seeking to prevent Adolf Hitler and the National Socialists from coming to power in Germany. That was to join the Socialist Party, which, along with Ernst Thälmann and his Communist Party, was the major obstacle for the Nazis. Hitler exploited the fear of Communism among the captains of industry, in the middle class and in the Christian population and sought to undermine the Socialist Party by associating it as an ally of the Moscow-loyal Ernst Thälmann.

In a speech on Wednesday, January 27, 1932 to German industrialists in Düsseldorf, Hitler said,

> It is a great honor for me that today Herr Trotsky urges the German Communists to form a coalition at any price with the Social Democrats, since the only real danger for Bolshevism (as Trotsky sees it) is National Socialism…. We have the firm resolve to destroy Marxism in Germany down to its very last root.

"In fact, we Social Democrats were opposed to both Adolf Hitler and Ernst Thälmann. If there could have been a union between the Social Democratic Party and the Communist Party, there might have been a chance of blocking Hitler's path to victory. We Social Democrats could not accept Thälmann's vassalage to Moscow. We fought against Thälmann almost as much as we fought against Hitler. Employing the strategy of the ancient Roman Consuls, Divida et Impera (Divide and Conquer), Hitler was successful in defeating both the Communists and the Social Democrats. I was a young idealist who believed that, if we could thwart the Nazi drive for political dictatorship, social democracy could be achieved in Germany. We all know what happened. Despite all our efforts, Adolf Hitler was successful in building a dictatorship. Socialists and Communists were the first inmates in the Nazi concentration camps. In the first thirty days of Hitler's chancellorship, Dachau was in operation. I was young and not in any leadership role. I later was drafted. After the war, there was created, out of the Soviet Zone where I found myself, a coalition of a Socialist and a Communist Party. We had much work to rebuild a nation destroyed by war, but we were confident that we could now create, on the ruins of National Socialism, a truly democratic socialist society. On Sunday, April 21, 1946, however, our Socialist Party Chairman, Otto Grotewohl, was coerced by the Soviet Occupation Force to form a coalition with Wilhelm Pieck, the Chairman of the Communist Party, and thereby was born the Socialist Unity Party, known as the SED. For all practical purposes, our Socialist Party was absorbed by the Communist Party and the Moscow-loyal head of the SED, Walter Ulbricht, ruled according to strict party discipline. Gradually our idealism faded and we found ourselves, for the purpose of survival, conforming to the party policies. Dissent was punished by expulsion from the party and the loss of economic security. As a theater director, I could maintain a low profile, but I had to obey when called upon to perform party functions. For instance, for several years, I was required to serve as the Eisenach Party Chairman. To have refused this party-imposed responsibility would have threatened my very existence and the livelihood of my family. I had a wife and a daughter to consider. Once that decision was made in 1946 to join with the Communists in building the socialist society, it could not be rescinded. No one yearned for martyrdom. Nevertheless, we have had our political martyrs. You may have heard of Robert Havemann, professor at the Humboldt University. Despite the fact that, because of his Communist idealism, he earlier had been a victim of National Socialist persecution, in March 1964, Dr. Havemann was expelled from the party and his teaching chair. His crime? He had challenged the Party line. Because there was a new breed of political jackals anxious to climb the Party ladder, I was able gracefully and gradually to ease myself out of the Eisenach Party Secretariat. There is something to the maxim that began to circulate regarding three attributes— Communist, honest, intelligent. One cannot possess all three distinctions simultaneously. If one is a Communist and intelligent, he's not honest; if he's honest and intelligent, he's not a Communist; if he's honest and a Communist, he's not intelligent."

Director Rückert became very pensive. Frau Rückert stroked her husband's hand. She knew better than anyone did what an intellectual and emotional toll her husband had paid over the years. Despite its sensitivity, I felt compelled to ask the question. "Director Rückert, if you had known then what you know now, what course of action would you have taken?" Director Rückert's countenance became very sad and with a long sigh he said, "I would not have taken the first step. There are many in our state who, in order to survive, chose, as I did, this sacrificium intellectum."

Although I am, and always have been, a non-smoker, I knew that cigarettes from the US were better currency than DDR marks. After a long afternoon and evening in Erfurt where I purchased many books, I arrived in Eisenach at about the midnight hour. I knew that my hosts did not retire before 1:00 a.m, and I had a house key. With the bag of heavy books, however, I did not want to walk the long uphill distance from the railroad station to Dittenberger Straße. I sighted a taxi and requested the driver to drive me to my destination. To my great disappointment, the cabbie replied, "I'm going off duty. I am accepting no more customers." I quickly countered, "But there's no other cab in sight. I'll be stranded." "I regret," he said and was about to drive off. I quickly reached into my shirt pocket and pulled out a pack of Marlboro cigarettes. "Not even for these?" I asked. The driver's eyes became big as saucers. The taciturn, lethargic cabbie suddenly became loquacious, and with a broad smile on his face, invited, "Get in!"

During my three-week residence in Eisenach, I decided to request an interview with Bishop Moritz Mitzenheim (1891-1977) whose office on the Pflugensberg was only a short distance from the Haus der Intelligenz, which was the social and cultural center for our summer school course. I knew that Bishop Mitzenheim had been a member of the Confessing Church during the Nazi era and, therefore, the strong opponent of Ludwig Müller, Hitler's handpicked choice as bishop to lead a national church, cooperating with and coordinated into the Nazi State. After the collapse of the Nazi State and its lackey, the National Church, the mantel of ecclesiastical leadership in Thuringia automatically fell upon Hitler and Müller's adamant antagonist, Moritz Mitzenheim. Ludwig Müller (1883-1945) committed suicide in Berlin on July 31, 1945.

As retired theater director and former Eisenach SED party chairman, Director Rückert had a telephone. He invited me to use his phone to contact the office of "The Thuringian Fox," as Bishop Mitzenheim, because of his political acumen, was nicknamed by the local inhabitants. After dialing the number 5226, I heard the voice of a female secretary. I introduced myself and requested an appointment with the bishop. After a brief pause, the secretary gave me a specific hour and day when I could meet with the bishop for a thirty-minute appointment. At mid- morning on the day of the interview, I was ushered into the bishop's office. To my disappointment, the church lawyer, Dr. Gerhard Lotz, also was present. I did not know Dr. Lotz and I was uncertain as to how candid Bishop Mitzenheim could be in his presence. Later, through another experience, I would discover that Dr. Lotz, if not an enthusiastic supporter of the SED political hegemony, was a realist to the point where the adage could be applied: "If you can't beat them, join them."

In the interview with Bishop Mitzenheim, his political realism came to the fore. "Dear Dr. Foster," the bishop said, "the church in the DDR finds herself in a unique situation that results from the war that Germany, as the aggressor, caused. We now pay the debt for our fanatical nationalism. The victorious allies agreed to partition Germany into zones of occupation. What is now the DDR state formerly was the Soviet occupied zone. According to the Yalta and Potsdam agreements, our homeland fell within the parameters of the Soviet occupied zone, which, since October 1949, has been the DDR. This state is an ally of the other socialist states within the Warsaw alliance, which is dedicated to building a socialist Europe on the platform of a Marxist/Leninist ideology. Because the Christian Church in Germany failed to resist Adolf Hitler and, in fact, many Christians actively supported Hitler and the national church under Hitler's sycophant, Ludwig Müller, Communist governments insist that the role of the church be restricted within her peculiar ecclesiastical orbit. We are free to preach the gospel in our churches, but our failure to respond to the evils that prevailed in the Third Reich has forfeited whatever prerogative the church might have had to address social or political questions. We must come to terms with the political realities as they now exist. Would any of the western capitalist powers risk a war to alter the current situation? I think not. Therefore, as the Church did in the Roman Empire for three centuries until the imperium of Constantine, and in many other hostile political environments, we come to terms with reality. Our reality is that we live in a political system based on Marxist/Leninist principles. The church in the DDR is neutral. She is not a church for socialism, nor a church against socialism, but a church that finds herself within the socialist context and that seeks to conduct her ministry within that given demesne. It was Otto von Bismarck, that archconservative founder of the Second Reich, which endured from 1871-1918, who instructed us that, 'Politics is the art of the possible.' The Roman Catholic Church in the East Bloc states finds herself confronted with the same dilemma that we Protestants face. In January 1950, Pope Pius XII addressed the question and arrived at the conclusion similar to ours. The pope proclaimed, 'History shows that Catholic and Christian inspiration can be realized in the largest variety of ethnic, economic and social experiences. The Church knows that social and political regimes and the various forms of civilization are by definition changeable. The Church is ready to live with all without tying her life to theirs.'

"Thus, you see, Dr. Foster," Bishop Mitzenheim continued, "we seek to apply Luther's theory of the two kingdoms to our current situation. The kingdom of God is in the world, but not of the world. The kingdom of the world may have many forms—Roman Empire, Medieval Latin Christendom, autocracy, democracy, capitalism or socialism. The kingdoms of the world come and go, as history reveals, but the Kingdom of God endures, as Saint Augustine instructed us in his grand classic, De Civitas Dei." I interjected, "You know, of course, Bishop Mitzenheim, that, ever since you signed the Wartburg Agreement with the SED First Party Secretary, Walter Ulbricht, on August 18, 1964, you have been described in the western media as 'The Red Bishop.'" "Yes, I am aware of my 'Red Bishop' title in the western media," Bishop Mitzenheim responded. "If the media means red in the sense of the blood of Christ or red as in Red Cross, I accept the sobriquet. It is not just in the West that I am branded 'The Red Bishop.' Some of my colleagues here in the DDR also subscribe to that title for me. They accuse me of breaking ranks with them and of establishing a separate Thuringian Regional Church modus vivendi with the State. Politics is the art of the possible. What is possible for the Christian Church in the DDR in our current situation?" The bishop continued. "Let me tell you to what I agreed in that Wartburg conversation with Walter Ulbricht. To the state's request for the church's assistance in providing medical assistance to our population, I responded affirmatively. The church in the DDR administers 54 hospitals and many facilities for handicapped and retarded children. I was willing to say that wherever the church can cooperate with the state in improving the health and welfare of our citizens, the church is prepared to offer her aid. Of course, I speak for the Thuringian church only, but I'm certain that other regional churches in the DDR would be prepared, at least in this regard, to follow our example. Sophisticated and expensive hospital equipment, provided to our church hospitals by western benefactors, we are prepared to lend, as needed, to the state hospitals. In the DDR, it is well known that medical treatment in the church hospitals is superior to that in state hospitals."

As Bishop Mitzenheim related this point, the account was called to my mind of a case in Berlin about which an SED party member told me concerning his party colleague. The colleague suffered a coronary and had to be rushed to the hospital. The SED functionary pleaded with the ambulance medical crew not to take him to a state hospital, but to one administered by the church. Bishop Mitzenheim continued, "In that Wartburg meeting, I promised that the Thuringian Church will cooperate with the state in those areas where she could alleviate suffering and improve the general health of our fellow citizens. The church's humanitarian ministry must not be contingent upon the particular political authority in power. As Dietrich Bonhoeffer preached, the church must be there for others regardless of the political context in which her ministry is conducted." "And what does the state offer as a quid pro quo?" I asked. Bishop Mitzenheim responded. "The state promises not to interfere in the church's ministry, to guarantee her independence and to respect her right to govern herself. There were other aspects that the party chairman agreed to take under consideration, but I'm not at liberty, at this time, to discuss them."

Later I learned that the September 9, 1964 proclamation of visitation rights for retired DDR citizens to visit relatives in West Germany and the limited permission of West German residents to visit relatives in the DDR was a result of the Wartburg Mitzenheim/Ulbricht meeting. Of course, that Bishop Mitzenheim could gain such a concession could not be publicized and had to be presented as though it were a gratuitous gesture emanating from the SED Politbüro. Before taking my departure from the Pflugensberg, Bishop Mitzenheim gave me a copy of an article he had written for the Thuringian Church newspaper, Glaube und Heimat. The article appeared in the April 21, 1946 edition. The bishop had written,

> In changing times, our church remains the same. Ideologies come and go. Political structures collapse. Cultures flourish and fade, but the Church remains. How is it possible that, in the midst of continuous transition, the Church remains the Church? It is not because of the loyalty of her members. Nor can her permanence be ascribed to brilliant leadership. That the

Church, despite human frailty, has weathered storms and survived hard times is due to that abiding message that has been entrusted to her; that gospel that is not of human origin, the eternal Word of God, the evangel of the crucified and resurrected Christ, the victor over sin, death and Satan. The Church will endure as long as she preaches this good news. What is the error that has caused the current confusion and destruction? The Church's link with her power center has been short-circuited. In addition, the race has declared its independence from God, has proclaimed its autonomy and is convinced that life's problems can be solved without God, and even against God. It is necessary to recognize these troubling points. The ministry of the Church is to call attention persistently to these errors and to urge conversion to the living God and to His eternal, new-life-creating word. If this maternal word of forgiveness and of comfort that the Church proclaims at all times is really heard, then wounds are healed, relations among individuals and nations restored to order. Hate will disappear and the cry for revenge will be muffled. Then forgiveness will be practiced, for each one lives having been forgiven. In all areas of human existence, new life becomes possible.

Bishop Mitzenheim retired in 1970. He was succeeded by the Reverend Bishop Ingo Braecklein (installed June 15, 1970). Bishop Braecklein in turn was succeeded in 1978, one year after Bishop Mitzenheim's death, by the Reverend Bishop Werner Leich. Bishop Leich (Bishop of Thuringia, 1978 to 1992) took a different view of the church's coexistence and cooperation with the State. In fact, according to Bishop Leich, one of his main duties was to reintegrate the Thuringian Church into union with the other regional churches. He said, "Because of her close association with the State, which was coined in the expression, 'The Thuringian Way,' the Thuringian Church had been isolated from other DDR regional churches. I was able to end this isolation." As a reward for ending the isolation, Bishop Leich was elected chairman of the Protestant Church League in the DDR, a position that he held from 1986 to 1990. It was while serving in this position that voices of dissent in the DDR grew ever louder and the peaceful demonstrations ever larger. With all due credit to Bishop Leich for his achievements, the accomplishments of Bishop Mitzenheim should not be forgotten or underestimated. Bishop Leich's tenure, it should be noted, was under different political circumstances than those that had confronted Bishop Mitzenheim.

Frau Giese and I corresponded via postcards. The day finally arrived when the excursion to Weimar was planned. The busses, transporting our student body, halted on the large square in front of the Franz Liszt Music University. Frau Giese was waiting. I swooped her petite form up into my arms in a big hug. Earlier, I had told Professor Richter and Frau Böttner that I wanted to spend the day with Frau Giese. The sites scheduled to be visited by the summer school participants I already had seen with Frau Giese in the summers of 1964 and 1965. Professor Richter and Frau Böttner agreed that I should spend the day with my Weimar guide. In fact, because of her frequent inquiries concerning the summer school course and her attendance at lectures open to the public, Frau Giese had become well known to Professor Richter and Frau Böttner. I noted that Professor Richter and Frau Böttner had developed an affection for Frau Giese and that my friendship with Frau Giese greatly pleased them. I was informed when to report to the square in the early evening for the return journey to Eisenach.

Frau Giese wanted to show me Tiefurt. We took the short bus ride to Tiefurt. We got off the bus on the single street that led to the park and the chalet. On that street, there was a small restaurant. Frau Giese said, "This is one of the few restaurants still privately owned. It was about 11:00 a.m., and we were ready for an early Mittagessen. As we sat at table, we talked about the many events that had transpired in the past year. "I was disappointed," Frau Giese said, "that the summer school course was transferred to Eisenach. I had counted on daily companionship. But you do plan to come to Weimar for some days at the conclusion of the course, don't you?" "Yes, I do," I replied. After a good Mittagessen, we walked to the Tiefurt Park. We passed a large house and a garden surrounded by a low wall. "This is the residence of Weimar's Oberkirchenrat." Frau Giese said. "An Oberkirchenrat is an office similar to Church Superintendent." I took note of the house, never dreaming that in future years I and my countrymen, whom I would guide in the DDR, would spend many a happy hour in the garden enjoying Thüringian sausages with Hans and Christa Schäfer, who would, some years later, assume the office of Oberkirchenrat and move into the attractive parsonage. Joining my US countrymen and me in those future picnics would be Christians from the various Weimar congregations.

Once in the park, Frau Giese and I delighted in the broad paths that led us under ancient trees to the Ilm stream. Benches offered opportunity to rest. There, in such a placid, natural setting, we conversed and renewed the friendship which, since 1964, had developed into a strong bond. I knew that Frau Giese was not in good health, but as long as I was in Weimar, she kept a steady pace and did not seem to grow weary. When we returned to Weimar, we went to the cemetery. For Frau Giese, all cemetery paths led to Oskar's grave. "This is where I shall be buried," she said. "When I am no longer alive and you come to Weimar, please come here and reflect on our friendship. I like to believe that somehow I will know that you are here." We stood in silent meditation before Oskar's grave. Finally, I said, "Frau Giese, whenever I return to Weimar, I shall come to this place and remember, and thank God for the friendship He has permitted us to know." Frau Giese's beautiful blue eyes welled with tears as she whispered in a sob-inflected voice, "Thank you." It was time to board the busses for the return to Eisenach. All the students had re-assembled on the square dominated by the equestrian statue of Karl August. I gave Frau Giese a hug and, as usual, when parting from her, pressed a sum of dollars into her palm. "Intershop currency," I whispered in her ear.

The evening before our departure from Eisenach, Professor Richter and Frau Böttner hosted a dinner dance for all participants. I exchanged addresses with many colleagues in the East Bloc states. Of course, in time, except for a few pen pals, the correspondence gradually died. The "Betreuerin" of the group to which I belonged was a young woman. She did not seek to brainwash us with SED propaganda and, in fact, was obviously embarrassed by some of the statements we heard from SED representatives. One evening, an SED spokesman sought to persuade the audience that the erection of the Berlin Wall had been necessary to forestall an imperialist assault on the DDR by aggressive, capitalist forces. The Berlin Wall was, in reality, a defense perimeter to protect the State of Workers and Farmers. The BRD and the other capitalist states sought to destroy the DDR by luring DDR citizens to the West with promises of material wealth and indulgent ease, a la John Bunyan's Vanity Fair and Valley of Ease. Therefore, to thwart an impending imperialist assault and to protect its own citizens from the sirens of materialist prosperity, the DDR was forced to erect the Berlin Wall and to seal its borders with the BRD. This particular apologia, I noticed, by regarding the faces of our "Betreuer" and especially the countenances of Professor Richter and Frau Böttner, was most embarrassing to our hosts. Only a few of the "Betreuer," nodding affirmation to everything the SED apostle said, were able to suppress reason in order to insure the victory of ideology.

Before taking my leave, I drew my "Betreuerin," Renata Weber, aside and quietly presented her a gift that I had purchased in the Intershop. I wanted to show my appreciation for her studious devotion to our group. She was very appreciative. "Dr Foster," she said, "you no doubt have noticed that some of my fellow graduate students, who acted as hosts along with me, were not to be trusted. I regret to inform you that some of them acted as agents, reporting to their political mentors on conversations and opinions expressed by our foreign guests. These graduate assistants have an insatiable appetite for success and power. They believe that the most certain road for them to achieve their goal is to execute directives assigned to them and to demonstrate enthusiastic support for state propaganda, especially in the presence of foreigners. After all, as our proverb has it, 'The young dogs only learn to bark by imitating the old dogs.' I'm certain that you are perceptive enough to know which of the student hosts were in Stasi service. As we say, 'You are able to recognize the bird by its plumage.' At first, I was concerned for you because I noticed how solicitous Herr Klein was toward you and how, with apparent sincerity, he sought to befriend you. We Betreuer know Herr Klein to be one of the more enthusiastic informers, and I thought that I must warn you concerning his duplicitous attention, but I noticed that your keen political vision had penetrated the cunning façade of guile. Without my warning, you somehow knew to apply the grassroots wisdom, 'that apparent new friends and old wine skins are not to be trusted.' Now that our course has ended, I know that I can trust you not to repeat to my detriment this commentary on the Berlin Wall. In contradiction to what you have heard, I relate the following joke, very well known here in the DDR:

Walter Ulbricht, SED Secretary, died and went up to the Pearly Gates. Saint Peter opened the gates and seeing Ulbricht, said, 'You have erred, you must go to the other place.' Disappointed, and reluctantly, Ulbricht descended to Hell. Three days later, there was a frantic knock on the gates of Heaven. Saint Peter opened the gates and there stood the Devil. 'What are you doing here?' Saint Peter demanded. 'You know that you can't enter here.' The Devil entreatingly looked at Saint Peter and implored, 'I'm the first refugee.'" We both laughed.

Gratified that her DDR jokes found such an appreciative reception with me, Fräulein Weber offered another humorous example that reflected the suffocating government surveillance of public opinion. Fräulein Weber related, "An intoxicated man sat alone at a table in a pub and talked to himself. 'We have to get rid of this war monger, but hanging is too good for him. If we don't soon get rid of him, he will cause World War III in Europe. He is the most detestable politician and his own people hate him.' Seated at a nearby table, two Stasi agents heard the castigations from the intoxicated narrator. 'All right,' the agent said, 'that's enough! Come with us.' The agents escorted their prisoner to the nearby jail. In the interrogation room, they demanded, 'Whom were you describing as a war monger, detestable and hated by his own people?' The drunkard replied, 'Konrad Adenauer, of course.' The Stasi agents looked at each other in great surprise and finally said, 'O, you were describing Konrad Adenauer. In that case, you may go.' In leaving the interrogation room, the man turned to his interrogators and asked, 'Whom did you have in mind?'"

"Just to assure you, Dr. Foster," our 'Betreuerin' said, "that many of us do not agree with much of what we have heard from SED apologists, and while we still have opportunity for private conversation, permit me to tell you another typical DDR joke: Two border guards, Karl and Fritz, seeking to wile away the long and boring hours, came into conversation concerning government policy. Karl asked Fritz, 'Fritz, what do you think of our government?' Fritz, never having been posted with Karl, of course, was wary of how he should answer. Finally, he said, 'Oh I guess my opinion is about the same as yours.' Whereupon Karl responded, 'In that case, I must arrest you as an enemy of the State.'" We laughed again. The Betreuerin added, "For us, humor is like a button whose function is to keep the collar from popping open." She continued, "You might ask that if I harbor such secret thoughts of resentment toward my government why, as a youth did I join the Thälmann Pioneers and later the Free German Youth, and why did I opt for the state Jugendweihe instead of confirmation in the Christian Church? My parents and I were concerned for my future. Our state does not admit to higher education those youth, who do not cooperate with the state's program for youth education. I have friends, very gifted, but because they did not join the Free German Youth or accept the state Jugendweihe, they were not admitted to university. My parents and I chose the course: 'If you can't beat them, join them.' I hope that you can understand and forgive my hypocrisy. We Germans have a proverb: 'Accommodation is the strength of the weak.' Another proverb that describes our limitations says, 'Goats must graze on the meadow on which they are tethered.' What would you do in my situation?"

I answered, "Never having had to face such a dilemma, I cannot respond to your query. Given the political reality that DDR youth must confront, I would not presume, without having had to walk in your shoes, to pass judgment on your decision." I repeated my thanks to our Fräulein Weber and wished her success with her studies. "Perhaps we shall see each other next summer. I hope to matriculate in the Summer School Course again," I said. "Aufwiedersehen."

I had learned from Fräulein Weber that Professor Richter's young son had been killed while riding his bicycle on a street in Jena. It seems that an inattentive driver had struck the youth. That Professor Richter, despite the grief that he suffered, carried out his academic and administrative duties with such patience and solicitude for course participants, greatly impressed me and increased my respect for him. I then went to say farewell to Professor Richter and Frau Böttner. "Thank you for being such gracious hosts," I said. "I hope that you will accept my matriculation for the course next summer," I added. "You're always welcome," Professor Richter replied. "Write to me early in the year and I will reserve a place for you." I then informed Professor Richter and Frau Böttner that, before the beginning of the 1967 Summer School, I was thinking of leading some of my pupils on a ten-day tour of the DDR. "I noticed," I said, "that there are forms for pupil and student group travel that provide a fifty percent reduction in the cost of train travel.

Where can I get such forms?" Frau Böttner spoke up. "I can send the forms to you." I then addressed Frau Böttner. "Frau Böttner, as a token of my gratitude for your gracious hospitality and generous assistance, I would like to present you with this gift." With those words, I handed Frau Böttner several packages of panty hose, which I had purchased in the Intershop, concealed of course by wrapping paper. A broad smile came to Frau Böttner's face. I'm certain that she knew what was contained inside the wrapping paper. Extending her hand to me, she said with an affectionate voice, "Thank you Dr. Foster." With a warm handshake, we said goodbye.

While I initially had been disappointed that the course had been transferred from Weimar to Eisenach, I was grateful for the opportunity of meeting the Rückert family and also for the privilege of getting to know Eisenach. On my very brief visits in 1964 and 1965, I had concentrated on the Wartburg. The three-week sojourn in 1966 afforded me time to visit on several occasions the Luther House, the birth house of Johann Sebastian Bach (March 21, 1685), the Reuter/Wagner museum and the historic cemetery. It is reported that Fritz Reuter was an alcoholic. Concerning this account, the epitaph he selected for his grave seems most appropriate:

> The Beginning and the End, oh Lord, they are Thine.
> The Span between, Life, it was mine.
> And if I erred, in the darkness lost my way,
> With Thee, Lord, is clarity, and Thy house Eternal Day.

It was difficult to say goodbye to the Rückert family. Late into each evening, Director and Frau Rückert and I had had discussions on topics ranging over politics, religion, history and literature. For me, Director Rückert's pessimistic prognosis concerning the future of the DDR was arresting. "In 1945," he said, "we socialists had hopes of building a socialist democracy out of the ruins of the Third Reich. But with the establishment of a Soviet dictatorship, the crushing of the workers' revolt on June 17, 1953 and the sealing of our borders with the West on August 13, 1961, and the subsequent erection of the Berlin Wall, our hopes were dashed. The propaganda optimists in the Politbüro persistently brainwash the public with the drumbeat that ours is the best of all possible societies, and we pessimists in our state fear that they are correct."

On that late Saturday evening, July 30, 1966, before my next day departure for Weimar, Director and Frau Rückert presented me with a large medallion, minted in 1917, the four hundredth anniversary of Martin Luther posting his ninety-five theses. On the one side of the medallion, the bust of Martin Luther is engraved with the dates 1517-1917. Above the bust in a semicircle are the words: "God's Word Endures In Eternity." On the reverse side of the medallion, directly in the center, is cast the Wartburg. Circling the medallion on the outer margin are the names Eisleben, Worms, Erfurt, Wittenberg, Eisenach, Coburg. Beneath each name is the coat of arms of that particular region. Between each coat of arms is the Luther Rose, Luther's coat of arms. As a student of the Reformation, I was very moved by such a valuable farewell gift. I was certain that this medallion was rare and I also was assured by this act of generosity that our friendship was appreciated by my hosts as much as it was valued by me.

Before I took an early train to Weimar, Frau Rückert set a breakfast table for me in the garden. At that time, I did not know that the Rückert family and that garden would constitute such a magnetic attraction in my life, drawing me with irresistible force back to Eisenach and to number 2 Dittenberger Straße. I sat in the garden and watched, transported, as the early morning sun cast its rays onto the Wartburg Castle. What an inspiring sight! I reflected on the long history of the Wartburg and how it had become a religious and cultural symbol in the history of Germany, as one scholar expressed it: "All Germany meets itself at the Wartburg." Taking one, long, last and nostalgic look at the citadel, which had been residence to saints, minnesänger, poets, philosophers, politicians and theologians, bathed in a brilliant sunrise, I departed.

As the train pulled out from the Eisenach station, I reflected on all I had learned during the 1966 International Summer School Course for German Language and Literature in this city that Luther described as "His beloved city." The Rückert family had taught me very much. To this day, I recall the language riddle:

We are it during life. During life, we are not it; they are it whom we carry to the grave, and even these are not it. While we live, we are it, but presently, we are not it.

(In German): Dieweil wie leben sind wir es eben; dieweil wir leben sind wir es nicht. Die sind es, die wir zum Grabe tragen und eben diese sind es nicht. Dieweil wir leben sind wir es eben; zur Zeit, noch nicht. The word key to the solution of this language riddle is: Verschieden. The word Verschieden means different. Earlier the word verschieden in the German language also was employed to describe death. For example, "He has died," would have been expressed, "Er ist verschieden." Thus, we are it (different) during life. But we are not dead (verschieden); thus we are not it. Those whom we carry to the grave are it (dead), but even they are not it (different), for they are all dead. While we live, we are it (different), but presently, we are not it (dead).

Frau Giese waited on the platform at the Weimar station. After a warm embrace, we took the bus to the hotel Elephant. The wait for a taxi simply was too time consuming. Each day, for the entire week, Frau Giese and I were able to pursue our goals in and around Weimar. We visited Bellvedere, the beautiful gardens on the outskirts of Weimar. Frau Giese took me to visit Frau Dorothea Schirow who resided in the Maria Seebach Home, a home for elderly artists and their spouses. Frau Schirow was the widow of a concert musician. Of course, before going to visit Frau Schirow, I purchased coffee and chocolates for her in the Intershop. Frau Giese and I also revisited Buchenwald. We stood for a long time before the cell of Pastor Paul Schneider, cell number 23 in the solitary confinement bloc. I was anxious to learn more about this Christian martyr, the first Protestant clergyman murdered by the Nazis. Frau Giese then took me to Schöndorf to show me the Saint Stephen's Church, a church built as a memorial to the circa 56,000 inmates who had died at Buchenwald. In the sanctuary, I was captivated by the artist's arrangement of the steel sculptured barbed wire that stretched from each wall of the chancel to the center, but there, in the chancel center, the barbed wire was broken by a large cross. The artistic image is dramatic. The tyranny, brutality, suffering and death that marked his crucifixion, Christ vicariously employs in mankind's behalf to break the barbed wire that surrounds us and threatens us with suffering and death. In the parsonage just opposite the church, we inquired after

Pastor Siegfried Urban, the shepherd of this congregation. Unfortunately, Pastor Urban was not at home. Frau Giese's description of Pastor Urban's sermons and his wonderful rapport with youth made meeting him one of my future priorities.

The week passed quickly. I was amazed at how energized Frau Giese was. I knew that she suffered from several serious illnesses, but our mutual, daily, strenuous schedule did not seem to tax her. In fact, when I suggested a slower pace, she smiled and said, "It's once a year only that I feel this rejuvenated. In our brief time together, we must not waste a second." Before leaving Weimar, Frau Giese presented me with a package that contained the porcelain, the silver coffee spoons and the silver ginkgo leaf that she earlier had mentioned in her June letter. Attached to the package was a card that read, "Weimar, July 1966. Dear good friend Foster. With all my being, energy and thought, I have selected these gifts for you and your family, and I request that you receive them with these sentiments. From your ever faithful, Frau Giese. I commend you to God." Once again we stood on the Weimar railroad platform waiting for the train to Leipzig. The scene of 1964 and 1965 was repeated. After a farewell hug and pressing dollars into her palm, I stood at the open train window and Frau Giese waved a large white handkerchief. We both realized that twelve months would elapse before I could return to Weimar. It was a sad moment.

On my way to Dresden, I stopped off to visit Professor Max Steinmetz and his wife once again. I had been given a letter of introduction from one of my professors at the University of Delaware, where I had received my Master of Arts degree in June 1955. The letter from Professor Walther Kirchner was addressed to his colleague, Professor Max Steinmetz, historian at the Karl Marx University in Leipzig. I visited Professor and Frau Steinmetz in their home, at 16 Stormthäler Straße, not far from the Battle of the Nations Monument, the monument erected as a memorial to "The Battle of the Nations" that marked the defeat of Napoleon in October 1813 by the allies, Russia, Prussia, Austria and Sweden. Over afternoon coffee and cake, we enjoyed a cordial conversation. Professor Steinmetz expressed interest in my dissertation, "Johannes Bünderlin: Radical Reformer of the Sixteenth Century." "In late October 1967," Professor Steinmetz said, "DDR historians will convoke a Reformation Congress in

Wittenberg to mark the 450th anniversary of Martin Luther's Ninety-Five Theses. Many scholars from the East Bloc states will be in attendance. M.M. Smirin, from the Soviet Union, will present a lecture on Thomas Müntzer. Your dissertation theme would fit very well into our program and your participation would provide us a representative outside the East Bloc. I am the chairman of the Reformation Congress and I herewith invite you to participate and to share with us your research on Johannes Bünderlin." I was thrilled at the invitation and immediately accepted it. Before my departure for Dresden, Professor Steinmetz and I exchanged addresses. He and Frau Steinmetz gave me a cordial send-off. "Please greet Professor Kirchner from me," he said. "Next summer you must visit us again and by that time our Reformation Congress Program will be in print."

After a few days in Dresden, where I was able to visit Frau Schulze again, (Rainer, having been conscripted into the army, was not at home), I returned to Freiburg. After visiting my friends in Freiburg, Manfred and Brigitte Otterpohl, Bernhard and Hildegard Hermann, and, enjoying several evenings with Herr Lindenberg and Herr Hützen in the Black Forest Inn, I departed for the United States. When I returned to my teaching duties at the Tatnall School in September 1966, I found a letter, dated August 3, 1966 from Maison Dr. Albert Schweitzer, Günsbach, Alsace, France, waiting for me. The letter was signed by a Dutch nurse who had worked with Dr. Schweitzer in Lambarene. Miss C. Gilver, during a European furlough from her duties in the Lambarene clinic, resided in Dr. Schweitzer's home in Günsbach, Alsace. She wrote,

> Dear Dr. Foster,
>
> Mrs. Martha Wardenburg sent me several weeks ago the text of the speech which you held in honor of Dr. Schweitzer's birthday. I want to thank you warmly for that fine speech. Yes, we witnessed one of the most fruitful lives ever lived. A life that was deeply rooted in love for Jesus and His teachings. That was the light in his life, the warmth and the wisdom. I wanted to write and thank you in May, but could not do so. Since a few weeks I am here in Dr. Schweitzer's home country for a little rest, and I want to thank you from here for your fine understanding, your noble speech, your gentleness.
>
> With kindest regards, Miss C. Gilver (Dutch Nurse)

On Thursday, October 6, 1966, the press reported that during the Christmas season, December 1965 to January 1966, 823,904 West Berliners were permitted to visit relatives in East Berlin. At Easter 1966, 510,433 West Berliners received permission to visit family members in East Berlin and at Pentecost, the number was 467,885. Despite the threat made by the DDR that no more travel concessions would be made before the West German government extended diplomatic recognition to the DDR, the agreement for West Berliners to visit East Berlin in the Christmas season 1966 to 1967 was signed with the specific statement that, "the existing juridical and political standpoints are not to be altered." My conviction was that the average citizens from the DDR and the BRD could come together and families remain in contact, the better the climate for an ultimate reunification of Germany.

A new year's greeting from Jo Tschakarowa from Sofia, Bulgaria, dated January 1, 1967, reminded me of the affable colleagues I had met at the Weimar Summer School Course. The "Cold War" often was the subject of our conversations. Jo wrote,

> I wish you a successful and happy new year. I am relieved concerning your promise that your son will not drop any bombs onto my daughter's head. Last evening, I read in Somerset Maugham that conversation is one of the greater joys in life. I would like to add to that observation that communiqués from far away also bring much joy.
>
> With many hearty greetings,
> Jo Tschakarowa

I received a letter from Professor Bernhard Töpfer, professor for medieval history at the Humboldt University in East Berlin, dated May 17, 1967. Through the good offices of Professor Töpfer, I was able to receive a stipend for August 1968 from the Humboldt University that provided me lodging and permitted me to conduct research in the history seminar at the university.

Summer in the DDR, 1967

In the summer of 1967, with six male pupils from the Tatnall School, I traveled to Freiburg. After some days in Freiburg, I proceeded with the pupils into the DDR. Our first stop was Eisenach where we resided in the Christliches Hospiz. The pupils and I were invited to visit the Rückert family for afternoon refreshments. Once again, from the Rückert garden, I marveled at the view one had of the Wartburg from this idyllic retreat. The afternoon stretched into the evening and the family insisted that we remain for dinner—Thuringian sausages cooked over glowing charcoals. Just after it was decided that we would stay for dinner, Rosi excused herself. While she was absent, Frau Rückert explained to me, "Carstans now is a Geheimdienstträger (a person who possesses classified information) and he is not permitted any contact with people from the West. Rosi telephones him to tell him to remain at the factory until she calls again to instruct him that our guests have departed. Carstans can get a meal at the factory." In each subsequent summer when I visited the Rückert family, I saw Carstans infrequently and for a fleeting moment, time only to say hello or goodbye. Had it become known in party circles that Carstans had contact with a professor from the US, his career would have been placed in jeopardy.

During our stay in Eisenach, I introduced my pupils to the Wartburg, to Saint George's Church, to the Luther Haus and to the Bach Haus. In the Luther Haus, I was delighted that Herr Quadron was present to guide us. Herr Quadron spoke English well enough to explain the various exhibits to my pupils. He pointed out to my pupils the text from Isaiah 7:9, printed in bold letters on the wall that I first had seen in 1964: "If you do not stand firm in faith, you shall not stand at all." Herr Quadron then guided us to the small attic room where, it is reputed, that the youth Martin Luther resided during his Eisenach attendance at the Saint George's Latin School. In the Bach Haus, one of my pupils, who was a musician, was struck by Lugwig von Beethoven's evaluation of Bach: "He should have been named 'Meer,' not 'Bach.'" The word "Meer" in the German language means "Ocean." The word "Bach" means "Pond."

As we stood at the foot of the Bürschenschaften Monument, I explained to my pupils that the student fraternities, made up of super patriotic young men, were opposed to the mandates of the Treaty of Vienna (1815) which, with few exceptions, called for the restoration of the German political geography as it had existed before Napoleon's conquests. From the students' point of view, such a policy prolonged political particularization and was in contradiction to the spirit of the age, which was "union and democracy, Einheit und Freiheit." I told the pupils that in the year 1967, the DDR would sponsor anniversary celebrations, the 900th anniversary of the founding of the Wartburg, the 450th anniversary of the publishing of Martin Luther's Ninety-Five Theses, the 150th anniversary of the Wartburg Bürschenschaften Convention and the 50th   anniversary of the Bolshevik Revolution. All of these events were interpreted by DDR historians as a historical prelude to the establishing of the first Socialist and Democratic Society on German soil, the DDR.

Before leaving for Europe, I had had the travel forms sent to me by Frau Böttner, stamped and signed by the Tatnall School headmaster. On the eve of our departure from Eisenach, I went with my pupils to the rail station to purchase tickets for our train travel in the DDR. There was no one waiting at the ticket counter. I presented the forms along with our itinerary to Erfurt, Weimar, Leipzig, Dresden, return from Dresden via Leipzig to Wittenberg and on to Berlin. The woman at the ticket counter said, "You are not eligible for a fifty percent group discount on the train ticket. You are six pupils and a teacher, a total of seven persons. In the DDR, a group is defined as ten or more persons." "I was unaware," I said, "that the DDR definition of group was ten or more persons. If we are not eligible for the fifty percent cost reduction, we shall have to curtail our travel. We must eliminate Dresden, Wittenberg and Berlin from our itinerary. That is very sad. The pupils probably never again will have the possibility of visiting such interesting and historic sites."   The woman reflected for a moment and then said, "Every Hinz and Kunz (Tom, Dick, and Harry) travels in our country with a discount. Why shouldn't you?" And with those words she issued us a ticket with a fifty percent discount for our entire itinerary. We thanked her profusely for having arbitrarily altered the prescribed definition of "group," and thereby making it possible for us to pursue our original travel plans.

In Weimar, Frau Giese waited. She shepherded us to the sites to which she first had guided me in 1964 and 1965. Once again, despite her many ailments, Frau Giese, with great enthusiasm, shared her profound knowledge of German culture, and especially of classical Weimar. A hearty and relaxed association immediately blossomed between her and the pupils. To observe this petite, elderly lady, with a sovereign command of her brigade, shepherding seven males about Weimar, was indeed an amusing sight.

After our brief stay in Weimar, we traveled directly to Dresden via Leipzig. I planned to stop at Leipzig on our way north to Wittenberg. In Dresden, we took a trip up the Elbe River to Saxon Switzerland on a paddle wheel vessel of the White Fleet. We visited the Zwinger Art Gallery and admired Raphael's Sistine Madonna. In Leipzig, we visited the Battle of the Nations Monument, and the Russian Orthodox Church, consecrated in 1913, marking the allied victory over Napoleon on October 18, 1813. We also took photographs of the Pleissenburg, the castle in which the Augustinian monk, Martin Luther, and the Dominican monk, John Eck, had had their famous debate in 1519. Wittenberg captured the pupils attention because they had heard much about the city in their classes with me on the Reformation.

In Berlin, we took advantage of a connection given to me by Maria, a colleague from Romania who had attended the summer school course in Eisenach in 1966. Maria had said, "If you go to Berlin, get in touch with Frau Charlotte Rhode. She lives on Friedrich Straße. Here is her address. Charlotte also speaks English and would be happy to act as a guide for you and your pupils." I had told Maria that I was considering bringing my pupils to the DDR. I wrote to Charlotte Rhode and informed her concerning the dates I would be in Berlin with my pupils. Frau Rhode responded that she would be happy to meet my pupils and me, and she invited us for afternoon refreshments in her apartment. It happened that on that August afternoon, the Communist World Youth Organization marched in a huge parade down Friedrich Straße. From Frau Rhode's third floor balcony, my pupils and I had a perfect bird's eye view of this massive demonstration of Communist youth from every continent. As we watched the parade, a loud knock was heard on the apartment door. Frau Rhode opened the door and there stood three girls, members of the Free German Youth (Freie Deutsche Jugend=FDJ) in their blue shirts with the gold-patched armbands. From the street level, and because of the mass of people, the girls had difficulty observing the parade. They then noticed Frau Rhode, my pupils and me standing on the balcony and they decided to request permission to join us on the balcony where they would have a much better view of the parade. Frau Rhode welcomed the new guests hospitably. The girls were the same age as my pupils. The fact that my pupils had had three years of German language instruction facilitated lively conversation. The parade went on for hours, and the youth drank many sodas (Frau Rhode and I drank coffee) and they ate all the pastry, the DDR girls also being invited to help themselves. After the parade had passed and the refreshments had been exhausted, the girls said that they must report to their group leader. Their corps was from Dresden. We exchanged addresses. One of the girls, Ute Döring, was especially pretty, with beautiful blue eyes and curly blond hair. For the next six years, we would exchange Christmas and Easter greetings. I also exchanged addresses with Frau Charlotte Rhode, and I thanked her for her generous hospitality. On each subsequent visit to Berlin, I could rely on an invitation for dinner or afternoon coffee at Frau Rhode's apartment.

After a few days in East Berlin, I escorted the pupils to West Berlin and put them on a plane to return to the US. I returned to Weimar to where, because the housing now was available for the Summer School participants, the course had been relocated in its original home. I was delighted to see Professor Richter and Frau Böttner again, and, of course, Frau Giese. Frau Giese and I looked forward to the next three weeks of spending at least part of each day together. I was housed in the Hotel Elephant, but as a Summer School participant, not as a tourist. Since the tuition for the Summer School had to be regulated to accommodate the majority of East Bloc students, and they were unable to afford an expensive fee, I found the expenses for the entire three weeks in Weimar for me, coming from a hard currency country, very modest.

One Sunday, Frau Giese and I took the bus from Goethe Square for the circa four-mile trip to Schöndorf, a suburb of Weimar. We wanted to attend Sunday morning worship service at Saint Stephen's Church, built as a memorial for those who had died at nearby Buchenwald. The church, consecrated on May 15, 1966 on the east slope of the Ettersberg, was situated on the same geography as the infamous labor camp, which had been erected on the west slope of the Ettersberg. The Protestant residents of Schöndorf wanted to name the new church with the name of the Preacher of Buchenwald, Pastor Paul Schneider, who had been murdered by a lethal injection in the camp on July 18, 1939. Church officials in Eisenach did not approve of this name. Other names considered were "Mountain Church," and "Luther Church." Finally, four weeks before the scheduled consecration, the name "Stephen" was selected, because Stephen had been the first Christian martyr. In this Schöndorf memorial church, Stephen, the martyr in Jerusalem, and Pastor Paul Schneider, the martyr in Buchenwald, were united. The exterior architecture of the church suggests a ship on an eastern course. I could not help but think of the passage in Mark 4:35-41 and in Matthew 8:23-27 that describes the boat in which Jesus and his disciples were sailing when a great storm threatened to inundate the boat. The ship of the church had been threatened with destruction by National Socialism and now, in a state that espoused atheistic materialism, the ship of the church was proceeding through a very dangerous storm, which showed no signs of abating. Years later, when I gained access to Pastor Paul Robert Schneider's sermons, I was particularly impressed by a sermon preached on January 28, 1934. From that time on, the architecture of the Schöndorf church and the sermon of Pastor Schneider were linked in my mind. Pastor Schneider would become The Buchenwald Apostle. Pastor Schneider had preached,

> Now, dear Protestant Church and you, dear Protestant Christian, are challenged to confess and to witness. Don't be a dumb dog, for the Savior says, only those who confess me before men will I confess before my Father. Now you are threatened, you, Christian, in your Church, by billows which rise against you from the Church and State (The National Church created by Adolf Hitler, the so-called "German Christians," against which the "Confessing Church resisted). We are apprehensive and we are afraid. We find ourselves in the

position of the disciples on the Sea of Galilee. We cry out, Lord, help us or we perish. We cannot imagine how that little defenseless ship of the Church can be preserved in the face of the powers and principalities in the world. But we remember that in this ship of the Church the Lord is with us, that this Church has the promise that the gates of Hell shall not prevail against her.

At the front of the sanctuary, a large cross breaks through the thorn-tipped steel barbed wire stretched across the chancel area. The red tile floor reminds the worshipper of the blood-drenched Ettersberg soil.

Frau Giese had told me about the pastor, Siegfried Urban (pastor from 1966 to 1993) and I looked forward to meeting him and hearing him preach. It was a very good sermon, filled with allegories, which enabled the pastor to preach about the contemporary challenges to faith from an atheistic regime by couching his message in the historical context of ancient Israel and the primitive church. Pastor Urban preached that the prophets interpreted the Babylonian Captivity of Judah as punishment for the nation's sin. Pastor Urban, in a grave voice then said, "A nation that sins so grievously is bound to come under Divine wrath. We now experience our Babylonian Captivity, and we deserve it!" At these words, there was absolute silence in the sanctuary. I noted the pained expression on many faces. Because he almost had died on the Eastern front, and because he possessed impeccable veteran credentials, Pastor Urban could say to a German congregation things that would not have been accepted from many other preachers. There was no reference to the present, but everyone drew the correct conclusion when it was pointed out that, by his faith and confidence in God, Daniel, in the Babylonian Empire, refusing to accept the privileges offered to him by a heathen political power and by repudiating the worship of pagan gods, ultimately was rescued and rewarded by Elohim, the one true God. Likewise, Christians in the Roman Empire, Pastor Urban emphasized, rather than bow before the imperial gods, accepted martyrdom.

Pastor Siegfried Urban and Claude in Schoendorf, near Weimar

After the worship service, Frau Giese introduced me to Pastor Urban and his wife, Ingrid. Frau Giese and I were invited to come for an afternoon coffee on the following Thursday. I bought a pound of coffee in the Intershop and we took the bus to Schöndorf. It was a very pleasant afternoon and I was delighted for the opportunity to have conversation with a DDR pastor. I asked Pastor Urban what motivated him to become a pastor. "I was a youthful recruit on the Eastern Front," he said. "The Red Army was on the offensive. It was the final stage of the war. Our units were in retreat. I was wounded and fell into a shell hole. I was alone and I could not staunch the bleeding from my wound. I knew that I would die in that shell hole in no man's land. With each second, I grew weaker. I committed my spirit to God and prepared to die. Just at that juncture, a medical team from one of our units passed by the shell hole where I lay. The team members saw me, staunched the bleeding and carried me to a field hospital where I could begin to recover. Now, what are the odds that on that vast front, where the units are retreating over hundreds of square miles, that a medical team should pass through that particular shell hole where I lay just minutes before I would have died from loss of blood? As I recuperated, I decided that my life had been miraculously spared and that I would dedicate the rest of my life to serving God in the Christian ministry."

Frau Giese and I were very impressed with Pastor Urban's story. In contrast to other churches where I had attended Sunday worship service, the attendance at Saint Stephen's was very good. I discovered that Pastor Urban had a great appeal to the youth. He was a skilled soccer player and frequently played with them. In addition, he took them on hiking and camping trips in the Thuringian forest. Pastor Urban cultivated the musical talents among his youth, creating a brass choir that every Saturday evening, following a tradition that can be traced back to Charlemagne (742-814), from the front steps of Saint Stephen's Church, by trumpet, bass horn and French horn, announced the coming Sunday. We also know that the Moravians, in obedience to Psalm 150, were employing trumpet choirs as early as 1764. Of course, the fact that Pastor Urban was so popular with the youth displeased the party officials who sought to discourage the young people from attending church. Frau Giese and I thanked our hosts and departed. During my stay in Weimar, we decided that we would attend Sunday worship service in Schöndorf. This was the first of many meetings that I would have with Pastor Urban up until his untimely death of bone cancer in 1993.

From Weimar, I wrote to Bishop Moritz Mitzenheim in Eisenach and requested another interview with him. Bishop Mitzenheim responded to my post with an invitation to meet with him at the end of July. I was invited for afternoon coffee by the bishop and his wife, Ella. I remember a pleasant summer day when we sat on the balcony of the bishop's home with a splendid view of the Wartburg, a view similar to the one I had had from the Rückert garden on Dittenberger Straβe. Frau Mitzenheim (Frau Ella, maiden name Heim, died on September 19, 1979) served the refreshments and added commentary to her husband's explanation of the State/Church relationship in the DDR. Mostly, Frau Mitzenheim nodded assent to her husband's comments. Because this interview took place on the balcony of the bishop's residence and not in the official administrative office of the Thuringian Church and because only the bishop, his wife and I participated, and we did not have to consider the presence of Gerhard Lotz, our conversation was more relaxed and natural.

Regarding the Christian Church and the DDR, Bishop Mitzenheim (died August 4, 1977) said to me:

> Now that we prepare to celebrate the 450th anniversary of the posting of Luther's Ninety-Five Theses, you no doubt have noticed what efforts our state is making to capitalize on this historic date. This date and anniversary celebration will call the world's attention to the DDR. Striving for international recognition and the hard currency that western tourists, who will flood into our country for this occasion, will bring, this opportunity to garner both recognition and convertible currency is not to be missed. The state's quest for international recognition and the desperate need for hard currency, plus the fact that most of the German Reformation sites are   on   the territory of the DDR, plays to our advantage. During this year of 1967, the Politbüro realizes that world attention is focused on the DDR. There must be, therefore, no impression that persecution of the church in the DDR is taking place or that there is a Kulturkampf between church and state.

> In October 1949, there were two major errors committed — one by the state and one by the church. The Politbüro assumed that now that a socialist German state had been created, the life expectancy of Christianity would be very brief. In fact, it was reported that, within the party circle, some expressed the conviction that within a generation the Christian Church in the DDR no longer would be a viable institution.

> The mistake on the part of the church in the DDR was the conviction, given the pressure for German reunification, the economic inferiority of the new state in contrast   to   western Germany and the lack of popular support, that the DDR would, in short order, collapse.

> The Christian Church did not fade away, as some members of the Politbüro predicted, and the DDR state did not collapse, as some churchmen believed it would. Therefore, we find ourselves, church and state, residing on the same territory and ministering to the same population. This is the reality that both church and state have had to confront. We were forced to search for a modus vivendi. Because I have been willing to affect a rapprochement between our Thuringian Church and

the DDR ruling party, I have been branded The Red Bishop in the BRD. As long as the red signifies the blood of Christ and/or the Red Cross, I accept the sobriquet. I would be a persona non grata in many circles in the BRD, and even here among some of my clerical colleagues, I am a pariah. Therefore, when you return to the BRD, I request that you greet all greetable persons.

My tenure as Bishop of Thuringia soon will end and so will my earthly pilgrimage, but I am prepared, without claiming the prophetic mantle, to prophesy that the Christian Church, as she did in the Roman Empire, will outlive the political state. And because I am convinced of faith's ultimate victory, I am prepared, so long as our Gospel is not compromised, to cooperate with the political authorities in improving the life of all of our fellow citizens. I subscribe to Saint Augustine's thesis in his great work, de Civitas Dei, 'Secular kingdoms come and go; the Kingdom of God is eternal.'

On Saturday, July 29, 1967, Frau Giese presented me with a small paperback book, "With Goethe Through The Year." The book contains a quotation from Goethe for each day of the year. Frau Giese inscribed the book: "To be read with friendly thoughts and meditation; Your old Frau Giese, Weimar, July 29, 1967." To this day (2012), this little volume occupies a special place on my desk and is read each day in fond memory of my dear Weimar guide and friend.

Time passed quickly and soon it was time for me to take my leave from Weimar. "But now that you plan to return to the DDR in October, it will not be a whole year before we can see each other again," Frau Giese said. I had received an invitation from Professor Max Steinmetz to attend and to present a lecture at the historical convocation to be convened in Wittenberg to mark the 450th anniversary of the posting of Martin Luther's Ninety-Five Theses. After the conclusion of the conference, on my way back to Frankfurt from Wittenberg, I promised Frau Giese that I would stop to see her in Weimar. Once again, I thanked Professor Richter and Frau Böttner for being such gracious hosts. "Will you come back next year?" Frau Böttner queried. "I would like to," I said. "May I register you now for next summer?" Frau Böttner asked. "Yes, you may," I said. "How else," I thought to myself, "could I acquire such an excellent education—residence for three weeks in Germany's Athens, access to language instruction, theater productions, almost daily concerts by artists from the Franz Liszt Music University, excursions to sites of cultural interest and daily interaction with colleagues from the East Bloc for such a nominal tuition?"

I returned to the US and began immediately preparing my lecture for the Wittenberg conference. At the same time, I had a significant transition to make. In the spring before departing for Europe, I had accepted an associate professorship at the West Chester State College beginning in September 1967. At the spring interview, I indicated to the college president and to the chairman of the history department that I would need to be absent for one week in October in order to participate in the Wittenberg conference. They agreed.

Fall 1967, Reformation Historical Congress

Before departing for Wittenberg, I received a letter, dated Monday, October 9, 1967, from Mrs. Lillie Ragazova from Bratislava. Lillie was a colleague whom I met at the International Summer School Course for German Language and Literature. She was one of the participants from the East Bloc states with whom one could converse candidly concerning political affairs, especially the lack of democracy in the East Bloc. Lillie wrote,

> Dear Claude,
>
> Today I received your card from September 30 with great joy. I thought of Goethe's words: "Out of sight, out of mind." Frau Giese wrote to me about your itinerary with your pupils, and about your departure for the US. I hope that you found your family healthy and that your son's first school day was successful. As I can notice from your correspondence, you enjoy your university vocation. It is pleasant that, after vacation, one may resume his daily tasks. You certainly are engaged in much preparation for Wittenberg. I would like very much a copy of your lecture. Perhaps you can send me a copy from the DDR, or perhaps you can take a detour per airplane to us. It is no problem. We would be very happy to host you. Frau Giese will be very happy when you visit her. The poor soul relies onyou as if you were her son.
>
> I have not much to report concerning my life. After my departure from Weimar, being alone once again was very difficult. I immersed myself in my work. The beginning of the school year was marked by many difficulties. I have completed, however, the difficult translation of the poetic description of my travel log. My two children have returned from their visits in foreign countries. My son was in Italy and my daughter was in Switzerland. Now I also am kept busy with household tasks.
>
> On September 8, we marked the second anniversary of my husband's death. You can imagine how sad this memorial makes me. Thus, I continue on life's path. I would welcome news from you concerning your activities. I am interested in everything.

I continue to correspond with our Weimar colleagues. Frau Giese's letters are wonderful. Jeanette writes regularly. Mademoiselle Cicile and Frau Boyle from Manchester have written twice. I have not heard from Kati. Have you heard from her? Frequently and with great pleasure, I think of Weimar. It was a beautiful time. I hope that friendships made there will endure.

If it is possible for you to spend a few days with us, inform me early so that I can plan an interesting program for you. Perhaps you could present a lecture at our foreign language school. I wish you much happiness and success for your lecture in Wittenberg.

Hearty greetings to your son and wife. I await your answer and remain with heartfelt greetings,

Lillie

P.S. My nephew traveled to the US. He is in Colorado Springs. I gave him your address. Thank you for the inquiry.

In October, I prepared to return to the DDR for the Reformation Historical Congress scheduled for Tuesday and Wednesday, October 24 and 25. On Monday, October 23, in Frankfurt, I got on the train headed for Leipzig. It was late afternoon and the train was crowded. I walked through one car after another seeking an unoccupied seat. No success. I had visions of having to stand all the way to Leipzig, at that time, including the Gerstungen border control, a journey in excess of five hours. Finally, when I almost had given up hope, I discovered an unoccupied aisle seat. An elderly woman sat at the window. "Is this seat free?" I asked. The woman nodded and said, "yes." I secured my suitcase in the overhead luggage rack and took the seat. Gradually, I came into conversation with my seat companion, Frau Hedwig Dette from Grimma, a town in the DDR between Leipzig and Dresden. I introduced myself. Frau Dette was, as she described herself, "travel mature" (Reisemündig). That meant that, according to DDR law, she was old enough to visit relatives in the BRD. Women over sixty years of age and men over sixty-five years of age were considered by DDR authorities "travel mature." DDR citizens in this age bracket were pensioners and the DDR, by permitting them to travel to the BRD, did not need to worry about losing workers. Frau Dette laughed, as she said, "Because we know that we can visit the West at age sixty, the DDR is the only country in the world where women are happy to grow older."

"I'm curious," Frau Dette said, "Why are you traveling to the DDR?" I answered, "I teach history. My major field of interest is the Protestant Reformation. I have been invited to attend and to present a lecture at the two-day historical congress in Wittenberg that will mark the 450th anniversary of the posting of Martin Luther's Ninety-Five Theses." Frau Dette looked at me in astonishment. "You mean," She asked, "that you have come all the way from the US to Wittenberg to attend a two-day congress?" "Well, with travel time and a visit in Weimar," I responded, "I will be absent from the university for one week." I could see that Frau Dette was nonplussed by my answer. She softly repeated to herself, as though struggling to comprehend, "all the way from the US to Wittenberg for two days!" I explained to Frau Dette that I first traveled to the DDR in the summer of 1964 and that I had visited Wittenberg in 1964, 1965, 1966 and 1967. I also told her that, in 1966 and 1967, I had attended the Summer School for German Language and Literature conducted by the Friedrich Schiller University of Jena. "Most of the German Reformation sites are on the territory of the DDR," I said. "I can't afford to spend three weeks living in first class hotels assigned to me by the DDR Travel Bureau, but, as a student, matriculated at the university for a very modest tuition, I am able, not only to have the advantage of university instruction, but also to have the time and the financial resources to become acquainted with German historical sites on the territory of the DDR." Frau Dette and I engaged in conversation throughout the entire journey from Frankfurt to Leipzig. Once again at Gerstungen, because of the strong coffee aroma that permeated the entire train, there was a long stopover while the custom officials checked luggage to ascertain which passengers were seeking to import more coffee, or other items forbidden or limited in quantity, than was permitted into the DDR.

Frau Dette told me that she was a widow, that she had two daughters, one unmarried daughter who resided with her and a daughter who was married and who resided in Bitterfeld. "I have sisters and brothers living in the BRD," she said. "I meet the requirements for travel to the BRD," she added, "I am 'travel mature.'" It was early evening when the train pulled into the Leipzig station. I helped Frau Dette with her suitcase. We both detrained in Leipzig. Frau Dette's son-in-law waited on the platform for her. I waited for my connecting train to Wittenberg. During the journey, Frau Dette and I had exchanged addresses. "If you come to the DDR next summer," she said, "come to visit me in Grimma. Near Grimma is Nimbschen, the convent where Katharina von Bora (1499-1552), the nun who became Martin Luther's wife, lived before she, with eight of her sisters on Easter Sunday night in 1523, fled to Wittenberg. After her mother's early death, Katharina's father, in 1504, having entered into a second marriage, where Katharina's presence was not wanted, placed his young daughter, as a bride of Christ, with Benedictine nuns in the Brehna convent near Bitterfeld. In 1508 or 1509, Katharina was transferred to Nimbschen. Only a few walls remain of what once was a thriving convent. Nimbschen is only a short walk from Grimma." "If I can return to the DDR next summer," I said, "I would like to accept your invitation." Frau Dette's son-in-law picked up her suitcase. We bade each other farewell. I watched Frau Dette and her son-in-law as they walked the long platform that led to the main concourse in the huge Leipzig head-in station. With more than twenty tracks leading into the station, Leipzig has the reputation of being one of the larger railroad centers in Europe.

I boarded the train for Wittenberg. After about a one-hour journey, I detrained in Wittenberg's small station. There were no taxis available. Following instructions that I earlier had received, and as I had done on my previous visits to Wittenberg, I walked along the street that led from the station until I came to the main intersection. At the intersection, I turned right onto the main street. From my visits to Wittenberg in the summers of 1964, 1965, 1966 and 1967, I knew the route and the Hotel Wittenberger Hof, where I had a reservation. Professor Max Steinmetz sat with a colleague in the lobby. I was greeted by Professor Steinmetz and introduced to Professor Gerhard Zschäbitz. "You must be tired," Professor Steinmetz said. "Get a good night's rest. We can meet at breakfast tomorrow and I then can brief you on our program." We said good night and I went to my room. I took a shower and fell exhausted into bed. Within minutes, I fell asleep.

The next morning at breakfast, I met many of the congress participants. I was the only US citizen at the congress. Most of the colleagues were from East Bloc states; a few were from the BRD. The theme of the congress was, "The World Impact of the Reformation." Professor Steinmetz, the host of the congress, opened the proceedings with a lecture on this subject. The presentations took place in the auditorium of the Luther Museum, the former Augustinian monastery and then later the Luther family residence. Professor Steinmetz, some years earlier, recognizing that there were two aspects of the evaluation of Luther in the writings of Marx and Engels, had begun to introduce a revised version of the first, the older, orthodox Marxist view of Luther and the Reformation. The old, orthodox view based on Friedrich Engels' book, "The German Peasants' War," published in 1850, stated that the Reformation and the Peasants' War constituted the first middle class revolution in European history. Thomas Müntzer, the leader of the peasants, was frustrated in his attempt to create, by revolution, a unified, democratic German state. Luther sided with the princes, opposed Müntzer and the peasants, and thereby postponed for centuries the realization of this unified state. Engels regarded Luther's conduct as a betrayal of the masses. He saw Luther as the lackey of the princes in their effort to maintain the status quo. Marx, Engels' compatriot, considered Luther's theological conservatism the major factor in the defeat of the peasants: the revolution failed because of theology.

The second view of Luther and the Reformation, which can be found in the writings of Marx and Engels, is the view that Professor Steinmetz and his school seized upon and sought to expand. The Reformation and the Peasants' War, taken together, were still regarded as the first middle class revolution in European history, but it is acknowledged that the bourgeois revolutionary forces were too weak in the sixteenth century to realize immediately a new middle class political and social order, not to mention, according to Marx and Engels' initial interpretation, the popular socialist democracy for which Thomas Müntzer and the common people were striving. The Reformation, nevertheless, provided the bedrock upon which all subsequent revolutions were founded. The Reformation afforded the necessary historical breakthrough out of medieval feudalism and into the new capitalist society and the series of bourgeois revolutions—Dutch, Puritan, American, French—which were to lead Europe to the threshold of contemporary socialist societies. Seen from this perspective, the hammer blows in Wittenberg in October 1517 posting the Ninety-Five Theses that initiated the Reformation were echoed exactly four centuries later in October 1917 by the salvos from the gunship Aurora that signaled the beginning of the Bolshevik Revolution. In this rendition of Marxist historical analysis, there is a clear line from Luther to Lenin. Supplementing this second version of Marxist historical writing, Marx wrote, "Germany's revolutionary past is theoretical; it is the Reformation. As at that time it was the monk, so it is now the philosopher in whose brain the revolution is born." In this second variant, the reformer is depicted neither as a traitor to the masses nor as a lackey of the princes, but rather as a herald of a new age.

The political development in post-World War II Europe would determine which interpretation of Luther and the Reformation would gain approval in the DDR. As Professor Faustus had instructed his attendant, Wagner: "The past, my friend is a book with seven seals. What you call the spirit of the ages is in reality the spirit of those in whom the times are reflected." The DDR, arrogating Luther and the Reformation for its own political and cultural needs, would not be the first specimen and, as the subsequent years demonstrate, not the last example where historical interpretation is made to serve the needs of the state.

From 1945 to 1961, claiming that the German bourgeoisie had supported Hitler and therefore had forfeited any right to political power, German Marxists called for a united postwar German socialist state. In order to combat the threat of partition and dismemberment, originating in American, French and British quarters, German Marxists turned to German history for examples of national union. They found in Thomas Müntzer and the Peasants' War the first attempt to unite the German people in a socialist democracy. Since Luther had opposed Thomas Müntzer and the peasants, and had supported the German princes, he was responsible, in the eyes of the Marxist historians, for the prolongation of German political particularization. Luther thus became associated with the divisive bourgeois forces, and those very forces, in the twentieth century as in the sixteenth century, appeared to prevent the unification of the German nation in a socialist democracy. Thomas Müntzer, on the other hand, became the hero for DDR Marxist historians. In some early DDR Marxist studies of the Reformation, the postwar phenomenon of the two rival German states was reduced to "Luther versus Müntzer." DDR Marxist historians continued until 1961 to call for German unification under the banner of a socialist society. As long as that summons prevailed, the Marx/Engels evaluation of Luther as traitor, lackey and reactionary also persisted. The international postwar political rivalry, the Cold War, the US policy of rollback and containment of international Communism (the Truman Doctrine, March 12, 1947), and the Marshall Plan (June 5, 1947) prepared the way for the establishment, in 1949, of a West German state (the BRD), under the supervision of the western allies. When the BRD, granted full sovereignty, was integrated into NATO (October 23, 1954) and the western economic community, and when it became clear that no unification of Germany within the boundaries of a socialist democracy, as envisioned by the DDR, would be possible, the DDR sealed its borders against the BRD on August 13, 1961, and turned its attention toward developing a separate and sovereign German socialist state. The new DDR constitution of April 16, 1968 described the DDR as "a socialist state of the German nation." The words by Johannes R. Becher to Hans Eisler's national anthem, which depicted a united German nation, now were taboo.

After the sealing of the borders between the DDR and the BRD on August 13, 1961, and the promulgation of the new DDR constitution on April 16, 1968, Johannes Becher's 1954 essay, Ein Deutschland ist, soll sein und bleiben (One Germany is, should be and remain), no longer would be applicable. Becher's exceptional admiration for Luther also appears in strong contradiction to the earlier Marxist interpretation of the reformer. Before the Steinmetz, Zschäbitz, Gerhard Brendler revision of the Marxist depiction of Luther, this earlier view castigated Luther as an enemy of the common man and lackey of the princes who, by his alliance with the ruling class, helped to defeat Thomas Müntzer and put down the Peasants' Revolt, thereby preventing the establishment of a socialist, democratic, united German state.

In contrast to this early Marxist portrayal of Martin Luther, Becher wrote that Luther's linguistic genius, revealed in the reformer's German language translation of the Bible, marked him as the creator of the modern German language. According to Becher, Luther's Bible translation was the necessary harbinger to unite the German people into a national community. Residing in many wide-spread districts and regions, and speaking a multitude of dialects, the German people, through Luther's Bible translation, were drawn together into a national community and bonded by the infrangible adhesive of the biblical word in a beautiful, unifying language.

Therefore, according to Becher, what Luther began at the Wartburg (late December 1521 to March 1522), namely the translation of the Bible into the German language, permits him to be considered the precursor preparing the way for a unified Germany and that lofty rock parapet, the reformer's Patmos, to serve as a symbol for the indivisible unity of the German nation. (See: Johannes R. Becher, Publizistik, Aufbau Verlag, Weimar, 1981, pages 280-294).

The new emphasis on building a socialist society within the boundaries of the DDR silenced the call for a unified German state and raised the appeal for socialist patriotism and the integration of the first socialist state in German history into the broad stream of the international proletariat. Recognizing that no state can be born in a vacuum, and taking very seriously Engels' affirmation that the German Reformation is the pivot point of German history, the DDR began to emphasize the second interpretation of the Marx/Engels evaluation of Luther: Luther was the herald of a new age. This explanation facilitated the building of a socialist society by enabling the DDR to enlist in its efforts a broader spectrum of its population, the majority of whom had been reared in the Lutheran tradition. By his revolt against the Roman Catholic ecclesiastical hierarchy, the bastion of medieval feudalism, Luther had liberated bourgeois ideology. Under the direction of Professor Max Steinmetz, the new DDR Reformation historiography spoke of a new theology as the necessary precondition for the birth of a new ideology. Thus, dialectically considered, the theology that caused the Peasants' War to founder was the conduit through which bourgeois revolutionary ideology was channeled.

"The spirit of those in whom the times are reflected," to repeat Professor Faustus, was clearly seen in 1967 at the 450th celebration of the posting of the Ninety-Five Theses. In one of the major presentations, Professor Gerhard Zschäbitz of the Karl Marx University in Leipzig and colleague and friend of Professor Max Steinmetz, read excerpts from his recent Luther biography. Professor Zschäbitz employed a Lenin quote to exonerate Luther from what Professor Zschäbitz considered unfair accusations made by some of his Marxist colleagues. Lenin had written that historical personalities might be judged by the present generation not on what they did not accomplish but, rather, compared with their predecessors, on what they did accomplish. Professor Zschäbitz then concluded that Luther was neither a traitor to the peasants nor a lackey of the princes. Luther was bound to his time and place on the historical stage, and he acted, as he had to, in conformity with his historical milieu. The presentations at the congress did not mean that the rehabilitation of Luther resulted in the neglect of Thomas Müntzer. Both figures are needed to represent reformation and revolution if the dialectical tensions of the sixteenth century, which gave birth to the first middle class revolution in European history, are to provide the reflection that the twentieth century seeks to discover. Luther is the herald of the new age and Müntzer is its hero. The emphasis on the ideological foundation provided by Luther does not deprive Müntzer of his historic mission, for Müntzer's mission (popular socialist democracy), though not viable in the sixteenth century, nevertheless provided a paradigm for future socialist societies and also demonstrated the limitations of bourgeois revolutions. In his play, "Thomas Müntzer: The Man With The Rainbow Banner," Friedrich Wolf expressed this view, as previously mentioned.

Under Professor Max Steinmetz and his two most loyal students, Gerhard Zschäbitz and Gerhard Brendler, DDR Reformation historiography no longer would regard Luther and Müntzer as contradicting each other, but rather as complementing each other. In the grand transition from medieval scholasticism and feudalism to the new theology of the Reformation and the birth of capitalism, both Luther and Müntzer are necessary. No Luther, no Müntzer. To employ Gerhard Brendler, "When a Luther spoke, could a Müntzer remain silent?" In its competition with the BRD for historical identity and its claim to be the heir to German culture, the DDR, with most of the German Reformation sites on its territory, laid claim to this pivot point in German history. This very claim, however, necessitated abandoning a view of Luther and the Reformation that was associated with treason, exploitation and subjugation. As Gerhard Brendler reminded his Marxist colleagues, "We must recognize that we are striving to build a socialist society in a baptized country."

It was this major adjustment to the political realities that confronted her that led the DDR to surrender the vision of a united Communist Germany and to concentrate on building a socialist state within the territory on which the Soviet Occupation force had permitted the state to be erected. This new political posture necessarily brought with it the new interpretation of the Reformation espoused by Professor Max Steinmetz and his disciples, Gerhard Zschäbitz and Gerhard Brendler. In the following year, April 6, 1968, the DDR would publish a new constitution that would embody the revised position, the DDR declaring itself to be, "The Socialist State of the German Nation Under The Leadership Of The Working Class And Its Marxist-Leninist Party."

I presented my lecture, "Johannes Bünderlin, A Radical Reformer of the Sixteenth Century," based on my doctoral dissertation. Johannes Bünderlin was a radical, fringe figure of the Reformation. The lecture was received well. I felt quite comfortable during the presentation because I was convinced, given Bünderlin's obscurity and the difficulty in locating his works, that most of what I was telling my colleagues was unknown to them. From where I stood at the lectern, I could see the bold letters over the door at the opposite end of the auditorium. The text from Hebrews 13:7, especially in this matrix of the Reformation, was an admonition to the epigoni: Remember your leaders, those who spoke the word of God to you; consider the outcome of their way of life, and imitate their faith."

Seated under those words in Luther's lecture hall were circa one hundred DDR historians, including their guests and a select group of lecturers from the various East Bloc states, all of which states were committed to atheistic materialism. "What a strange phenomenon!" I thought. At the conclusion of my lecture, being the only historian from the US present and realizing the acrimonious atmosphere that existed between East and West, I made certain to thank Professor Steinmetz for the invitation to attend and for the hospitality I enjoyed. I also was careful to express my thanks to Professor Anton Blaschka and Dr. Helmut Deckert, who had provided me with copies of Bünderlin's works.

During the conference, I was approached by two reporters who requested me to give a radio interview. I was hesitant because I knew that, after a few questions concerning the conference, the reporters would pose questions concerning the contemporary political scene. That very morning, DDR newspapers railed against "The Dirty American War in Vietnam." I knew that the reporters would seek to lead me into a criticism of the US government's policy in Southeast Asia. Although I believed that it had been a mistake for the US to have become involved militarily in Vietnam, and I was greatly disturbed that the Pentagon had begun, in February 1967, to employ "Agent Orange" to defoliate the forests in order to deprive the Vietcong of cover, I certainly would not make such statements on DDR radio. To the reporter's request for an interview, I asked for time to reflect on the matter. Later that afternoon, I mentioned the invitation that I had received from the reporters to Professor Steinmetz and explained to him that I did not want to be discourteous or seem uncooperative but, at the same time, I did not want my words used for propaganda purposes. Professor Steinmetz said, "I understand. Neither do I want my guests to be placed in an awkward position. I will speak to the reporters." Later I learned that Professor Steinmetz said to the reporters, "Professor Foster is my guest at this historical congress that celebrates the 450th anniversary of the beginning of the German Reformation. If you wish to interview Professor Foster concerning his Reformation research and how he incorporates his research in teaching the Reformation in the US, you may. Do not, however, present questions to him of a political nature." I gave the interview. There were no political questions. The reporters, though no doubt disappointed, had gotten the message.

The conference ended and I prepared to take the morning train, on Thursday, October 26, to Weimar. Professor Steinmetz informed me, with a wink, that the local authorities had arranged for me to be chauffeur-driven to Weimar. The journey from Wittenberg to Weimar took more than two hours. I knew that during this journey I would have to be very circumspect in my conversation. I was picked up at the hotel by two men. They placed my suitcase in the trunk of the car. I was invited to take a back seat, behind the two escorts. Of course, ever since Professor Steinmetz had informed me that I was to be chauffeured to Weimar, the question that occupied my mind was: "Why would such special transportation be provided for me, which was not provided for the other congress participants?" It did not take long before my political antenna began to vibrate with the conviction that my escorts were "Stasi" (State Secret Police). They were well trained to guide the conversation into channels that could enable them to discover one's political persuasion. They no doubt had been commissioned by their superiors to present me with a selected litany of political questions that would enable the "Stasi" to project my political profile. They pretended that they had a genuine interest as to why I, as the only US historian at the conference, would make such a strenuous effort to travel to Wittenberg for a two-day historical congress. They were as amazed, as Frau Dette had been, at my adventure. I kept the conversation centered on the topic of the Reformation, that I taught this subject and that sources for my research were to be found at archives and universities in the DDR, that my Ph.D. dissertation investigated the radical Reformation and that Professor Steinmetz, whom I knew, because of his SED party affiliation and position, to be untouchable by these two "Stasi" lackeys, had invited me. I made it clear that my association with Professor Anton Blaschka and Dr. Deckert, whom I had mentioned in my lecture, was an academic one only. Of course, I did not mention the names of any other DDR acquaintances. I enthusiastically described to my escorts my visits to the Wartburg, to Erfurt, to Weimar and how pleased I had been to have been able to participate in the summer school curriculum sponsored by Jena's Friedrich Schiller University and conducted in Weimar. I wanted my "Stasi" escorts to see in me a naïve, pedantic egghead, a bookworm so immersed in the sixteenth century that he was totally oblivious to contemporary international events. By the fact of my four visits to the DDR in 1964, 1965, 1966, 1967, my "Stasi" escorts knew, of course, that

I had been cleared for a DDR visa at the official state travel bureau in Berlin.

When the escorts began to pump me for my reaction to the daily DDR headlines concerning the war in Vietnam, where the conflict was described as a "Dirty, American imperialist attempt to subjugate a small nation," I gave a vague answer expressing the conviction of all people for peace and international collegiality. I sought to strike a delicate balance, not to make any statement that could serve to fodder the DDR propaganda mills and, at the same time, to maintain an irenic, neutral position, which remained opened to bipartisan dialogue. By the glances that my escorts exchanged with each other, some frustrating, some revealing impatience at having to spend two hours in the presence of a "political dunce," and some of surprise at my expressions of admiration for the DDR's preservation of historical monuments and the promotion of German classical culture, I perceived that my naivety strategy was parrying successfully their propaganda probes.

Finally, we arrived at the market square in Weimar, on which square is located the Hotel Elephant, where Frau Giese and I had agreed to meet. I got out of the car. My "Stasi" escorts also got out, took my suitcase from the trunk and wished me a pleasant journey home. Frau Giese had spotted us and, not knowing that my companions were "Stasi," ran to greet me. There we stood on the market square in affectionate embrace. Why this US professor was in warm embrace with a petite, elderly DDR female citizen, I left as a riddle for my "Stasi" escorts that they could ponder all the way back to Wittenberg.

It was shortly before noon. We entered the hotel and proceeded to the dining room. I was scheduled to take the late afternoon train to Frankfurt. "This will be our last meal together," I said, "until next summer." "Yes, I know," Frau Giese said with a note of pathos in her voice. We had a very good meal accompanied by a good Rhine wine. After the waiter had cleared the table and we continued to sip our wine, Frau Giese said to me, "My physician tells me that I am not well, that my health is in serious decline. In fact, I probably do not have many more days. When you return next summer, I may not be alive." Her voice faltered slightly and then Frau Giese added, "I do not fear death. In fact, before we met, I desired to go to my dear Oskar. I still desire to go to him, but our friendship has given purpose to my life. Ever since our first meeting in the park, where I became your guide and, if I may be so bold to say, your Weimar mentor, I no longer was alone. Our friendship provided me with a new vocation, rejuvenated me, and death no longer was as attractive to me as it earlier had been. I read in the works of my beloved Dr. Albert Schweitzer the sentiment that I'm trying to express. Dr. Schweitzer wrote, 'Sometimes our light goes out but is blown again into flame by an encounter with another human being. Each of us owes the deepest thanks to those who have rekindled this inner light.' I could ignore the rude remarks of insensitive youths, who regarding me seated alone in the park, howled their resentment of the aged, 'cemetery vegetable.' For them the elderly merely take up space and diminish the food supply."

Frau Giese never before had spoken so bluntly about death and I had to conclude that her physician had given her a realistic and pessimistic opinion of her life's expectancy. She sighed and said, "For some our meeting in the park may appear to have been a mere coincidence, but I believe it was providential. Our friendship has given purpose and joy to these last years of my life. Our beloved Dr. Schweitzer also had an observation on such experiences: 'Coincidence is the divine pseudonym which our dear Lord selects when He wishes to remain anonymous.'" While still in a somber silence as Frau Giese's words weighed heavily on both of us, she pushed a plastic envelope across the table. "Please take this with you," she requested. "If I should die before you return in the summer, I do not want these letters to be lost. Upon my death, the vultures will flock into my flat seeking anything of value. These letters are the only thing of value in my little room." I noticed that inside the plastic envelope there were three paper envelopes. Frau Giese invited me to open the envelopes and to read the letters. At the top of each letter was stamped: "Dr. Albert Schweitzer, Lambarene, Republique Gabonaise." I was very curious. The first letter was dated Sunday, February 16, 1964 and was addressed to Frau Giese.

Dear Sister Elsbeth,

At the beginning of January, the beautiful, irenic angel, which you sent to us and which brought joy to all of us, arrived. The angel inspires us with peace. To achieve such a posture of serenity is a tall task, and you have undertaken to accomplish such a goal. Everything arrived intact, not exactly at Christmas, but our celebrations are not confined to a specific date. We celebrate whenever a festive occasion arises. How beautiful Weimar must be in Winter! Each year, with great nostalgia, I think of Christmas in winter. Here, Christmas comes at the hottest season of the year. Dr. Schweitzer sends his thanks. He rejoices over your generosity and he repeatedly remarks, with great feeling, how charitable people are toward him. In reflecting on the great goodness extended to him, Dr. Schweitzer is able to forget the exceptional burdens which he daily bears. Dr. Schweitzer's health, thank God, is good, but the many hours he must work cause him excessive fatigue.

I also thank you, dear Sister Elsbeth, and I heartily greet you.

Your Mathilde Kottmann

A postscript in his own hand is added to the letter by Dr. Albert Schweitzer:

I heartily thank you for such a lovely and interesting present. The photograph of the elderly Liszt is wonderful. Here everything is well. The clinic never ceases to expand.

With best thoughts,
Albert Schweitzer

The second letter was written on Wednesday, September 16, 1964, one year, almost to the day, before Dr. Schweitzer's death on Sunday, September 5, 1965.

Very Honorable Sister Elsbeth,

With the charming flower greeting from Goethe's meadow in Weimar, you brought much joy to Dr. Schweitzer and I wish to thank you in his name. How beautiful the celebration must have been in Goethe's house (August 28) which marked the 215th anniversary of his birth. Your description of the festivities is very arresting. I can appreciate your yearning to have had Dr. Schweitzer at this event. In 1957 and in 1959, on the anniversary of Goethe's birth, I had the great pleasure to be with Dr. Schweitzer in Frankfurt at the poet's birth house.

The house and the courtyard were bathed in candlelight and exquisitely decorated with flowers. Thank God, Dr. Schweitzer is well. It is astonishing what he, at his age, is able to accomplish. Daily, after a full day's work, Dr. Schweitzer provides us with a beautiful homily. Majestically he improvises a prelude to the choraleand then all, who are assembled in the dining hall, join in singing. Dr. Schweitzer then reads a passage from the German language translation of the Bible. He then reads the same passage from the French language translation. In conclusion, Dr.   Schweitzer recites the Lord's Prayer in the German language. On Sunday evenings, recordings of concert music are played.

> With every good wish, I heartily greet you.
> Your Charlotte (last name illegible)

A postscript by Mathilde Kottmann reads:

> Hearty greetings, dear Sister. Your letter is so cheerful. You write a lively description and I rejoice that you so kindly inform us. I thank you and greet you.
>
> Your Mathilde Kottmann

The third letter was written on Tuesday, August 3, 1965:

> Very Honorable Sister Elsbeth!
>
> I must begin this letter with the plea that you will forgive us for the long delay in confirming the arrival of your post, and the birthday greetings for Dr. Schweitzer, for which He heartily thanks you. It is only gradually that we are able to respond to the January avalanche of mail, and we still have not completed the task. The Christmas ornament you obviously made yourself, and it reflects very long and painstaking hours devoted to your handicraft. Please accept our heartiest thanks, and we send you warmest greetings from Lambarene.
>
> Edith Lenel

Frau Giese gazed steadily at me as I read the letters. "Frau Giese," I said, "I cannot accept these letters. These letters constitute very precious memories for you." "Dear friend, you must take them," she replied. "When I die, they will be lost. They'll be carried off by someone not able to value them. You know how to appreciate them. Please take them." "I can't bring myself to take such a precious gift from you, Frau Giese." "You must! You must!" Frau Giese urged. "Otherwise they'll be lost. I can't stand the thought of them being lost. Please! Please! Take the letters." I struggled with my emotions. I knew that Frau Giese was correct, that upon her death anything of value in her room would be expropriated by human vultures. I sensed how much these letters meant to her, how she read and re-read them. Frau Giese imploringly looked at me and kept repeating, "Please! Please! Please!" "Alright," I said. "On one condition, I'll take the letters. I'll keep them for you." "Yes," she softly sighed, "keep them for me."

At the train station, I pressed a large amount of dollars into Frau Giese's palm. Holding her in affectionate embrace, I whispered into her ear, "Happy birthday in a few days." The train that was to transport me from Weimar to Frankfurt pulled out of the Weimar station. Once again, Frau Giese stood on the platform and waved a large white handkerchief. Leaning out the window, I kept her petite figure in sight as long as I could. Finally, distance caused her to fade from view. I wondered if we ever would meet again. I returned to teaching at the West Chester State College. Frau Giese and I once again took up our correspondence. At the beginning of the year 1968, I received a letter from mutual friends informing me that on Thursday, December 21, 1967, Frau Giese had been found dead in her room. Near the end of January, I received a small package from Weimar, stamped December 20. Inside the package was a paperback book, a brief biography of Johann Wolfgang von Goethe. One day before she died, Frau Giese had mailed this present to me.

I wept. I had lost one of the more loyal and affectionate companions of my life. I knew the location where Frau Giese would find her final resting place next to her beloved Oskar, whose grave I had visited with her on many occasions. I sought to alleviate my grief with verse:

He stands silently at her grave
remembering summers past.
He had been enriched
for all she gave
with blessings which would ever last.

And now beneath the stone she lies,
that fair form returned to earth.
He thought about her life,
a happy ray
of joy, of love and mirth.

Her petite body,
frail and old,
had at last surrendered to the years,
though in Weimar's streets, he sees her still,
and brushes away his tears.

He walks in the park
where they often walked,
she always by his side.
He sits on the bench where they always talked,
and where she first offered to be his guide.

Each summer he meets her at the Ilm
where the bridge joins shore to shore.
At twilight he sits alone,
where quiet nature memory does restore.

This summer tryst
he will ever keep
as long as God grants life,
for in some transcendent union he knows
she is sister, mother, wife.

Still in a meditative mood at the news of Frau Giese's death, I wrote a poem about the marker at the head of the path where Frau Giese and I turned off the main footway to follow the side trail to Oskar's, and now her grave. The epitaph reads,

You blessed eyes what you have seen;
Be it as it may have been,
It was indeed beautiful.

I wrote,

You blessed eyes—
What you have seen
Be it as it may have been,
It was indeed beautiful---
The epitaph incised in the stone,
a description of life and love
many years since flown.
The green moss rooted in the lettered incisions
blurs the inscription
on the stone's weather-worn, gray face,
conveying its nostalgic farewell to earth
of the two who lie here,
who lived and loved at another time and in another place.
And we frail children of time
recognize in this marker
nature's eternal cycle and rule of rotation,
for as we supplant others, we shall be supplanted
by the next generation.
Thank we then heaven as the grave us
from earth doth wean.
For it was indeed beautiful
What our blessed eyes have seen.

Summer school in 1968, a year of revolution

Before traveling to Wittenberg in October 1967, I had alerted the editors of the journal, The Christian Century, that I could submit an account of my observations of the Wittenberg conference. The editors wished to publish my account as close as possible to the Reformation anniversary date, October 31. Before departing for East Germany, I submitted an article that was published in the October 25, 1967 number of the journal— "The Wartburg: Symbol of a Synthesis," to be followed by a second article upon my return to the United States.

Frau Hedwig Dette, the lady I met on the train on my journey from Frankfurt to Wittenberg in October 1967, wrote to me on December 12, 1967,

> Very Honorable Mr. Foster,
>
> In a separate post I have today mailed a Saxon Christmas Stollen (cake). I hope that you will receive it at Christmas and that you enjoy it. I heartily thank you for   your greetings from your native country. I was delighted to hear from you. What   is "Heart of Amish Land?" Is it a congregation or a colony? In any case, the "Heart of Amish Land" demonstrates that in the US one can find more than skyscrapers, glamour girls and playboys. If you should come to Saxony next year, I hope to be able to host you here in Grimma. Today I wish you a happy Christmas and a healthy new year.
>
> Frau Hedwig Dette

During the 1967 summer school course in Weimar, I had met Luitpold Steidle, the Weimar mayor. Mayor Steidle was very anxious to cultivate contact between young people from East and West. In the summer of 1967, he hosted a reception for my pupils and me with DDR youth in the Weimar City Hall. Mayor Steidle and I had several very fruitful and interesting conversations. Over the course of the years, our acquaintanceship developed into a friendship. Mayor Steidle wrote to me on December 21, 1967,

> Very Honorable Mr. Foster,

With great joy I received your very informative letter of November 30, 1967. Your letter is a new witness for me as to how intensively you occupy yourself with the cultural events of our German Democratic Republic, and especially with the humanistic traditions of our German history. Unfortunately, it was not possible to meet you in Wittenberg at the 450th anniversary celebration of the Reformation, and to hear your lecture, about which I since have heard…. I include with this letter the special New Year Greeting of our city. May you enjoy happy and recuperative Christmas days, the best health in the coming year, and may your worthwhile goals be realized in the New Year and in an extended future.

With a special feeling of camaraderie, I greet you.

Steidle

On the same date on which Mayor Luitpold Steidle wrote to me, December 21, 1967, my dear friend and Weimar guide, Frau Elsbeth Giese died. Weimar friends wrote to inform me of Frau Giese's death, and from Frau Giese's half sister, residing in Schwerin, I received a card, dated January 7, 1968, that conveyed the same sad news. Frau Valisha Schumacher (maiden name Giese), wrote,

From my sister's voluminous correspondence with you, I have a picture of the spiritual kinship that existed between you and her. The friendship with you was my sister's great joy. I wish to thank you and your family for this exceptional friendship.

Your, Valisha Schumacher

In the summer of 1968, I once again registered for the Summer School Course in Weimar conducted by the Friedrich Schiller University in Jena. Once again, I met Professor Hans Richter and his assistants, Dr. Beyer and Frau Elfriede Böttner, who so effectively administered the curriculum. I was housed in the Hotel Elephant, but as a student matriculated in the Summer School Course. The tuition that I had remitted for the course included room and board. This meant that I resided for three weeks in one of the more expensive first class DDR hotels where, had I resided in this hotel as a tourist, the cost of a three-week occupancy would have exceeded by far the tuition that I had paid for the Summer School Course. There also were course participants from the Soviet Union, Czechoslovakia, Romania, Poland and Lithuania housed in the Hotel Elephant. After registering my arrival with Professor Richter and Frau Böttner and unpacking, I went immediately to the park. I passed the bust of Alexander Pushkin (1739-1837) at the head of the park path that led to the Ilm Bridge. I remembered how Frau Giese had told me that from her window she could see this entrance to the park that had become familiar and endeared to us.

I descended the path and crossed the bridge. There stood a bench on the very spot where Frau Giese and I first had met in the summer of 1964. It seemed that I still could hear her response to my remark, "I don't want to take up your time." Frau Giese had responded, "Young man, I don't have a thing to do." To which I answered, "Madame, please come with me." And thus began our association that would develop into a beautiful friendship. I sat on the bench and reflected on the many fruitful hours and conversations Frau Giese and I had shared. She had been such an excellent guide that I now was able independently to find my way about Weimar and to appreciate the cultural and historical significance of each site visited. I no longer needed to ask that question, which had initiated our relationship: "Pardon me, could you please tell me how I might get to the cemetery?"

After a period of long, nostalgic meditation, I set off for the cemetery. Not far from the cemetery entrance on Poseckscher Garten, a florist is located. I purchased a plant that I could place at Frau Giese's gravesite. I wanted a more permanent decoration than a cut flower arrangement could provide. I then walked the path that I, with Frau Giese, so often had walked. Once again, as was our custom, I paused at the large, erect stone marker, which stood opposite the fountain and at the head of the path that branched off to the left in the direction of Oskar's grave. I read again the words from Goethe's Faust incised in the stone:

You blessed eyes, what you have seen,
Be it as it may have been, it was indeed beautiful.

I then turned into the side path and followed its descent to the grave. Frau Giese had left instructions. On the stone marker which bore the name Alice and Oskar Rommeis now also was incised, "Elsbeth Giese 1893-1967." Across from the grave, on the opposite side of the path, was a plot into which refuse was deposited. I retrieved a sharp-edged branch, burrowed in the soft earth and place the plant in the cavity. From the nearby fountain, where buckets were suspended on a metal frame, I took a bucket, filled it with water and watered the plant and the ivy that covered the gravesite. I stood for a long time in silence before the grave, thanking God for His servant, Elsbeth Giese.

The summer school course provided a rich curriculum of German language and literature. Each evening the course participants met on an informal basis in the Haus der Intelligenz on Mozart Straβe. Usually an author would read from his or her works or a government official from Berlin would present the SED interpretation of current political events. For me, as a US citizen, the sessions with the political briefings were most painful, frustrating and annoying. While I was not in total agreement with my government's foreign policy, I found the highly selective and censored information that was provided by DDR political missionaries biased and distorted.

One theme presented made me uncomfortable. Speaker after speaker depicted US society as a jungle where violence ruled. They pointed to the assassination of President John Kennedy on November 22, 1963, the assassination of Martin Luther King on April 4, 1968 and to the assault on Robert Kennedy on June 5, 1968 that caused his death on June 6. In contrast to socialist societies, capitalist societies, especially the US, because of the powerful gun lobby, permitted easy access to weapons. In the case of Martin Luther King, the SED political interpreters emphasized the racial discrimination in the US. Even though painful, it was informative to hear how my nation was evaluated in the eyes of others and how social turmoil and the civil rights protest in the US provided grist for their Communist propaganda mills.

Beginning in 1967, other crises in the West that played into the hands of DDR propaganda included the student protests in the BRD, in France, and in the United States. In the protest rally in West Berlin, on June 2, 1967, against the visit of the Iranian Shah, Mohammed Rez

Pahlavi, the student, Benno Ohnesorg, was shot and killed by a West Berlin policeman. This death of a young theology student caused violent student protests throughout the BRD. The students protested against the established social and economic order in the BRD. The new generation protested against their elders—elders now in control of the society—who had permitted the rise of National Socialism. The United States' policy in Vietnam also was protested. Student strikes and occupation of university buildings caused chaos in many BRD university centers. Students in the United States, who protested the United States' conduct in Vietnam, borrowed tactics of revolt from their German and French peers.

Some BRD media reports suggested that the student rioters were receiving clandestine financial support from the DDR. The charismatic leader of the student protest movement, Rudi Dutschke (July 30, 1940- December 24, 1979) had emigrated from the DDR to the BRD. The situation in the BRD became even more inflamed when, on Saturday, April 11, 1968, on the West Berlin Kurfürstendamm, Josef Bachmann attempted to assassinate Rudi Dutschke. Dutschke suffered a serious head wound. Protests erupted in all BRD university centers. In Munich, two people were killed in the protest rallies.

Although the head wound did not kill Rudi Dutschke, it seriously impaired his ability to speak and to remember. The wound also subjected him to violent seizures. Rudi Dutschke died in Aarhus, Denmark on Monday, December 24, 1979. In 2009, Hosea Dutschke, Rudi's son, wrote an account of his father's death. Hosea, in December 1979, was eleven years old. According to Hosea's report, Hosea, his younger sister, Polly, his mother, Gretchen, and his father Rudi, had cut a Christmas tree and were preparing for Christmas when Rudi suffered an epileptic seizure that caused his death. Hosea Dutschke wrote, "I kept begging, 'Papa, wake up,' and I prayed for the first time in my life. My mother begged the emergency medical team, which she had called, to persist in attempting to revive Papa. The physician finally told my mother that further efforts to revive my father were futile."

Rudi Dutschke is buried in the Berlin/Dahlem Lutheran Church cemetery, the former parish of Martin Niemöller (January 14, 1892- March 6, 1984). Dutschke's grave lies on an exterior wall of the sanctuary, not far from the burial site of Prelate Kurt Scharf (October 21, 1902-March 28, 1990), the former Chairman of the Council of the Lutheran Church in Germany. At the last All-German Annual Church Convention, convoked in Berlin on July 19, 1961, (just 26 days before the borders between East and West Germany were sealed by DDR authorities), and attended by 20,000 Christians from both the BRD and the DDR, Prelate Kurt Scharf probably spoke too candidly about religious and political freedom. On September 1, 1961, he was forced to emigrate from the DDR.

Later I visited the grave sites. As I stood at the graves of these two ardent advocates for their respective causes, one, Prelate Kurt Scharf, seeking to retain the unity of the Lutheran Church throughout the German nation, and appealing for tolerance for the Christian faith in the DDR-—and the other, Rudi Dutschke, who emigrated from the DDR to the BRD and who sought to challenge what he considered to be the monopoly of wealth and political power in the hands of a BRD clique, I thought that it was appropriate that these two former DDR residents, championing their respective causes, one in the DDR and one in the BRD, should find their final resting place in proximity to each other. Josef Bachmann, who sought to assassinate Rudi Dutschke, committed suicide in prison in February 1970.

In contrast to the uproar among students in the West, the DDR universities remained islands of tranquility. The speakers at our evening sessions in the International Summer School Course for German Language and Literature never failed to exploit the news from the West for propaganda purposes. Of course, nothing was reported concerning the rebellion of workers and students in Poland in March 1968. In Warsaw and Krakow, thousands of students demanded democratic freedoms for their country. The students were soon joined by the workers. Although the Catholic bishops pleaded for moderation and compromise, the Communist Party reacted with a very hard line. Twelve hundred and eight ringleaders were arrested, among them 365 students. On March 30, 1968, the authorities closed the Warsaw University until the student body had been 'purged.'

One of my Polish colleagues at the Weimar International Summer School Course for German Language and Literature, commenting on the student/worker revolt in Poland, said to me, "We have a rule for unorthodox thinkers in Poland: If you think it, don't say it; if you think it and say it, don't write it; if you think it, say it and write it, don't sign it; if you think it, say it, write it and sign it, don't be surprised."

Because every effort was made in the presentations to divorce United States government policy from peace loving US citizens, I am certain that Professor Richter earlier had informed the party propagandists that a US citizen was in the audience. I heard statements concerning the dirty US war of aggression in Vietnam and in the same time context the claim that most US citizens did not support such criminal activity. Of course, the DDR interpretation of the news was no different from that which my East Bloc colleagues heard in their respective media. My colleagues had difficulty disguising their boredom at what they already had heard repeated ad nauseam. From time to time, for the sake of objectivity, I would raise a question, but always within the context of desiring instruction, never in the context of confrontation or contradiction. After all, I thought, you don't challenge the lion in his den. Because I, as a private US citizen, never was associated with US foreign policy, I was able to pursue my studies and my friendly associations with my East Bloc colleagues in an amiable environment.

On one occasion, I sat in a lecture next to an engineer from the Soviet Union who participated primarily in the language instruction courses. I took notes. The Russian engineer also began to take notes. His ballpoint pen, however, failed. After repeated attempts to resuscitate the pen, he gave up trying to take notes. Observing his predicament, I offered him one of my pens. He smiled his gratitude and resumed recording. In the coffee break, after the lecture, we sat together and chatted. During our conversation, he returned my pen to me. "Keep the pen," I said. "I have an ample supply." To my surprise, given the national pride exhibited by many Russians in their nation's space achievements, especially vis à vis westerners, my table companion held up his failed pen and, with a cynical smile, said, "We can launch Sputniks into space, but we can't produce a dependable ballpoint pen."

The Russian engineer than added, "You've heard, of course, of the Nikita Khrushchev prediction." "No," I responded. "I did not know that Khrushchev had made a prediction." "O yes," the engineer responded. "Khrushchev predicted that, within the next generation, the Soviet Union will have overtaken and left far behind the capitalist states. The Russian people would, indeed, like to catch up with the capitalist states, but under no circumstances do the people wish to pass the capitalist nations." "But I always thought," I answered, "that it was the goal of the Soviet Union and the Warsaw Pact nations to overtake and leave the capitalist states far behind."

"To catch up to, yes," the engineer inserted, "but not to pass; under no circumstances to pass."

"Why not pass?" I inquired. "Because if we passed you," my conversation partner said, with laughter in his voice, "you would see the holes in the seat of our britches."

East Bloc humor reflected this situation. The story was told of the US tourist, who, on his last day with his tour group in Moscow got up very early to go to Red Square to use up his film. He promised to meet the other members of the tour later at breakfast in the hotel. After breakfast, the group was to be driven to the airport for the return flight to the US. At that early hour, except for a solitary figure struggling with two heavy suitcases on the far side of the square, there were no people. The tourist preoccupied with photographing forgot about the time. Suddenly, he remembered that he was to meet his group. He glanced at his watch. Panic seized him. His watch had stopped. Frantically he turned to the figure with the two suitcases who, in the long interval, had progressed across the square and was in the immediate vicinity of the tourist. "Pardon me," the tourist said, "can you tell me what time it is?" The man placed his giant suitcases on the ground, rolled up the sleeve of his left arm and studied his watch. He answered, "It's now 5:04 and 32 seconds a.m. Temperature is 22 degrees Celsius; at 3:00 p.m. this afternoon, there will be a thunderstorm. Sunset will be at 9:37 and 40 seconds p.m. According to Keplerian epicycles, the planets in our universe approach the ultimate arch of their circuit." The tourist stood astonished. "Wow! What a watch!" he exclaimed. "That must be the most expensive Swiss watch that is made." The Russian, proud of Soviet technology answered, "This is not a Swiss watch, but a Soviet watch, manufactured here in our Soviet Union." The tourist responded, "I must congratulate you on your technology. We have no watch to compare with yours." Gratified with the compliment of Soviet technology, the Russian strained to pick up his suitcases and to continue his journey. In so doing, he grunted, "The batteries still are somewhat heavy." When subsequently I told this joke to my Polish host in Poznan, Eugene Wachowski, he roared in laughter and big tears of ecstatic humor rolled down his cheeks, and he exclaimed, "Bolshaia Technika!" (Big Technology).

In subsequent conversations with East Bloc colleagues, the general truth revealed in this humor and the above comment by the Russian engineer repeatedly was affirmed. Spending for military equipment was the priority in the East Bloc states and the investment for articles of domestic consumption was curtailed severely by the military monopoly of the national budget. The financial support supplied to North Vietnam by the East Bloc nations, as well as the huge sums invested in cosmopolitan, Communist insurgent movements, placed great strain on the treasuries of the respective East Bloc states. This policy of building a huge military force, subsidizing North Vietnam and Communist revolutions on every continent, forced the East Bloc states to choose guns rather than butter. "That's why," my DDR friends insisted, "we must wait seventeen years for a telephone, ten years for an automobile and ten to fifteen years for a simple three-room flat. Our currency, outside the Comecon neighborhood, is worthless. Even if we were permitted to travel to the West, without financial support from relatives or friends residing in the West, such a journey would be financially impossible. "You have seen the intershops here. In Poland, they are called 'PEWEK.' The government in each East Bloc state holds a monopoly on such markets. They are stocked with the best quality goods produced in the West, but these centers accept western currency only. What an insult these shops are to DDR citizens! We work hard to earn our wages, but the currency in which we are compensated is worthless in markets where foreigners only, or DDR citizens with access to western currency, can purchase goods. Can you appreciate the resentment that these shops engender in most of the population? These shops are government administered and the hard currency profits are poured into Party coffers."

Two of my more interesting table companions were Anna Zoricakova from Levoca and Lillie Ragazova from Bratislava, both very patriotic women from Czechoslovakia. Anna and her husband Stefan, whom I later would meet on a visit to Levoca, were devout Roman Catholics. Of course, they had to be very circumspect concerning their religious sentiments. Lillie Ragazova and her husband (deceased September 8, 1965), had been reared in Orthodox Judaism, but, after the Soviet Union had established hegemony in Eastern Europe, they had become zealous members of the Czech Communist Party. Anna and Lillie, as Slovakian patriots, were polite to each other, but the ideological canyon that separated them was too deep for them to become friends. In 1968, Lillie was torn by her loyalty to the International Communist Movement, directed from Moscow, and her devotion to Alexander Dubček and his innovation of the Prague Spring. During the summer school session and before the invasion of Czechoslovakia by the Warsaw Pact nations on Tuesday, August 20, 1968, the increasing tension between Prague and Moscow was reflected in Lillie's personality (usually cheerful), now registering deep depression and concern.

Lillie confided in me, "Despite the frequent gaps between theory and practice, what my husband and I described as Communism's childhood diseases, we were convinced that, with time, all would work out well. My husband died on September 8, 1965. If my husband could have witnessed, what I now witness, namely, the pressures being placed upon our nation and the increasing threats against our leader, Alexander Dubček, coming from our 'fraternal Communist allies,' he would be as disillusioned as I now am with the international leadership of the Communist Party. In fact, in protest against the intimidation now directed at my country from our European Communist fraternity, I have resigned from the party and returned my Party Membership Card to Party officials in Prague." I frowned. "I know what you're thinking," Lillie said. "If I quit the party, how did I get chosen to be in the Czech delegation? There is a very simple answer. There are so many resignations, the party leadership is overwhelmed and it will take months before all the resignations can be processed. In the meantime, not knowing that I resigned, my university and local party leadership approved my application for the summer school course. In a month or so the local leaders will discover that they sent an ex-party member for continued study in the DDR. There's a certain humor in all this, n'est pas?"

Lillie added, "Apropos our Prague Spring, have you heard the joke concerning the two Communist dogs?" "No," I replied. Lillie continued, "There were two Communist dogs, one Czech and one East German. At every opportunity, the East German dog went to Prague. His buddy in Prague could not understand why his East German pal came so frequently to Prague. Finally, the Czech dog said to his companion, 'In East Germany you have the highest living standard in the East Bloc, you have access to more consumer goods and you earn better wages. Why, at every opportunity, do you come to Prague?' "The East German dog replied, 'To bark!'" Lillie then renewed her invitation to me to visit her family— "If you come to Czechoslovakia to visit Anna Zoricakova, you also can visit me."

Since I frequently had purchased items for Frau Giese in the Weimar Intershop behind the Hotel Elephant, I was familiar with these establishments. These outlets were made as inconspicuous as possible. The authorities must have known what a psychological burden the presence of such centers placed on the general population. Intershop humor was illustrated by the following query and answer:

> What is the place called where one Politbüro member is found?
>
> Answer: An alley.
>
> What is the place called where several Politbüro members may be found?
>
> Answer: A street.
>
> What is the place called where many Politbüro members may be found?
>
> Answer: An Intershop.

One evening as I sat on the bench along the Ilm bank, on the bench that Frau Giese and I used to like to call "ours," I was approached by an intoxicated man. He requested money from me. I didn't answer him. He then became belligerent and began to demand money from me. It was getting dark and there was no one else in sight. Would I be forced to physically defend myself? An idea flashed into my mind. In Weimar was stationed a large contingent of Soviet troops and civilian personnel. I knew that the Weimar citizenry had great fear of "Big Brother." Despite years of Russian presence in Weimar, there had been very little integration of the Red Army personnel with the native population. I had learned enough Russian to ask the question, "Do you speak Russian?" Looking directly at the aggressive pest, I asked in my best Russian, "Do you speak Russian?" The eyes of the bore became saucer-large. His face registered shock and fear. In an instant, he was sobered, turned quickly on his heels, and hurried from the scene. My one question in the Russian language had resolved what could have resulted in a nasty altercation.

On Tuesday, August 13, 1968, I accepted Frau Hedwig Dette's (the lady I met on the crowded train in October 1967) invitation to visit her in Grimma. I took an early express train to Leipzig and there I transferred to a commuter train that would take me to Grimma. Following Frau Dette's instructions, I walked the circa one-half mile from the Grimma rail station to Frau Dette's residence, 1 Kuntz Straße. I presented the gifts that I had purchased in the Intershop to Frau Dette. Frau Dette's unmarried daughter, Anni, who resided with her mother, offered to lead me to Nymschen, the convent where Katharina von Bora (1499-1552) had lived until she, with eight other nuns, at Easter in 1523, escaped the convent and went to Wittenberg. In June 1525, Katharina married Martin Luther. It was a pleasant, countryside walk to Nymschen. "As you see," Anni said, "there's only a few walls still standing. Of course, on this site in the sixteenth century, there was a well-populated convent."

We returned to Frau Dette's residence. Frau Dette, along with her married daughter, Ilse, who had arrived from nearby Bitterfeld, had prepared a tasty midday meal. We engaged in conversation, Frau Dette, Anni and Ilse briefing me on life in the DDR. "Being elderly," Frau Dette said, "I could emigrate to relatives in the BRD. When we met last

October on the train from Frankfurt to Leipzig, I was returning from visiting relatives in West Germany. I do not want to leave my Grimma home. I have lived in this house for many years. My husband and I raised our two daughters here. My husband is buried a short walk from our home and I frequently can visit his grave. No, at my age to move into an entirely new environment, far from daughters and from my husband's grave, holds no attraction for me."

Following the afternoon coffee and homemade pastry, I thanked my hostesses for a pleasant afternoon and prepared to return to Weimar. At that juncture, Frau Dette walked to the desk against the living room wall. She drew back a curtain above the desk. Behind this veil were several bookshelves. She requested Anni to take a particular volume from one of the shelves, a very large, heavy book. "My husband was a great admirer of Martin Luther," Frau Dette said. "This book was one of his prized possessions. After our train conversation of last October, I decided to present this book to you. There is no one in my family who can appreciate this volume as much as you can. I know that with you this book, so beloved by my husband, will find a friendly home. I'm old and do not have many more years. I would like to be assured that this volume is in a safe refuge."

I opened the book. The book contained a selection of Martin Luther's homilies, and had been published in Dresden, in fraktur, in 1888. On the first page of the volume, Frau Dette wrote, "In memory of your visit in Grimma, August 13, 1968. Frau Hedwig Dette." I was overwhelmed by such a precious gift. The volume occupies an honored place in my study.

Professor Hans Richter, knowing my interest for the Reformation, presented me with a book from his library, "The Man With The Rainbow Banner," (Der Mann Mit Dem Regenbogen Fahne) by Friedrich Wolf. This book is the German text of the play, based upon Friedrich Engles' study, "The German Peasants' War," which Wolf had written concerning Müntzer. I thanked Professor Richter for his generosity in presenting me a book from his private collection. Professor Richter smiled and said, "You are the most consistent foreign participant in our summer school course. Knowing your interest in the Reformation, I believe that you will appreciate this dramatic treatment of the German Peasants' War."

After the summer school course concluded, I traveled to Berlin. Through the good offices of Professor Bernhard Töpfer at the Humboldt University, I had received permission to do research in the history seminar at the university. I had a room in one of the university-owned residences, and I planned to spend a couple of weeks pursuing my research and engaging in conversations with my DDR colleagues. In the history seminar library were rich sources that facilitated historical research. On one long shelf were copies of Einheit, the official SED political voice. As I scanned the various numbers of this journal, an interesting phenomenon presented itself to me. In the editions from 1950 to 1956, almost every article had for its first reference a quotation from Joseph Stalin. Photographs of Stalin, with laudatios for his omniscient achievements in practically every discipline, were plentiful. In the numbers of Einheit after 1956, there were no references to Stalin. A main boulevard in East Berlin underwent a name change from Stalin Allee to Karl Marx Allee. The statues of Stalin in East Bloc cities were removed.

On the morning of Wednesday, August 21, 1968, having gotten off the streetcar and walked to the university, I noticed that a police cordon surrounded the entrance. I had my passport plus permission from the Rector to enter the university. With this documentation, I passed easily through the cordon. All other persons without documentation were requested to clear the courtyard, situated immediately before the entrance. I later learned that, with the exception of the main Unter den Linden entrance, all entrances to the university had been closed. Why? While at my desk in the history seminar room, a DDR colleague came to inform me. In a grim voice and with clouded countenance, my colleague said, "Today the Warsaw Pact nations, with the exception of Romania, have invaded Czechoslovakia. The Red Army has occupied Prague. Alexander Dubček has been arrested. The rumor is that he has been transported to the Soviet Union. There are so many western tourists now in East Berlin that our government fears protests in solidarity with the Czech people. There are several hundred students from France here. Given their predisposition to build barricades and to call for revolution, our government is nervous about possible demonstrations on the streets of East Berlin." My colleague continued, "We knew something had to be done about Dubček. His 'Socialism with a human face' or as some call it, 'The Prague Spring,' had to be terminated, and now it has been by what Günter Grass calls 'Tank Communism.' The Czech experiment—lifting of censorship, permitting his countrymen to travel to western nations, promoting student and professional exchanges with western universities and institutions, permitting western books, newspapers, magazines, films and theater productions into Czechoslovakia—set a very bad example for the Warsaw Pact States. In those states, the question from the populace naturally arose, 'If the citizens of Czechoslovakia can enjoy such privileges, why can't we?' On any given weekend, thousands of DDR citizens who reside near the Czech border were streaming to Prague to have access to uncensored news and to see western films and stage productions. Of course, here in the DDR, we can see some western films, but only those that reveal the exploitation, corruption and brutality in the capitalist countries. By his arbitrary democratic course, Dubček was undermining the cohesion of the East Bloc alliance. Something had to be done." We now know (2012) from documents that have become available that Brezhnev considered Dubček's experiment with democratic socialism as "creating a Hothouse atmosphere for the counter revolution." Brezhnev telephoned Dubček on August 13 to reiterate the Communist Bloc warning concerning liberalization in Czechoslovakia. In this conversation, Dubček offered to resign. Irritated, Brezhnev replied, "You should avoid grasping at such extreme measures." Brezhnev added, "Sascha (the name Brezhnev used for Alexander), you must also understand my position." (a veiled reminder of the proverb that in a stork-ruled society, the frogs are permitted a limited sovereignty only.)

My German colleague continued, "For us, however, it is very painful to see German troops once more, although not penetrating, poised on the Czechoslovakian border. It is reported that Brezhnev assured his supporters in Czechoslovakia that no German troops would be included in the occupying force. In confidence, Brezhnev is reported to have said, 'Our German comrades were offended that we excluded them from participating in the occupation.' You can imagine the enmity our action of mobilization on the Czech border will create among the

Czech people. The official party line to justify the invasion is that the Czech people, recognizing that Dubček was leading them toward economic dependence on the West, requested the Big Brother in Moscow to save them from this course and to remove Dubček. That our propaganda ministry actually disseminates such an interpretation demonstrates how gullible it considers the general public to be. We are told that the Czech people called for help and that the Warsaw Pact invasion of Czechoslovakia is in response to this call for help. The Soviet Press is able to interpret all events in favor of and in conformity with Politbüro propaganda, to turn every story so that the superiority of Communism over Capitalism is assured. For instance, it was reported that during a visit to the Kremlin by President Jimmy Carter, Leonid Brezhnev challenged the US president to a footrace around the Kremlin campus. President Carter won the race. The Soviet Press reported, 'Comrade Brezhnev ran a very strong race. The American President only managed to come in second from last.'"

As the Red Army occupied Prague, large banners could be seen with the inscription, 'LENIN, AWAKE; THEY HAVE GONE MAD!'" I thought of my Czech colleagues with whom I had studied just a few weeks earlier in Weimar. Especially, I thought of Anna and Lillie. I remember the concern they had expressed for their nation and for their leader, Alexander Dubček. In late August 1968, a colleague whom I had met at the Weimar International Summer School Course for German Language and Literature wrote to me from Bucharest, Romania,

> Dear Mr. Foster,
>
> Perhaps this is the last letter that I will be able to write to you. The events in Czechoslovakia probably will have an impact on us. You know that I have suffered much from the Russians and this time I may not survive. I am very sorry that I could not present to you the novel that I wrote. Even though it may not be Nobel Prize-worthy or compete with Pasternak, my novel depicts the life of those who have to live under tyranny.
>
> I had hoped to emigrate as quickly as possible, but it appears now to be too late, but I don't give up hope. If I could get to Vienna, could you recommend me to your friends in West Germany who would be willing to help me? I will not be a burden to anyone. I have technological gifts and could earn my

own way. I hate to bother you with this request. You live in a free world and perhaps cannot understand my dilemma. Because of my mother and her illness, I have postponed the decision to try to emigrate. Now it is perhaps too late. Thank you for the photos. They are good company as I confront the growing danger.

Waiting for your post, I greet you,

Maria

I wrote to Maria and, because I suspected that correspondence was intercepted by government officials, I sought to express myself in very cautious language. I did not receive any future post from Maria. I can only assume that her letter, expressing her desire to emigrate, had been read by the authorities, and that was sufficient to place her under surveillance.

During the Weimar Summer School Course, I met several colleagues who solicited my help to assist in their emigration to the West. Because the course duration was three weeks only, however, it was impossible to determine whether or not the requests were genuine or an attempt to entrap me. As long as I resided in the DDR, I remained non-committal. Because all course participants exchanged addresses with one another, this exchange was not suspicious.

Dubček subsequently was released from his Moscow internment and, after being ousted as Party Chairman on Thursday, April 17, 1969, and expelled from the Communist Party on Sunday, September 28, 1969, he was permitted to reside in Bratislava as a "non-person," that is, no public recognition or mention of his name. (Alexander Dubček, as a result of an automobile accident on September 1, 1992, died of his injuries. He is buried in Bratislava). After I had returned to the United States and was engaged in teaching my courses at the university, I read the news concerning the Czech student Jan Palach who, on Thursday, January 16, 1969, to protest the invasion of his homeland, engaged in self immolation on Wenzel Square in Prague. Three days later, Jan Palach died as result of this act.

Not only was the invasion of Czechoslovakia by the Soviet Union, Poland, Hungary and Bulgaria with 27 divisions (300,000 troops, 2,000 artillery pieces, and 7,500 tanks), the biggest military operation since

World War II in Europe, a shock to the world, it also revealed a glaring vacuum in western intelligence surveillance. In the NATO headquarters in Brussels, not a single document could be found that warned of the impending invasion of Czechoslovakia.

On December 10, 1968, Professor Karl Barth (May 10, 1886-December 10, 1968) died in Basel. I remembered with great gratitude the invitation that Professor Barth extended to me in 1957 to participate in his seminar in the restaurant Bruderholz in Basel, not far from his residence. What an enriching experience that seminar had been in my graduate education! When I recalled how impressed Herr Lindenberg had been that one of his residents in the Carl Mez Heim had been invited to attend the seminar of one of Europe's great scholars, I had to smile.

Eastern Europe, 1969

In the summer of 1969, I accepted an interim teaching post at the Saint Ursula Gymnasium in Freiburg. The gymnasium was named for the popular Saint Ursula who, because she refused to sacrifice her chastity to the chief of the Huns who had invaded Köln, was martyred in that city in 452. The position was offered to me by Frau Dr. Maria Wölfle (Maiden name Settele, 1904-1989), director of the gymnasium. Ever since my teaching tenure at Kepler Gymnasium (1957 to 1958), when I had become acquainted with Professor Eugen Wölfle, Frau Maria Wölfle's husband, I remained in contact with the Wölfle family and each summer, on different occasions, I was invited to share in family activities. Professor Wölfle and his wife were very devout Roman Catholics. Because she embodied traditional Catholic orthodoxy, my colleagues at the gymnasium called their director, "Maria the Catholic." Early on the morning of Monday, July 21, as I walked to school from my "broom closet" in the Carl Mez Heim, I saw the banner headlines by the chief editor of the Bild newspaper, Peter Bönisch: "DER MOND IST JETZT EIN AMI," "The Moon is now an American!" Neil Armstrong and Edwin (Buzz) Aldrin landed on the moon at 3:46 a.m. middle European time." That day at the gymnasium my pupils wanted only to discuss this amazing achievement. "Alright," I said, "but you must discuss this theme in the English language only." I was teaching the English language and I thought that the excitement engendered by the moon landing would encourage even the more reticent pupils to speak up.

At the same time that the largest daily newspaper in Germany (circulation 5.3 million copies) announced, "The Moon Was An American," I recalled the statement by the publisher Axel Springer that explained the phenomenal success of his publication: "At the end of the war, it was clear to me that the German reader under no circumstances wished to be placed under the burden of the necessity to think. It was upon this principle that I established my publication." Axel Springer's recipe for success soon would be imitated by media monopolies around the world.

After completing my teaching tenure in Freiburg, I once again traveled to the DDR where I was enrolled in the Weimar University Summer School course. A year had passed since the "Prague Spring" had been crushed by the Warsaw Pact invasion, but this subject remained the main political topic of discussion. I was anxious to learn how my colleagues from Czechoslovakia would interpret this event. The SED Party officials who came to address the summer school participants in the Haus der Intelligenz on Mozart Straße had no easy task. Against the silent and sullen resentment of the Czech participants and the critical frowns of participants from England, France, Denmark, the Netherlands, Norway and Sweden, the propaganda merchants had no chance of selling their wares. In private discussions with my Czech colleagues, I learned of their great antagonism toward the Warsaw Pact action. "Leonid Brezhnev insists that we called for help," one of my Czech colleagues said. "Let me give you our version of that call. Late one evening, a couple walked across the historic Charles' Bridge that spans the Moldau River in Prague. An intoxicated man fell off the bridge into the river. He began to scream, 'Help! Help!' The couple walked to the edge of the bridge and called down to the drunkard, 'Shut up! You'll have every Russian in the Soviet Union here!'" The same colleague went on to say, "Now we have a Soviet puppet government. Nothing can be decided in Prague. Even our weather report first will have to be approved by the Moscow Politbüro. The current humor describes our situation: A ship sank in the Pacific Ocean. Only two men and one woman were able to survive and made it to an island. What would happen if both men were Italian? One would murder the other male in order to have the female for himself. If the two males were French, they would agree to live together a trois. If one male were English and the other German, they would move to a neighboring island and permit the woman to live alone on her island. If the two males were Russian, they would write a letter, place it in a bottle and throw it into the surf. The content of the letter would request instructions from the Politbüro."

Out of the "Prague Spring" was born the "Brezhnev Doctrine." The doctrine states that whenever any member of the Communist community is in danger of breaking out of that circle and pursuing an independent course, it is the obligation of the other alliance partners to coerce the prodigal back into his proper position as a member of the body. Regarding the subjugation of Czechoslovakia by the Warsaw Pact nations, I thought of the observation of Ecclesiastes 1:9: "There is nothing new under the sun." At the subjugation of Melos by the Athenian League in 406 B.C., Thucydides records the Athenian ambassador's address to the Melians: "Of the gods we believe and of men we are certain that by a necessity of their nature, where they have the power, they rule." As the East Berlin propagandists sought to justify the Brezhnev Doctrine and to dismiss the self-immolation of the student Jan Palach on Wenzelplatz on January 16, 1969, in protest to the Soviet domination of his country, as the act of a mentally disturbed young man, I could see stern disagreement on the faces of the Czech male participants. One of the Czech colleagues who sat next to me most every evening, after listening to the propaganda fed to us each evening by SED representatives sent from Berlin, whispered to me, "Whose bread I eat, his song I sing." Some of the Czech female colleagues wept, but as inconspicuously as possible. One of the women who wept was Anna Zoricakova. Anna also had participated in the course in the summer of 1968. We arranged once again to become table companions. I inquired about Lillie. I had hoped that Lillie also would return for the 1969 summer school course. Anna looked very sad. "No", she said, "Lillie could not return. She suffers from cancer and now resides at the cancer clinic in Kosice which her brother, chief physician, administers." This news caused me great sadness.

Anna and I had become friends. When we were alone at table, Anna expressed her true feelings. Because there was never a contradictory voice heard from the Czech delegation, Anna feared that some western participants might believe that the Czech people actually petitioned the Soviet Union to intervene and to remove Dubček. "You must understand," she said, "we are all professional people. To sustain our families we must be professionally employed. If any one of us were to challenge the official propaganda presentations made here concerning the events of last August, he or she would run the risk of losing his or her position at home. We have an adage, 'Only fools boldly declare what intelligent people are thinking.' It's bitter, indeed to have to maintain silence in the face of such lies about our people and about our beloved leader. Despite the fact that Alexander Dubček was replaced as Party Chairman on April 17, 1969 and gradually is being transformed into a non-person by the new Moscow-loyal Czech party bosses, we Czechs still consider him to be the leader of our nation. We knew, of course, that the Renaissance he brought to us in the Prague Spring probably could not endure. Now, once again we are in the straight jacket of Politbüro propaganda and censorship, and Moscow's apparatchiks control our national, political and cultural life. In every publication, our media seeks to glorify our new masters, but we Czechs know the adage, 'When culture's sun declines, even dwarfs cast long shadows.' We also knew that Dubček's days in Prague were numbered. Dubček now resides in Bratislava with his wife. No one is permitted to mention his name in public without risking party disfavor. Therefore, whenever Dubček and his wife attend concerts, an interesting scene takes place. When Dubček and his wife enter the concert hall, the people in the audience, without a word, and in discrete silence, stand up and remain standing until Dubček and his wife have been seated. Is that the gesture of a people who summoned the Warsaw Pact to save them from this man?"

One of our excursions in the summer of 1969 took us to Jena to a production of Friedrich Schiller's play, Don Carlos. In the scene in which the Marquis von Posa, who is sympathetic to the cause of the Netherlands' independence, (the Netherlands at the time being under subjugation to Philip II, King of Spain), pleads with Philip II to lift the ban on liberty and free expression:

> Show the way to Europe's monarchs.
> A stroke of the pen from your royal hand
> And the earth will be re-created.
> Sire, grant liberty of thought!

At these words, there was a burst of spontaneous applause. The actors had to wait until the applause ceased before they could continue their lines. Everyone understood that this spontaneous applause in the middle of a dialogue was a way of registering protest to state censorship. Members of this audience never would have built barricades or publicly have risked the displeasure of state officials, but in the anonymity of a darkened theater, they could vent their pent up frustration for they immediately applied a scene that described tyranny in the sixteenth century to their own unhappy condition. My Czech colleagues, who sat near me, maintained a sullen silence. Fearing the same kind of reaction to Friedrich Schiller's play, the Nazis had banned Don Carlos during their twelve-year rule. Once more, the definition of dictatorship was confirmed: "Dictatorship is a form of government where all fear one and one fears all."

Anna from Levoca and Lillie from Kosice both invited me to visit their respective cities. "Levoca's claim to fame," Anna said, "is that the Catholic Church houses the sculptured wood masterpiece of the Last Supper by the medieval artist, Master Paulus. This artistic treasure was displayed at the New York World's Fair in 1964-1965. My husband, Stephen, teaches in a school for the blind, located immediately behind our residence. I teach music and the German language in Kosice, which means that several times a week I must take the long bus ride to that city. If you come to Levoca, you may stay with us. We have room." I knew that Lillie Ragazowa now resided in the Kosice Cancer Clinic. At the conclusion of the 1969 Weimar International Summer School Course for German Language and Literature, I flew from Berlin to Prague and then from Prague to Kosice. Through correspondence with Lillie, I knew that she was taking treatment for cancer. The treatment prevented Lillie from matriculating in the Weimar summer course in 1969 as she had hoped to do.

Lillie's brother met me and drove me to the clinic. I spent two days there visiting with Lillie. The clinic had a guest apartment that was made available to me. The last visit with Lillie was deeply impressed on my mind. She already had become very ill and her brother told me that her condition was terminal. I sat next to her bed and read Psalms to her. Although, as a young woman and as a result of the trauma of having lost her family at Auschwitz, she had abandoned the traditions of her ancestors, had embraced atheistic materialism, and had sought to fulfill her spiritual yearning by replacing Moses with Marx. On the threshold of death, Lillie returned to her ancestral roots. As I read, "Though I walk through the valley of the shadow of death, I will fear no evil, for Thou art with me," Lillie gripped my hand. Tears emerged from under her closed eyelids, perhaps because of pain, but perhaps also because of joy as Lillie found comfort in the ancient scriptures of her people. Lillie asked me, "How is it that you, a Christian, are so familiar with the scriptures of the Jewish people?" I explained to her that Christianity believed that these scriptures testify concerning Jesus of Nazareth who Christians consider to be the Messiah. I gave her the illustration of Isaiah, chapter 53. As I read the passage to her, I could not help but think of Philip and the Ethiopian eunuch, recorded in the Book of Acts, chapter 8, verses 26-39. "Who is the Suffering Servant?" I asked. "Christians believe that this text is a prophecy concerning the coming Messiah, even if the prophet himself did not comprehend the full meaning of his words." Lillie was silent for a long time. Finally, she said, "It's interesting that you, a Christian, made such a long journey to visit me and to read to me from the Bible. I have not heard the biblical text since my youth." The time had arrived when I had to take my leave. I read one more scripture verse to Lillie: "As for me, I am poor and needy, but the Lord takes thought of me" (Psalm 40:17). As I read the words slowly and deliberately, Lillie lay with eyes closed in the attitude of prayer. When I finished reading, Lillie opened her eyes. I leaned over the bed and placed a kiss on her cheek. She responded with a faint smile and a "Danke schön." Lillie's brother stood at the foot of the bed, and, although he daily confronted death in the clinic, his eyes brimmed with tears. Just before entering Lillie's brother's car in which he would drive me to the airport where I would board a flight to Prague, I looked up to the balcony that adjoined Lillie's room. Lillie stood on the balcony and waved to us. I could only imagine the great effort it took to enable her to go from bed to balcony. The memory of our meditating upon the Psalms together and Lillie waving farewell remains with me until this day. At the beginning of the year 1970, I received a letter from Lillie's brother informing me that she had died. I have an inner conviction that she died in peace.

In the summer of 1969, Bishop Mitzenheim granted me another interview. As at our second meeting in 1967, the bishop invited me to his home at the afternoon coffee hour. During this conversation, as in 1967, only the bishop, Mrs. Mitzenheim and I were present. We sat on the balcony with a view of the Wartburg. It was a magnificent full view of the historic castle. I related to Bishop Mitzenheim my experience at the Wittenberg Historical Congress of 1967. The bishop had followed the development of Marxist interpretation of the Reformation. "It's refreshing," he said, "to note that Professor Max Steinmetz and

Gerhard Zschäbitz have arrived at an interpretation of the Reformation movement that discredits the earlier pejorative attacks on Luther as a lackey of the princes. I am very pleased that you, as an American, could witness this transition at Wittenberg in 1967, and that you yourself had opportunity to present your research."

Bishop Mitzenheim continued. "On the question of the dissolution of the national church union (June 10, 1969), there was no possibility of retaining such a union that sought to sustain the association of the regional churches in West Germany and the DDR regional churches. The political confrontation between East and West and the assertion daily to be seen in our press that the church in West Germany is a NATO church, subservient to the capitalist and military interests of the western powers, made it impossible for churches in the DDR to remain in union with our fellow Christians in the West. Even if the charge is untrue, the daily drumbeat of propaganda made it impossible, as long as we remained in league with churches in the BRD, for churches in the DDR to conduct their ministry apart from government suspicion and hostility. I know there are those in the West who believe that we should have resisted more energetically the design of our government to destroy the National German Church Union. My reply to the critics is that their critique comes from the safe haven in the West. In my talks with the First Party Chairman, Walter Ulbricht, I have been able to gain certain concessions that alleviate conditions for our DDR population. Fighting a battle that, in the long run, could not be won, namely, seeking to retain a National Church Union, would have cost me leverage in the petitions to Ulbricht on behalf of our people."

Bishop Mitzenheim continued, "After the adoption of our new constitution on April 6, 1968, in which the DDR is described as the first socialist state of the German nation, totally segregated from the capitalist state of the BRD, the arbitrary dissolution of the National Church Union by the DDR Politbüro came as no surprise. As long as hope for reunification was alive, the National Church Union was less vulnerable, but now that hope, with the increasing belligerent Cold War stance between East and West, has been abandoned. A National Church Union between two sharply segregated states is an anomaly. We Christians in the DDR must come to terms with the political reality that prevails. We must seek to live and to conduct our ministry within the context in which we find ourselves. We anticipate no rescue mission from the West."

One area of Bishop Mitzenheim's influence with Walter Ulbricht I personally experienced. As I stood on the Eisenach train platform waiting for the 3:00 p.m. train that would take me to Frankfurt/Main in West Germany, I was approached by a man and a woman with a girl whom I would estimate to have been about ten or eleven years old. "Excuse me, sir," the man said, "I assume that you are traveling to West Germany." Since Eisenach was the last station in DDR Thuringia before the border checkpoint, Gerstungen, the assumption was obvious. In Eisenach, all passengers without valid travel documents for the BRD would have to get off the train. "Yes," I replied. "I'm traveling to Frankfurt/Main." Noting my camera and the red, white and blue address shield on my suitcase, the man asked, "Are you an American?" "Yes," I replied. Hesitantly and imploringly the man then said, "May I request a great favor of you?" "What sort of favor?" I inquired. Pointing to the girl, the man said, "This is our eleven-year-old niece, Inge. She is traveling to Hanau, the station before Frankfurt. Because she must travel alone, would you be so kind as to accompany her? We are apprehensive as to what might occur in Gerstungen. We do not trust the authorities. Let me explain. Inge has resided with us since age three. When the border between the DDR and the BRD was sealed, Inge's parents were in the BRD. Rather than return to the DDR, they decided to file for Inge's emigration to the BRD. All attempts failed and in the meantime, the period of grace in which DDR citizens in the BRD could return home without penalty had expired. After the expiration of the grace period, my sister and her husband faced punishment if they returned to the DDR. They remained in the BRD, but without their daughter. Appeals to the Office for German Affairs in Bonn and to many political leaders all ended in failure and endless procrastination. Finally, Inge's parents appealed to Bishop Mitzenheim. What Bonn and the politicians could not accomplish, Bishop Mitzenheim executed. We were notified by authorities in Erfurt, our regional capital, that Inge's exit visa could be picked up this morning at the Eisenach police station. I went to the police station this morning, but the official in charge claimed that he had received no exit visa for our niece from Erfurt. On my motorcycle, I raced to Erfurt to get the visa. There I was shown a signature on a certified letter that the visa had been received in Eisenach. I raced back to Eisenach and returned to the police station with this confirmation. The police chief searched in his desk, but found no exit visa. By this time, it was early afternoon and the train departure was scheduled for 3:00 p.m. The visa was valid for that train on this particular day only. I then asked permission to make a telephone call. 'Whom do you wish to call?' The officer asked. I replied, 'I wish to call Bishop Mitzenheim whose office is only a few blocks from here. It was Bishop Mitzenheim, in personal consultation with SED Chairman Ulbricht, who arranged for the issuing of this visa for our niece. Bishop Mitzenheim should know that the visa cannot be located.' The police official once again searched his desk drawer and, in this search, he found the visa, one hour before train time. This whole affair has caused us great stress and we are worried that at Gerstungen the authorities may be plotting difficulties. An eleven-year-old should not have to confront such anxiety. If you would be so kind to sit with our niece, it would relieve our apprehension. If an American witness is present, there is less likelihood that the border officials will cause her problems." "Certainly, I will sit with your niece," I said.

There were no problems at the border. The visa was in order and was honored by the border authorities. As we traveled on to Frankfurt, Inge told me about how her parents had sought for years by appeals to gain permission for her to emigrate to her parents in the BRD. It was only after an appeal to Bishop Mitzenheim that the process for Inge's emigration began to proceed. "It was Bishop Mitzenheim," she said, "who was able to gain from Chairman Ulbricht consent for our family reunion. When my uncle told the Eisenach police captain that my visa had been arranged by Chairman Ulbricht and Bishop Mitzenheim, the police captain immediately found the visa." At Hanau, I helped Inge with her luggage. Her parents waited on the platform. What a reunion! Parents and child reunited after years of separation and political chicanery. The parents thanked me profusely. I quickly re-boarded the train, for the next stop was Frankfurt, my destination. Inge and her parents waved goodbye.

As I thought about this story, I realized that the "Red Bishop" of Thuringia (The Thuringian Fox) quietly was able (with no trumpet before him) to unite many families. Perhaps the Wartburg meeting of August 18, 1964 did not reap any political advantages for the church in the DDR, but it certainly harvested tremendous advantages in terms of Christian humanitarianism. If, on the face of the Wartburg meeting, there were no obvious great advantages for the church, there were incalculable beneficent gains for individuals and families in that Bishop Mitzenheim was able to exercise a genuine Dietrich Bonhoeffer definition of the Christian Church, namely, "To be there for others."

As I reminisced about my meeting with Bishop and Mrs. Mitzenheim on their balcony with the spectacular view of the Wartburg and the huge tower cross that dominated the landscape, I recalled Bishop Mitzenheim saying, "That cross has an interesting history. The Nazis removed the cross. After the Red Army occupied Thuringia at the departure of the US forces in July 1945, I became acquainted with Iwan Sosonowitsch Kolesnitschenko, the commandant of the Red Army in Thuringia. There were always many matters for discussion between the occupying military force and the church leadership. Finally, one day, I mustered up courage to request General Kolesnitschenko for permission to replace the cross on the Wartburg tower. The general frowned, but gave no answer. Finally, he said, 'Return in one week.' One week later, I stood in the cavernous chancery before the general as he sat at his desk signing papers. 'I came concerning the Wartburg cross,' I said. 'May it be restored to its proper place?' 'All right,' the general grunted, 'dismissed.' I left with permission to replace the cross on the Wartburg tower, but, of course, the Christians in Thuringia had no means to achieve such a feat. We had no motorized equipment, no cranes, no steeplejacks. Without equipment, it would be impossible, with a huge, heavy cross, to scale to such a height. As I pondered all possibilities, that afternoon to my astonishment and to the amazement of Eisenachers, Red Army crane-mounted trucks and teams of military steeplejacks with ladders and scaffolding arrived at the Wartburg. Within a few hours, the soldiers had bolted the cross securely to its tower pinnacle and there you see it today."

Bishop Mitzenheim noted my surprised look. "Wait, there is more to the story," he said. "About one week later, General Kolesnitschenko summoned me to his office. 'I did you a favor,' he said. 'Now you must do one for me. My wife is not well and we have two children. I'm instructed that the nurses trained in the church's medical facilities are the best qualified. Find me one of your nurses who is willing to reside in our home, to care for my wife and to look after our children.' I replied, 'Thank you very much for restoring the cross to the Wartburg. I will do my best to find a nurse.' After inquiring in our church's medical administration, a nurse informed me that she would be prepared to accept the position, and what a wonderful result this association would have! The nurse, let us name her Anna, adapted to her new environment. She performed her office so well that she soon was considered a member of the family. Not only did nurse Anna provide excellent medical care, she also played with the children, taught them the German language and they taught her the Russian language. What a wonderful example nurse Anna was. By her Christian witness and compassion, she demonstrated to our former enemy that not every German was a Nazi. I noticed that after nurse Anna moved into the Kolesnitschenko home, the general's attitude toward me became significantly friendlier."

The bishop continued, "After several years of commanding the Red Army in Thuringia, the time came for General Kolesnitschenko to be relieved of that command and to return to the Soviet Union. A reception was given in honor of the parting general. I was invited. During the reception, General Kolesnitschenko asked me, 'Bishop Mitzenheim, did you ever wonder why I consented to replacing the cross on the Wartburg tower? After all, among the duties of a Red Army commander, there is no provision for erecting crosses. 'Yes, General,' I replied. 'I often wondered why you were willing to restore the cross to its original place, and even to employ Red Army equipment and personnel to do it, but I was too timid to ask.' General Kolesnitschenko then said, 'Well let me tell you the story of how your request gained my consent. I thought about your request for one week. The automatic answer to the petition should have been "No." The Red Army is the military force of a Marxist-Leninist state and has no interest in promoting Christianity. The answer to your request was clear—No. Each morning, however, as I shaved and saw my face reflected in the mirror, a disturbing thought penetrated my mind. This invasive thought gave me no peace until finally I capitulated before it. 'General Kolesnitschenko,' I implored, 'may I know what that thought was?' 'Yes, you may,' the general replied. 'It was this—what would my mother say?'"

Bishop Mitzenheim continued, "What a marvelous witness this unknown Russian peasant woman from a remote village in the vast Soviet Union had been for her son," I thought. "Although his mother long had been deceased, this Soviet general wished to honor her memory in performing an act that he knew would please her, namely, restoring the cross to its proper elevated station. It was with a clear sign of emotion that General Kolesnitschenko related this story to me. I thanked him for this revelation. We shook hands and bade each other farewell. I learned later that nurse Anna periodically visited the Kolesnitschenko family in their native land."

I then asked Bishop Mitzenheim if he regretted his pronouncement of cooperation and coexistence with the Communist government that he had made at the August 18, 1964 meeting with Ulbricht. "No," he responded. "My position, in contrast to some of my fraternal critics in the West is similar to Bismarck's 'Realpolitik,' that is, policy must be based on reality, on the actual, existing situation, not on the idealistic environment created in your imagination. As I told you before, we are aware that no western state will challenge the status quo in order to liberate us. We must come to terms with the political reality of our condition and so long as we are free to preach the gospel in our churches, our policy remains, a church not for socialism, not against socialism, but a church that finds herself called upon to conduct her ministry within a socialist society. Again, with Bismarck, we have learned that politics is the art of the possible."

On October 9, 1969, The Christian Century published an essay that I wrote based on my continuing conversations with historians in the DDR and from what I was able to learn during my summer residences in the land of Luther: Reformation and Revolution: The Maturing East German View.

On Tuesday, October 21, 1969, Willy Brandt, chairman of the Socialist Party of Germany (the SPD) became the first post-World War II Socialist Chancellor of the BRD. "It will be interesting," I thought, "to see how relations between the BRD and the DDR now would proceed." I continued to participate in the summer school courses well into the 1970s. In the summers of 1969 and 1970, I was housed with other participants in the Christian Inn, just across the street from the Wieland Square. The inn could accommodate about fifty people. There was one bath on the ground floor. Toilettes were at the end of the corridor on each floor. Throughout the evening, a line formed outside the bathroom, each person eagerly waiting his or her turn to get in the bathtub. I waited until midnight or later. At that hour, the bathroom usually was unoccupied.

1970-1972

A new friend in Weimar and a visit from the FBI

On February 1, 1970, Lilli Monossova wrote to me from Leningrad on a card with the monument of Peter the Great:

> Honorable Colleague,
>
> I thank you very much for your thoughtfulness and the beautiful card and stamps.
>
> My daughters and my husband are elated with the stamps. I wish you in the New Year health, joy and success. For a period of time, I could not write. The news of Lillie's death, though not unexpected, nevertheless was devastating. I thank fate that I was permitted to know her. Lillie (Ragazova) will remain alive in my heart.
>
> With hearty greetings from Leningrad,
>
> > Lilli Monossova

Lillie Ragazova was a cheerful and affable colleague in the Weimar Summer School Course in 1967 and 1968. Mrs. Monossova, other colleagues and I shared a wonderful esprit de corp during the summer semester. Lillie Ragazova belonged to our group.

On Wednesday, February 4, 1970, Anna Zoricakova, who was attending a music seminar in Leipzig, wrote to me at my home address,

> Dear Professor Foster,
>
> Many hearty thanks for the gift. Yesterday I received a letter from my husband in which he wrote that the package, with its wonderful contents, arrived safely. On February 24th, I will depart for home. The university city, Presov, is about 70 Kilometers from Levoca, not far from Kosice. Last summer we drove with you in the vicinity of Presov.
>
> In July, I again will participate in the Weimar Summer School Course. I would be very happy if we could meet again. Perhaps my husband (Stefan) will come to Weimar for a few days at the conclusion of the course. At the end of the course, you could come with us to Levoca.
>
> I greet you heartily,   Anna Zoricakova

On Tuesday, April 20, 1971, Professor Max Steinmetz, chairman of the History Department at the Karl Marx University in Leipzig, wrote to me,

> Dear Mr. Foster,
>
> Hearty thanks for your letter and for the postcard from Newark, Delaware. I received your letter within one week of it being posted. The post seems to take   longer going in the opposite direction. I thank you for your friendly assistance. I would like to have the book by Abraham Friesen. Unfortunately, at present, we have a limited number of dollars, only a few west marks and some other west European currency.... For purchases in the US we need dollars and they are in short supply. If you could purchase the book for me, I would be very grateful. When you come in the summer, I will be immersed in work and will not take a vacation on the Black Sea until September. I will be available to reimburse you in our currency or to purchase books here for you. I am very happy about your impending visit and I look forward to stimulating conversations. My Müntzer biography certainly will be published before you arrive. Let me know in good time when you will come. You can bring the film about the Friesen biography with you or mail it to my department at the university. We all are well as I hope that you are. With many hearty thanks and best greetings,
>
> Your, Professor Steinmetz

In the summer of 1971, once again traveling on my own, I resided for a few days in the Youth Hostel Maxim Gorgi in Wilden Graben in Weimar. The men's shower room had a pipe protruding from the ceiling. The pipe had no showerhead and consequently the water fell in a narrow, vertical line. When several people were trying to shower at the same time, the person immediately under the pipe had access to water. The others had to be content with the water that splashed off the body of the person under the pipe. One morning, as I stood before the mirror in order to shave, I noticed that the man at the sink next to me grimaced in pain each time he pulled his razor across his face. I learned later that he was from Czechoslovakia. I surmised that his pain was caused by a dull razor. I, therefore, offered him a blade from my dispenser and squirted shaving crème into his palm. He placed the blade in his razor, lathered his beard and, as he made the first stroke with a sharp blade, I saw his eyes light up and with a loud voice he exclaimed, "Wunderbar"!

Each summer I re-visited the friends I had made in the DDR—the Rückert family in Eisenach and Frau Ilse Weissenborn in that city, a catechetical teacher in the Lutheran Church. Frau Weissenborn's confirmands had met with my pupils of the same age in 1967. DDR and US youth hiked in the Thuringian Forest and enjoyed picnics together. In Weimar, each summer, I visited Frau Dorothea Schirow in the Maria Seebach Retirement Home, Mayor Luitpold Steidle and Pastor Siegfried Urban and his family. In Dresden, I visited Rainer Schultze and through Rainer I met Frau Pommrich and her daughter Edith Krummreich and Edith's daughter, Freya Klier. I also met Peter, Frau Pommrich's unmarried son who resided with his mother at 2 Schilling Straβe. In conversations with these friends, I was able to get a picture of life in the DDR that I believe few of my countrymen could imagine.

In August 1971, while visiting Frau Schirow, shortly before she died, she presented to me a book from her collection, Christus für uns heute, Bonhoeffer Auswahl: Christ for us today, a Bonhoeffer Anthology. Whenever preparing lectures on Dietrich Bonhoeffer, I have resorted to re-reading this volume. Frau Schirow's body was cremated and her ashes buried in the grave with her husband in the plot reserved for artists near the Russian chapel in the Weimar cemetery.

On Sunday, August 1, 1971, I visited Dr. Herbert Hintzenstern and his family in their residence, Shakespeare Straβe 10, in Weimar. Dr. Hintzenstern, Editor of the Thuringian Church Newspaper, *Glaube und Heimat*, had explained to me on other occasions the state's censorship of all media. It was my custom to present a cash gift from Christians in the United States to Dr. Hintzenstern in order to assist in keeping the church newspaper solvent. It was on this occasion that Dr. Hintzenstern presented me with a paperback book about Johannes Falk (1768-1826), Weimar's great humanitarian.

The Tuesday, September 28, 1971 edition of *Neues Deutschland*, the official voice of the SED in the DDR, reported, "On Monday, the Reverend Ralph Abernathy (March 11, 1926-April 17, 1990) arrived for a visit in the DDR. The Reverend Abernathy is the exceptional leader of peace-loving Americans and the successor of Dr. Martin Luther King. Dr. King was murdered by imperialist reactionaries. The Reverend Abernathy was released from prison a few weeks ago. The guest was heartily welcomed at the Berlin/Schönefeld Airport by leaders of Church and State." In the same edition, Neues Deutschland reported that, on February 2, 1971, in a New York City rally, the Reverend Abernathy, along with American Communists, had condemned racism and the imperialist war in Vietnam.

The September 29, 1971 edition of *Neues Deutschland* reported that a banquet was hosted to honor the Reverend Ralph Abernathy, the representative of the subjugated black population in the US, by the DDR Peace Council. At the banquet, prominent leaders of Church and State bestowed the DDR Peace Council Medallion on the Reverend Abernathy. Professor Albert Norden, member of the Central Committee of the SED recalled his experience with racism in Nazi Germany. "We are opposed to racism because it was a hallmark in the aggressive war (1939-1945) that cost the lives of twenty million Russians and six million Poles, as well as many other victims. DDR citizens see in Nixon and the Pentagon the heirs of Hitler, who transform Vietnam into a battlefield and who exploit and subjugate twenty million black citizens in the US." The report continued, "Deeply moved, the Reverend Abernathy thanked Professor Norden with a fraternal hug."

As the Peace Medallion was bestowed on him, the Reverend Abernathy said, "My heart overflows with joy. Today you make me feel like a human being. You move me to tears." Then he added, "I live in a society that persistently seeks to persuade me that I am less than human, unable of achieving anything of value. But, ever since I became an adult, I have not ceased to struggle for equality and justice for black people in the US. Be assured that, as long as I live, I will not relent in my efforts to imitate my close friend, Dr. Martin Luther King, in the struggle against racism, imperialism, poverty and injustice, not only in America, but in the entire world."

In the same edition, under his signature, the Reverend Abernathy placed the call: "Freedom For Angela Davis! Ralph Abernathy, President of the Southern Christian Leadership Conference, Atlanta, Georgia,

USA." He added, "I appeal to my DDR brothers and sisters in the struggle against the three evils—racism, poverty, war—never to relent. I am deeply impressed by the yearning for world peace among DDR citizens. I greet you with the challenge of our movement, 'Right On, Stay the Course, Power to the People.'"

In its Thursday September 30, 1971 edition, *Neues Deutschland* reported the Reverend Abernathy as saying, "From now on, I belong to the movement that calls for international recognition of the DDR." In a press conference at the Berlin/Schönefeld Airport, just before his departure, the Reverend Abernathy said, "As pastor and theologian, I am of the opinion that the DDR embodies that for which the world is striving. Seven years ago, when I accompanied Dr. Martin Luther King on a European trip, we resided in West Berlin. From there, we made a short visit to East Berlin. During this current visit, I resided in East Berlin and made a short visit to West Berlin. After only a few hours in West Berlin, I was homesick for the DDR. Too much in West Berlin reminded me of conditions in the US." From his prominent hosts from Church and State, the Reverend Abernathy took his leave on September 30, 1971.

As I read these reports, I could not but think of how cleverly the East Bloc Communist propaganda used the Civil Rights struggle in the United States to divert attention from the violation of civil rights in the East Bloc. "As Pastor and theologian," to quote the Reverend Abernathy, he should have demonstrated some concern for Christians in the DDR who were confronted with discrimination, and even persecution. He failed to demonstrate any concern for those who were killed at the Berlin Wall and other border locations. The DDR visit of the American Civil Rights leader, and the paeans of praise that he so effusively heaped upon that state, proved to be a propaganda coup for the DDR regime. My friends in the DDR inquired of me, "How can religious and political leaders in the United States be so naive in their pronouncements concerning foreign affairs?"

In the summer of 1972, at the conclusion of the summer school course, I traveled to the Frankfurt Airport to pick up a small group of US citizens. I guided them into the DDR. I also took my eleven-year-old son, Stephen Mark, along. In traveling to the DDR each summer, I had learned that cigarettes made in the US, in certain situations, were more valuable than DDR currency. My wife's sister, Charlotte Lively, was married to Ronald Lively, an executive in the Philip Morris Company. This gentleman supplied me with a generous amount of cigarettes. In order to pass through DDR customs, I distributed cartons of cigarettes equally across the members of our group. Each person was permitted his own personal quantity, and, although no one in our group smoked, we were able to transport an abundance of cigarettes into the DDR for those special situations when a pack or a carton of cigarettes could open doors that otherwise might have remained shut.

Our residence in Weimar was in the Ernst Thälmann Youth Hostel on Windmühlen Straße. From the bus stop on Steuben Straße, it was about one half mile to the hostel, but all uphill. Each person in our group carried two suitcases. Stephen struggled with his heavy suitcases. As we left Humboldt Straße to turn right into Windmühlen Straße, a woman came along pushing her bicycle up the hill. Noting the ten-year-old child (Stephen Mark would turn eleven on August 3, 1972) struggling with his suitcases, the woman scolded me. "Why do you permit that child to carry such heavy suitcases?" she demanded. "Madame," I said, "each of us has two suitcases and two arms. Each person must carry his own suitcases." Hearing my answer, the woman said to Stephen, "Give me the suitcases." With that, she placed Stephen's suitcases on her bicycle and conveyed them all the way to the front door of the Ernst Thälmann Hostel.

Realizing that Stephen had a difficult struggle with his suitcases, I greatly appreciated the woman's kind act. Before we had departed Frankfurt in the BRD, I had purchased a sack of oranges on the railroad concourse. Unzipping the bag into which I had placed the pouch, I pulled the sack of oranges out of its secluded chamber, handed it to the woman and said, "Danke schön."

A broad smile replaced the scolding frown that had been on the woman's face when she had demanded, "Why do you let that child carry two heavy suitcases?" The woman could not have known that her considerate act of helping Stephen would be rewarded by a sack of oranges, in 1972, a rare treat in the DDR. Realizing from our conversation in English and from our youth hostel address that we were Americans whose residence in Weimar probably was to be of short duration, the woman immediately issued an invitation to us. "I am Hilde Bredenbröcker. I reside just across the street with my family. After you get settled and have free time, I would like to invite you for refreshments in our garden." A couple of days later, Ines, the Bredenbröckers' twelve-year-old daughter, came to the hostel and invited us for afternoon refreshments in the Bredenbröcker garden. This was to be the beginning of a friendship that endures until today. The afternoon refreshment invitation was extended to the evening meal. Uwe, Ines' older brother, grilled Thuringian sausages. Otto, the husband of Hilde and father of Ines and Uwe, came home from his dental practice. Because they had lessons in the English language at school, Ines and Uwe were able to communicate with us and to act as translators for their parents. Frau Bredenbröcker cultivated many sorts of roses in the garden. "There are three hundred roses that bloom in my garden," she said with pride. Sitting in Frau Bredenbröcker's garden, surrounded by the pleasant aroma of 300 roses, an aroma that integrated well with the smell of Thuringian sausages simmering over a charcoal grill, I thought of my first visit to Germany as a Fulbright Grantee in 1955 and of the visit we Fulbright students paid to the Rhöndorf home of Chancellor Konrad Adenauer. He also prided himself on his rose garden, and he, as Frau Bredenbröcker, had many varieties. During our ten-day residence in Weimar, we were several times invited for refreshments in the garden. I guided my group to the Luther sites in Erfurt, just a short distance from Weimar. Of course, I led the group to those sites to which Frau Giese had led me. I also had the group accompany me to Frau Giese's grave where I told them the story of how Frau Giese and I had met and how rewarding, enriching and informative our friendship had proved to be for me. I also told the Bredenbröcker family about Frau Giese. Before we departed Weimar, we exchanged addresses with the Bredenbröcker family. Frau Bredenbröcker requested that I lead her to Frau Giese's grave. After reaching the spot, Frau Bredenbröcker said, "Frau Giese is buried quite near our family plot. Whenever I come to the cemetery to attend our gravesite, I'll also take care of Frau Giese's grave for you. Now, for these many years since 1972, Hilde has retained Frau Giese's grave in good order. Whenever I return to the site, I notice how well kept it is, with a plant or fresh flowers adorning the location. Each subsequent summer, I was invited with my countrymen to enjoy the hospitality of the Bredenbröcker family. After our picnic in the garden, we would assemble in the large dining room where a piano stood. Otto particularly loved to hear and to sing German folk songs. Two ladies who frequently joined my summer group, Maryann Tustin and Helen Harrop, were accomplished pianists. Maryann (deceased July 31, 2006) was a music teacher and Helen also was an elementary school teacher. Seated at the piano, they alternated playing the German folk songs that the group lustily sang. I observed Otto seated in his large comfortable chair. At the sound of the music and song, he beamed in delight. Frequently, touched by the sentiments in many of the folk songs, his eyes glistened with tears. In the course of her many visits in the Bredenbröcker family, a deep friendship developed between Maryann and the family.

During the summers of 1967, 1968, 1969, 1970, 1971 and 1972, while attending the summer school course, my residence had been in the Park Hotel in 1967, and the Hotel Elephant from 1968 through 1972. Later in 1972, I resided with my group in the Ernst Thälmann Youth Hostel. In 1973, I was assigned residence in the Christliches Hospiz (Inn), on Amalien Straße, just opposite the Wieland Platz. The inn was a cozy environment. Frau Leupoldt, the hostess and her assistant, Frau Mühseler, were most accommodating. I enjoyed residing there.

Claude with Otto and Hilde Bredenbröcker, Weimar

Realizing that accommodations in the inn, being very modest in price, would permit me to spend three weeks in Weimar with a group of my friends and acquaintances who very much wanted to visit the

Reformation sites, I began to plan to bring eight to twelve people each summer on such a tour. I knew that somehow I would have to deflect the insistence of the DDR travel bureau in Berlin that sought to place tourists from capitalist states in the most expensive hotels. I mentioned this problem to Mayor Luitpold Steidle who had been most hospitable in arranging meetings between my pupils and DDR youth. "Book your accommodations now for next year with Frau Leupoldt," Mayor Steidle recommended. "Later, when you write to the travel bureau to procure your DDR visa, include in your letter the statement that, because the Mayor of Weimar, Luitpold Steidle, already has booked accommodations for you in the Christian Inn, you will not need the reservation services of the Berlin travel agency. The bureau, of course, will regret that it cannot place you in the most expensive hotels, but it will have no reason not to grant you a tourist visa."

Another very fortunate connection came my way. In 1972, in my conversations with the Bredenbröcker family, I discovered that Frau Hilde Bredenbröcker was a friend of Frau Augst, the woman in charge of the Weimar branch of the DDR Travel Bureau. Their friendship dated back to their school days. "I'll introduce you to Frau Augst," Frau Bredenbröcker said. One day, Frau Bredenbröcker escorted me into Frau Augst's office. The two women embraced each other. I was introduced. "Dr. Foster plans to come next summer with a group of his countrymen. Frau Leupoldt has reserved rooms for him in the Christian Inn. Mayor Steidle supports this reservation. We want to make certain that there is no holdup in Berlin." Frau Augst answered, "Dr. Foster, write to me when you apply for your visa. I will call Berlin and expedite the matter."

Thus, with the support of Mayor Steidle and Frau Augst, the central Berlin Travel Bureau gave up its attempt to place my group and me in expensive Inter Hotels. The following summer, and for all the subsequent summers in which I led groups to the DDR, we resided in the Weimar Christian Inn.

I became better acquainted with Mayor Steidle. He invited me to his home for dinner. He introduced me to his hospitable wife. In the course of the evening, Mayor Steidle, who had been born in Bavaria and raised in the Roman Catholic faith, revealed that he still considered himself a Roman Catholic Christian. "I was, after all," he explained, "elected mayor as a member of the Christian Democratic Party." Of course, the mayor knew and he was aware that I knew that in addition to the SED ruling party, four other parties participated in the government—the Christian Democratic Party, the Liberal Democratic Party, the National Democratic Party of Germany and the German Farmers' Party. In the DDR political system, these four parties were apportioned candidates and districts in the country that, under the supervision of the SED, they were permitted to administer. Weimar was a Christian Democratic Party region. Therefore, with five political parties in the Volkskammer and districts of the country where each party might have its respective administration, the appearance of a democratic state was preserved. This arrangement was in harmony with Walter Ulbricht's statement to his colleagues at the founding of the DDR state, "It must have the appearance of a democracy, but we must retain all power in our hands." Mayor Steidle also held powerful credentials for after he was taken prisoner at Stalingrad in February 1943, he joined the organization in the Soviet Union, Freies

Deutschland, an organization made up of captured German officers who broadcast over the front to their comrades to surrender to the Red Army, that Hitler had lost the war and that they should not sacrifice their lives for a madman whose egotistical mania drove them on into certain death. Mayor Steidle earlier had given me an autographed copy of his book, Entscheidung an der Volga (Decision at the Volga), which he wrote on his return to Germany. The dedication reads, "For Professor C. Foster, In sincere companionship and with all good wishes, Weimar, July, 1970, Luitpold Steidle." "I wrote this book," he declared, "to defend our action in seeking to persuade German soldiers to surrender. I was a major at Stalingrad. I had to send my men into certain death in obeying the commands that were coming to us from the Führer's headquarters. I had to ask myself, 'Can I justify what amounts to mass suicide to satisfy the ego of a commander who is safely ensconced under concrete bunkers hundreds of miles from the front?' The answer to this question finally became clear to us all, and despite Hitler's insistence that we should fight to the last man, General von Paulus and his officers decided on surrender. That was my first act of disobedience and, as a Wehrmacht officer trained in the Prussian tradition, it cost me much anguish. My second act of disobedience was actively to seek to persuade my comrades on other fronts, who continued to sacrifice their lives, to disavow Hitler and to surrender. Of course, if we had been captured by German units still fighting, we would have been executed as traitors, but treason, as Tallyrand said, is a matter of chronology; yesterday's traitor is today's hero. If Great Britain had defeated the thirteen colonies, Benedict Arnold, instead of being sentenced to death by a colonial court, would have been decorated by his majesty's government. Does blind obedience to a dictator in a hopeless situation take precedence over disavowing that obedience in order to save the lives of those whom the dictator willingly and callously sacrifices to his ego?"

During each summer residence in Weimar, I was invited by Mayor and Mrs. Steidle for a dinner. The mayor presented me with photos of some of his meetings with colleagues in Berlin. On August 29, 1971, he had written on the back of a photo that he had taken of the dining area in his home, where we had had many stimulating conversations: "Dear Professor Foster, Thank you for your greetings from Freiburg. In the meantime, I hope that you have returned home safely. Soon I shall write a letter to you. My wife and I greet you and your family most heartily. The photo is in memory of our pleasant hours together. Your Steidle."

In this same summer of 1972, on Monday, June 19, I visited Frau Dette once again in her home in Grimma. Frau Dette presented a children's storybook by Wilhelm Busch to me to give to our son Stephen; "Hans Huckebein, The Unfortunate Raven." Frau Dette wrote in the book: "In memory of June 19, 1972 for Stephen Foster, Hedwig Dette, DDR."

I received a letter from the DDR Historical Society, dated October 26, 1972:

> Very Honorable Professor Foster,
>
> The DDR Historical Society will sponsor a conference from December 12-15, 1972 in Dresden. As you can see from the enclosed program, the theme of the conference will be questions related to German history within a world historical context. We are cognizant of the fact that such a theme is of importance not only to DDR historians, but also to historians from other nations. Therefore, we are anxious to have historians from other nations participate in our conference. We would be very happy if you, colleague professor, would accept our invitation to participate in our conference. We will assume all expenses for your accommodations in Dresden. Please indicate at what border point you will enter the DDR so that we can arrange to have your visa for pick up at that border entrance.
>
> With collegial greetings,
>
> Professor J. Streisand - President

In the autumn of 1972, I received a telephone call from the office of the Federal Bureau of Investigation requesting an interview. I consented and a few days later, two FBI representatives called at our home on Taft Avenue in Wilmington, Delaware. Sitting in our living room, we, at first, engaged in small talk, but I knew that two FBI representatives did not come to discuss the current football season and express admiration for the winning ways of the University of Delaware football team. "We note," they said, "that you spend each summer in the DDR." I was surprised that my annual visits to the DDR would be of interest to the FBI. "Yes," I replied. "I guide US citizens to the German Reformation sites, and after the group returns to the US, I remain in the DDR to study the German language and literature and to conduct research." "In the course of the years," one agent remarked, "you must have met very many interesting people. We note that you have received invitations to lecture at historical congresses convened in the DDR, that your lectures have been published there, and that you have studied at the Humboldt University as a guest of that university's history faculty. Would you like to share with us some of your interesting encounters?" With this remark, my political antenna shot high into the air.

"My contacts," I responded, "are with colleagues who study in the same discipline in which I teach and research. There is, I am certain, nothing in these relationships that could be of interest to the FBI." The other agent then replied, "But you know Bishop Moritz Mitzenheim of Thuringia and his associate, Gerhard Lotz, who we believe is a mole inside the Church. When you studied in Eisenach in the summer of 1966, you resided with the family of Richard Rückert, the retired theater director and former Eisenach SED party chairman. You also know Professor Max Steinmetz, the leading historian at the Karl Marx University in Leipzig and high-ranking SED member; you also know Professor Steinmetz's colleagues, Gerhard Zschäbitz and Gerhard Brendler. You know Mayor Luitpold Steidle of Weimar, and you and your pupils from the Tatnall School have enjoyed his hospitality, and you and your pupils have attended picnics with youth in Weimar hosted by the mayor. You know Klaus Trostorff, director of the Buchenwald Memorial Museum. You often take your groups to Erfurt. Outside Erfurt is a major Soviet base. We also know that you receive, subscription-free, copies of literature published in the DDR; for example, the official SED newspaper, *Neues Deutschland* and the propaganda magazine, *Neue Heimat* as well as the CDU Union magazine publication, *Standpunkt*. With all these connections, Dr. Foster, we are convinced that you are in a position to assist your nation in the Cold War."

I was astonished that these two agents possessed so much information about my contacts in the DDR. I realized that my voluminous correspondence with friends and colleagues in the DDR had come to their attention. Of course, I knew that my correspondence to friends and colleagues in the DDR was subject to DDR state scrutiny, and now it was clear that my post also was subject to FBI surveillance. After recovering from the shock provoked by the rude revelations that I had heard, I repeated my former statement: "My relationship with all these associates and friends is based on professional interests only. We assist one another and contribute to one another in our academic pursuits. There is no political agenda. I am not prepared to enter into any agreement that could, if detected, place my colleagues and friends in the DDR in grave danger. I am a patriotic American and I love my country, but I am unwilling to betray colleagues and friends in the name of patriotism, especially when I have no access to information that could be relevant." One agent broke in, "Dr. Foster, you must permit us to evaluate what is relevant and irrelevant. We are not looking for military secrets from you. You are in a most strategic position to evaluate the mood of the populace and, with your inside access to high-ranking party members, to gage the esprit de corps of DDR Communism." There was a long pause. Finally, I said, "I'm sorry gentlemen. Espionage is not my vocation." The representatives departed, no doubt disappointed in what for them was a stubborn refusal by me to accept my responsibility as a good citizen and ardent patriot.

From December 12 to December 15, 1972, during a sabbatical leave, I attended the Fifth Historical Congress of the DDR convoked in Dresden. At dinner, I sat at table with Professor Karl Drechsler from the Academy of Sciences in Berlin and some of his colleagues. One of the colleagues was Dr. Margot Hegemann, a specialist in the history of Romania. The gentlemen colleagues excused themselves to go to search for a colleague who had not arrived and who they feared might have gone to the wrong banquet hall. Dr. Hegemann and I were alone at table. "I understand," Dr. Hegemann said, "that your area of specialty is the Protestant Reformation." "Yes," I answered. "I wrote my dissertation in this area and I prefer to teach this subject." Dr. Hegemann then continued, "The Reformation played a large part in my early education. My mother was very devout. She taught me the catechism, the traditional hymns and her favorite Bible verses. Each evening before she tucked me into bed, my mother and I kneeled and prayed together." Dr. Hegemann had a very nostalgic look on her face, nostalgia and pathos combined. Then, in a subdued and sad voice, she said, "Of course, I don't pray anymore, but I never go to bed without thinking about those childhood evenings at my mother's knee." I was astonished that this lady, whom I had met for the first time, would, as a member of the SED, be so candid with me concerning her childhood religious training, an experience that I could discern from her voice and facial expression, she held in fond memory. "Well, Dr. Hegemann," I said, "Perhaps you are what the Jesuit scholar, Karl Rahner, would describe as an 'anonymous Christian.'" Dr. Hegemann laughed lustily. "O please," she said, "don't mention that possibility in the presence of my SED colleagues. I'm afraid they would not understand."

Dr. Hegemann and I exchanged addresses and promised to keep in touch with each other. Of course, because we knew that our correspondence might be read by the Stasi and Dr. Hegemann's position could be jeopardized, we had to be circumspect when referring to religious faith. Our exchange had to appear academic and when we wrote concerning Luther's doctrine of grace, our discussion had to be carefully couched within the framework of Luther's dispute with the papacy and in no way suggest a personal reliance on God's grace. During my summer visits to the DDR and at various conferences, I saw Dr. Hegemann. When opportunity presented itself, we continued our conversations on Christianity, and especially on Luther's theology in which Dr. Hegemann as a child had been thoroughly trained by her mother. It was clear from the yearning for faith that Dr. Hegemann exhibited in our discussions that she was not at all a Marxist. Her mother had died. As a girl, in the chaos of the post-war Soviet occupied zone of Germany, she had to make her way. She was intelligent and soon was enlisted by SED talent scouts. Livelihood and professional opportunity were contingent upon Party loyalty. "Once caught up in the strong current of Party ideology and conformity," Dr. Hegemann said, "it's almost impossible to extricate oneself from that flood. Promotion, security and recognition are very enticing, but they must be purchased at the price of sacrificium intellectus."

On December 21, 1972, the BRD and the DDR signed a treaty that granted diplomatic recognition to the DDR and provided for the exchange of ambassadors. The Hallstein Doctrine had been replaced by Willy Brandt's Ostpolitik. In 1974, the US granted diplomatic recognition to the DDR, and in August 1975, the Helsinki Accords constituted another step in the recognition of the postwar realties.

On Saturday, January 27, 1973, in the Majestic Hotel in Paris, the US and Vietnam signed a treaty that ended the Vietnam War. Everyone knew that the treaty provided for a quick exit for the US from Southeast Asia, but provided no guarantee for the security or independence of South Vietnam. A US news team, filming in South Vietnam, announced to the world, "Now the war finally is over." A South Vietnamese woman responded to the proclamation, "Which war has ended? Perhaps the American war; but ours?" The staggering losses, 56,000 US combat deaths, 135 billion dollars and the incalculable casualties among the Vietnamese demonstrated once again that foreign policy decisions are too important to be left to politicians with little or no knowledge of history or foreign cultures. On Tuesday, January 23, 1973, just four days before the US/Vietnam treaty was signed, Lyndon Baines Johnson died. His decision to invest overwhelming US military forces in the war made him "the most hated man in America," and dictated his decision not to seek the nomination of his party for another term as president.

One of the more controversial decisions during the war was the employment of Agent Orange, a sobriquet for the herbicide to defoliate the forest areas that offered cover to the Vietcong. It would take years before the Pentagon would concede that the more than 20 million gallons of chemicals sprayed had an adverse effect on the health of US troops fighting in the regions where Agent Orange was used. It is now admitted that exposure to the chemical caused cancer and the number of American troops who subsequently contracted and died from cancer caused by Agent Orange cannot for certainty be known.

Reflecting on this tragic chapter in American history, I wrote,

AGENT ORANGE

He must soon die
News terse and clear.
Predicted death.
Predictable fear.
The best of his youth
to his country he gave.
His country prepared him
an early grave.
Agent Orange,
Nam's incense,
enshrouds the forest
like a halo dense.
Kill the trees,
destroy the rice.
Annihilate the enemy
at any price.
Knowing only the soldier's fare,
he breathed for months
the turgid air.
He survived the war,
the enemy's might
and came back home
to a future bright.
But Nam's incense
was with him still.
It poisoned his lungs,
eroded his will.
Young must he go,
cut off not by foe,
but by his own nation.
Who shall declare
his generation?

Traveling with my countrymen, 1973-74

In the summer of 1973, I conducted a tour of the German Reformation sites for ten of my countrymen. We visited Eisenach and walked up the forest path to the Wartburg. From our base in Weimar, a few days later at breakfast, I announced that if the weather were good, we would visit Erfurt, just a twenty-minute train ride from Weimar. As we breakfasted, the rain stopped and the sky began to clear. "Good," I said. "It will be pleasant weather. We can travel to Erfurt." From the Steuben Straße bus stop, we took the bus to the rail station. Looking at the bus schedule posted at the bus stop, one member of our group remarked, "Dr. Foster, there's another bus after the one we plan to take that would get us to the station in time to catch the train for Erfurt. Why do we always come early to the bus stop and take a bus before the bus we could take later? If we took the later bus, we would not have to wait so long at the station."

"True," I said, "but what would we do if one of these busses does not come, which is not an unusual occurrence in the DDR. I plan to take the earlier bus, and if it does not arrive, we still can take the later bus that may get us to our destination on time."

After arriving in Erfurt, I led my group through the old city. We walked across the Krämer Bridge and along the banks of the Gera River. Finally, we came to the Augustinum, the former Augustinian monastery. We entered the gothic church. As we entered the sanctuary, in the narthex we noticed a large table on which a guest book had been placed. A typed notice next to the guest book invited each guest to sign the book and to provide his or her nationality. In this fashion, the administration could take note of how many guests found their way to this famous site associated with Luther and the Reformation, and from what cities and nations the guests had come. On behalf of my group, I signed my name and the date of our visit. We proceeded into the nave, admiring the exquisite stained glass windows, some, especially those in the chancel area, dating from the fourteenth century. In the presbytery, I pointed out the white stone on which Martin Luther had prostrated himself in September 1506 in order to take his Augustinian monastic vows.

Having completed our tour of the sanctuary, we walked to the quad area where, beneath a blanket of green grass, the friars of former ages lie buried. Surrounding the quad, under gothic stone arches, was the cloister's ambulatory where for centuries friars silently had made their rounds, immersed in meditation and prayer. From the ambulatory, a door provided access to the upper rooms of the former monastery, now a museum area. We climbed the steps and proceeded through the rooms, studying each exhibit illustrative of Luther's residence in the Erfurt friary, with brief interludes, from 1505 until 1512. While I once again studied the seal of a black cross on a red heart situated on a white rose and surrounded by a blue background that Luther had designed as his personal emblem, I heard loud footsteps on the highly polished timbered floor.

Suddenly, standing in the doorway that gave access to the room in which my countrymen and I were studying the various exhibits, stood a beautiful blond, blue-eyed young woman. Looking directly at me and with a smile that captivated everyone in the room, the young woman called out, "Dr. Foster!" and rushed into my arms. She wrapped her arms about me and gave me a hug and then a demonstrative kiss on the cheek. Then, stepping back from the tight embrace, our faces only inches apart, she asked, "Dr. Foster, don't you recognize me? I'm Ute Döring from Dresden." "Ute!" I exclaimed. "Is it possible? I haven't seen you since 1967. At that time, you were a thirteen-year-old watching a parade with my pupils and me from Frau Charlotte Rhode's balcony in Berlin. That was six years ago and now you are a beautiful young woman."

"I have every Christmas and Easter card that you wrote to me, Dr. Foster," Ute said. "My parents and I were always pleasantly surprised by your gifts, and especially the delicious fruit cakes that you sent to us at Christmas." As Ute and I stood immersed in vivacious conversation, my countrymen stood about us and looked on with great curiosity. Especially when I noticed Bob McMichael, a dear friend, who regarded me with great suspicion on his countenance, I realized that I had better interrupt my conversation with Ute and provide an explanation for my group. Later Bob would tell me what his initial reaction was. "I didn't know what to think. When I saw that beautiful, young blond wrap her arms about you in such an affectionate embrace, I was stunned."

I asked Ute to permit me to explain the situation to my group. Everyone, especially Bob, was relieved to learn that the hug and kiss I had received from Ute were the expressions of an innocent friendship. Now it was time for me to satisfy my curiosity. "Ute," I asked, "what are you doing in Erfurt?" Ute answered, "I have never been to Erfurt. My fiancé was conscripted into the army. This morning he had to report to his training center that is not far from Erfurt. I accompanied him by train from Dresden to the boot camp where we had to say goodbye until he has his first leave. Having never been in Erfurt, I decided that before I returned to Dresden, I should visit this old city and its historical sites. When I entered the church, I saw the guest book and, as I was writing my name in the book, I happened to look at the entry immediately above my signature. You can imagine how amazed I was to read, 'Dr. Claude Foster and countrymen, USA.' I asked the custodian, who was working in the narthex, whether or not this gentleman still was in the building. The custodian told me that you and your group had gone to the second floor museum rooms. I ran immediately to the stairs and came searching for you."

After having completed her story, Ute gasped, "Dr. Foster, isn't it remarkable that, having not seen each other since 1967, we meet in Erfurt?" "It is extraordinary," I replied, "especially when my countrymen and I only made our decision to travel to Erfurt after the weather cleared. Had the weather not improved, we would not have come and you and I would not have met. You were in this region for just one day. Consider the percentages. There are 365 days in the year. On this very day, you traveled from Dresden to Erfurt, and we traveled from Weimar to Erfurt. There are 24 hours in the day, and on this single day at this specific hour our paths cross in this particular building. This encounter encourages one to believe in Providence. Our meeting under these circumstances lends credence to Dr. Albert Schweitzer's adage, "Coincidence is the pseudonym which God employs when He wishes to remain anonymous." Ute joined our group. I invited her to return with us to Weimar. "I will ask Frau Leupoldt if she has a room available for you," I said. "In that case you can stay overnight in Weimar and accompany us the next day to Dresden. We had planned to visit Dresden later, but, with you as a guide, we will travel to Dresden tomorrow." Ute agreed and, after returning to Weimar, a room was made available to her. The next day, we journeyed to Dresden. From my earlier visits to Dresden, I was familiar with the center of the city and with the White Fleet that ferried passengers up the Elbe River to Saxon Switzerland. Saxon Switzerland is the region near Dresden where high rock formations remind one of the Alpine landscape in Switzerland. The reunion with Ute was very pleasant. We thanked her for guiding us and then we went to our respective families where previously we had arranged overnight accommodations.

On a later visit to Dresden, while returning on the ship that conveyed us from Saxon Switzerland to the center of the city, I noticed a man in long and intense conversation with some members of my group. Of course, in those days, DDR citizens were anxious to have conversations with people from the West. I casually walked past the group in order to discern the theme being discussed. The DDR citizen was probing the Americans to discover details about their stay in the DDR. I recognized immediately that the man was a member of the Stasi, the DDR secret police. On a pretext of calling attention to a castle on the Elbe bank, I interrupted the conversation. I then drew some of the group aside and reminded them of instructions I earlier had given each person. Never mention names of your DDR hosts. Never reveal that you are residing overnight with a family. This last point was important because our residence accommodations were in the Weimar Hospiz, not with a private family in Dresden. Conceivably one could, by taking the earliest train from Weimar to Dresden and the latest train from Dresden to Weimar, spend most of the day in Dresden and still be able to return late to Weimar. We permitted the Stasi agent to believe that this was our plan. Of course, we planned to remain overnight in Dresden where we were hosted by several families. Perhaps the agent suspected that we intended to remain overnight in Dresden, and, after we left the ship, he followed us. He kept a block behind so that we would not notice that we were being trailed. I had to discover a way to shake off this undercover leech. From the pier, we walked toward a main street, Ernst Thälmann Straße. At that intersection, when we turned the corner into Ernst Thälmann Straße, we would be out of sight of our pursuer. At that point, I instructed the group to stop and to look at the books on display in the window of a large bookstore. When the agent turned the corner in hot pursuit, he was startled to see us standing in front of the bookstore. Of course, he could not stop because that would have made his trailing us too obvious. He proceeded slowly down Ernst Thälmann Straβe, always looking back to see if we resumed our march. At the corner was a streetcar stop. I saw a streetcar coming. It halted to discharge and take on passengers. At the very last minute before the streetcar doors closed and the trolley proceeded, I hustled my group onto the car. Under full speed, we passed the Stasi agent standing frustrated on the sidewalk. The next stop was too far away for the thwarted stalker to catch up with us. This was a good lesson for naive Americans. The group had not realized that this deputy had been pumping them for information.

During my summer visits to Dresden in 1966 and 1967, I had paid a short visit to Frau Schultze, but, because he had been conscripted into the army, I did not see Rainer. Rainer wrote to me in 1968 and informed me that his mother had died, and that after he had been discharged from military service, he had moved into an apartment near the city center and closer to his place of employment. Upon my next visit to Dresden, he invited me to visit him at his new address. I did visit Rainer at his new address, Number 2 Schilling Straβe, and on that occasion, I met his fiancée, Bärbel, who resided at the same address. One floor below Rainer's apartment was the residence of Frau Pommrich. Frau Pommrich invited Rainer, Bärbel, and me to dinner. At this dinner, I became acquainted with Edith Krummreich, Frau Pommrich's daughter, Freya Klier, Edith's daughter and Peter Pommrich, Frau Pommrich's son, who resided with his mother. Frau Pommrich prepared a wonderful meal. For more than twenty years, Frau Pommrich had been employed by Metropa, the caterer for diner service on passenger trains. Frau Pommrich was able to put a variety of food on the table, dishes that usually were available only in the dining rooms of the most expensive hotels. When I commented on the variety and quality of the food, Edith smiled and said, "Mother possesses the vitamin most essential here in the DDR, vitamin B." Everyone laughed at Edith's remark for we all knew that in DDR parlance the "B" stood for the first letter of the German word "Beziehungen," "Connections." It was Frau Pommrich's connections with her colleagues at Metropa Catering that enabled her to acquire such variety and quality. Connections and hard currency were able to achieve what appeared to be unachievable.

Throughout the year, by sending presents at Christmas and on other occasions, I kept in touch with friends in Dresden. I asked Edith what I could send to her mother, Frau Pommrich. "Your mother makes a great effort to provide us with such a delicious meal during our visit in Dresden," I said. "I would like to send her a present from the United States, but I'm not certain as to what I should send." Frau Pommrich was short of stature, corpulent, with very stout legs. Edith responded, "What my mother really would like and needs, especially for the Dresden winter (as you see we have no central heating), are pantyhose. Mother's size is so large that pantyhose to fit her are almost impossible to find here." "All right," I said, "for Christmas I will send pantyhose." Back in the US, I decided to stop at a department store to purchase the pantyhose for Frau Pommrich. That was the only item that I intended to purchase. Upon entering the store, I asked a female clerk if she could direct me to the largest size of pantyhose. She gave me a suspicious glance and then pointed to an area where pantyhose were on display. I selected the biggest. The brand name was "Big Mama." I took twelve packages of "Big Mama" pantyhose from the shelf and proceeded to the cashier. As the cashier rang up my purchase, I could see that she was thinking, "What a pervert he must be!"

Claude with Frau Helene Pommrich

In Dresden, at Frau Pommrich's, we had experienced what vitamin B could accomplish. Once, while visiting Professor Max Steinmetz in Leipzig, this fact was brought home to me. As I sat at afternoon coffee with Professor and Frau Steinmetz in their residence at 16 Stormthäler Straβe, workers were at the task in the adjoining room of extending the size of Professor Steinmetz's study. On the garden side of the study, where room for expansion existed, the workers had removed the wall and were hammering the additional floor space into place. Professor and Frau Steinmetz explained, "When we first sought to enlist these workers for this job, we were told that they were booked up for the next twelve months. We did not want to wait such a long time. Therefore, we offered to pay for the work in West German Marks. Even that attractive offer was not sufficient to change the schedule. The foreman said that if we would provide west cigarettes and if Frau Steinmetz would prepare a warm midday meal for them, they would give our request priority. Yes, Dr. Foster, in our society it is vitamin B and hard currency that open doors."

To illustrate the frustration that DDR citizens faced when, without hard currency, they had to wait their turn in the long queue for house repairs, the following humorous tale was told: Upon requesting a plumber to schedule repair work, the customer was told that the first available appointment would be in two years on January 15. In quiet resignation, the patron asked, "Morning or afternoon?"

Of course, I knew about vitamin B from my experience with the DDR Travel Bureau. Until the Weimar Mayor, Luitpold Steidle, intervened on my behalf, the travel bureau insisted on booking me in the most expensive hotels. When I wrote to the travel bureau that Mayor Steidle had made my reservations for me in Weimar, and when Frau Augst, the director of the Weimar branch of the State Travel Bureau, called Berlin on my behalf, the bureau dropped its insistence on placing me in the Hotel Elephant.

During a visit to Stotternheim, an agrarian region just outside Erfurt, I once again discovered the importance of having hard currency at one's disposal. As my group and I sat in the Stotternheim parsonage and enjoyed refreshments, especially the excellent pastry baked by Pastor Ulrich Nagel's mother-in-law, the pastor related to us the frustration his congregation faced in seeking materials to repair a leak in the church's roof. "At every rain," Pastor Nagel said, "water penetrates through the apertures in the roof. We must place buckets in the transept at the left front of the sanctuary. Several times our farmers have driven their tractors to the nearby state depot, the only source of building supplies, but to no avail. Each time our congregational members are repulsed with the lie that no materials are available. Of course, materials are available, but not for the church and not for payment in DDR currency."

Each person in our group had brought dollars from his or her respective congregation. I had told the members of the group that we could assist churches in the DDR with gifts of hard currency. We gave Pastor Nagel a sum of dollars. The Stotternheim farmers once again drove their tractors to the state depot and once again requested construction materials to repair the church roof. Exasperatingly the foreman at the depot scolded, "How many times must you be told that we do not have the materials you request!" Thereupon Pastor Nagel, who had accompanied his farmers to the depot, asked, "Not even for dollars?" The depot foreman looked stunned. Then he asked, "Do you have dollars?" "Yes," Pastor Nagel replied, "and we are prepared to pay in dollars for the materials." Miracle of miracles! What never had been available for DDR currency suddenly became available for dollars.

In my earlier visits to Stotternheim, I had discovered the Swedish granite marker that had been erected in the field to designate the supposed place where the 22-year-old student, Martin Luther, had experienced the lightning bolt that caused him to cry out, "Saint Anna, help me; I will become a monk!" From the Stotternheim parsonage, Pastor Nagel and I guided my countrymen to the monument. Incised in the granite, we read, "Ex Thuringia Lux (Out of Thuringia came the light). Here the young Martin Luther was shown the path, July 2, 1505." Another inscription reads, "The starting point of the Reformation." "Sometimes," Pastor Nagel said, "it is impossible to come here with guests because the Red Army uses these fields for tank maneuvers. Fortunately, the stand of trees around the monument protects it from being knocked over by an errant tank. After what happened in our village, I have no confidence in the driving ability of Soviet tank crews. Our neighbor's house, which is situated on the corner of an intersection, now has no wall or roof on the street side of the dwelling. A tank, trying to negotiate the turn from one street into the other, hooked the side of the house and pulled that section of the house to the ground. The members of the crew, apparently unaware of the fact that they had pulled down the side of a house, drove on to rendezvous with their fellow tank crews here on this plain."

On September 16, 1973, Gunter Hutschenreuther, Professor at the University for Construction and Architecture in Weimar, wrote to me. Renata Hutschenreuther, his wife, also was professor at this university. In the group that I guided in the summer of 1973 to the DDR, there were several very attractive coeds that drew DDR young men like blooming flowers draw bees. During our three-week residence in Weimar, one of these young men, Jürgen, who was attracted to Valentine Pupo, one of the coeds in my group, was the son of the professors Hutschenreuther. On one occasion, Jürgen, on behalf of his parents, invited our entire group for a picnic in the Hutschenreuther garden. We spent a very pleasant evening with the Hutschenreuther family. I knew from Hilde Bredenbröcker, who resided not far from the Hutschenreuther home, that the professors were "Party People," Gunter, CDU and Renata, SED. Therefore, I alerted my people to avoid political topics in our conversations.

In 1974, I was invited to participate in the historical congress convoked in Leipzig to mark the 450th anniversary of the German Peasants' War (1524-1525). The invitation came from Professor Gerhard Brendler from the Academy of Sciences in East Berlin, noting, "All your expenses in the DDR will be borne by the Academy of Sciences." I presented a lecture: "The View of Thomas Müntzer in American Historical Writings." Professor Max Steinmetz once again was the host for the convocation. Professor Steinmetz also gave the keynote address at an evening banquet—an excellent address. On this occasion, I was able to renew acquaintances that I had made in Wittenberg in 1967 and to become acquainted with other DDR colleagues. My lecture subsequently was published in the symposium protocol volume.

On Friday, August 1, 1975, thirty-five nations met in Helsinki, Finland to seek to ease tensions between the East and West Blocs in Europe. The western nations, including Canada and the United States, agreed to recognize the borders in Europe as they then existed as de jure. This meant renouncing all claims for a revision of the borders in Eastern Europe. This point had been a goal of Soviet policy ever since the end of World War II, which saw the Soviet Union in possession of former eastern Polish territory, also of East Prussia, and Poland in possession of the former German Silesian territory. As a quid pro quo, the Soviet Bloc agreed to ease travel restrictions to the West for citizens in the various East Bloc states, to promote family reunion for those families separated by the East/West borders and to demonstrate greater respect for human rights.

1976, Sorrow in the DDR

On August 18, 1976, the twelfth anniversary of the Wartburg meeting between Bishop Moritz Mitzenheim and Walter Ulbricht, a meeting in which Ulbricht had promised that the state would respect the independence of the Christian Church, a shocking scene on the main square of Zeitz, (Saxony/Anhalt) just outside the Saint Michael's Church took place. The Reverend Oskar Brüsewitz, forty-seven years old, pastor in Drossdorf/Rippicha, drove the short distance from his village into the city, parked his trabant, and opened the trunk from which he took several placards that he set up against his car. Then he took a canister of gasoline from the car's trunk, poured the gasoline over his body and lit a match. Passersby sought to smother the flames. Rushed to the hospital, Pastor Brüsewitz died five days later. Why did the pastor engage in such an act? The DDR media depicted him as mentally ill. If the public could be convinced that the suicide was the act of a mentally deranged person, the question of a dramatic protest against the state's attempted coordination of the church into an atheistic state system could be parried. Also to be avoided was discussion of Pastor Brüsewitz's questioning of his ecclesiastical leaders who permitted, with increasing tolerance, state encroachment into the life of the church. For Oskar Brüsewitz the Christian Church in the DDR had become a twentieth-century model of the Laodicaean Church whose witness the risen Christ accused of being like a lukewarm liquid, and therefore, would be spewed out of His mouth (Revelation 3:16). Because the witnesses to this self-immolation immediately became involved in seeking to smother the flames, they only had vague remembrance of the messages on the placards. According to the best recollections, the posters complained about the DDR's atheistic brainwashing of the youth, and perhaps a call for ecclesiastical resistance to the state's erosion of the Christian witness. The police arrived quickly on the scene and the placards were removed and were never seen again.

Some years after Pastor Brüsewitz's death, Frau Ursula Brandschwei, one of my Weimar hostesses, at my request, telephoned Frau Christa Roland Brüsewitz and petitioned permission for me to visit and to interview her. In her trabant, Frau Brandschwei drove me from Weimar to Drossdorf/Rippicha. Frau Brüsewitz resided in a house near the church in which her husband had conducted his ministry. Pastor Brüsewitz's grave is located only a few steps from the church in the church cemetery. Frau Brüsewitz said, "We were married in December 1955. I lived with Oskar for twenty-one years. My husband was not mentally deranged. Yes, he was depressed, but the depression was caused by the state's policy of undermining the church's youth training program and the failure of his ecclesiastical leaders to support him in his effort to confront the political authority on behalf of freedom for his church. We often discussed these problems and in the testament he left behind, he accused the local political leaders that by intimidation, by threats of not admitting the youth to higher education and by promises of material gain, they were eroding my husband's attempt to provide Christian education for the youth. The pressures to accept Jugendweihe, whereby the youth swear allegiance to their socialist Fatherland, instead of Christian confirmation, are almost irresistible. Membership in the Thälmann Pioneers and in the Free German Youth is made prerequisites for admission to the university and for career development. In these organizations, the youth are systematically brainwashed in Marxist atheistic ideology. Our daughter, Esther, despite the fact that she earned excellent grades, was not admitted to upper grades, which would prepare her for the university. Persistently, my husband contended with the local political leaders against these discriminatory practices directed at Christian youth, and he petitioned his ecclesiastical superiors for support. On both fronts, he met with repeated frustration. Oskar's protests began to draw the attention of the Stasi. There was a report that Stasi chief Erich Mielke was considering expelling him from Saxony/Anhalt, a device the Nazis had employed against Confessing Church pastors, the most famous case being that of Pastor Paul Schneider. Despite the grandiose language in the Helsinki Accords of August 1975— which Erich Honecker had signed—concerning human rights, the real situation in the DDR was in sharp contrast to the spirit of that document. Even if there had been a way of calling attention to our plight, the world would not concern itself with the complaints of an unknown village pastor. Our church leaders were too anxious to preserve a modus vivendi with the state, an unholy alliance between "throne and altar" which too frequently, in the history of our country, caused the Christian gospel to be diluted and the Church to become the handmaid of the state. My husband came to the conclusion that only a desperate act, which would shock the world, could draw attention to the state's subjugation of the church. "Before setting out on his mission, my husband insisted that our entire family (our two daughters, Esther and Dorothea (Dörle), Oskar and I (our thirteen-year-old handicapped son, Matthias, had died on November 2, 1969 of a muscular disorder) should breakfast together. I thought his insistence odd because never before had he been adamant on that point. Perhaps it was the Losungen for the day, I reasoned, that he wanted us all to share. Oskar opened the small paperback volume of the Losungen (Daily Scripture Readings Published by The Moravian Church In Herrnhut, Germany) and said,

> Psalm 82:3: "Give justice to the weak and the orphan; maintain the right of the lowly and the destitute."

> I Corinthians 12:26: "If one member suffers, all suffer."

> Reflection: "My neighbor's burden also is my burden. The burden which encumbers him, I bear with my neighbor. Lord, permit Thy light to shine in my heart in order that its brilliance might cause my brother to rejoice."
> Fritz Schmidt König."

Frau Brüsewitz continued, "Oskar read the words so deliberately, with such feeling that the children and I felt a certain sadness, perhaps induced by the pathos in his voice. Almost with a sigh, Oskar repeated, 'If one suffers, all suffer.' At breakfast, he was particularly affectionate with me and the children and we sat at table much longer than usual. Oskar requested Esther to play his favorite hymn on the piano; 'Dear Lord, Take My Hands.' Finally, he hugged each of us with a lingering embrace and then returned to his study. Later I saw him place two posters in his trabant, posters on which he had worked alone. Usually he enlisted Dörle to help him with posters. I saw him get in his car and start his trabant. The sound familiar to every DDR resident—the shifting gears in a trabant motor—was the last sound from my husband's auto, still a witness to life, I was to hear as he drove away. Later that morning, police officials called at the parsonage to inform me that Oskar had been taken to the hospital. The shock and worry that Esther, Dörle and I registered convinced the police that we had no knowledge of Oskar's intentions. At about the same time our neighbors delivered a letter to us that Oskar had requested them to bring to me later in the day. It was his farewell letter to his family. Near Oskar's body was found a banner with the inscription: 'The Church in the DDR accuses the State of discriminating against the Christian youth.' The physicians were quite candid. Given the extent of the burns on his body, Oskar was given no chance for recovery. Five days later, on August 23, he died."

Oskar Brüsewitz's self-immolation, as protest against the state's erosion of the Christian witness in the DDR and against lethargic church leadership that mounted no vigorous resistance to combat the atheistic octopus that was entangling and devouring the Christian youth, drew national and international attention. By his suicide protest, the village pastor had provoked a scandal that could not be concealed nor explained away, and that proved most embarrassing to state and church officials. One prominent DDR church official regretted the impact this act might have upon the Church/State dialogue, which was difficult enough without such dramatic protest." After the collapse of the Communist government in East Germany, this same official was quoted as saying, "Oskar Brüsewitz was a precursor of the coming political transformation. Only later did I comprehend his mission." Other DDR churchmen expressed the concern that the West critics would exploit the self-immolation of Pastor Brüsewitz to increase their anti-Communist propaganda.

In a 1993 interview, Pastor Brüsewitz's Bishop, Friedrich Wilhelm Bäumer, expressed regret that he had not sought more diligently to listen to the complaints of Pastor Brüsewitz concerning the Communist discrimination against Christian youth. Recently declassified Stasi records reveal that Pastor Brüsewitz, rather than finding a sympathetic listener in his bishop, discovered an ecclesiastical official who sought to coerce him to conform to a modus vivendi that his synodal superiors had established with the state. In the 1993 interview, Bishop Bäumer said, "I am continuously in dialogue with Brother Brüsewitz and I repeatedly ask him why he committed suicide, but there never is an answer to my question. What remains is my inner disquietude that will never permit rest, because I was Brother Brüsewitz's confidant and I failed to discern his psychological anguish."

Four weeks before the fatal date of August 18, 1976, and because local Party leaders were becoming increasingly annoyed with Pastor Brüsewitz's complaints, Bishop Bäumer suggested to Pastor Brüsewitz that perhaps a transfer to another parish would solve the problem. Pastor Brüsewitz, however, apparently interpreted this suggestion not as a solution, but as a punishment for his resistance to the Communist authorities with whom his own ecclesiastical administrators were too anxious to cooperate. In the 1993 interview, Bishop Bäumer expressed regret that he did not give closer attention to Pastor Brüsewitz's charges and that he did not more actively support his pastor against the Communist Party persecution.

Today on the Saint Michael's Church Square is a stone mosaic with the date 1976, a tribute to the self-sacrifice of Pastor Oskar Brüsewitz. The Newspaper, *Neues Deutschland*, which in 1976 was the media organ for the SED, in August 2006, issued an official apology for its 1976 editorial that dismissed Pastor Brüsewitz's act as the deed of someone mentally unbalanced. The current editors wrote, "We regret the pain that the editors of *Neues Deutschla*nd, (in August 1976) with their denigrating editorial, caused the family and friends of Pastor Brüsewitz. This guilt remains indelible. In deep shame and regret, we also confess that not one of the thousands of letters received protesting the despicable editorial ever was published." Thirty years later, August 2006, one historian concluded, "As Dietrich Bonhoeffer today is the positive symbol for the Church in the Third Reich, one day Oskar Brüsewitz will be assigned this role for the church in the DDR."

Frau Brüsewitz commented, "If only for a brief period, Oskar accomplished in death what he was unable to achieve in life, namely a world focus on Church/State relations in the DDR." I thought of the self-immolation of Jan Palach on January 16, 1969 on Wenzel Square in Prague in protest to the crushing of The Prague Spring by the Warsaw Pact on August 20, 1968. In order to protest the subjugation of his nation and to shock a complaisant and indifferent world, which too easily had come to terms with the events of August 1968, the student Jan Palach took such dramatic action. Frau Brüsewitz continued, "The authorities prevented publication of funeral arrangements. But by word of mouth and telephone calls, many people were informed. Checkpoints were set up around our village to intimidate those who might want to attend the funeral. The autobahn near Rippicha was limited to one lane and the speed limit reduced to enable the police better to control the traffic and to thwart those wishing to attend the funeral. In Zeitz, all the flower shops were closed. Despite all these efforts by the authorities, many people assembled for the funeral. Six brother clergy carried the coffin the short distance from the church sanctuary to the grave." Frau Brüsewitz then led Frau Brandschwei and me to Oskar's grave. We stood in silence reflecting on the mental anguish that this village pastor had had to endure.

In September 1976, I received an obituary notice from Anni Dette. The envelope, rimmed in black, alerted me to the possibility that my dear Grimma hostess, Frau Hedwig Dette, had died. Frau Dette's daughter, Anni had written the notice on September 8, 1976. I recalled my meeting with Frau Dette on the train, Frankfurt to Leipzig in October 1967. In my mind, I reconstructed our stimulating conversation that made the long journey from Frankfurt to Leipzig pass quickly. I recalled accepting Frau Dette's invitation to visit her at her residence on 1 Küntz Straße in Grimma. I picked up the beautiful volume of Martin Luther's Kirchen Postille that she had presented to me during my visit to her home on Tuesday, August 13, 1968. I remembered that Frau Dette had said that this volume was one of her deceased husband's prized possessions, and that she wanted me to have the book because she was certain that with me the publication would find a friendly home. I recalled visiting Frau Dette on several subsequent occasions in the years following 1968. I remembered the terrible blow to the family when the news arrived from the BRD that Ilse's son, Frau Dette's grandson, had been killed in an automobile accident. Klaus, a dentist, had managed, illegally, to cross the border into West Germany (BRD). Soon after having won his freedom, Klaus had lost his life in an automobile accident. A notepad found on Klaus' desk was sent to Ilse. Apparently, the last lines that he had written before his untimely death read, "I seek and I seek and I seek, not entirely without success — but I seek, and I seek, and I seek." Klaus had hoped to prepare the way for his parents to emigrate to the BRD.

Frau Dette and Anni had written to me with what cruelty the DDR state punished the family of one who had fled the Republic. Ilse and her husband resided in Bitterfeld where her husband was employed in the Leuna Chemical Industry. Reflecting on the information that I received from the family, I wrote the following meditation:

TEARS IN BITTERFELD

The telegram message,
brief as a Roman dagger,
pierced her heart.

"Klaus killed—
last night in automobile accident.
Can you attend funeral?"

The raised letters on the thin paper,
like a branding iron,
burned a deep wound into her heart.

"Klaus, dear Klaus," she wept,
and sank into her chair
under the burden of grief.

No, she may not attend the funeral.
East Berlin rejects her visa application
for travel to West Germany.

No, his body may not be buried
in the hallowed soil of his socialist Fatherland.

Three months ago, he had crossed the border illegally.
Did his mother know of his plans?
DDR functionaries suspected she did.

No permission to attend the funeral of a son
who fled the Republic.

No permission for the Republic fugitive
to be interred in the soil of his native land.

Farewell then, dear son,
from within the alienation which estranges Germany from Germany.
Only in my thoughts may I, your German mother,
accompany her German son to his
narrow, modest house in German soil.

The smoke from the chemical chimneys
hangs low in the cold, leaden, winter sky.

The mother sits before a window,
looking westward through the dull gray.
Silent tears,
the only witness to grief in Bitterfeld.

In a few years, at age sixty-two,
she would have emigrated to her son.

"T'were better had he remained with her," she thought,
"for now more than barbed wire separates us."

"He cannot return to me,
and I cannot go to him.
Only in some transcendent world
which knows no borders
or political ideologies
will I find him again."

She sighs and whispers his name,
and the frigid winter air bears her lament
before an indifferent race.

Production schedules must be met.
A brigade of blue-shirted Free German Youth marches past,
Skis slung over their shoulders.
A baby cries in the adjoining apartment.
No one notices the tears in Bitterfeld.

1976, Religious Persecution

Because my countrymen and I resided for the entire three-week stay in the Weimar Hospiz, our visa, which I had to procure at the Weimar police station within twenty-four hours of our arrival in Weimar, was issued for the Erfurt region (Bezirk) only. This I found too confining. I complained that we had not traveled such a great distance to be confined to the Erfurt bailiwick. "We want to visit Leipzig, Dresden, Wittenberg and Berlin," I said. "Then you must book hotel accommodations in those precincts," was the answer of the official. I knew, of course, that outside of Weimar, the State Travel Bureau would assign us to the most expensive hotels. It was only vitamin "B" with Mayor Steidle and Frau Augst that thwarted the travel bureau from booking us in the Hotel Elephant. "We can reside in Weimar and visit Berlin, Wittenberg, Leipzig or Dresden just for the day," was my argument. "Leipzig is only two hours by train from Weimar, and if we take the earliest train from Weimar to Berlin and the last train from Berlin to Weimar, we could visit Berlin inside one day. The same plan would also work for Wittenberg and Dresden." The police official responded, "But Leipzig, Berlin, Wittenberg and Dresden are outside the Erfurt district and your visa is valid for the Erfurt principality only."

I must have looked disappointed. I said, "If you wish to encourage western tourists to visit your country, you must not put such restrictions on them. I will not be able to persuade my countrymen to accompany me to the DDR if we are to be confined to the Erfurt borough." The official understood my argument. "All right," he said. "I will give you a visa for the entire Republic, but, unless you book in a hotel, you must limit your visit to areas outside the Erfurt Bezirk to one day." I knew that this was a major concession and that the official actually had altered regulations to accommodate us, as the clerk in the Eisenach train station had done when she sold us train tickets at a group rate. But I also knew that in the next summer I might not find such an indulgent police official. I must find a permanent remedy to this limitation. Fortunately, a solution, once again based on vitamin "B," was forthcoming.

Professor Karl Drechsler and a colleague, Dr. Dieter Lange, from the East Berlin Academy of Sciences came to the US to conduct research in their respective disciplines. Professor Drechsler was preparing his manuscript on the US between the anti-Hitler coalition and the Cold War, which was published under that title by the Akademie Verlag in East Berlin in 1986. Professor Drechsler's study of Kennedy and Khrushchev would appear later in 1999. At the end of their sojourn in Washington, D.C., and before their departure for the DDR, I invited both DDR colleagues to Wilmington, Delaware where I resided at that time. I gave them a tour of the Wilmington area. Among other sites, we visited the Dupont powder works that now comprise the Hagley Museum along the banks of the Brandywine River. We also visited Longwood Gardens in Kennett Square, Pennsylvania. During the few days in which Professor Drechsler and Dr. Lange resided with my family, I mentioned the problem of the visa that restricted my group to the Erfurt district. Professor Drechsler suggested a solution. "Inform me in advance on what day you will arrive in Weimar. On that day, I will send my secretary to Weimar with personal invitations for your countrymen to visit and to hear lectures at the Academy of Sciences. Since official invitations from the Academy can be accepted only if one has a visa valid for the entire Republic, the Weimar police must issue a non-restrictive visa. My secretary will explain the situation to the Weimar police official. Berlin takes precedence over Weimar; the Academy over the Weimar Police bureaucracy."

This was a brilliant resolution to the problem. "Never mind," I thought, "that none of my countrymen would have been able to understand a lecture in the German language." In fact, while in Berlin, I did not take the group to the Academy. We utilized our time in Berlin to go sightseeing. I met Frau Astrid Assmann, Professor Drechsler's secretary, at the Weimar train station and together we walked the few blocks to the police station. Frau Assmann explained to the police official that Dr. Foster and his group were invited guests to the Academy of Sciences. She opened her briefcase and produced the official invitations, whereupon the Weimar official expeditiously issued us unrestricted visas. Vitamin "B" once again had demonstrated its vitality.

Sometime in the early 1970s, I received a telephone call from the chairperson of the Women's Association of the First Baptist Church in Kennett Square, Pennsylvania. The chairperson informed me that at an evening session of the association the guest speaker would be Mrs. Jurina Turnska from Prague, Czechoslovakia. Knowing of my interest in the East Bloc (I had addressed the association on an earlier occasion concerning the witness of the Christian Church in the East Bloc), the chairperson invited me to attend the meeting when Mrs. Turnska was scheduled to speak. Mrs. Turnska was the widow of one of the professors at the Johannes Amos Comenius Theological Seminary in Prague. Mrs. Turnska presented a very interesting lecture on the relationship between the Christian Church and the Communist State of Czechoslovakia. Her command of the English language was quite good. Later, I discovered, she also could speak the German language. After her presentation, Mrs. Turnska and I had a long discussion. She invited me to visit her on my next visit to the East Bloc. This invitation would lead to my being introduced to faculty members at the Comenius Theological Seminary, for, although her husband was deceased, Mrs. Turnska maintained close contact with her husband's colleagues. We exchanged addresses and I promised to visit Prague at the earliest opportunity. Since I already had invitations to visit Anna Zoricakova and her husband, Stefan, in Levoca, I decided that, at the end of my summer residence in the DDR, I would travel from Dresden to Prague to visit Mrs. Turnska and then fly from Prague to Poprad in Czechoslovakia where Anna and Stefan would pick me up and drive me to their home in Levoca. When I was certain that I had time and means for a visit to Czechoslovakia, I wrote to Mrs. Turnska.

Anna and Stefan Zoricak

She responded enthusiastically to my plans and agreed to meet me at the Prague Central Rail Station. I also alerted Anna and Stefan when I planned to travel to Czechoslovakia.

Jurina gave me a very thorough tour of Prague and arranged a luncheon where I was introduced to faculty members at the Comenius Theological Seminary. In the course of our conversation, I mentioned that my doctor father was Professor Otakar Odložilík who, before 1948 had been a professor at the Charles University in Prague. I did not think it diplomatic or necessary to mention that Professor Odložilík had been forced by the Communist Party to surrender his chair in the history department. Professor Odložilík was successful in receiving an exit visa that enabled him to accept a position at London University. From London, he was called to Columbia in New York and from Columbia, he was invited to join the faculty of the University of Pennsylvania where I met him in 1958. When I mentioned Professor Otakar Odložilík and that he was my doctor father, the Czech professors expressed their envy. Some of them had studied with Professor Odložilík before he was removed from the Charles University faculty. I could see that Professor Odložilík still was held in the highest esteem by Czech intellectuals.

Jurina accompanied me on the bus trip to the airport and saw to it that I got on the correct flight to Poprad. I planned to spend ten days in Levoca. "I'll meet your return flight," Jurina said. After about a one and one-half-hour flight, I arrive in Poprad. Anna and Stefan awaited me at the small Poprad airport. In about one hour, we drove from the airport to Levoca. Stefan spoke only the Slovak language. Anna and I conversed in the German language. Anna and Stefan resided in the center of the small town of Levoca, only a few blocks distant from the Roman Catholic basilica in which the sculptured wooden altarpiece of the "Last Supper" by Master Paulus is housed. During the visit in Levoca, Anna and Stefan drove me to the mountain lake country of the High Tatra Mountains. Anna and Stefan had two other guests, a married couple from Leipzig, Dr. and Mrs. Herbert Schramowski. Anna had met the couple during her summer visit to Leipzig. Apart from giving instruction in the German language, Anna also taught piano. Dr. Schramowski and his wife Sigrid are accomplished pianists. Dr. Schramowski taught at the Karl Marx University in Leipzig. As a result of their meeting in Leipzig, Anna invited the Schramowskis to visit Levoca. Thus, this visit in Levoca also brought me into a friendship with Herbert and Sigrid that endures until today.

Early on Sunday morning, Stefan drove his car out of the garage that was situated under Anna and Stefan's apartment. We drove the circa twenty miles to Spišská Nová Ves where we attended the Roman Catholic worship service. Because we arrived early, we were able to get seats. Soon after our arrival, the sanctuary was crowded and many people had to stand in the aisles and in the narthex. I learned that, with a short time interval, there were six Masses celebrated each Sunday morning, one after the other. At each service, the sanctuary was filled with worshipers. I estimated that the sanctuary could accommodate circa two hundred people. The priests, who resided in the nearby parsonage, took turns celebrating Sunday Mass on a rotating basis. Stefan and Anna preferred to attend the Mass celebrated by the senior priest, who also was a friend. Anna and Stefan earlier had informed Father Vladka that they would bring guests to the service. After the service, Anna and Stefan introduced Sigrid and Herbert Schramowski and me to Father Vladka. Father Vladka then invited us to the midday meal in the parsonage, and what an excellent meal it was! Two women cooks in the rectory kitchen supplied us with one tasty course after another. The beverages for the meal—wine or beer. The excellent Czech beer, Pilsner, which usually could be found only in the most expensive hotels that catered to tourists from capitalist countries, was in ample supply in the rectory. Because the Communist regime desperately needed hard currency, the general Czech population had to forego consumption of one of its nation's better earning exports. Pilsner beer, with the exception of being available in the first-class hotels, was exported to the western capitalist markets.

It was during this meal, in conversation with the priests, that I was briefed on discrimination and persecution that the church had to endure at the hands of the Communist state. The very fact that Anna and Stefan, as employees of the state, rather than attend worship in the Levoca Catholic Church, only three blocks from their residence, drove to Spiŝská Nová Ves to attend church now became clear. "To attend church in Levoca, where we are well known, would place our professional position at risk," Anna said. "Our state does not condone teachers attending Christian worship services. Practicing our Christian faith by attending church, in defiance of the well-known state antipathy toward the church, would be considered a provocation and could lead to dismissal and loss of livelihood." In Weimar, I had noted that Anna was one of the many East Bloc participants at the International Summer School Course for German Language and Literature who took advantage of being in a foreign country to attend worship services in the historic Herder Church.

Father Vladka then related how some parents, intimidated by local political officials, had withdrawn their children from his catechetical class. "The state has many weapons at its disposal," Father Vladka said. "For instance, one of my male parishioners, the father of a boy in my catechetical class, was told by his foreman at the factory, where this father is employed, that unless he withdrew his child from my class, the promotion, with significant increase in wages, which earlier had been promised to him, would be given to someone else. The local Party chief told the father that if his child were not withdrawn from the class that the boy would be denied admission to the vocational school that he had hoped to attend. In the face of such pressure and discrimination, it is very difficult for Christian parents to practice their faith and to train their children in the Christian tradition. Nevertheless, I still have a class, though reduced in number of catechumens."

Father Vladka added, "You may know the case of the Hungarian Cardinal, Josef Mindszenty, who, after the 1956 Hungarian uprising against the Communist rule, to escape arrest by the Soviets, fled to the US embassy in Budapest, and resided there until, in September 1971, because of poor health, he was permitted to emigrate to the Vatican. The conflict with the Marxist state concerning the education of children that Cardinal Mindszenty faced in Hungary, we face in Czechoslovakia. As Cardinal Mindszenty claimed as early as 1946, that parents have the right to decide how their children are to be educated, we also affirm. The official Hungarian state response to Cardinal Mindszenty was documented in June 1950 and is to this day also the official state policy in Czechoslovakia.

Anna then spoke up. "Professor Foster, I told Father Vladka that you would like to return next summer with a group of your countrymen, that after you visit sites in the DDR you plan to take the train from Dresden to Prague and, after some days in Prague, to have your Prague acquaintances drive you here to Czechoslovakia. Father Vladka would like to invite you and your group for a Sunday midday meal here in the parsonage. Father Vladka also would like to make a request. You notice that the four young priests who assist Father Vladka have no clerical collar. Clerical collars are not to be found in all Czechoslovakia. When you return next summer, would you please bring several clerical shirts and collars for our young priests?" I promised that I would. When Anna translated my reply to Father Vladka's petition, the four young priests, who sat at table with us, beamed with excitement.

One evening a young priest from a village not far from Levoca visited Anna and Stefan. I was introduced. Stefan, following his daily evening custom, took a cigar box from on top of a cabinet in the dining room. In the box was a short wave radio. With this radio, Stefan could listen to western newscasts in the Slovak language. "This is our window to the outside world," Anna said. After I had been introduced to Anna and Stefan's guest, Father Stefan Stakov registered his disappointment with statements, broadcast over the Russian radio, which the Reverend Billy Graham had made during the American Evangelist's recent visit to the Soviet Union. "Christians in the Soviet Union," Father Stakov said, "face daily discrimination and persecution, yet the American Evangelist was too anxious to compliment his Communist Party hosts and too reticent to criticize the policy of discrimination and persecution that cries out to heaven for redress. We in Czechoslovakia experience a similar persecution that the famous evangelist, with his cosmopolitan congregation, could have condemned or at least exposed to the world. He failed to do so. Your countryman seemed more eager to please his hosts than to succor his fellow believers."

Father Stakov continued, "Don't Christian leaders in the capitalist western countries know about the persecution and discrimination that their fellow believers behind the Iron Curtain face on a daily basis? For instance, on Tuesday, May 6, 1975, Jozef Cardinal Mindszenty of Budapest, died in Rome. From the date of the popular revolt of the Hungarian people against their Soviet masters in the autumn of 1956, which was drowned in great bloodshed by Soviet tanks, in order to avoid arrest and possible execution, Cardinal Mindszenty had to reside in the Budapest US Embassy until September 28, 1971. It was only on this latter date, because of failing health, that the Cardinal was granted amnesty and permitted to leave Hungary for residence at the Vatican. As far as we can discern here in Czechoslovakia, the brutal persecution of Christians in the Communist states is not a priority of western publicity, and the World Council of Churches, anxious not to offend the East Bloc delegations at the Council, prefers to discuss problems in Asia and Africa."

For me, as a US citizen with ties to evangelical Protestantism, this critique was painful, and it registered on my mind. Later, as I observed western church leaders visiting the East Bloc states, I had to conclude that the critique was valid. In East Berlin, for example, the Reverend Ralph Abernathy, Dr. Martin Luther King's successor as the director of the NAACP, took opportunity to describe in most disparaging terms the slow pace of the civil rights struggle in the US while at the same time lavishing praise on the DDR for having achieved such a high level of democracy. Not a word of criticism did the Reverend Abernathy utter concerning the discrimination against the Christian Church in the Communist East Bloc. Nor did the Reverend Abernathy complain on behalf of those killed at the wall whose only crime was the desire to emigrate from East Germany to West Germany. In employing an East Bloc platform to criticize discrimination in his native country, the Reverend Abernathy may have succeeded in embarrassing his nation so that the campaign against discrimination in the US might have been accelerated. (The East Bloc media persistently proclaimed that it was the Cold War competition between the Soviet Union and the US for Asia and Africa that forced the US to expedite the Civil Rights movement. To woo the African and Asian populations away from trysting with Moscow, so the argument went, it was necessary for Washington to become a more attractive suitor. East Bloc media, therefore, ascribed to the Communist East Bloc much of the credit for the success of the US Civil Rights legislation). But what about the people of the DDR who waited in vain for a word on their behalf from the US Christian leader. Christians in the East Bloc were forced to conclude that their dilemma was not a priority for western political and religious leaders.

At home in the US, preparing for the next summer trip to the DDR and Czechoslovakia, I remembered the request of the priests in Spiŝská Nová Ves. I telephoned a boyhood friend, now a Catholic priest and pastor of a large parish in Wilmington, Delaware. "Joe," I said, "this is Sonny Foster. We haven't heard from each other in many years, but I have heard from our mutual friends, our former teammates, what you have been doing." Joe inserted, "Sonny Foster, a voice from our old neighborhood! I've heard that you're a professor at West Chester University! Given the pranks of our youth, none of our neighbors would have predicted that one of us would become a priest and the other a professor! What's on your mind?" That was the opening for which I waited. "Joe," I said, "I need the shirt off your back." After a pause, came the expected answer, "What?" I then explain to Joe (Father Hazard) that I planned another trip to Czechoslovakia and that his spiritual confreres in that Communist country were unable to procure clerical garb. "You certainly have an ample supply of clerical shirts and collars. Since all the priests in Czechoslovakia need the vestments, we need not worry about size. Your size is bound to fit someone." "O.K." Joe responded. "When would you like to pick up the shirts?" "I can come to the church office tomorrow morning," I said. "One other request," I added. "Please write out the address of the shop where you purchase your clerical shirts and collars. In addition to what you can give me. I also will purchase some." The next morning, I was able to pick up Joe's clerical shirts. Unfortunately, just before I arrived, Joe received an urgent call to the deathbed of one of his parishioners. The church secretary met me and delivered the shirts and the vestment shop address. I left a note expressing thanks for the shirts on behalf of the Slovakian priests.

Priests at Spišská Nová Ves

Each summer, I instructed the persons traveling with me to take an extra suitcase of clothes that we then distributed to people in the countries visited behind the "Iron Curtain." In this particular summer, each person also purchased a clerical shirt that we presented in Spišská Nová Ves. What rejoicing! The young priests were beside themselves with joy! In the course of guiding my countrymen to the German Reformation sites each summer from 1967 to 1992 (with the exception of 1978 in which summer I was recovering from surgery), I discovered a technique that helped to expedite clearance for us at the DDR Gerstungen border check point. I knew that the border custom officials did not speak English and that they were accustomed to checking people who sat in stressful silence in the train compartment. Each compartment could accommodate eight people. The absolute silence in the train as the guards approached revealed the fear-induced apprehension that had seized the passengers. I instructed each person in my group to put a wad of chewing gum in his mouth, to talk fast, loud and incessantly while at the same time chewing the gum. We handed our passports to the guards to be stamped. I noticed that the guards were most uncomfortable in an environment of loud, cacophonic sounds. They stamped our passports as quickly as possible, throwing only a cursory glance at our luggage, without checking the contents. As the guards proceeded down the corridor, I heard one say to his colleague, "I can't stand those chewing gum chewers."

One day while traveling on the train from Berlin to Weimar, I was seated next to a young black woman. We came into conversation. She told me that she was a scholarship student from Zimbabwe. I knew that DDR policy was to bring many students from Asia and Africa to study in the DDR. These students would one day be leaders in their respective native states and, having received a free education in the DDR, they would be friends of the state that had trained them. The young woman told me that, during the few days' vacation, she was traveling to Weimar to visit a friend, a fellow student from Zimbabwe. She said, "My friend in Weimar also has a scholarship at the University for Architecture and Construction. She and I traveled to the DDR together. I study oral surgery in Berlin." Noting that her German conversation was limited, I asked the young woman if she spoke the English language. "O yes, much better than German," she said. "In Zimbabwe, I attended a Methodist Missionary School founded and supported by Methodist Churches in the US." I smiled and replied, "Perhaps we should speak English. I'm an American." "You're an American?!" she gasped. We both laughed.

I knew that foreign students studying in the DDR were able to visit West Berlin. I asked the young woman if she had been to West Berlin. "O yes," she said. "When my friend in Weimar came to Berlin to visit me, we crossed over into West Berlin to see the city. As citizens of Zimbabwe, we can cross through the checkpoints to West Berlin. Our East German fellow students are very envious of us. West Berlin is fabulous. We went into big department stores and just stared at the supply of goods." "Did you purchase anything," I asked. "O no," she replied. "We could not afford to purchase anything. Our stipend is in East German currency." Just before we arrived in the Weimar station, I placed, unobserved by other travelers, a twenty dollar bill on the small window shelf next to my seat companion. I said, "The next time that you go to West Berlin, you may purchase something." Startled at the sight of the money, the young woman spontaneously cried out, "God bless you!" I do not believe that the other passengers who heard this loud exclamation knew for what reason such a blessing was invoked. On the platform, the other young woman from Zimbabwe waited for her friend. We exchanged addresses. "I will write to you when I expect to be in Weimar next summer," I said.

The next summer I alerted the Zimbabwe students when I would be at the Hospiz with my group. I told the women in my group about the Zimbabwe students. The women packed extra suitcases with very attractive clothing. When we arrived in Weimar, I went to the dormitory where the young students waited for me and returned with them to the Hospiz. The women in my group took the Zimbabwe guests into one of the larger rooms, unpacked the suitcases and had the students try on the clothing. Seated outside in the reception room, I could hear the squeals of delight coming from the fitting room. The students completed their education and returned to Zimbabwe. Some years later, I received an invitation to attend a wedding in Harare, Zimbabwe. The oral surgeon was about to marry. Although I could not attend the wedding, I sent a gift and some weeks later, I received a handsome wedding photograph of the bride and groom.

Claude and the two Zimbabwe students

1977-1979
Margarete Schneider and Aimé Bonifas

In the fall of 1977, I received a sabbatical leave. I was invited to participate in an historical congress in the DDR convoked at the Karl Marx University from October 10 to 11. Professor Max Steinmetz, who had been pleased with my lecture in Wittenberg in 1967, and who, in that year of 1977, was elected rector of the Karl Marx University, had invited me. Realizing that my DDR colleagues were very curious of how their historical research was evaluated in western historical studies and also aware of the fact that very few western historical studies were known in the DDR, except to a certain few elite scholars, Professor Steinmetz being among the elite, I prepared a lecture in the German language on the subject: DDR Reformation Historical Scholarship As Evaluated In American: Historical Writings, A Synopsis. The lecture was very well received and copies of the annotated bibliography that I placed on the table next to the lectern disappeared in short order. The lecture was subsequently published in the symposium protocol volume.

After the congress, I took the train to Prague where I visited friends. My Czech friends still were suffering from the shock of August 1968 when the Warsaw Pact nations, under the rationale of the Brezhnev Doctrine had invaded Czechoslovakia and ended the "Prague Spring" promoted by Alexander Dubček. There were many moving stories of the chaos and suffering this invasion had caused. One particularly sad story was the case of a young woman who suffered a coronary and who was being rushed to the hospital in an ambulance. Soviet tanks had blocked off the street that the ambulance crew had taken to get the woman to the hospital. By the time clearance was procured for the ambulance to proceed, the woman had died. The Czech people had not forgotten Jan Palach, the student who, on Thursday, January 16, 1969, at the top of the Saint Wenzel Square, out of protest against the invasion and a return to a tyrannical government, engaged in self-immolation.

I flew from Prague to Poprad where Anna and her husband Stefan picked me up and drove me to their home in Levoca. One October evening we sat before the television and watched the celebration in Moscow of the 60th anniversary of the Bolshevik Revolution. Martial music, singing, speeches and endless parades marked the festivities. Having visited most of the states in the East Bloc and having been in contact since 1966 with colleagues from all East Bloc states, I knew that the population of those respective countries under Soviet hegemony did not share in the euphoria of the 60th anniversary celebration. The picture of the Soviet Union as the great bastion of socialist humanitarianism was belied by the brutal suppression of popular dissent: Berlin, June 17, 1953; Poland and Hungary in 1956; the Berlin Wall, August 13, 1961; the invasion of Czechoslovakia, August 1968, and the persistent reports of the Gulag that filtered through to the West. Stefan and Anna, both well-educated teachers, expressed their dismay at the celebration of a tyrannical system that subjugated them and their nation to the will of the "Big Brother" in Moscow.

In January 1978, I had to have major surgery. Sometime in 1976, I began to suffer from high blood pressure and I consulted my physician. On a few occasions, while lecturing, I felt that I was about to faint. These experiences, of course, caused me great concern. The physician diagnosed my condition as hypertension. The prescribed medication helped to control the high blood pressure, but the pressure always remained above normal. "You're working too hard," my physician said. "Slow down. Get more rest and sleep." I responded, "Doctor, I'm following the same routine that I have pursued for years. Why would my work habits now provoke hypertension?" "You're older," my physician answered. I sensed, however, that the physician was not satisfied with his own answer. After several hospital visits during which many tests were made, the diagnosis remained the same— "hypertension, cause unknown." Finally, in a conversation with a colleague, a specialist in urology, my physician related my particular case. The urologist answered, "It sounds to me like an adrenal tumor. These tumors normally do not show up on standard x-rays. They can be detected by an angiogram." My physician sent me to Cooper Hospital in New Jersey to a Japanese physician who was a specialist in angiogram technology. Our son, Stephen, drove me to the hospital. The angiogram revealed a tumor in the left adrenal gland. I had surgery to remove the benign tumor and from that point on, my anatomy returned to normal. After a couple of weeks at home, I was able to return to my university responsibilities. I did not travel to Europe in 1978.

In the summer of 1979, while visiting a museum in Weimar, my group and I came into conversation with the woman guide in one of the exhibit rooms. Discovering that we were US citizens, the woman begged us to visit her and her family in her flat in the center of Weimar. We agreed to visit her and her family. I told my group to be cautious. When we arrived at the flat for a coffee hour, the family members immediately described to us their woes. They showed us a letter that they had written on October 29, 1977 and had risked mailing to the Chairman for German Affairs in Bonn, West Germany. The letterhead read,

> To Those Concerned About Human Rights. Request Permission To Emigrate From East Germany.
>
> On August 3, 1976, my son, Walter, twenty-two years old and I, forty-nine years old, and I on behalf of my younger children, Christine, seventeen years old and Wolfgang, fourteen years old, filed application to emigrate from East Germany. We wish to become citizens of West Germany. We have not yet received an answer to our application. A letter to local authorities and

two letters to the Party Chairman, Erich Honecker, remain unanswered. We reminded Mr. Honecker that he had affixed his signature to the Helsinki Accords and that we now invoked those very rights that he had approved in Helsinki.

Since we do not wish to remain in this state, we cannot comprehend why we are forced to stay. We appeal, therefore, to the United Nations Charter of Human Rights and fervently petition that we be permitted to renounce our East German citizenship. According to the charter, such a right may not be denied to us. Because we are convinced and practicing Christians, life in East Germany is not only made difficult for us, it has become intolerable. My son completed high school, but, because he had not participated in the State Confirmation Ceremony, all future educational opportunity has been denied to him. He has procured a position as a hospital worker in a Catholic hospital in Erfurt. After we had submitted our application for emigration, state authorities promised my son opportunity for continued education if he would withdraw our application. We shall not consider withdrawing our application. We recognize that our steadfast determination in this matter will have dire consequences for us. Recently my son was picked up at his place of employment by the security police. He was placed in an interrogation room, forced to partially disrobe, questioned for 8 hours by various interrogators. He was thrown against the wall and was not permitted as much as a glass of water. The interrogators also threatened him with imprisonment. There were no witnesses and who will believe the word of a 22-year-old against that of the security service? Although she has the ability to pursue higher education, my daughter will have to take whatever job she can find. The political pressure, the arbitrary and continuous psychological persecution and the constant fear has transformed our life here into intolerable affliction. We, therefore, desperately plead for your help. In the hope that you will assist in ending our torment, forever grateful.

Family Signature

After some weeks of checking with my Weimar friends who knew the family and could reassure me that the case was a valid one, I agreed to carry the letter to West Germany and to mail it from within West

Germany to authorities in Bonn. About two years later, permission to emigrate to West Germany was granted.

On October 16, 1978, the voice of Cardinal Pericle sounded from the papal palace over Saint Peter's Square in Rome: "Annuncio vobis gaudium magnum, HABEMUS PAPAM!" (With great joy, I announce to you, We Have a Pope). The election of the Archbishop of Krakow, Karol Cardinal Wojtyła, to the Roman Pontificate would prove to be a major factor in the subsequent history of the twentieth century. Taking the Pontifical name of John Paul II, this Polish pope would be the first non-Italian pope since the Pontificate of Hadrian VI, who died in 1523. On the threshold of the election, Poland's Primate, Cardinal Archbishop of Warsaw, Stefan Wyszynski, urged his fellow cardinal, "If the Lord calls you, you must lead the Church into the new millennium. If you are elected to the Chair of Peter, I beg you, do not decline." Well aware of the 1848 prediction by the Polish poet, Juliusz Slowacki,

> Behold there is coming the Slav Pope—
> brother of the nations.
> As rulers distribute weapons,
> he disseminates love's salutations.
> While petitioning for the world
> in its dismal, dark hour,
> he will gain Heaven's mercy through
> the sacraments' mystic power

Cardinal Wojtyła obeyed what he regarded to be the Divine summons and the fulfillment of poetic prophecy,

Pope John Paul II proved to be one of the main personalities whose policies and influence were major factors in the demise of Communism in Europe. Later in 2004, my hostess in Poznan, Ursula Wachowska, who, with her husband had been leaders in the Solidarity Movement in Poland, arranged for me to interview Lech Wałęsa. In that interview, the former Solidarity leader told me, "Without the inspiration and support that Pope John Paul II provided to the Polish nation throughout the 1980s, Solidarity's victory over the Polish Communist Government could not have been achieved."

In the late 1970s, while residing in Freiburg, before setting out for my annual visit to the DDR, my friend Bernhard Hermann and I took a few of my countrymen to Alsace/Lorraine for a day's outing.

Claude and Bernhard Hermann in later years

We visited Dr. Albert Schweitzer's birthplace in Kaysersberg and his boyhood home in Günsbach. In Günsbach, we stopped at the home that Dr. Schweitzer had built for his retired nurses—the nurses who had worked with Dr. Schweitzer in Lambarene. In 1952, Dr. Schweitzer was the Nobel Peace Prize recipient. With the monetary reward that accompanied the prize, Dr. Schweitzer expanded his mission and built the Günsbach home for his retired staff. We rang the doorbell. An elderly lady opened the door, one of Dr. Schweitzer's former nurses. She welcomed us into the house and introduced us to another nurse who also currently resided in the house. The ladies were very hospitable. They showed us through the residence. We saw Dr. Schweitzer's briefcase, his cape and hat. Also in the house was the organ that had accompanied him to Lambarene. One of the nurses showed us a large filing cabinet. "Here's where we have filed Dr. Schweitzer's voluminous correspondence," she said. An idea struck me. I remembered Frau Giese telling me that occasionally she had written to Dr. Schweitzer and to Mathilde Kottmann, his nurse. I asked our guide if she would please open the file cabinet and search in the drawer marked with the capital letter "G." "Is there a letter in that drawer from a Frau Elisabeth Giese in Weimar?" I asked. The nurse flipped through the file cards and, sure enough, there was the name Elisabeth Giese. "Oh, there are quite a few letters from her to Dr. Schweitzer and Mathilde Kottmann," our guide said. The guide pulled the drawer out of the cabinet and placed it on a table so that I better could see the letters. "Yes," I said, "this is Frau Giese's handwriting. I would recognize it anywhere." I then told the guides about my meeting with Frau Giese and how she had been a great admirer of Dr. Schweitzer and how, at my last meeting with her, Frau Giese had given me her correspondence from Lambarene. I felt a great satisfaction to know that Frau Giese's letters to Dr. Schweitzer and to Mathilde Kottmann are filed permanently in the Günsbach archives. I thought of the miles that this correspondence had traveled, from Weimar to Lambarene, from Lambarene to Günsbach, and of the persons it once had connected, an unknown little lady in Weimar with the great medical missionary of the twentieth century.

During the summer of 1979, while residing with a group of my countrymen in Weimar, I read the notice posted on the door of the Herder Church that on Wednesday, July 18, Frau Margarete Schneider and Pastor Aimé Bonifas would speak on the fortieth anniversary of Pastor Paul Schneider's Buchenwald martyrdom. I attended with my countrymen. The sanctuary of the church was filled to capacity. I had read the paperback book that Frau Schneider had written concerning her husband: "Der Prediger von Buchenwald" (The Preacher of Buchenwald). I also had read Pastor Aimé Bonifas' autobiographical account of his labor camp experiences: "Détenu 20 801" (Prisoner 20 801). To hear these two persons speak was indeed a rare privilege. Speaking freely, without notes, the 75-year-old widow of Pastor Paul Schneider captured the rapt attention of the capacity audience. In subsequent years, I would have the privilege of hearing Frau Schneider speak on many occasions. Her sovereign command of her subject, her sound knowledge of scriptures, and her most pleasing personality, enabled her to speak freely and to win the attention and affection of every audience. Pastor Bonifas had had his presentation translated from the French language into the German language, and, although he read his remarks, his presentation, rich in content, was no less arresting. I wanted very much to introduce myself to Pastor Bonifas and to thank him for his book. After the program, I sought Pastor Bonifas on the church square. Night had fallen and there were many people. In the darkness and on the crowded square, my search for Pastor Bonifas was in vain. I returned to the Hospiz where I resided with my group. As I entered the lobby, there stood Pastor Bonifas in conversation with Fräulein Leupoldt, the hostess. I noted that Pastor Bonifas had difficulty expressing himself in the German language. I waited at some distance until they had concluded their conversation and then, in my elementary French, I introduced myself to Pastor Bonifas. "I wish to thank you for the account of your labor camp experiences that I have read in German," I said. "I regret that your book is not in the English language. I would like my students to have access to this story." Pastor Bonifas smiled and said, "Why don't you translate the book into English?"

Claude and group at the Weimar Hospiz, Summer 1979; Frau Leupoldt on left

I hold the copyright. If you wish to translate the book, you have my permission." We exchanged addresses.

I requested Pastor Bonifas to send me official written permission to translate Prisoner 20 801.

Later that summer, while visiting Czechoslovakia with my countrymen, we enlisted friends in Prague to drive us to Levoca. Stefan had arranged housing for the group in the boarding school for blind pupils where he taught, located just across the street from Stefan and Anna's residence. The pupils had gone to their respective homes for the vacation period. I resided with Stefan and Anna. Each morning, after breakfast, we drove to the High Tatra mountains. The lakes were crystal clear and the air a pleasure to breathe. After one such all-day itinerary, we returned at dusk to Levoca.

I requested the key to the school from Jurina Turnska, to whom I had entrusted the key. Jurina was our hostess from Prague, who drove one of the cars in which we had traveled from Prague to Levoca. Jurina replied, "Carla has the key. This morning, before we departed, Carla asked me for the key because she had forgotten her purse. She wanted to return to her room to get her purse." "Didn't I return the key to you?" Carla asked Jurina. "No," Jurina replied, "I don't recall your returning the key to me." Carla searched her pockets and purse. Jurina searched her pocketbook and pockets. The key could not be found. What now? We couldn't enter the school without the key. The door and all windows on the ground floor were locked. Hans-Walter Brandschwei, one of our drivers from Weimar, and I noticed that a window on the third floor at the rear of the school was open. Fortunately, there was a scaffold that reached to the third floor. During the day, workers were touching up some of the stucco surface of the exterior wall. Hans-Walter and I climbed up the scaffold and entered the school through the open window. We then descended to the ground floor, but, since, without the key we couldn't unlock the door, we opened a window. The window was about three feet from the ground level. The men had to lift the women to the window, pushing them by the buttocks through the window while Hans-Walter and I, gripping them under the armpits, pulled them into the school. Fortunately, for the most difficult case of a portly woman with pronounced buttocks, her husband stood at the ready. But even the husband, given his wife's weight and the angle of entrance, needed help from some of the young men to push his wife through the window. We couldn't refrain from laughing as, grunting and groaning, the males on the outside of the school and Hans-Walter and I on the inside pushed and pulled the squealing woman into the school.

By the next morning, Stefan had located a colleague who had an extra key. We had been using Stefan's key. Stefan came with his colleague's key. We assembled in the yard to plan our itinerary. Carla came to me and in a quivering voice said, "Dr. Foster, I found the key. It was buried in the cloth lining of my purse." "You mean," I said, "that the whole time Hans-Walter and I climbed up the scaffold to the third floor and while we were pushing and pulling people through the window, you had the key in your purse?!" With a deep blush, she said, "yes." I laughed. "Well," I said, "this experience will make this visit to Levoca unforgettable."

For an older married couple in our group, Stefan and Anna had arranged accommodations with neighbors who resided across the street from Stefan and Anna's flat and next to the school. The couple were assigned the front room on the ground floor in the residence. There was a sofa in the room that was to serve the couple as sleeping accommodation. The sofa partially blocked access to an adjoining room. The homeowners had gone away for the weekend, and the American couple thought that they were the only residents in the house. We returned at nightfall from our itinerary. It was a very warm evening. The next morning, I was briefed by the couple concerning their nocturnal excitement. "Because it was so warm," the husband said, "we decided to sleep in the nude. As we lay in bed, I heard a key turn in the front door lock. The front door opened immediately into our room. A man and woman came in and stumbled over our bed. Realizing that there were two bodies in the bed, the woman screamed something in a language I had never heard and then swiftly ran across our bed into the room behind ours. The man, in a somewhat less loud voice, exclaimed also in a foreign language and walked across our bed, trying, of course, not to step on us. We quickly put on our pajamas and could not sleep the entire night, wondering who these strangers were and why they were in the room next to ours. The next morning we were up and out bright and early." When the homeowners returned that morning, they explained to Stefan and Anna, and I translated for the benefit of the American couple. The homeowners had rented the rear room to a couple from Hungary. We were unaware of this fact, and the couple from Hungary was unaware that the American couple occupied the front room. When the Hungarian couple came home late at night and had to walk across the bed, trying to avoid stepping on nude bodies, they were as shocked as the American couple was. We all laughed.

Soon after returning home, I received a letter from Pastor Bonifas from his home in Nîmes, France with notarized permission to translate Détenu 20 801 into the English language.

Cher Monsieur,   Nîmes, September 2, 1979

Our meeting in Weimar in July truly was a fortuitous happenstance.

I write this letter in reference to my book Prisoner 20 801 in order to confirm that, should you wish to translate the work into the English language, you have my permission. The book has enjoyed three printings in the French language; three printings in the German language and one printing in the Spanish language. I hold the copyright of the original French edition (Détenu 20 801) and I grant you permission to translate this edition into the English language.

I thank you for your interest and I trust, Cher Monsieur, that you will accept my cordial and devoted sentiments.

Aimé Bonifas
(my translation)

Because my long time friend, Mildred Van Sice, has a better command of the French language than I do, I invited her to join me in the translation venture. Aimé provided us with several copies of his French text. During the week, Mildred and I independently translated the French text into English. Of course, with my university duties, I could devote only a few hours daily to the task. On Saturday morning, I drove to the home of my friends, Delmer (Bud) and Mildred. Mildred and I sat at the kitchen table, drank coffee and compared our respective translations. Remarkably, sometimes we had word for word the same translation. In other cases, we had employed various synonyms. We discussed each sentence and agreed on what we considered the best translation. We followed this procedure until the translation was completed. We sent a copy of the translation to Pastor Bonifas, who is able to read the English language, to gain his reaction. Pastor Bonifas wrote to us, "I never thought that I would speak such beautiful English."

Initially the Southern Illinois University Press published our translation as Prisoner 20 801: A French National in the Nazi Labor Camps. After all copies of the book had been sold, the Southern Illinois University Press decided not to reprint the text. Since I employed

Prisoner 20 801 as a collateral reader in some of my courses, I retrieved the copyright for the English language version. The book continues to be reprinted by the West Chester University Press. Students respond very well to the book.

While translating Détenu 20 801, I compared the French language text with the German language translation by Gerhard Lotz, the Thuringian lawyer whom I had met in Bishop Moritz Mitzenheim's office in 1966. Lotz's German language translation bore the title, Häftling 20 801. One day I came upon a scene in Détenu that Lotz had deleted from his translation. I was surprised because the German title of the work purports to be an unabridged translation of Détenu, that is of the complete French text. There is no notice that the text has been abridged. The deletion reflected the political situation in Europe between 1945 and 1989. One of the more prominent slogans that blanketed the DDR was, "Learn from the Soviet Union!" The Soviet Union was depicted as the cradle of the Bolshevik revolution from which would emerge that child, which, as an adult, would introduce the "messianic" age of world socialism, the classless society, freed from the exploitation of man-by-man. Membership in the Society for Soviet/German Friendship was one way of promoting one's career and of demonstrating one's loyalty to and enthusiasm for the Marxist/Leninist ideology. Given the political reality that existed in the DDR, it was impossible to include in the DDR edition of Détenu 20 801 the following scene:

> During a rather peaceful afternoon, I heard prolonged wailing coming from the lavatory barrack. We had developed a certain insensitivity to the suffering of others, but these cries rent the soul, and I went to see what was happening. Many inmates had gathered to witness the summary execution of four German kapos, or chiefs. After an absence of several months, a work group, assigned to work outside of Buchenwald, had just returned to the camp, and the Russian members of the group were avenging themselves of the mistreatment inflicted by their kapos. The SS did not interfere because, once the group was dissolved, the kapos lost their privileges. These acts of revenge, although not openly encouraged, were inherent in the system that devoured its most "loyal" servants. What occurred was inconceivable. The Russians, armed with metal rods, had

deliberately disemboweled their victims; when they lost consciousness, the Russians threw a bucket of cold water on the kapos to revive them so that their suffering could be extended. All afternoon they agonized, subjected to the taunts of their executioners, until death freed the fallen chiefs or until a physician   inmate gave them a lethal injection. I quickly turned away from this nauseating scene, but the smell of blood and the butchers' gleeful exultation remained with me for a long time.

From Weimar, I called Gerhard Lotz. He invited me to his Eisenach home. Herr Lotz suffered from terminal cancer, and he lived for only about one year after our interview. We enjoyed a cordial conversation. I told Herr Lotz that, in translating Détenu 20 801 and comparing the original with his German translation of the text, I had discovered a deletion. I then said that I believe that I know why this scene had been deleted, but I wanted my suspicion confirmed by you, the translator. Herr Lotz smiled at my observation and without commenting on my question simply replied, "You're correct." "Did you discuss the deletion with the author," I inquired. "Yes, I did," Herr Lotz responded. "I told Aimé that to publish the book in the DDR we must delete this episode. We wanted very much to publish the book and were able to persuade Aimé that the greater benefit for the general public in reading this book should not be lost because of the omission of one brief story."

At West Chester University, in the academic year 1979-1980, Maria Wachowska chose to take one of my courses, "The Bible in History." Coming from Adam Mickiewicz University in Poznan in Communist Poland, she was aware that no such course ever would be offered during the Communist era at her university. Maria, therefore, decided to register for this course. On the first day of the class, I entered the lecture hall with a copy of the class roster, each student listed alphabetically. I read each name to ascertain whether or not each student was present and also to begin the process of associating the student with his or her name. When I reached the end of the student roster, I noticed the name "Wachowska," quite different from most of the names on the roster. I knew that it was a Polish name and I did my best to pronounce it correctly. When her name was called, Maria gave me an approving and appreciative smile indicating that I had pronounced her name correctly. After the lecture, Maria introduced herself to me and told me that her year at West Chester University had been arranged by one of her father's colleagues, Dr. Russell Sturzebecker. Maria's father, Eugene Wachowski, professor of Athletics at Mickiewicz University and Professor Sturzebecker served together on an international sports committee. As a result of this contact, the two professors were able to arrange for Maria to study for one year at West Chester University.

Cardinal Karol Wojtyła, archbishop of Krakow had been elected Pope on October 16, 1978, taking the pontifical name of John Paul II. The Pope's first visit to the United States came in early October 1979, in the autumn semester in which Maria was enrolled in my course. A welcome for the Pope in the Philadelphia area was planned by his host, Archbishop of Philadelphia, John Cardinal Krol, who had Polish ancestry. One week before the pontiff's arrival in Philadelphia, Maria requested permission to be excused from the lecture so that she could journey to Philadelphia to see the pope. On this occasion, I became aware of the different approach to study that students behind the Iron Curtain had contrasted with the attitude of most of my American students. Most American students would have cut class with no explanation offered. Of course, I gave permission. I was persuaded that a rally for the Pope that would draw thousands of Roman Catholics to Philadelphia was more important for Maria's US experience than one fifty-minute lecture.

Although Maria spoke, read and understood the English language well, I decided to facilitate her study by requesting Polish friends of mine to lend her a Bible in the Polish language. With the Polish text, Maria was able to remain current with the class in the reading assignments. Occasionally, Maria visited my family and before she returned to Poland, I invited her to lunch at the local Pizza Hut. She invited me to come to Poland. "Dr. Foster," she said, "you visit Germany each summer and Poland borders on Germany. You could come to visit my family." I made a vague promise that someday I would visit her and her family, which I did.

The other result of that July 18, 1979 evening in the Herder Church in Weimar was my biography of Pastor Paul Schneider, *Paul Schneider: The Buchenwald Apostle, A Sourcebook on the German Church Struggle*, West Chester University Press, which I published in 1995. After hearing Frau Schneider's presentation, I was anxious to learn more about Pastor Schneider. When I returned home to the United States, I checked publication catalogues, but to my consternation, with the exception of one thin volume excerpted from Frau Schneider's book, *Der Prediger von Buchenwald*, there was nothing available. I wrote to Frau Schneider and requested an interview for the following summer. Frau Schneider invited me to visit her in Dickenschied, an agrarian village on the Hunsrück between Trier and Bingen. I wrote to Frau Schneider and requested her to reserve a room for me in the local hotel. Frau Schneider responded, "Dear Professor, in Dickenschied there is no hotel; you will reside with me."

I resided with Frau Schneider in her cozy home. Upon arrival in Dickenschied, I discovered that Frau Schneider had a family archive in which she had accumulated family memorabilia, including many of Pastor Schneider's sermons and the correspondence between her and Pastor Schneider, especially the correspondence they conducted during Pastor Schneider's incarceration in the Gestapo prison in Koblenz and in his last imprisonment at Buchenwald. "Frau Schneider," I asked, "How did you retrieve the letters to Pastor Schneider that you addressed to him at Buchenwald?" Frau Schneider answered, "On July 18, 1939, at 6:30 p.m., I received a telegram from the Buchenwald Commandant. The telegram read, 'Paul Schneider, born August 29, 1897, died today at 10:40 a.m. In case transport of the body at the family's expense is desired, request for transport must be made within 24 hours at the Weimar mortuary; otherwise the body will be cremated.' Pastor Gerhard Petry happened to be visiting in the Dickenschied parsonage when the telegram arrived. He immediately volunteered to go with me to Weimar. Ernst Schmidt, a Simmern cabinetmaker, who owned a Mercedes and a small trailer, at the request of Superintendent Gillmann, agreed to drive us. We drove all through the night and arrived at Weimar on Wednesday, July 19, at 10:00 a.m. From the Weimar Police Station, we called the Buchenwald administration and were informed that we could pick up the body at noon. I purchased a casket that was placed in the trailer. At the camp gate, two SS guards, one on each running board side of the car directed us to the building where Paul's body had been placed. Two inmates transferred Paul's body from the rough wooden bier, on which he lay, to the casket. After I was permitted to spend some minutes alone with Paul's body, the casket was sealed and I was instructed that it was not to be opened. I protested that our children wanted to see their father's body. The answer was that only under the condition that the casket remained sealed would the body be released. I then requested my letters that I had written to Paul and they were handed over to me. One must keep in mind that the Nazis had not yet perfected their system. It was July 1939. Later they would not release bodies of the deceased to relatives nor return correspondence that had been received by an inmate."

Each morning, Frau Schneider and I read the Losungen together plus selected Old Testament and New Testament texts. Then we sang a hymn and only then did we eat breakfast. The breakfast nook in the small dining room is situated between the kitchen and the spacious living room. When many guests were hosted, which often was the case, the large living room table could be extended to accommodate them. Most of the time, Frau Schneider and I were alone and therefore we ate our meals in the breakfast nook. On the wall opposite from where I sat there was a large portrait of Pastor Schneider by the artist, Rudolf Yelin. The portrait became widely distributed and probably is the portrait most associated with Pastor Schneider. During my first visits to Dickenschied, I set up my video camera on a tripod in the breakfast nook. Frau Schneider sat at the end of the table with the portrait of Pastor Schneider as background. Beginning with her first encounter with the student Paul Schneider, I requested Frau Schneider to relate the history of her family. For about one hour each morning, Frau Schneider recounted her story. Seeking more details, I would ask questions. I then was permitted to read the correspondence and to view the photographs that related to the time frame that Frau Schneider had covered in her account. Frequently, as we read the letters or looked at the photos, Frau Schneider would remember details or anecdotes that she had not mentioned in the videotaping. All supplementary material that she provided, I recorded in writing.

After lunch, Frau Schneider took a nap. During that time, I was able to consolidate the materials of our morning session. After coffee and pastry in the afternoon, Frau Schneider and I frequently walked the circa five blocks to the cemetery. There, on a bench next to Pastor Schneider's grave, we continued our conversation—my endless questions and Frau Schneider's patient answers, based on her remarkable memory and detailed descriptions of events, which only a person with firsthand knowledge could know, made these conversations rich indeed. After our evening meal, we watched the television news and drank a glass of wine. At about 9:30 p.m., Frau Schneider retired. I wrote and read for another hour before retiring to the comfortable guest room, in which hung a large painting of a young lad lying asleep on a broad field under a brilliant blue sky. The painting set the proper mood for the guest room. Each summer, for years, until the manuscript was completed, this procedure was followed. During these summer periods on which Frau Schneider and I worked on the biography, I continued to conduct a 3-week tour of the German Reformation sites for my countrymen. After the tour, I then was free to travel to Dickenschied where Frau Schneider and I resumed our work.

Connections continue to develop, 1980-1985

In the summer of 1980, while residing with my group in the Christliches Hospiz in Weimar and frequently visiting the Bredenbröcker family, Hilde Bredenbröcker introduced us to her guest from Hattingen in the Ruhr area of West Germany, Fräulein Annelore Schmidt. Hilde and Otto Bredenbröcker had cared for Annelore's aunt (her father's sister) in her old age. Hilde and Otto resided in Frau Schmidt's home and were in the process of purchasing the home while at the same time providing the nursing care that the elderly lady needed. On her deathbed, in gratitude for the faithful care that Hilde and Otto had provided, Frau Schmidt canceled the balance of what still was owed for the purchase of her home. Annelore's father, Dr. Hermann Schmidt and his wife Edith, were very grateful to the Bredenbröckers for the service they had rendered. The two families became friends. As a citizen of West Germany, Annelore had been in Weimar only on the occasion of her aunt's funeral. Hilde asked me if Annelore might join my group in our travels and visits to the various Reformation sites. I, of course, was happy to include Annelore in our group. Annelore and my 10-year-old daughter, Charissa, became immediate friends.

As in each summer, in the summer of 1980, I took the group to Berlin. On the train, we sat in a car with children from a Weimar elementary school. In my group were Helen and Bob McMichael. Helen was a retired elementary school music teacher and a marvelous pedagogue. Because Helen, walking up and down the aisle, led the children in chorus, singing folk songs, the 3-hour train ride to Berlin passed quickly. The children responded enthusiastically to Helen's energetic conducting. They particularly loved to sing "O McDonald Had a Farm." As I watched Helen's zeal engender enthusiasm in the children and heard the whole train coach resounding with youthful German voices singing American folk songs, I thought, "What an antidote to the Cold War! Here in this railcar, representatives from each hostile camp are joined together in harmony and friendship." This happy scene called to mind the adage: "International relations are too important to be left to politicians." Because of their encounter with Helen, these children would have returned to their school and to their homes prepared to contradict the propaganda image of the ugly American. I remember having read in Der Pionierleiter (The Pioneer Leader, 1960, Number 20), the following: "Our teachers and our pioneer leaders must awaken in our children a hatred for the USA imperialists and their lackey, the Adenauer state." Another DDR publication for teachers had urged teachers to instruct their pupils, "The American democracy is nothing other than a brutal dictatorship of powerful industrialists and economic arrogators under whom the entire USA political system is subjugated." Their experience with Helen on the train to Berlin would make it difficult for DDR pedagogues to persuade their pupils of the truth of this propaganda.

On our return from Berlin to Weimar, we took the last evening connection. Almost all the passengers on the train were Red Army soldiers returning to base in Weimar and Erfurt. Most of the soldiers were inebriated. In the dining car, bottles of beer were sold. There was a deposit charge on each bottle. When the bottle was returned to the dining car bar, the cash deposit was returned to the purchaser. Most of the intoxicated soldiers had many empty bottles on the seat and floor of their respective coach and made no effort to return them. Perhaps they would not have been able to walk to the dining car. Charissa noticed that empty bottles, returned to the dining car, brought a refund. She began to go through the train gathering up all the empty bottles she could find, and there were many to be had. When the soldiers noticed this 10-year-old girl collecting bottles, they began to help her. The dining car may have been too distant for them, but they collected the empty bottles in their car and turned them over to Charissa. The soldiers even nicknamed her, "Flaschen-Fräulein—Bottle Maid." It was an amusing scene to observe jovial, deep in their cups, Red Army soldiers, defenders of Communism, promoting the wealth of a 10-year-old capitalist. I mused, "In the midst of the Cold War between the Soviet Union and the United States with all the media vitriol with which each camp attacks the other, this gesture of cooperation indeed was refreshing." By the time the train arrived in Weimar, the Red Army had made a significant contribution in promoting the wealth of the capitalist Bottle Maid.

In a Sunday evening worship service in the Weimar Kreuz Kirche, the Weimar Youth Minister, Herr Wolfgang Kerst, announced that on the following morning (Monday), the Christian youth would travel to

Buchenwald in order to tidy up the museum area and the surrounding landscape. I thought that such activity would be ideal for my ten-year-old daughter. Charissa thereby would be placed together with East German youth, and the opportunity to perform constructive service in the immediate vicinity of Buchenwald, I was certain, would make a lasting impression on her.

After the service, I approached Herr Kerst and requested that Charissa be permitted to join the East German youth under his supervision in the Buchenwald project. Herr Kerst seemed very uncomfortable with my request. He replied, "We depart Weimar very early in the morning," apparently hoping that such a remark would discourage me from pursuing my goal. I replied, "We get up early; the early hour provides us no problem." Then Herr Kerst, quite uneasy with my persistence, added, "We depart from the railroad station that is quite some distance from your residence in the Hospiz." I countered, "I can bring my daughter at the early hour to the station." Now Herr Kerst began to stammer, searching for still another reason why it would be unfeasible for Charissa to join his group. Of course, I knew why Herr Kerst did not want Charissa to join the East German youth. The Party emphasis was "Abgrenzung" (differentiation)—that is, as far as possible preserve segregation between the youth from western capitalist states and the DDR youth. Finally, I bluntly said to Herr Kerst, "Herr Kerst, you spoke in your remarks this evening about the necessity of promoting an ecumenical spirit among Christians, an ecumenical spirit that transcends political boundaries. May Charissa join your youth group tomorrow at Buchenwald or not?" The direct question left Herr Kerst no room to evade the request. Embarrassed, because he realized that I knew that he was seeking to discourage Charissa's participation, and that I also was aware of why he didn't want her to be in close association with East German youth, Herr Kerst blurted out, "O, of course, your daughter may join us."

I took Charissa to the rail station early on Monday morning and she traveled with the DDR youth to Buchenwald. In the evening, after working all day at Buchenwald, the youth were treated to a Bratwurst cookout on the lawn of the Saint Stephen's Church in Schöndorf. The evening ended with singing to the accompaniment of various instruments. The opportunity to spend the day with DDR youth, cleaning the environment of the Buchenwald Camp, made a lasting impression on the 10-year-old American girl.

It was not long after this experience that I received a dinner invitation from Herr Kerst. My friends in Thuringia had warned me to be cautious when meeting with Herr Kerst. They were convinced that Herr Kerst was an agent for the Stasi (State Security). I went to his residence. I noticed that he resided on Immanuel Kant Straße, in one of the more attractive neighborhoods in Weimar. I thought to myself, "How is it that a youth minister can afford to reside in such an exclusive neighborhood?" I also was told by my East German friends that, while travel restrictions from the DDR to the BRD were very severe, Herr Kerst seemed to be able to travel frequently to the BRD. Herr Kerst introduced me to his wife and to another guest, Professor G. Fink, theology professor at the Humboldt University in Berlin. From the conversation, I could detect the subtle approach that was invoked to lure me into discussing my frequent visits to the DDR and the associations I had formed over the years. I was careful to mention only high Party functionaries and the associations that were well known to the authorities through my participation in historical congresses. The food and wine were good, but the investment of time and expense on the part of my hosts, I'm certain, did not bring the dividends they had hoped to receive.

In the autumn, I received a letter from the Humboldt University, Theology Faculty, dated October 21, 1980.

> Very Honorable Colleague,
>
> I was most pleased to meet you in Weimar. I remember gladly our meeting in the Kerst garden. I especially want to thank you for the translation of the two articles that, for my Holocaust research, are very important. In anticipation of the planned Reformation ceremonies (1983, the Quincentennial of Martin Luther's birth), your Reformation research will be of great interest for me. A few days ago, Bruno Schottstädt sent me a copy of his interview with Harvey Cox. I am happy to learn that you also know Bruno Schottstädt.

You are planning a trip to the DDR in the summer of 1981. Permit me to request that you inform me concerning the dates of your visit so that we can arrange a meeting.

With friendly Greetings
    Your G. Fink

After the collapse of the DDR and the investigation into the files of the Stasi, it was discovered that both Professor Fink and Wolfgang Kerst had acted as agents for the Stasi. This revelation cost Wolfgang Kerst a position in the Thuringian Church to which he had aspired. Professor Fink also did not escape censorship from his university colleagues.

The reference in the letter to Bruno Schottstädt reminded me of the visit to Pennsylvania that Bruno and his wife made, and which afforded Lois and me the opportunity to host them for several days. I had met Bruno earlier in Berlin. He was pastor of the Protestant Church in Marzahn, a suburb of Berlin. Because he apparently was an ardent CDU member and enjoyed close relations with Gerald Götting, the CDU chairman and leading government official, the Christians in Berlin-—and even the non-Christians and party members whom I knew-—referred to Bruno as "The Red Pastor of Marzahn." Bruno's enthusiastic support of the government was rewarded by permitting him and his wife to travel to the United States. One of the objectives of the journey was to visit the Amish and Mennonite communities in Pennsylvania, Ohio and Indiana, and to prepare an article to be published later in the DDR. Another objective was to write an article on his observation of life in US metropolitan centers. I later read these articles published in the DDR media. Bruno's article on life in the US metropolitan centers was very negative. He emphasized the poverty, crime and the pedagogical chaos that prevailed in the inner city schools. Throughout the article, there was the subtle suggestion of contrast between DDR cities and US cities. Large DDR cities, benefitting from the advantages of the socialist society, did not suffer from the blight brought about by an unbridled and aggressive capitalism—a capitalism monopolized by an elite group that controlled the economic and political forces of the nation.

While Bruno and his wife visited us in West Chester, I arranged for him to speak on our university campus, to the university and borough residents. On the evening of his address, the large room was filled to capacity. Bruno's remarks were tape-recorded. After he had completed his remarks, members in the audience, some of whom had relatives in the DDR, asked penetrating questions about the DDR church/state relationship. Bruno realized that the usual DDR propaganda would not satisfy an audience that was more sophisticated than audiences he usually addressed. I sat at the table, next to the podium on which the tape recorder had been placed. Bruno looked at me and requested, "May we turn off the tape recorder?" I turned it off. Bruno then proceeded to abandon the party line propaganda and to present satisfactory and credulous answers to the auditors' questions.

It was during the 1980 summer that we planned for Hilde and Otto to visit the United States in the spring of 1981. Hilde had reached her 60th birthday and, as DDR citizens humorously said, had become "Travel mature" (old enough to travel to western capitalist states). Otto was 79 years old. Travel mature alone, however, would not have enabled Hilde and Otto to receive permission to journey to the United States. Fortunately, Otto had a niece residing in Illinois. On the basis of a visit to a family member, they had a legitimate reason for applying for permission to visit the United States. On behalf of Otto's niece, I wrote a letter of invitation to Hilde and Otto in the German language and sent the letter to Otto's niece, Nancy Kraemer, in Illinois. Nancy signed the letter and forwarded it to Weimar. With this invitation from a family member, Hilde and Otto were granted permission by DDR authorities to travel to the United States. Hilde and Otto received a US visa, pro forma, from the US embassy in East Berlin. Of course, gaining permission from DDR authorities and the possession of a US visa still left one grand obstacle to be overcome—the roundtrip airfare. Hilde and Otto would fly Lufthansa from Frankfurt to Philadelphia. DDR currency had no value in western capitalist states. I, therefore, telephoned each person who had accompanied me to the DDR since 1972 and who had enjoyed the hospitality of what we fondly called the "Bredenbröcker Guesthouse." I explained that I was collecting for Hilde and Otto's roundtrip airfare and would appreciate whatever contribution could be made for this cause. I issued this request once only and within two weeks, I had sufficient funds to cover roundtrip travel expenses from Europe to the US, and even a surplus that, upon their arrival, I gave to Hilde and Otto for per diem.

During the spring of 1981, after plans for Hilde and Otto's US visit had been completed and before Hilde and Otto arrived in the United States, I happened to enter a delicatessen in Wilmington, Delaware. A woman clerk waited on me. I noticed that the clerk spoke the English language with a distinct German accent. I inquired, "Are you from Germany?" The clerk responded, "Yes." "What part of Germany?" I asked. The clerk responded, "O, you've never heard of the remote, little town of my origins." "Well, perhaps I have," I said. "Have you ever heard of Rudolstadt?" the clerk countered, satisfied that her answer would stymie my curiosity. "Yes I have." I said. "In fact, one week before I returned to the United States last August, I visited friends in Rudolstadt." The clerk's mouth dropped open. "You were in Rudolstadt in Thuringia!" she exclaimed. "Yes," I replied. "My friends in Weimar, Hilde and Otto Bredenbröcker took me and my countrymen to visit Hilde's brother, Karl Brömel, and his family in Rudolstadt. The Brömel family operates a bakery that has been in their family since the sixteenth century. I've never tasted such delicious pastry; nothing to compare with it." The clerk became greatly excited. "You visited Karl Brömel!" she exclaimed. "I went to school with Karl and Hilde! They were my neighbors! As children, we played on the slopes of the Heidecksburg (medieval castle promontory). When the war ended, I was in the US zone. I married an American soldier and came to the United States with my husband. Because my former home is in the Communist zone, I lost contact with my childhood friends. How are Karl and Hilde?"

I then told the clerk, who now introduced herself as Alberta Smith, that Hilde and her husband were to visit me in April and May. "All my countrymen in the West Chester area who enjoyed Hilde and Otto's hospitality in Weimar have planned a reception for our guests on a Saturday afternoon. It would be wonderful if you would attend. I won't tell Hilde that you're coming. Let your meeting with a childhood friend be a surprise." In her voice, face and body language, I could detect the great excitement that this news caused Alberta Smith. "I would be delighted to come," she replied with exuberance. I drew a map, directions on how to drive from Wilmington to my West Chester residence. I marked the date and time of the reception and gave Alberta my telephone number.

I shall never forget that spring Saturday afternoon in 1981. All my countrymen who had been with me in the DDR, who had been hosted by Hilde and Otto, and who resided within convenient driving distance to our residence, assembled. It was a beautiful spring day and we were able to set up tables and chairs in our spacious garden. Hilde and Otto were overwhelmed at the number of people who came to honor them on this occasion. In the midst of the conviviality, Alberta arrived. She approached Hilde and said "Guten Tag." Hilde looked at Alberta for an extended time and then with a voice quivering in deep emotion, she cried, "Alberta!" Both women fell into each other's arms and wept. It had been almost forty years since they last had seen each other.

I thought, "What are the odds of my meeting Alberta Smith in a large city of Wilmington, Delaware in a delicatessen of which there are hundreds in the city? What are the odds that I would meet in Wilmington the Rudolstadt childhood friend of Hilde Brömel Bredenbröcker a few weeks before Hilde was scheduled to make her first visit to the United States?" Once again, I was compelled to assent to Albert Schweitzer's observation: "Coincidence is the pseudonym which God employs when He wishes to remain anonymous."

Because they could not speak or understand the English language, Hilde and Otto had requested their friend, Annelore Schmidt from Hattingen in West Germany to accompany them on their journey to the United States. This greatly facilitated matters, because when I could not be present with Hilde and Otto, Annelore, who has a fine command of the English language, could be the translator. Annelore resided with our friends, Bud and Mildred Van Sice. Otto and Hilde resided with us. The three guests arrived on a Saturday afternoon. I had arranged with friends, Ken and Della Fisher, who had Amish friends in Lancaster County, for my guests and me to visit an Amish worship service. I thought that it would be interesting for my German guests to hear the German language as spoken by the Amish. This "old Bible German" fascinates German tourists who visit the Lancaster County area. It is as if the language were frozen in the time of the seventeenth and eighteenth centuries.

In arranging for our visit to the Amish worship service on Sunday morning, I had failed to allow for the fact that Hilde, Otto and Annelore first needed time to overcome the jet lag. On benches with no back support, we sat in a large room of the Amish farmhouse, surrounded by our hospitable hosts. The service lasted several hours and I felt great empathy for Otto as he fought to hold his eyes open. Once, when sleep overwhelmed him, he almost fell off the bench. From that point on, terrified that he might end up on the floor in front of the speakers, Otto sat wide-eyed, fighting off slumber. At the conclusion of the service, in a remarkably short time, our hosts converted the room that had served as a sanctuary into a dining hall. A great variety of food was served. After expressing our gratitude to our hosts, we exited the farmhouse. As we got into our car to drive away, Della remarked, "One automobile and fifty buggies and horses."

I was astonished to read in the press that on Thursday, March 18, 1982, Dr. Philip Potter, Secretary General of the World Council of Churches, received an honorary doctorate degree from the Humboldt University in East Berlin. My astonishment was not based on whether or not the Secretary General deserved such an honor, but rather on the fact that, given the political realities that prevailed in the DDR—an atheistic state that discriminated against its Christian population and was guilty of the deaths of many of its citizens killed at the Berlin Wall or at other border crossing points with the BRD—that the Secretary General of the World Council of Churches would accept such an honor from the DDR. Of course, the fact that the leader of the World Council of Churches accepted such an honor from the DDR was very good for DDR propaganda. It would blunt the accusation that the DDR discriminated against the Christian Church. In reflecting on this honorary promotion for the World Council of Churches' Secretary, I was moved to write the following observation:

God Doesn't Love A Wall

Barbed wire border,
like a crown of thorns pressed upon the nation's brow.
Anguish, tears, death, separation its citizens endow.

The mine explodes, the dogs pursue,
automatic weapons chatter.
Indifferent executioners retrieve the lifeless form.
Does it matter?

Apparently not, for in the news
the soccer scores demand attention.
In East Germany the World Council of Churches assembles
in ecumenical convention.

Politicians and theologians toast one another in convivial revelry.
The mine explodes, the dogs pursue, and once again Christ is going to
Calvary.

As the High Priest of the World Council of Churches receives in East Berlin
an honorary doctor's gown,
a few blocks away a fellow Christian bleeds to death on Germany's Golgotha
ground.

When I returned to the DDR in the summer of 1982, my Christian friends still were very annoyed with the Secretary General. "What planet does he live on?" they asked. "Doesn't he know what goes on in this country in regard to the Christian Church? How could he accept the warm hospitality of the Politbüro executioners?"

In the summer of 1983, the "Luther Year," I conducted two successive tours for my countrymen of three weeks for each tour. In the Luther Year, it was quite obvious that the DDR had revised drastically its original view of Luther as "an enemy of the people and the lackey of the princes." In a meeting of Party officials with the Thuringian Bishop, Werner Leich, at the Wartburg on Thursday, April 21, 1983, Erich Honecker hailed Luther as a great figure in German history and he urged his fellow DDR citizens to visit the Wartburg in order to strengthen their national loyalty and love of homeland. On his part,

Bishop Leich gained the promise from the SED Chairman—"All citizens of the DDR, including Christians, will not suffer vocational or promotional discrimination because of their religious faith." This promise was ignored by party officials. Another topic of great sensitivity was the Christian Peace Movement, Swords to Plowshares. A few weeks before this Wartburg meeting, forty students, active in the Jena Swords to Plowshares Movement, had been deported to the BRD. Since the year 1980, two national committees had been at work preparing celebrations to mark the quincentennial birth of Germany's great son—a state committee, under the leadership of Erich Honecker, and a Church committee, under the leadership of the Lutheran Church in the DDR. The fact that the First Party Secretary of the SED had assumed the chairmanship of the State Luther Committee drew from the BRD chancellor, Helmut Kohl, the cynical remark: "The goal is to expropriate German history, to take over its identity from the Middle Ages to Frederick the Great.... Imagine a republic that officially considers itself atheistic has a Luther year and Honecker, the head of State, is the president of the Luther Committee!"

One major event of that summer was a rally on the open fields of Stotternheim where the Swedish Granite Memorial now marks the spot where, on July 2, 1505, the 21-year-old law student Martin Luther, terrified by a ferocious thunderstorm and lightening strike, made the vow: "Saint Anna! Help me, I will become a monk!" On Saturday, July 2, 1983, at the invitation of the Weimar Oberkirchenrat, Hans Schäfer, my countrymen and I attended the memorial service. A lectern was erected near the granite memorial and loud speakers were mounted on the trees surrounding the memorial so that the thousands assembled on the fields could hear the speakers. Special music was provided and Reformation hymns were sung, especially "A Mighty Fortress Is Our God." How inspiring at that historic spot to hear from a chorus of thousands this stirring hymn! In our group was the Reverend Dr. Robert Young and his wife Louisa. Dr. Young was pastor of the Westminster Presbyterian Church in West Chester, Pennsylvania. In previous summers, I had been invited with my group for a picnic at the Tiefurt home of Oberkirchenrat Hans Schäfer and his most hospitable wife, Christa. Tiefurt is a small suburb of Weimar. Before the July 2 celebration, our group had enjoyed the annual picnic in the Schäfer's

Tiefurt garden. At that picnic, Hans invited Bob Young to bring a brief greeting from Christians in the US during the July 2 worship service in Stotternheim. I was to be the translator. Bob greeted the large congregation, "I extend hearty greetings to Christians in the German Democratic Republic from Christians in the United States." I translated, "Christen in der DDR begrüsse ich herzlich von Christen in meiner Heimat." Bob looked at me quizzically. He had not heard the German translation of the United States. During the course of his homily, Bob mentioned the United States several times. Each time I translated, "Meiner Heimat," "my home country." Later, I explained to Bob that each day in their media, DDR citizens read only negative news concerning the United States. I did not want the audience to hear the words "United States," for those two words always were burdened by the most negative propaganda. "Heimat" is a very innocent, neutral and endearing word for the German ear. Out of this association with Hans Schäfer, the Westminster Presbyterian Church and the Pastor Paul Schneider Memorial Church in Weimar became sister congregations. After the fall of the Berlin Wall, the pastor of the Pastor Paul Schneider Church, Ulrike Ross, came several times for visits to the Westminster Presbyterian Church in West Chester. Hans and Christa made several visits to the United States, and after Christa's death in 2004, Hans continued to visit in West Chester. At the beginning of each new year, Hans continued to supply some friends in the US with the German language edition of Die Losungen, a daily devotional reading published by the Moravian Brethren in Herrnhut, Germany. The year 2012 marked the 282nd annual publication of Die Losungen. Hans died of cancer in January 2012. Requiescat in pace, dear friend.

In the first group that I guided to the DDR in the summer of 1983, there was an elderly lady (Mrs. Helder) who for many years had taught catechetical classes in her Lutheran Church. Her daughter, who is a nurse, was in one of my history classes at West Chester University. The daughter told her mother about the journey to the German Reformation sites. Mrs. Helder then called me and asked if she might be included in my group. I met with her and her daughter. From our meeting, I knew that travel to the DDR and the strenuous activity of climbing up to the Wartburg and walking long distances would be too difficult for her. I related to her my reservations. "O please Dr. Foster," she begged. "All my life I've wanted to visit the sites that I discuss with the pupils in my catechetical classes. This is the only opportunity I will have to fulfill my dreams. I will adjust to any requirements you suggest, but please permit me to join the group." I was at a loss. How does one say "no" to such an impassioned request? I reflected. Then I answered, "If your daughter will accompany you and you do not insist on trying to do everything the group does (some things will be too strenuous for you), you may join our group."

Once in the DDR, I discovered that, with a little ingenuity, Mrs. Helder was able to participate in almost all activities. In Eisenach, for instance, in our visit to the Wartburg, I notified the museum administration that we had an elderly lady in our group who was unable to make the steep climb to the castle. I received permission to have her driven to the castle entrance on a road usually blocked off to traffic in one of the automobiles in which we had traveled from Weimar. We were able to employ this solution in almost every case; where the group walked, our elderly friend was able to ride. In this manner, she participated in almost every undertaking. Our last stop was East Berlin. After visiting the historic sites, the Pergamum Museum, the Berlin Dom, the French Huguenot Church, Saint Hedwig's Cathedral, the Brandenburg Gate and a sightseeing boat ride on the River Spree, we took refreshments in the flat of Frau Charlotte Rhode. Now we were prepared to cross over into West Berlin through the check. At the checkpoint, each member of the group surrendered his exit card to the border patrol officer. This card had been issued to us along with the visa that each person had received from the DDR Berlin Travel Bureau and was required to be turned in upon exiting the territory of the DDR. Mrs. Helder could not find her exit card. I had to keep the group together. Everyone had to wait until Mrs. Helder found her exit card. The guard was adamant. We could not leave his post until the exit card had been turned in. We searched through Mrs. Helder's luggage. No card could be found. I noticed that the tension provoked by this situation was causing Mrs. Helder to become very upset. I tried to reason with the guard. "Surely you can understand that an elderly person, who does not speak German and who has spent 3 weeks in the DDR, might have lost the exit card." The guard remained intransigent. I then requested, "May I speak to your senior officer?" The guard went to the office behind the counter. Soon the subordinate returned with his senior officer who was in charge of the checkpoint. "You must return the exit card," the senior officer said, "before you are permitted to cross the border. That's the rule." How often had I heard that word in the DDR!-Vorschrift! (rule).

"But the lady has lost the exit card," I countered. "Tuts mir leid, (I regret,"), the officer replied. Having visions of being forced to remain in the DDR, Mrs. Helder, seated on a bench, began to tremble. Recalling the stress-provoked coronary death of the BRD citizen, Rudolf Burkert, on Sunday, April 10, 1983 at the Berlin/Drewitz border station, and the tension-evoked coronary death of Heinz Moldenhauer on Tuesday, April 26, 1983 at the Wartha/Herleshausen border point, deaths that had caused very bad publicity for the DDR in the international media, I said to the senior officer, "Herr Oberst, you see that elderly lady trembling. She has a heart condition. Permit me to remind you that if this elderly person, because she lacks a simple exit card, should suffer a coronary attack on your watch, you bear full responsibility." The senior officer then said, "She may leave."

That evening in a West Berlin hotel, I lay in bed reading. Mrs. Helder and her daughter shared a room next to mine. There was a knock on my door. I opened the door and there stood Mrs. Helder and her daughter. "We found the exit card," they exclaimed. "What?" I responded. The daughter explained. "Each night before mother goes to sleep, she reads a passage from her Bible. She had placed the exit card as a bookmark in her Bible. We never thought to look in her Bible for the card." We laughed.

In the second group that I guided in the DDR, in the quincentennial year of Martin Luther's birth, there was a lady, Maggie Smith, whose story should be related. The story begins with an incident that occurred in the autumn of 1982. Not far from our residence in West Chester, the Pocopson Home, a state-administered facility for the elderly and infirmed, is located. In the fall of 1982, the Pocopson Home sponsored a picnic for residents, their family members and friends. The youth in our neighborhood were enlisted as volunteers to assist in serving the food and drinks to the residents and their guests seated at tables set up on the broad green. Our daughter, Charissa, 12-years-old, was among the youthful volunteers. It was a Saturday afternoon. I was at home. The telephone rang. I answered. On the line was a Pocopson Home employee who announced to me that Charissa had been bitten on the wrist by a dog belonging to one of the residents. I drove immediately to Pocopson Home, about one quarter of a mile from our residence. There, I was met by the dog's owner and her sister, Maggie Smith. Maggie had come to visit her sister, a Pocopson Home resident. When the sister moved into the Pocopson Home, she had to entrust her dog to Maggie. Each time that Maggie visited her sister, she brought the dog along so that her sister could enjoy the company of her pet, and, of course, the pet could enjoy being with his original mistress, if only for a brief time.

It so happened that, when Charissa came to the table where Maggie and her sister sat, Charissa's act, in passing a plate to Maggie's sister, was interpreted by the dog as an aggressive gesture, and he bit Charissa on the wrist. Maggie was very apologetic. "Please," Maggie said to me, "have your daughter treated immediately. I'll take care of any expense you incur." I took Charissa for a tetanus shot. The wound was not deep, and it healed quickly. A few days later, Maggie telephoned to inquire about Charissa. In the meantime, she had learned that I was a professor at West Chester University. In the course of our conversation, I related to her that my favorite courses were the Reformation and Modern German History. It was then that Maggie said, "My ancestors came from Germany. In fact, I have a certificate that was given to my grandfather, but the language is German and no one in our family can read the text." I responded, "You frequently visit your sister at Pocopson Home. You pass my residence on your way to the Pocopson Home. Sometime, when you plan to pay a visit, call me, and if I am at home, you can bring the certificate and I will translate it for you." Maggie was very excited about my offer. One day she called and stopped at our home with the certificate. The certificate was in a beautiful frame. The German text was a commendation for her paternal grandfather for his many years of service on the German Railroad System at Waltershausen in the State of Thuringia. I was familiar with Waltershausen, a small town in the DDR, not far from Gotha and Weimar. "It's possible," I said to Maggie, "that your ancestors may be mentioned in the Waltershausen archives or in the church archives."

I copied the name of the grandfather. Subsequently, I wrote to Ilse Weissenborn, a catechetical teacher in the Eisenach Lutheran Church, whose youth earlier had hiked with my pupils, and with whom I had remained in correspondence. Whenever I took a group to Eisenach, Ilse treated us to coffee and pastry, and sometimes she accompanied us on our visit to the Wartburg. Eisenach is not far from Waltershausen. I requested Ilse to check with the Waltershausen Town archivist in order to glean information concerning the family of Hans Schmidt. It was discovered that the roots of Maggie's grandfather's family could be traced back to the sixteenth century. Maggie was thrilled with the news conveyed to me by the Waltershausen Town archivist. She requested permission to join our tour in the summer of 1983.

At that time, Maggie was about seventy years old and obese. I knew that she would not be able to keep pace with our walking tours. Fortunately, Dr. Anton, Hilde Bredenbröcker's neighbor, provided us with a wheelchair, and we were able to take Maggie for sightseeing in the Weimar park and around the town. Weimar friends drove us to Waltershausen. There, we met the archivist who provided Maggie with a book that traced her ancestry back to the sixteenth century. The archivist took us on a tour of Waltershausen. He pointed out a small castle. "One of your ancestors, an architect, built this castle. He also built this stone bridge over the stream that leads to the castle. Look here! You see the capital "S" in the keystone of the bridge, the first letter of his last name." Maggie was moved to tears as she looked upon the beautiful handiwork of ancestors she had never known. "I'll show you one more contribution to our town of Waltershausen from your ancestors," the archivist said. He led us to the town center. There stood the Lutheran Church. The archivist said, "This church was built by one of your ancestors in the eighteenth century." Once again, Maggie's eyes brimmed with tears as she sensed that intangible bond that bound her to her forebears. Regarding Maggie's deep emotion as she looked upon castle, bridge and church, permanent memorials to her ancestors' residence in this small Thuringian town on the edge of the Thuringian Forest, I could not help but muse, "This story and this scene became possible because of a dog bite!"

In the second group that I guided in the summer of 1983 was also mother and daughter, Elinor and Carla Antes. Carla had been in a group that a few years earlier I had guided. Carla knew that her maternal ancestors had come from a village near Levoca and in the vicinity of the town of Käsemarkt. She also knew that they had migrated to Germany, but she did not know where they had settled in Germany. We traveled from Levoca to Käsemarkt.

Claude's group visiting Czechoslovakia; Anna Zoricakowa in dark sweater

Before my group arrived in Levoca, I had requested Stefan and Anna to inquire where the "Aboshi family" had lived. Anna and Stefan had located the house and also had discovered that one branch of the family still resided in a village near Käsemarkt. It was a remarkable scene. In the members of the Aboshi family that we visited, the elderly woman in the family had a clear resemblance to Elinor. I spoke German to Anna, and Anna spoke her native Slovakian with the family members, and in this manner, Elinor and Carla were able to communicate with relatives they now had met for the first time. The residents of the house, where the other branch of the family had resided, permitted us to go through the house and to become acquainted with the place where family members had lived for many years. In the nearby cemetery, we were shown the graves of those ancestors who had never emigrated from the village. The Slovakian Aboshis were able to provide us the German address of the relatives who had emigrated. When we returned to the DDR, we contacted the family residing in Saβnitz on the island of Rügen in the Baltic Sea. Responding to an enthusiastic invitation, Elinor, Carla and I traveled to Saβnitz for a three-day visit. My group remained in Weimar under the tutelage of Weimar friends. It was quite a meeting in Saβnitz. Elinor's parents had emigrated to the US, but a brother had been left behind in Europe. That brother's son is named Joseph Aboshi. Therefore, Elinor and Joseph are cousins. Joseph's aged parents were still living in Baabe, not far from Saβnitz. Joseph drove Elinor and Carla to Baabe for a visit with Elinor's aunt and uncle. Both the US branch and the German branch of the family have remained in correspondence.

In the autumn of 1983, I was invited to participate in the historical convocation hosted by the East Berlin Academy of Sciences to mark the quincentennial of Martin Luther's birth. Realizing that my East German colleagues had immediate access to Reformation sources and that it would be difficult to present any informative lecture to them on a sixteenth-century German Reformation theme, I decided to select a topic that I was convinced would be informative as well as interesting for them. The title of my lecture was, "The View of Martin Luther in American Historical Writings." Beginning with the 1930s, I reviewed the major monographs and most important articles, from both Protestant and Catholic historians and theologians on the person of Martin Luther. I prepared an annotated bibliography and made many copies of it. Because western historical writings were hardly known in the German Democratic Republic (except for some of the elite Party member historians), I was convinced that such a topic would be of interest to my DDR colleagues. And it was. Within a few moments after my presentation, the fifty copies of the annotated bibliography, which I had placed on the table next to the lectern, had disappeared.

Throughout my contact with DDR colleagues, I noticed the great desire for access to western publications. The lack of the availability of western scholarship for the East Bloc universities was not merely because of ideological restrictions. There also was a financial reason.

East Bloc universities simply could not afford to purchase literature published in the capitalist states. This fact was illustrated to me when I learned that the Humboldt University in East Berlin subscribed to the Archiv für Reformationsgeschichte (Journal for Reformation History), published in the West. Other DDR universities did not receive this journal that was kept in a locked section of the library and available only by the grace of the librarian's key. Students from other DDR universities, who needed access to the journal, could request that the journal be sent via inter-library loan to their particular university. The inconvenience, however, was very frustrating. The waiting period was long and then, when received, the loan period very brief. Some students, rather than wait indefinitely for the inter-library loan to function, traveled a long distance to Berlin where they knew that the particular western publication that they needed for their research might be located. It always was best to confirm via a telephone call that the publication was in fact on hand and not in inter-library loan transit.

One of my colleagues, Günter Mühlpfordt at Halle University, did extensive research on the sixteenth-century Anabaptist movement. Halle University did not receive the leading US publication in this field of study, "The Mennonite Quarterly Review." It would be impossible to mail copies of this journal to Günter's domestic address. He did not stand in good favor with the party. Innocently and in good humor, Günter had mentioned the role that weather played in major historical events. "For instance," he said to his students, "suppose it had rained on that day in Red October when the Bolshevik Revolution took place. Rainy days are not conducive to revolutions. There may never have been a revolution." Günter was reported to the rector and his teaching privileges were canceled. He still was permitted to research and publish, but no longer teach. Because he was out of favor with the party, I, therefore, mailed copies of the journal to the Halle University History Department, not to Günter's home address. Günter's colleagues knew that the journals were intended for him and they saw to it that the journals found their way into his possession.

In late 2011, I inquired at the Berlin Bureau, which is the custodian of the DDR Stasi documents, whether or not my name appeared in the secret police records. On February 4, 2012, I received post from the

Berlin Office. My name is recorded one time in the former Stasi records. The single entry refers to: (1) My regular participation in the Summer School Course for the German Language and Literature, conducted by the Jena Friedrich Schiller University, in which the report reads, "Uses this opportunity to maintain contact with ideologically weak intellectuals;" (2) My association with Professor Dr. Günter Mühlpfordt. Immediately after the name of Professor Mühlpfordt, some subsequent words in the record are stenciled over in black, and thus cannot be read; (3) In the same record, there also is reference to my contact with Professor Dr. Max Steinmetz. And, immediately after Professor Steinmetz's name, there are once again words that have been buried under a thick black cover, making them illegible.

It was during this quincentennial convocation that Gerhard Brendler, Director of the Church History Department at the Academy of Sciences, approached me with a petition. Gerhard had prepared a Luther biography, *Martin Luther: Theologie und Revolution*, for the quincentennial. Despite old guard objections, the biography had been published. The old guard Communists took umbrage at the revised view of Luther that appeared in the biography. Gerhard, following his mentor, Max Steinmetz, presented Luther as the herald of a new age, not as the enemy of the peasants or the lackey of the princes as the original Marxist view had depicted the Reformer. "Herr Kollege Foster," Gerhard said, "would you consider translating my Luther biography into the English language? I would like to see it published in English." I responded, "Dear Colleague Brendler, unless we can find a publisher willing to publish the biography, I do not want to undertake the project. I do not want to invest time and effort in a fruitless endeavor. Provide me several copies of the biography. I will send copies to US publishers to ascertain if there is interest in the US for the publication of such a study." This was done. For about one year, there was no response to my inquiry. Then a call came from Oxford University Press in New York. "Professor Foster, we would like to publish this text in English," the editor said. "Are you prepared to undertake the project?" I responded that I would gladly translate the work so long as no time restraints were placed on me. It was agreed. Within a few days, I received a contract from Oxford University Press and I began the translation. I later learned that the Oxford University Press editors had requested Reformation scholars to review the book and to comment on the worthiness of publishing an English translation. I later learned that one of the reviewers, Professor Carter Lindberg of Boston University, strongly recommended that Oxford University Press publish my English translation of the Brendler book.

The very title of the book revealed the new Marxist interpretation of the Reformation that had begun with Max Steinmetz. Brendler earned his Ph.D. under Professor Steinmetz's tutelage. The word "Theology" in the book's title placed before the word "Revolution" indicated that theology did not thwart revolution as Marx originally had maintained, but, in fact, theology could be the motor for revolution. In the sixteenth century, it was not revolution that produced a new theology, but rather the leaven of a new theology that fermented into revolution. Gerhard told me how he had had to fight for his thesis against the old guard in the Party who would have none of his revisionism. The DDR, home of most of the Lutheran Reformation sites, in the quincentennial year of Luther's birth, needed a Luther biography. Brendler's work was the only one available. By the time the Old Guard discovered the content of Brendler's Luther biography, it was too late to produce another biography. In addition, Professor Horst Bartel, director of the Academy of Sciences, Professor Max Steinmetz, senior professor at Karl Marx University in Leipzig and the new generation of historians in the DDR, supported Brendler. By 1983, it had become apparent that the Old Guard had mismanaged the development of the DDR, and a new and restless youth was anxious to replace the Party fossils.

After extending the itinerary of one of my groups from the DDR into Poland in the 1980s, Hilde Bredenbröcker gave me the address of one of her childhood schoolmates, Ursula Techner, who resided in Ludwigsfelde, a suburb of East Berlin. Because the train journey from Weimar to Poznan (with transfer in Berlin), was about 7 hours, it was best to spend an overnight in the Berlin area and, on the next day, take the train for the 3-hour trip to Poznan. We contacted Ursula from Weimar and inquired as to whether or not she and her husband, Rudi, could accommodate our group for dinner, overnight, and breakfast. Ursula and Rudi were pleased to accept us. They knew, of course, that we would reward them with hard currency. It was not hard currency alone, however, which motivated this charming couple. They were sincerely affable and anxious to share time with US citizens. We checked our large suitcases at the East Berlin rail station, and took only what we needed for one night in Ludwigsfelde. Ten people checking luggage took longer than we had anticipated, and we ran the risk of missing the local train for Ludwigsfelde. Rather than waiting in a long line to purchase tickets, I herded the group onto the train without tickets. It was about a thirty-minute trip on this commuter train to Ludwigsfelde. It was the evening hour, and the train was crowded. I saw the conductor at one end of our car collecting tickets, and I moved our group into the adjoining car. As the conductor worked his way through each car, I retreated with my group into the adjoining car. Finally, we were in the last car, and the conductor was at the opposite end, making his way toward us. "Ten people without tickets and ten Americans in this suburban area of Berlin would be hard to explain," I thought. Just when the conductor was about ten feet from us (and we were at the very end of the last car), the train stopped at the Ludwigsfelde station, and we hurried off.

We spent a delightful evening with Ursula and Rudi and their daughter, Suzanne, who came to meet us from her nearby flat. Rudi was one of those prisoners of war held in the Soviet Union for whose repatriation Chancellor Konrad Adenauer had negotiated in 1955. "Soon after the war, the Red Cross informed me that Rudi was alive," Ursula said, "but we had to wait until 1955 for our reunion." The Techner residence offered one extra bedroom, where two or three of the group could sleep. Rudi had built an addition onto the house that accommodated the males in our group. There also was sufficient space for sleeping on the living room floor. In the spacious backyard, Rudi had constructed an outdoor, solar-heated shower. Two barrels were placed on a platform about ten feet high. Garden hoses fed water into the barrels. Spigots at the base of the barrels released the solar-heated water. Only a few in our group dared to take a shower. I took a shower, and I thought, "Fortunately it is summer!"

The next morning, after breakfast, we took the commuter train to the East Berlin train station, picked up our luggage, and boarded the train for Poznan. The visit with Ursula, Rudi and Suzanne was mutually beneficial. We had convenient and convivial stopover accommodations on our way to Poland, and the Techners had the benefit of the hard currency we provided for their purchases in the Intershops. We agreed that whenever I was on my way to Poland via Berlin, my group and I would be welcome to overnight in Ludwigsfelde.

Connections between USA and Europe, 1986-1988

Each summer that I resided in Weimar with my group, I was in the habit of taking them to the Sunday 6:00 p.m. organ concerts in the Herder Church. The program was arranged by Professor Johannes Ernst Köhler, professor at the Franz Liszt Music University in Weimar and organist at the Herder Church and his wife, Hannelore. Professor Köhler usually presented the last concert in the summer series. His concerts always were played to a full sanctuary of music lovers who particularly anticipated Professor Köhler's improvisation of the music of Johann Sebastian Bach. The idea occurred to me; why not invite Professor Köhler and his wife, Hannelore, who also is an accomplished organist, to the United States. The Köhlers were very receptive to the idea. Professor Köhler frequently gave concerts in all the East Bloc states, and he had once visited the United States in the mid-1970s. Because his concerts would draw large audiences and most of the honorarium he received would end up in the DDR state's coffers, I was persuaded, given the desperate need for hard currency in the DDR, that Professor Köhler and his wife could receive permission to visit the United States.

In conjunction with the Reverend Dr. Robert Young, pastor of the West Chester Westminster Presbyterian Church, I invited Professor Johannes Ernst Köhler and his wife to the United States. Dr. Young and his wife, Louisa, arranged for a seminar for organists in the greater Philadelphia area. On Saturday, April 12, 1986, the renowned Franz Liszt Music University professor conducted a seminar for organists. Professor Köhler demonstrated his improvisation technique and provided an analysis of Bach's organ works. On Sunday, April 13, at 4:00 p.m., Professor Köhler gave an organ concert at the Westminster Presbyterian Church. We alerted music directors in Washington, Baltimore, Chicago, Cleveland, New York and Philadelphia, and in a very brief period, a concert tour schedule was in place. Professor Köhler was well known by organ masters in the United States, and as soon as they were alerted concerning his visit to the United States, they immediately requested to have him play in their respective concert halls. Professor Köhler presented concerts in Baltimore, Washington, New York and Chicago.

Whenever I had visitors from Germany, I took them on a tour of the so-called Pennsylvania Dutch Country. Of course, the people residing in the region are not "Dutch," but "Deutsch," (German). Beginning in the eighteenth century, German emigrants were coming to the United States. The first newspaper published in Philadelphia was printed in the German language. Many Amish families subsequently settled not far from Philadelphia in the beautiful farm belt of Lancaster County. Since these Germans never returned to Germany, they continued to speak that German dialect, which they brought with them. The German language in Germany continued to evolve, but not among the Amish in the New World. Therefore, when a German tourist in the twenty-first century hears the German language as spoken by the Amish, the tourist is quite amused. When I toured the Amish country with Professor and Mrs. Köhler, I was able to engage an Amish farmer in conversation. The Köhlers joined in and were delighted to hear their native language as it would have been spoken in the Palatinate region of Germany in earlier generations. This conversation with the Amish farmer greatly pleased them and they frequently referred to it.

On Saturday, April 26, 1986, the nuclear accident at Chernobyl occurred. "This accident," as one commentator reflected, "made us fear the Russians' shoddy construction and administrative lethargy more than their military might." In the light of the nuclear accidents at Three Mile Island (1979), Chernobyl (1986) and Fukushima (2011), the critique of nuclear power plants has been repeated by those who insist that the dependance on nuclear power plants constitutes too great a risk for the human race and nature. During our brief visit to Poland in the summer of 1986, heeding the warnings of nuclear proliferation, our group studiously avoided eating garden vegetables.

In the summer of 1986, Ursula Wachowska, a Poznan representative in the Polish Congress (SEJM), and her husband, Eugene Wachowski and their daughter Barbara, offered to drive us along one of the routes that served as a pilgrim way for the many thousands of pilgrims in their annual summer march to Częstochowa. Barbara Wachowska, now Mrs. Karandyszowska, is the younger sister of Maria Wachowska. Maria was a student at West Chester University from 1979 to 1980 when she attended my lectures on the Bible in History. Years later, Dr. Young arranged for Barbara to reside in a rent-free apartment, and I organized a tuition-free semester for her at the university. Early one evening, Ursula Wachowska, with the aid of loud speakers, addressed the thousands of pilgrims bivouacked on the fields of an hospitable farmer. I also was introduced and was invited, on behalf of US Christians and our group, to extend greetings. Barbara translated my remarks.

In the autumn of 1986, six years after I had begun my research on the life and ministry of Pastor Paul Schneider, I met Frau Luise Löwer from Dierdorf, Germany. How did this meeting occur? One day, at the West Chester University, seated in my office that I shared with a colleague, Dr. Irene G. Shur, the telephone rang. Irene picked up the receiver and began an amiable conversation with one of her many friends. I was reading and writing and preoccupied with my own affairs when I noticed that Irene raised her left hand high in the air and pointed at me. Since I could hear only what Irene said and not what her conversation partner was saying to her, I could not comprehend the meaning of this gesture. Irene then interrupted her conversation with the caller and said to me, "Claude, Kurt Strauss is on the phone and needs someone to entertain his guest from Germany for a few hours this afternoon. He asked me, but I have classes. You are free and speak German. Could you host the lady?" "Yes," I replied. "I'll be happy to show the guest about our campus." Irene then resumed her conversation. "My colleague, Dr. Claude Foster, will entertain your guest. When will you come? Good. No problem. Goodbye." Irene then turned to me and said, "Claude, Kurt will drop off the guest in front of our building at 1:00 p.m. and return to pick her up at 4:00 p.m. Kurt must take his wife for therapy at the hospital and does not want his guest to have to wait for a long period in the hospital."

At 1:00 p.m., I stood in front of our office building, Main Hall, on High Street. A large Cadillac drove up. Kurt Strauss, a tall, thin gentleman got out and his passenger also got out of the car. I had never met Kurt Strauss. I knew that he was a member of the West Chester University Board of Trustees, a very successful businessman and a philanthropist. "You're Dr. Foster, I assume," he said. "Yes, I am," I responded. Speaking then in the German language, Kurt Strauss said, "This is my guest, Frau Luise Löwer." Frau Löwer and I shook hands.

"Welcome to West Chester University," I said to her in the German language. "Thank you," Frau Löwer responded. Kurt Strauss interjected, "I'll leave you two together and I'll meet you here at 4:00 p.m. Kurt Strauss got into his car and drove off. Turning to Frau Löwer, I suggested that I give her a tour of the campus. She welcomed my suggestion. After the campus tour, I invited Frau Löwer to coffee and we continued our conversation on the topic of the Confessing Church during the Nazi era. Frau Löwer was very impressed that I had begun the task of writing a biography of Pastor Paul Schneider. As soon as we discovered our mutual interest, we regretted that we had a few hours only for conversation. When Kurt Strauss came to collect his guest, I asked him if it were possible to spare Frau Löwer for another afternoon. "Yes, I suppose so," he said. "Here is my number. Give me a call and we can arrange another meeting. Frau Löwer will be here for several weeks." Subsequently, I was invited to a reception for Frau Löwer in the Strauss' Coatesville, Pennsylvania home. Frau Löwer and I met again and were able, over a longer period of time, to become better acquainted. I was curious about how Frau Löwer and Kurt Strauss knew each other. I asked, "Where did you meet?" Luise (we agreed to be on a first name basis) answered, "Kurt is a native of Dierdorf, my town. When the Nazis came to power, he, as a young man, succeeded in emigrating to the US. All his relatives remained in Dierdorf and subsequently were murdered in the genocide that is known as The Final Solution. After the war, I sponsored a movement to erect a plaque in the city in memory of the Dierdorf Jewish citizens murdered by the Nazis. Kurt heard of this effort on the part of a Protestant Christian to revere the memory of the Jewish victims, many of whom were his relatives. I discovered that Kurt had visited Dierdorf after the war and his US address was known to some of my acquaintances. I sent him an invitation to attend the dedication of the plague in our city park. He thanked me, but he was unable to attend the dedication ceremony. Some months later, the doorbell rang. I opened the door. There stood a tall, slender gentleman. 'I'm Kurt Strauss,' he said. Thus began a beautiful friendship. We talked for most of the morning and it was on that occasion that Kurt invited me to visit his family in Coatesville. Little did I realize that my visit to the US would bring me into contact with an American history professor who is writing a biography about Pastor

Paul Schneider, one of the first Christian martyrs in Nazi Germany. The next time you come to Germany, you must come to visit me in Dierdorf. Dierdorf is not far from the sites where Pastor Schneider conducted his ministry."

In April 1987, my colleague, Irene Shur, who introduced the curriculum devoted to the study of the Shoah at West Chester University, and I sponsored a conference at the university: "Resistance to the Third Reich." We invited Klaus Trostorff, Director of the Buchenwald Memorial Museum in the DDR, Aimé Bonifas, author of Prisoner 20 801, from France, and Jurgen Glenthoj, a Protestant pastor from Denmark. Each guest presented his experience of resistance to the Third Reich.

Juergen Glenthoj, Aime Bonifas, Klaus Trostorff

The conference took place on April 9, 1987, the anniversary of Dietrich Bonhoeffer's execution at Flossenbürg concentration camp. Bonhoeffer not only was a member of the resistance movement against Hitler, he also was involved in the conspiracy to assassinate Hitler. Klaus resided with Lois and me. Aimé, and his daughter who accompanied him, resided with Mildred and Bud Van Sice, friends of mine in Wilmington, Delaware. Because Mildred speaks the French language, this resident arrangement was most convenient for Aimé and his daughter. I believe that Jürgen resided at Irene's home. On the afternoon of April 9, Main Hall at West Chester University was filled to capacity. On that day, we may have violated the fire code for the building that permits a specific number of people in a given space. Since diplomatic relations between the US and the DDR had been established, the DDR ambassador attended. A West German consular officer attended, as did French and Danish embassy personnel. Each guest, Aimé, Klaus and Jürgen was presented with a US flag. The West Chester Kesher Synagogue sponsored an evening of reflection with our European guests. Most of the people in the respective audiences were unaware of the heroic efforts on the part of Danish Christians to save Jews in Denmark by transporting them across the straits to Sweden.

While visiting friends in Freiburg in the summer of 1987, I called Luise. She invited me to Dierdorf. From Dierdorf we drove to Hochelheim and Dornholzhausen where Pastor Schneider had conducted his pastorate in these two villages from 1926 to 1934. After acquiring the key from the Hochelheim custodian family, who resided near the church, we entered the sanctuary. In Dornholzhausen, we also gained access to the church through the friendly help of the custodian in that village. On prominent display in both churches were scripture verses that pertained to the martyr's sacrifice. In Hochelheim, the parsonage was located near the church on the main road that led through the village. A narrow street opposite the parsonage, Friedhofs Weg, led to the nearby cemetery where Pastor Schneider's parents lie buried. Noting the grave marker, I read the death dates for Elizabeth Schnorr Schneider, (August 8, 1863-September 8, 1914) and Gustav Adolf Schneider (January 13, 1858-January 13, 1926). Having discovered in my research that Elizabeth Schneider suffered from severe arthritis, I was struck by the epitaph verse: Romans 12:12: "Rejoicing in hope, patient in tribulation, continuing instant in prayer."

After speaking with residents of Hochelheim and Dornholzhausen who had known Pastor Schneider, we drove to the Hunsrück on the left side of the Rhine River where Pastor Schneider conducted his pastorate from 1934 to 1937 in the villages of Dickenschied and Womrath. On October 3, 1937, after having preached in Dickenschied in the morning, he was arrested in the evening on his way to preach in Womrath. After having become familiar with the wider geography in which Pastor Schneider ministered, Luise and I found Frau Schneider at home, at number 19 Paul Schneider Straße in Dickenschied, an address that I knew very well, residing part of each summer there while working with Frau Schneider on the biography, *The Buchenwald Apostle*. In 1979, I had discovered that apart from E.H. Robertson's abridged English text (1956) of Frau Schneider's book, *Der Prediger von Buchenwald*, there was no English language publication concerning the ministry and martyrdom of Pastor Schneider. Through Luise's kindness, generosity and chauffeuring ability, having achieved a broader knowledge of the people to whom Pastor Schneider ministered and the agrarian landscape that steeled his character, now, more than ever, I was determined to provide my countrymen with a biography of this brave Christian pastor. Frau Schneider, with her warm hospitality, welcomed Luise and me, and we spent a pleasant afternoon with her. After my return from the DDR, I was scheduled to return to Dickenschied to resume with Frau Schneider our preparation of *The Buchenwald Apostle*. On the drive back to Dierdorf, Luise expressed her great pleasure at having met Frau Schneider.

While residing in the Christliches Hospiz in Weimar each summer, I came into contact with many interesting people. One of those persons had been Klaus Trostorff, the director of the Buchenwald Memorial Museum. Klaus Trostorff, a member of the German Communist Party, had been an inmate at Buchenwald. Along with the Socialists, the Communists were Hitler's greatest political enemies in the Weimar Republic. Once Hitler was appointed chancellor and was granted dictatorial powers by the Reichstag, the Communists and Socialists were hunted down and sent to concentration camps. When Klaus discovered that I was writing a biography of Pastor Paul Schneider, who was murdered at Buchenwald on July 18, 1939, for readers in the United States, he became very cooperative in assisting me in locating documents housed at Buchenwald.

One day on my way to the Weimar cemetery where I frequently went to read or write, I passed two elderly women seated on a bench enjoying the rays of a June sun. As I passed them, my ears picked up a dialect that I had not heard before. I was curious. I approached the women and engaged them in conversation so that I could hear more clearly their dialect. I discovered that they were from East Prussia. At the end of the war, the German population in East Prussia was driven westwards and these two women, who were sisters, landed in Weimar. "We have been here ever since 1945," they remarked. Pointing to a second floor window in the building across the street, they said, "Our room is up there." I learned that one of the sisters was eighty-eight and the other one ninety years old. I knew from my friendship with Frau Giese that the elderly were regarded by aggressive youth, desperately searching for a place to live, as "cemetery vegetables." "Why don't they just die instead of taking up space and diminishing the food supply?" was the query of an impatient, frustrated and aggressive young generation. "The elderly should not neglect their duty to die!" From these two frail, shabbily clad women, I was certain that not much of the food supply was being diminished by them. I thanked them for our conversation and pressed a large amount of dollars into the palm of the older sister with the instructions, "During the winter you can use these dollars in the Intershop to purchase juice so that you can be fortified with vitamin C."

The following summer I also resided for a period in the Hospiz. Once again, I made my way to the cemetery. As I went through the Poseckscher Garden, I noticed the two sisters seated on their bench. I approached them and began a conversation. They did not immediately recognized me. Finally, they said, "You are the American professor whom we met last year!" Then the younger sister, now eighty-nine years old, told me, "During the winter, we cannot sit here on our bench. We must remain in our room, but as spring approaches and the sun's rays are warm enough, I say to my sister, 'Let's go sit on the dollar bench.'" This statement pleased me very much and I said, "Well we don't want to have to relinquish that description of your bench." Thereupon I pressed another large sum of dollars into the palm of the older sister.

The next summer I looked for the sisters on their bench, but the bench remained unoccupied. Finally, I asked a young mother, whose children were playing in the sandbox next to the path, if she knew anything about the two elderly sisters who daily sat here in fair and warm weather. "Yes, I knew them," the young woman replied. "They died in the winter; first the older sister and then ten days later, the younger sister. They were inseparable and, living together for so long in one small room, the one could not survive long without the other." I went on my way with nostalgic sorrow. I would frequently pass the bench, usually unoccupied, but never could I pass that bench without thinking of those two sisters cozily seated in the sun's warm rays on their dollar bench.

In the summer of 1987, I once again was with a group of my countrymen in Weimar. On a pleasant August Sunday afternoon, we were enjoying a picnic in the Bredenbröcker garden. Hilde told me that her neighbor, Dr. Waldemar Anton, a leading gynecologist in Thuringia, desired a conversation with me. I remembered that Dr. Anton, in the summer of 1983, had supplied us with a wheelchair for Maggie, so that she could accompany us on our walks about Weimar. Because Dr. Anton knew that the two men who occupied the second floor of the house in which he resided with his wife, Karin and his daughter, Beatrice, were Stasi agents and that they might have concealed recording devices in his residence, Hilde and Dr. Anton agreed that he would come into his garden at the same time our picnic was taking place in Hilde's garden. In a brief conversation over the garden fence, Dr. Anton requested me to come to his residence and to enter through the basement door that faced onto Windmühlen Straße. "The door will be unlocked," he said. I followed his instructions. Once inside the house, Dr. Anton led me up the stairs to his living room. He put a recording of classical music on the record player and turned up the volume, and we quietly conversed in the background of loud music. He told me that after he filed application for emigration to the BRD in 1984 (an application that he renewed in 1985, 1986, and 1987) for himself and his wife and daughter, he was subjected to systematic persecution. After the 1984 filing, he received a visit from Party officials. At first, the visitors were very polite and praised him for the contribution his expert medical services made to the Weimar population. When he refused to withdraw his emigration application, however, the visitors became agitated and began to threaten him. Dr. Anton suspected that his telephone had been tapped. Some of his professional colleagues at the hospital kept a safe distance from him, lest they come under suspicion. Frequently, he was summoned to the police station where renewed attempts were made to intimidate and to persuade him to withdraw the emigration application. The two Stasi agents who resided in the second floor apartment of the house went about devising all manner of annoyance for the Anton family. Finally, Dr. Anton wrote a letter of complaint to the Weimar Housing Authority.

When the annoyances continued and, in fact, were increased, and he had received no response from the Housing Authority, he wrote a second letter that he said he intended to mail in September. He showed me a copy of the letter that he had dated September 15, 1987. "August is vacation month," he said, "and there is no point in mailing the letter at this time." Dr. Anton wanted to convey a copy of this letter to his parents-in-law in Frankfurt in the BRD. They, in turn, would forward the letter to the Ministry For All German Affairs in Bonn. Dr. Anton said, "I cannot risk mailing this letter in Weimar. The Stasi has a sharp eye on the post between the DDR and the BRD. If the letter were intercepted, it would be destroyed and my family and I would be at risk for increased persecution. I want the authorities in Bonn to know that while they will be hosting Erich Honecker in September on his five-day state visit in the BRD, there is no compliance in the DDR with the terms of the Helsinki Accords pertaining to the right of emigration for restoring family unity. Most of our relatives reside in the BRD. Honecker signed those accords in August 1975. Now, my great plea to you, Professor Foster," Dr. Anton said, "is, would you be willing to carry this letter on your person and to deliver it to my parents-in-law in Frankfurt?" With that request, Dr. Anton handed me a copy of the letter to read. The letter was addressed to the director of the Housing Authority and a copy was directed to the Weimar Political Council:

Honorable Frau Director Pasch!

Unfortunately I am forced to call your attention to the intolerable, chaotic conditions that prevail in the house we share with other renters at number 7 Windmühlen Straße (a large 2-story-house and a full basement).

On August 16, the resident, Friebe, tapped into our basement electrical cable. His section of the basement is only one and one-half meters from our basement area, and he has his own electric outlet. This action caused an overload on our electrical system and short-circuited the electricity in our entire residence. I had to pay for the repair to our electrical system. The basement corridor lights are connected to our electrical cable, and they are deliberately left burning all night by the two residents, even when no one is in the basement. The noise coming from the basement is intolerable. Even on the weekends, the resident Krüger hammers and uses machines whose noise makes it impossible for us to remain in our residence.... Herr Friebe and Herr Krüger alternate in their noise-making projects. Each one seeks to outdo the other in their macabre-like variety of selecting that which causes the loudest noise. In addition, there is a continuous slamming shut of the basement door—a slamming shut that sometimes goes on until midnight and causes our entire residence to vibrate.

In the letter, Dr. Anton goes on to complain that on a Sunday afternoon, a motor bike was parked outside the Anton's residence and the throttle repeatedly was opened to full power, causing intolerable noise. The Anton's television antenna had been mysteriously damaged so that no television reception was possible. Dr. Anton pointed out that the acts of Herr Friebe and Herr Krüger were serious violations of the law, and especially of Article 215 of the DDR Constitution.

In fact, such conduct was punishable as Rowdyism under Article 215. Dr. Anton concluded the letter with an urgent appeal for justice:

Because of these deliberate acts of disturbance, I also am hindered in my professional activity as a physician which, of course, could have ominous consequences. Once again, I earnestly plead for intervention by the authorities.

Waldemar Anton, M.D.

I agreed to carry the letter to Frankfurt and to deliver it to Erich and Lucia de Haß, parents-in-law of Dr. Anton. This visit in the de Haß residence, at number 9 Breslauer Straße, would be followed by more visits to this elderly couple who were forced to spend their declining years in the anguishing effort to gain emigration for their daughter, son-in-law, and granddaughter.

In the summer of 1987, my group and I also traveled to Poznan. Maria, her family and her friends waited for us at the Poznan train station. When the train arrived, and because we had so much luggage, the women in the group got off the train carrying what they could and the men then hurriedly passed luggage through the opened windows. Professor Wachowski and several other men, waiting on the platform, loaded the luggage onto a large baggage cart. The men pushed and pulled the cart to waiting automobiles where it was packed into the trunks of many cars. This luggage transfer made a great impression on us and taught us to admire the efficiency with which the operation was carried out, an efficiency that through years of confronting crowded and confining conditions, had been honed into a fine skill. After an excellent dinner in the flat of Maria's parents, where we were introduced to Maria's family, her parents, Professor Eugene and Mrs. Ursula Wachowski, her grandmother, her sister Barbara and Barbara's fiancée, Wojtek Karandyszowski and Maria's husband, Mirek Lewicki and family friends, we were assigned to the respective families where, two by two, we could find our overnight accommodations. The next day, Maria's husband, Mirek, Barbara's fiance, Wojtek, and two other family friends came with autos and in the four automobiles, we began our itinerary through Poland. Barbara accompanied us as translator. We visited Krakow and many other sites in southern Poland.

One of the places we visited was Niepokalanow. I remember having read that Pope John Paul II, on Sunday, October 10, 1982, had canonized Maximilian Kolbe, the founder of this monastery, and that the friary possessed a museum. Before his final arrest, Father Maximilian had been detained with thirty-seven of his friars in various internment centers from September 17, 1939 to December 8, 1939. From December 9, 1939 until his arrest on February 17, 1941, Father Maximilian again administered Niepokalanow, which had been transformed into a machine repair depot, a farm and a refugee center.

After a circa three-hour drive from Poznan, we arrived at Niepokalanow. We were introduced to the receptionist, but we were told that no one was available to give us a tour in the English language. "Today we have guides who can present the tour either in the Polish or in the German language," the receptionist told our hosts. I then said, "Give us the guide who can speak German." I reasoned that I could then act as a translator for my group. The receptionist dialed a telephone number and in a brief time, Brother Jerome Maria Wierzba appeared. Brother Jerome was very affable and we immediately felt very comfortable in his presence. We learned that Brother Jerome had been born in Germany in 1912 where his father had been employed in a mine. After Poland reappeared as a sovereign nation on the European map in 1919, the Wierzba family had returned to Poland. Although Brother Jerome's German was distinctly that form of the language that had been in vogue in the early twentieth century, he was easy to comprehend and I had no difficulty in translating for my countrymen. We began making our way through the museum. At each exhibit, there was a brief, printed description in the Polish language. Brother Jerome then would add commentary to the description and we soon learned that his knowledge of each exhibit was inexhaustible. With anecdotes and many references to conversations with Saint Maximilian, Brother Jerome enriched our visit. It did not take us long to discover that Brother Jerome had come to Niepokalanow in 1932, educated in polygraphics, and that he worked in the press center of the friary. After Saint Maximilian returned to Poland from Japan in 1936 and before his final arrest by the Gestapo on Monday, February 17, 1941, Brother Jerome served as Saint Maximilian's secretary. Finally, I said to Brother Jerome, "Brother, it's impossible to assimilate so much information in one afternoon. If I return to Niepokalanow next summer and remain here for an extended period, will you make yourself available to me?" We had learned that the monastery had a guesthouse for pilgrims. Brother Jerome's face shown with joy in that beautiful smile that everyone came to admire. "Yes," he said. "As far as I am able, I would be happy to provide you with all the information you desire." We exchanged addresses. Because he was charged with the ministry to the poor, Brother Jerome had a telephone in his room. I recorded the number.

Barbara then accompanied us to Zakopane, remaining with us there for a brief period. She then returned by bus to Poznan. Our group stayed overnight in a hotel on the Polish side of the border with Czechoslovakia. From there we planned to cross the border. On the Slovak side, Stefan and Anna Zoricak, with friends, would wait for us and drive us to Levoca. At about 5 a.m., on the day of our departure from Poland, I was awakened by a heavy rainfall. I looked out the hotel window and saw a long line of people in rain gear and under umbrellas huddled along the sidewalk. The line extended for about one city block. "What are so many people doing at 5 a.m. lined up in a teeming rain?" I thought. My curiosity got the best of me. I dressed and went out to see what the attraction was that convoked so many people in such bad weather. I crossed the street and walked to the head of the line. There, in a cubicle, sat a woman distributing two rolls of toilet paper to each customer. My Polish friends had warned me, "If you travel by train, don't expect to find toilet paper in the train lavatories. As soon as it is placed there, it is stolen."

After I returned to the United States, I read all the literature I could locate on Saint Maximilian, both in English and in German. I discovered many contradictions and some information that did not correspond with what I had learned from Brother Jerome. In one of my phone conversations with Brother Jerome, I mentioned that, in all the literature that I had read, I had not found any treatment of Saint Maximilian's mission and martyrdom that covered his entire life and which was written within the historical context of the twentieth century. Brother Jerome agreed with me that such a work did not yet exist. "Brother," I said, "if you are willing, we could write such a biography. I cannot undertake such a task without you and the assistance of the Niepokalanow friars and priests, but, if you are willing to collaborate with me, we can produce such a biography." Brother Jerome responded with enthusiasm. "Yes," he said, "such a biography is needed."

On October 22, 1987, Erich and Lucia de Haß wrote to me, from their Frankfurt am Main address, concerning their appeal for help from BRD authorities. Erich and Lucia de Haß sought assistance in Bonn to gain permission from the DDR for their son-in-law, their daughter and their teenage granddaughter, Beatrice, to emigrate to the BRD. Ever since the signing of the Helsinki Accords in which, in exchange for the Western Allies' de facto and de jure recognition of the post-war borders in central and eastern Europe, the Soviet Union and her satellite East Bloc states had consented to facilitating the reunion of families. Once this concession became known in the East Bloc states, and especially in the DDR, the authorities were inundated with applications for emigration to the West. Of course, the DDR had no intention of permitting so many of its citizens to emigrate to the BRD. By interminable delays in processing applications, by intimidation and by promises of future privileges, the DDR sought to stem the tide of thousands seeking to leave for the West. On behalf of their daughter, granddaughter and son-in-law, Erich and Lucia de Haß appealed to various government agencies in Bonn. Thinking that he could possibly help them, I gave them the address of Pastor Aimé Bonifas. Aimé, because of his resistance to National Socialism and the fact that he had been an inmate in Hitler's labor camps, and was the author of *Häftling 20 801* (*Prisoner 20 801*), which enjoyed a broad readership in the DDR, was highly esteemed. During his visits to the DDR, Aimé was hosted by Gerald Götting, Chairman of the CDU political party, and second to Erich Honecker in the Politbüro. Through their many efforts, the family was permitted to emigrate to the BRD in 1988, primarily I am convinced, through the intercession of Pastor Aimé Bonifas.

On June 18, 1988, while residing at the Hospiz with my group, we met Pia-Monika Nittke from Magdeburg. This association, which developed into a friendship with Monika and her daughter Elisabeth, led ultimately in 1999 to an important publication, *Poetic Allegories*, a book of my poetry, which I published with our West Chester University Press.

The Berlin Wall comes down

About 1985, I had begun translating Gerhard Brendler's Luther biography into the English language. The biography was published in 1991. I translated about one third of the book in one year. I had accepted the translation task on the condition that no time line was set for completing the work. After all, I had professional responsibilities at the university and frequently was invited to present lectures before civic and ecclesiastical audiences. Each summer, while residing in Weimar in the DDR, I traveled to the East Berlin Academy of Sciences where Gerhard served as director for the Church History Department. We earlier had agreed that he would make himself available to me for at least one week each summer so that we could review my translation. Gerhard could understand and read the English language, but he would not have been able to translate a book from the German into the English language. During my one week in Berlin, while working on the translation, I was the guest of the Academy of Sciences. I resided in the Johannes Hof, all expenses paid.

We sat at a large table in Gerhard's office. While he looked at his German text, I read to him my English translation. "Gerhard," I said, "wherever you disagree or have a question, you must interrupt me." Because I had taken great pains to translate very carefully, there were few interruptions. Gerhard was most pleased with the translation. That first summer's review covered one third of the German text. The following summer, we occupied ourselves with the second third of the biography. In the summer of 1989, we almost had completed the final review before I had to return to the United States. Because I had been granted a sabbatical leave for the autumn of 1989, Gerhard and I planned to meet in November in his Berlin office to complete our work.

On November 9, 1989, the Berlin Wall was opened. A few days later, I arrived in West Berlin and was astounded to see so many East Berliners and other DDR residents roaming Kurfürstendamm and crowding the shops where they wished to spend their one hundred West German marks welcome money, distributed by West Berlin banks. Because the regular banks were overwhelmed with people waiting for their welcome money, the municipal government stationed trailers (mobile banks) strategically throughout the city to help relieve the pressure. Because of the masses of people, Kurfürstendamm was closed to traffic. More than 300,000 people flooded the center of West Berlin. Despite the serious phenomenon of sudden liberty on display, there was a humorous side to the spectacle. The DDR residents were easy to identify. Most of them had either an orange or a banana in hand. Oranges and bananas were rare in the DDR. Once in West Berlin, the DDR citizens stormed the fruit stands.

The vain gestures at reform that the Politbüro daily made to the DDR population were unable to stem the tide or to silence the increasingly loud chorus for democracy and unification (Freiheit und Einheit). These words were the same revolutionary code words that the student fraternities had invoked in the 1817 Wartburg Congress. What once had been expropriated for DDR propaganda (the student revolutionary activity of 1817) now was turned against the Politbüro. Token reforms and a rearrangement of political furniture inside the Politbüro could not satisfy the masses, and the attempt at reform verified Alexis de Tocqueville's (1805-1859) observation: "The most dangerous moment for a tyrannical regime usually occurs when it seeks to reform itself." The continuous reports of economic and social progress issued by the Politbüro were belied by the obvious economic and material decline in the DDR. After 40 years of residence in the DDR, the population sided with the Roman philosopher, Seneca (4 B.C.-65 A.D.): "People believe their eyes more than their ears."

The S Bahn trams (elevated train) from Friedrich Straße (border point between West and East Berlin) to the Zoological Garden (Zoo) in West Berlin were jammed with travelers. Traveling from Friedrich Straße to Berlin Zoo, the travelers were empty handed, but the return journey from Berlin Zoo to Friedrich Straße, saw each person burdened with packages of every description. Carrying a heavy suitcase, I managed to squeeze onto one of the cars where people were pressed together as sardines in a can. Gerhard waited for me at the Friedrich Straße station and, after passing through border control, which the DDR officials still pretended was necessary, we walked the four blocks to the Johannes Hof.

Because I wanted to be certain that I could retrieve souvenir pieces of the rapidly disappearing wall, one afternoon, after having completed my session with Gerhard in his office, I walked along the wall's perimeter between Potsdamer Platz and the Brandenburg Gate with Charlotte Rhode. Ever since Charlotte hosted my pupils and me in 1967 when, from her balcony, we had viewed the International Communist Youth Parade, each subsequent summer she extended warm hospitality to my group and me. Charlotte and I collected the fragments, which were being chipped out of the body of this massive 28-year-old concrete giant. The sound of hundreds of chisels and picks assaulting the stubborn, reinforced cement echoed along the wall in a never-ending demolition staccato. Charlotte and I were quite content with the pieces we were able to collect.

Not long after the autumn of 1989, I received the very sad news that Charlotte had been struck by a truck and killed. Across a broad boulevard from Charlotte's flat was a grocery store where she purchased her groceries. It was while crossing this boulevard that she was struck. All of my countrymen, who had enjoyed the generous hospitality that Charlotte each summer had extended to us, were deeply grieved by the news of her death.

That autumn of 1989 remains unforgettable. By the time I had arrived in Berlin in late November, after I had spent some days with Frau Schneider in Dickenschied working on the biography of Pastor Paul Schneider, the Berlin Wall had been opened and was in the process of being dismantled. The SED worked frantically to shore up its collapsing political edifice. Everyone sensed that, despite the presentation of new faces and novel ideas, the once sovereign party could offer cosmetic illusions only for the new political realities. The SED state was doomed.

On November 9, 1989, the Chancellor of the BRD, Helmut Kohl, had been paying a state visit to Poland. When he received the news that the Berlin Wall had been opened, he cut short his visit and returned to Bonn. Before the Chancellor returned, in a conversation with Lech Wałęsa, Wałęsa said to Kohl, "If the DDR opens the Berlin Wall, you may have to erect a wall yourself to prevent the BRD from being inundated by DDR citizens." Such an impending danger, no doubt, hastened the process for German reunification.

The monopoly of power that the Politbüro had possessed for forty years had led to an intolerable arrogance. As in a Greek tragedy, hubris became the cardinal sin that must lead to inevitable destruction. Once again, history confirmed the observation of Sophocles (495-406 B.C.) that those blinded by their own arrogance and ambition are to be identified with his prediction: "God first blinds those whom he has determined to destroy."

From Gerhard's office in the academy, we could look out onto a broad boulevard and see the masses and hear the chants. Before the fall of the wall, the chant had been, "We want out." Now the chant became, "We remain here." Finally, in a crescendo of voices, the chant became, "Germany one united nation." These three variations demonstrate the course of the revolution. When it appeared that there could be no hope of challenging the political status quo, the chant was, "We want out." When the wall was opened and it became apparent that the mass movement had, in fact, forced the government to alter policy, the refrain became, "We remain here." Now that the window of opportunity for German reunification was open, the chorus became, "Germany, one united nation." It was indeed a surrealistic scene. While Gerhard and I sat in tranquil isolation in his office and discussed Luther and the sixteenth-century Reformation, on the streets outside the academy, a twentieth-century revolution was taking place. Each day and each demonstration further eroded the last, fragile foundation on which the SED state was anchored. Reflecting on my status as a guest residing in the Johannes Hof, one of Berlin's better hotels, and having all my expenses paid by the Academy, I said to Gerhard, "I have a guilty conscience." "Why?" Gerhard asked. "Because," I responded, "I have the feeling that the DDR is spending its last dime on me." Gerhard laughed. "That may be true," he asserted.

Gerhard and I realized that we were witnessing the death throes of the DDR State. The great irony was that the state that claimed to be the heir of Lenin (1870-1924) and the guardian of his testament now was in the process of fulfilling his prophecy. Lenin had written, "The stage for revolution is erected when those below no longer will, and those above no longer can."

Gerhard suggested that I attend the SED party rally scheduled for the evening of December 3, 1989 on the campus outside the party headquarters in the center of East Berlin, not far from Alexander Square. Because the number of members attending was anticipated to be great, the meeting had to be scheduled on the large campus adjoining the building. It was a crisp December evening. In the meantime, since November 9, 1989, the Honecker cabinet had resigned and Egon Krenz, Honecker's crown prince, was seeking to retain political leadership and to prevent a massive exodus from the party. Because of the revelations, however, emanating from Berlin/Wandlitz, an exclusive, suburban enclave for party members only, Krenz's efforts were in vain and his tenure as party leader ended that night after only a few days on the job. The Wandlitz discoveries revealed that the party elite resided in homes stocked with delicacies from the West. It also came to light that SED leaders held secret Swiss bank accounts that contained thousands of West marks and US dollars. These exposures proved to be a catastrophic blow to the SED leadership. The rank and file members found the following adage most appropriate concerning their leaders, for while the leaders demanded sacrifice on the part of the population to build the socialist society, they themselves indulged in luxury and affluence: "They preached water, but they themselves drank wine."

The campus was floodlighted. Even before Krenz exited the party headquarters to come to the lectern, mounted on the outdoor platform, it was obvious what reception he would get. Did he really believe that, in the light of the hypocrisy on the part of party leaders, now exposed, he could maintain leadership and prevent a mass exodus? Did he really think that he could persuade the vast audience that he had disassociated himself from his former colleagues in the Politbüro and their policies—policies that he had helped to draft? Did he think that he could negate the truism of the Arab proverb: "No one can emerge from an onion patch without smelling like an onion?" Was he living in a fool's paradise?

Hanging from the top of the party headquarters building was a large sheet on which a characterization of Krenz's face had been painted. Krenz has unusually large teeth. The cartoon-like depiction portrayed Krenz with a bonnet on his head and a broad grin, revealing huge teeth. The caption above the cartoon read, "Grandmother, what big teeth you have!" Of course, everyone knew the story of Little Red Riding Hood, whom the wolf, disguised as the grandmother, sought to lure into his embrace in order to devour. Krenz came to the lectern, but his words were drowned out by defiant shouts, whistles and the chant, "We don't believe you anymore." Despite repeated efforts to placate the crowd, he could not silence the angry calls for his resignation. Krenz left the platform. A few hours later, he resigned all political functions. Observing the vain attempts of the Politbüro and its leaders to retain political power by opening the borders between the DDR and the BRD, and by promising democratic reforms, I thought of the ancient German proverb: "The oats arrive too late after the horse already has died." Mikhail Gorbachev had warned his DDR Communist colleagues, who had resisted adopting a policy of Glasnost and Perestroika in the DDR, with a grim prediction: "He who comes too late is punished by history."

From Berlin, I traveled to Leipzig. I wanted to visit my friends, Herbert and Sigrid Schramowski, but I also wanted to observe the now famous Leipzig demonstration. Each Monday afternoon at 5:00 p.m. in the Saint Nicholas Church, only a short distance from the Karl Marx Square, a brief worship service with prayers and Bible reading was conducted. In the spring of 1989, a modest number of Christian youth, promoting disarmament and peace, in the "Swords to Plowshares" movement, assembled in the church, lit candles, prayed for peace and then sought to carry their message to the streets. They were set upon by the security police, forced into vans and driven to some remote interrogation center, far from public surveillance, where they were physically and psychologically abused. Upon being released, often with fractured limbs and missing teeth, they regrouped and chanted, "Next Monday we'll come again and we'll bring someone with us." And so it occurred. From a modest number of "Swords to Plowshares" youth in the spring of 1989, the number increased each Monday until it reached into the thousands. By November/December 1989, tens of thousands of demonstrators dominated the Leipzig streets. The proverb, "From the smallest spark often springs the greatest conflagration," was verified in the Swords to Plowshares movement. I thought of the parallel with Luther's Ninety-Five Theses, a solitary monk requesting in the Latin language a debate on the validity of indulgences, and from that spark sprang the conflagration that spread throughout the world. In Czechoslovakia, at the same time in 1989, the Velvet Revolution was taking place. Vaclav Havel, the most important leader of that revolution, with his Charter 77 Compatriots, described the Velvet Revolution: "The struggle for freedom is reflected in the ocean. The solitary wave hardly can make an impact, but when waves unite in a giant swell, they create an irresistible force." The police and army personnel, who threatened to use force to disperse the Leipzig demonstrators, disappeared.

The service in the Saint Nicholas Church began at 5:00 p.m. The church, with its three balconies, accommodates several hundred people. One had to arrive at the church by 4:15 p.m. in order to squeeze into the overcrowded sanctuary. The organ played and hymns were sung. There was scripture reading, prayer and a brief homily. Before members of the congregation departed the church to proceed to Karl Marx Square—a few blocks distant—where they would join the thousands of demonstrators who had assembled, they heard the strong admonition from the pastor: "Keine Gewalt-No Violence!" Sigrid and I arrived at the Saint Nicholas Church at about 4:00 p.m. (Herbert was to join us later at a designated spot). Observing the overflow congregation in the sanctuary, and recalling the failed attempts to overthrow Communist dictatorships (the DDR, June 17, 1953, Hungary and Poland 1956, The Prague Spring, 1968), Sigrid commented, "Only when the fruit is ripe does it fall from the tree. I am convinced that this time our revolutionary fruit is ripe." Because I wanted to video the entire sanctuary, we took our seats in the third balcony at the rear of the sanctuary, near the organ. From that vantage point, I was able, with my camera, to do a complete sweep of the sanctuary. At about 4:45 p.m., when the organist began to play, the sanctuary was completely occupied with people standing in the aisles and wall to wall. When we came out of the church, we entered a sea of humanity; all streets leading to the church were crowded. The human tide slowly moved toward Karl Marx Square where it fused with more masses already assembled on the square. Bodies were pressed together as people continued to arrive not only from Leipzig and its environs, but also from areas some distance from Leipzig.

Standing on the elevated platform outside the Opera House were the cultural and religious leaders of Leipzig. Each one gave a short, but firm admonition before the demonstrators were to begin their march around the inner city: "No Violence!" The superintendent of the Leipzig area Lutheran Church spoke as did the senior Roman Catholic Bishop. Finally, Kurt Mazur, a person known and respected by all Leipzigers, having conducted the Leipzig Gewand House Orchestra for many years, spoke and implored his fellow Leipzigers: "No Violence!"

The demonstrators then began their march. Sigrid and I met Herbert at the agreed place and time. In order to view better the march, we went up to the pedestrian bridge that spans the wide boulevard near the main rail station. From that height, we had a commanding view of the march and demonstrators, walking shoulder on shoulder and rank on rank, a mass of people covering the entire boulevard from curb to curb, passed below us in an unending stream. In order to avoid the temptation to vandalize the building that housed the Stasi headquarters and that lay on the march route, leaders of the demonstration and "Swords to Plowshares" members stood on the balcony of the Stasi headquarters under brilliant searchlight illumination—a clear message to the demonstrators that violence would not be tolerated, not even against the foe so hated by the general populace.

As Sigrid, Herbert and I watched the flow of never-ending waves, many individuals carrying candles (ergo, the "Candle Revolution"), I thought of the massive non-violent movement in India that had been led by Mohandas Gandhi (1869-1948) and I concluded that European revolutionaries had learned something from Gandhi who had taught, "What is gained by violence can only be retained by violence." An old proverb also determined the pacific course of the November Revolution: "When violence is invoked—justice is on crutches." Members of the Swords to Plowshares Movement told me that they had learned much from the Civil Rights Movement in the US and that they were aware that Dr. Martin Luther King had been influenced by Gandhi's movement of passive resistance. They said, "We are convinced that great historical movements project their shadow into the future. That certainly was true for the passive resistance movement in India and for the Civil Rights Movement in the US. We believe our movement also is projecting its shadow into the future. Despite the arrest and beatings to which we are subjected, we are convinced with Seneca, 'that courage increases with every glance at the greatness of the undertaking.'"

In addition, the Swords to Plowshares members who were largely responsible for setting the liberation movement into motion may have recalled Martin Luther's pamphlet—Admonition to Peace—written on the verge of the 1525 Peasants War in which pamphlet Luther pleaded for a peaceful resolution to the antagonisms that existed between the peasants and the feudal barons. Luther wrote, "Let the spirits collide but restrain the fist."

After the fall of the wall, I was inspired to write this poem:

> Torn and tortured, by barbed wire and concrete rupture,
> the anatomy of the nation.
> Naked puncture throbbing with pain
> from mine and machine gun pulsation.
> Rude division defying reconciliation.
>
> Shrapnel sentinels, automatic dispensers of death,
> like sutures on a jagged scar,
> survey its length and breadth.
>
> Of course, we know the explanation.
> Security of the socialist state from alien infiltration.
>
> But DDR citizens, like moths flapping about the light in frenzied animation,
> are allured by the shining demons of capitalist exploitation.
>
> "Against your will," says the Party, "we must save you from the West's
> economic Hell.
> Settle down, adjust, be content, and believe the story we tell."
>
> "What! You want to leave?
> You want to take the risk inherent in the freedom of motion and of speech?
> You actually want to experience the theoretical liberties we preach?"
>
> Man's insatiable appetite for freedom provokes again the eternal,
> invincible call—confirming the poet's observation—
>
> "Something there is that doesn't love a wall."

Forever Connected to Europe

In the summer of 1990, after my visit in Germany, I returned to Niepokalanow prepared to spend as long as I needed to interview all the friars and priests who had known and worked with Saint Maximilian. I took my video camera to record my interviews with the friars. I interviewed Brother Jerome many times. The interviews were conducted in the German language. With the Polish brothers who did not speak German, Brother Jerome acted as interpreter. Of course, Brother Jerome was the first person I interviewed. He told me how he had decided to enter the Niepokalanow friary and how he ultimately became secretary to Saint Maximilian. Brother Jerome related many anecdotes that nowhere were documented. Then Brother Jerome introduced me to the friars who had known and had worked with Saint Maximilian—Brother Ivo, Brother Juventyn, Brother Pelagius, Brother Felicissimus, Brother Jerimiasz and Father Jerzy Domanski. I interviewed each one on several occasions and in each subsequent summer, spending part of every summer at Niepokalanow from 1990 until 2001, when the manuscript was completed.

Brother Jerome with Claude

In July 1990, I met Prince Drucki-Lubecki at Niepokalanow. The prince had fled Poland in 1939 and returned only after the fall of the Communist government in 1989. It was the prince's desire to live out his remaining days in the friary that his generous land grant had made possible. The prince related to me the details of his land grant to Saint Maximilian that provided the land on which the Niepokalanow friary is built. Prince Drucki-Lubecki said, "I met with Father Maximilian and his brother, Father Alfons on July 11, 1927. The priests were seeking a location near Warsaw to build a publishing center. At that time, their friary was in Grodno, but that was a remote area far from good transportation and distribution facilities. On condition that the Franciscans would install a pew—reserved for my family—in the chapel to be built, would promise to maintain the chapel, to celebrate twenty-four Masses annually for the living and deceased members of my family, and to celebrate one Mass on the anniversary of my father's birth and one Mass on the anniversary of his death (in total 26 Masses), I offered to grant them a portion of my estate in Teresin, near Warsaw. Because the property offered is on the main rail line between Warsaw and Poznan, this is an ideal location for their friary and publishing center. The Kolbe brothers were ecstatic at my liberality. They immediately began to make plans to build and to move from Grodno. The Franciscan Provincial, however, rejected my terms. When the Kolbe brothers came to announce to me that the Provincial had rejected the terms, they were very discouraged. In their anticipation of having my terms accepted by the Provincial, they had erected a statue of the Virgin Mary on the proposed site. I told them that they would have to remove the statue. Father Maximilian then spoke up and said, 'Prince, once the land has been dedicated to the Immaculata, we cannot remove the statue. That would be a travesty. Permit the statue to remain. Your estate then will be under the protection of the Mother of God.' Father Maximilian's remarks drove a dagger deep into my conscience. At birth, my parents had placed me under the protection of the Virgin Mary. My full name is Jan Maria Drucki-Lubecki. I could not bring myself to reclaim what, in good faith, had been dedicated to the Virgin Mary. I said to Father Maximilian and Father Alfons, 'I give you the land without conditions. I would not have given it to the Provincial.' Father Maximilian and Father Alfons threw up their hands in exaltation and exclaimed, 'Praised be Jesus Christ and His Holy Mother!' That is how this land grant became the Niepokalanow Friary, now the largest

Franciscan Friary in the world." Two weeks after this interview, the prince died and, as he desired, he is buried in the friary cemetery.

With the aid of Father Jerzy Domanski, (1919-2007) who had served, in turn, as Militia Immaculatae International President, editor of Rycerz Niepokalanej and as Guardian of the Niepokalanow Friary, Brother Jerome and I were able to make steady progress in the preparation of our manuscript. An August 31 email from the Sisters Minor of Mary Immaculate, domiciled at Niepokalanow, informed me that Father Domanski died on August 28, 2007 at 5:10 p.m. on the Feast Day of Saint Augustine, and that the funeral would take place at Niepokalanow on September 3.

In the summer of 1990, when I again traveled with my group from Weimar to Berlin to Poland, we planned to check our big luggage at the East Berlin rail station and take only what we needed for one night to Ludwigsfelde, a suburb of Berlin. To our great consternation, the area for checked luggage could not accept any more baggage. Many gypsies recently had arrived in Berlin and, with their many bundles and suitcases, had occupied all space in the checked luggage department. Fortunately, Charlotte Rhode, our Berlin hostess, was with us. Her flat was too small to accommodate so many suitcases, but she had the keys to the apartment of friends, who currently were not in Berlin. The apartment was not far from the station. In many taxis, we drove to the apartment and deposited the luggage. Then we proceeded to take the commuter train (this time with tickets) to Ludwigsfelde. We spent a pleasant evening with the Techner family, and we returned to Berlin the next morning. Charlotte met us. We got our luggage from the apartment and proceeded to the East Berlin rail station in order to take the train to Poznan. We noticed that the checked luggage department was closed. LICE! Apparently, among the many bundles that the gypsies had checked, lice were present, and now the entire luggage department had to be fumigated. We breathed a sigh of relief. What a blessing that we were unable to check our luggage on the preceding afternoon. At that time, we were frustrated, but, by having to store our luggage elsewhere, we escaped having our luggage subjected to the lice invasion.

In early December 1990, I received a telephone call from Father Hugh Campbell, pastor of the Saint Maximilian Kolbe Church in West Chester, Pennsylvania, only a fifteen-minute drive from my residence. Father Campbell related to me that Franciszek Gajowniczek (1901-1995) was currently visiting the Kolbe Church. Franciszek Gajowniczek was the Auschwitz inmate for whom Father Kolbe had sacrificed his life at that concentration camp in August 1941. Mr. Gajowniczek was in the United States in order to visit those congregations that were named after Saint Maximilian Kolbe, and to visit the Militia Immaculatae retreat centers. Father Campbell knew that I was working on a Kolbe biography with Brother Jerome Maria Wierzba, Father Kolbe's former secretary. Father Campbell invited me to come to the church and to interview Mr. Gajowniczek. I immediately drove to the church and was able, through an interpreter, to interview him. Mr. Gajowniczek confirmed the information that I already had gathered from witnesses and sources. It was, however, very reassuring to hear from the primary person involved in that Auschwitz scene, when Father Kolbe left the inmate ranks, approached the co-commandant Karl Fritsch, and implored the SS officer to permit him, a Franciscan priest without dependents, to die for the husband and father, Franciszek Gajowniczek. A photograph, taken during my interview with Mr. Gajowniczek, is published in my Saint Maximilian Maria Kolbe biography, *Mary's Knight: The Mission and Martyrdom of Saint Maksymilian Maria Kolbe* (Polish spelling of the name). After surviving Auschwitz, Franciszek Gajowniczek made an annual retreat to Niepokalanow. There in prayer and meditation, he reflected on the sacrifice made on his behalf. Franciszek Gajowniczek requested that he be buried in the friary cemetery. At his death on March 13, 1995, this request was granted.

In the group of my countrymen whom I led to the German Reformation sites in the summer of 1991 was a West Chester University librarian, Mrs. Dorothy Nettles. One day, at the circulation desk (probably in the spring of 1990) in the library, Dottie (as we called her) heard my conversation with her colleague, Emma Brown. Emma had been in the group that I had guided to the DDR in 1972. Emma and I talked about that trip to Germany. Dottie said, "My father was German. He emigrated to the US and here he married my mother. Unfortunately, my father died when I was eight years old. I remember that my father received post from Germany. After my father's death, my mother put the letters in a box in the attic. My mother now also is deceased, and the letters still are in the attic." I then said, "You have the letters. If you will bring some of them to the university, I would be happy to translate them for you." "That would be wonderful," Dottie responded. A few days later when I again was in the library, Dottie approached me and said, "Professor Foster, I have some of my father's letters on my desk, if you have time to look at them."

Dottie and I went to her desk. I began to translate one of the letters addressed to her father from his relatives in Flacht-Weissach, Germany. In the course of the following weeks, whenever I was in the library, I translated the letters. I noticed that the letters came from various relatives and in conclusion greetings were extended to Hermann Gottlieb Döhmler (Dottie's father) from many family members. I told Dottie that the many relatives mentioned in the letters indicated that she probably still had relatives in Flacht-Weissach, relatives she never had met. I told Dottie that when I returned to Germany in the summer of 1990, I would check in the Flacht-Weissach telephone book under the name Döhmler. While visiting my friends, Hermann and Rosi Hützen in Freiburg, I went to the Freiburg main post office and consulted the telephone book for Flacht-Weissach. There were about five listings for the name Döhmler. I copied the telephone number under each listing, and from the Hützen residence, I called the first listing. A woman answered the phone. I introduced myself and related that I was calling for my colleague in the US. I explained that I had been translating letters for her, letters that had been addressed to her father, Hermann Gottlieb Döhmler. The woman to whom I spoke then said, "Hermann Gottlieb Döhmler was my husband's uncle." The woman gave me her current address and I promised to write to the family for Dottie once I had returned to the US. In the summer of 1991, Dottie joined my group and, before traveling to Weimar, I took her and my group for a two-day visit with her father's relatives. The Döhmlers were exceptionally hospitable and very happy that they now had met their American kinsman. The meeting was very emotional and tears of joy were shed. Dottie (now in retirement) continues to remain in correspondence with her Flacht-Weissach relatives.

In January 1992, I received notice from my friends in Dresden that my beloved Dresden hostess, Helene Pommrich had died. This communique caused me great grief. The annual visits in Frau Pommrich's apartment, where I, with my group of countrymen, enjoyed such generous hospitality, would remain a lasting memory of a most lovable personality. Reflecting on Frau Pommrich's irenic and modest personality, I thought of Jesus' assurance: "Blessed are the meek, for they shall inherit the earth; Blessed are the peacemakers, for they shall be called the children of God." (Matthew 5:4,9) In the summer of 1992, I traveled to Dresden and Editha led me to Frau Pommrich's grave.

Each summer, I continued to work on my research of Paul Schneider (Germany) and Maximilian Kolbe (Poland). At the monastery in Niepokalanow, I went to Brother Jerome's room each evening after dinner so that we could review what we had done on that particular day in the archives. One evening I suggested to Brother Jerome that he visit me in the US. He was overwhelmed by the thought. "Never, in my wildest imagination," he said, "did I ever anticipate that I would be able to visit the US." We made the arrangements in the summer of 1992. In the autumn of 1992, Brother Jerome made his visit to the US. He spent six weeks as my guest and for a period he also was hosted by the Saint Maximilian Kolbe Congregation in West Chester in the parish manse. As soon as Brother Jerome's travel plans were completed, I notified various churches, colleges and civic groups that I believed would be interested in hearing Brother Jerome speak about his experiences in Nazi-occupied Poland and concerning his close relationship with Saint Maximilian.

Invitations came from many quarters from people who were eager to hear Brother Jerome. Brother Jerome possessed a plethora of anecdotes with which he enriched his presentations. On most occasions, he spoke German and I translated. On a few occasions, when a Polish/American was available, Brother Jerome spoke Polish and his message then was translated from Polish into English. At the end of each presentation, Brother Jerome, in his strong baritone voice, sang the song that Father Kolbe had taught his Niepokalanow Franciscan friars and priests, "I'll See Her Some Fair Day." Everywhere, whether before Catholic or Protestant congregations, civic or university audience, Brother Jerome was welcomed with enthusiasm and his presentations never failed to arrest the attention of his auditors.

When I picked him up at the Philadelphia airport, Brother Jerome carried a small suitcase and a plastic bag that contained his toothbrush, toothpaste, razor and shaving crème. The plastic bag was beginning to come apart. I told Brother Jerome that we must purchase a sturdy, carry-on bag for his return trip to Poland. One afternoon I decided to drive Brother Jerome to Valley Forge Memorial Park, not far from my West Chester residence. I wanted him to see this historic site, General George Washington's headquarters, and to be informed about the significance of Valley Forge in the colonial war for independence. On our way to the park, however, it began to rain. I decided to postpone our visit to the park until we had fair weather. Since we were not too far from the Exton Mall, a large shopping center, I decided to use this opportunity to purchase a carry-on bag for Brother Jerome. In the luggage section of one of the department stores, Brother Jerome and I found ourselves alone with a female clerk. Noting Brother Jerome's black Franciscan Conventual habit and that he did not speak English, the clerk asked me, "Where is the Brother's monastery?" I replied, "You probably never have heard of his monastery." "Perhaps I have," the clerk responded. I then said, "My friend is from the Franciscan friary, Niepokalanow, about twenty-five miles west of Warsaw." The clerk smiled and replied, "I was there one week ago." Astounding!! Then the clerk explained. "I visited relatives in Warsaw and they insisted that I should see the Niepokalanow basilica, chapel and museum." When I translated for Brother Jerome what the clerk told me, his countenance became even brighter than it usually was and he said, "Praise Be Jesus Christ!" After exchanging pleasantries with the clerk, I purchased a small leather bag in which Brother Jerome, on his return flight, would be able to accommodate his carry-on items.

After leaving the department store, we walked along the main corridor of the mall. People stared at this frail, black-clad friar with the angelic face, a face that reflected an inner peace and tranquility. Suddenly, a woman, passing us in the corridor, approached Brother Jerome and placed a kiss on his cheek while pressing a twenty-dollar bill into his hand and, in a soft voice, making a request. Realizing that

Brother Jerome did not understand her, the woman addressed me, "Please ask the Brother to pray for my terminally-ill sister." "Brother Jerome will pray for your sister without your having to give him money," I said. "Write your sister's name." Taking a pen from her purse, the woman wrote the name on a small piece of paper and insisted that Brother Jerome take the money. "The Franciscans do good work," she said. Placing another kiss on Brother Jerome's cheek, the woman continued on her way. Quite some distance from us, she stopped, turned around and said with a loud voice, so that all passing could hear, "You don't see many saints at Exton Mall!"

One of the churches, Saints Simon and Jude, in West Chester, where Brother Jerome spoke was completely occupied during the late Saturday afternoon Mass. After the service, as we stood in the narthex in order to enable people to greet Brother Jerome, Sister Francina, who resided in the convent adjacent to the church and who taught in the parochial elementary school, approached with a request, "Could you please arrange to have Brother Jerome visit my terminally-ill sister in the West Chester Hospital?" I said that we would arrange a visit. Sister Francina then supplied her sister's name and room number. Soon after this conversation, Brother Jerome visited Mrs. Margaret Murphy, who was dying of cancer. The physicians had alerted the family that nothing more could be done for the patient and the family should prepare itself for the inevitable. Brother Jerome requested to be left alone with the patient who may or may not have been aware of his presence. After a long time, Brother Jerome emerged from the hospital room. We went our way. The sequel to this story was to take place two years later in 1994 when Brother Jerome visited me for the second time.

Many people helped me host Brother Jerome. The Saint Maximilian Kolbe Church in West Chester where, in December 1990, I had interviewed Franciszek Gajowniczek, provided a period of room and board. Various families also hosted Brother Jerome for a day or two. Some of his hosts took him to New York, and to the Atlantic seashore. I remember with what enthusiasm Brother Jerome described his visit to the top floor of one of the twin towers in New York. I recalled this description when, on September 11, 2001, the twin towers were destroyed, one month after Brother Jerome's death. I accompanied him on a visit to the Delaware and Maryland seashores and on a trip to

Washington D.C. and to the Shrine of the Immaculate Conception. One Friday evening, just before leaving my home to attend a dinner, provided by friends, given in honor of Brother Jerome, I remembered that our hostess for that evening had told me that she planned to serve her favorite meat dish. Shortly before departing, we quickly called the Catholic churches in West Chester until we finally contacted a priest who, over the telephone, gave Brother Jerome dispensation for that evening.

On our way to the Philadelphia airport where Brother Jerome was to board his return flight for Poland, he commented, "Professor, do you realize how much money I have?" "No," I replied, "but from what I observed over a six-week period of people pressing dollar bills into your hand, I know that it must be a significant amount." "Well," Brother Jerome continued, "I have several thousand dollars for my mission to the poor, and more than fifty percent of the funds came from Protestants." "That's a great sign of ecumenicity," I said, "when Protestants wholeheartedly support a Franciscan mission to the poor!" During his visit, Brother Jerome read the documents in the German language that I had collected for my research and biography on the life and ministry of Pastor Paul Schneider. "Pastor Schneider, in our church, would be a candidate for canonization," Brother Jerome said.

In February 1993, I received the news that I was dreading—the obituary for my friend, Pastor Siegfried Urban, pastor of Saint Stephen's Church in Schöndorf, a suburb of Weimar. During my annual visits to Weimar, I had met many people who knew Pastor Siegfried and Mrs. Ingrid Urban. Among these people were some who were quite close to the Urban family. They related to me a story that was known by an inner circle of friends, but never openly discussed. Because of his popularity with the youth and a well-attended worship service each Sunday, the political authorities offered Pastor Urban and his family permission to emigrate to the BRD. While other DDR citizens, who sought to escape to the BRD, were being shot at the Berlin Wall and other border crossing points, the DDR state was willing to grant emigration to a pastor who was very popular with the youth. When Pastor Urban knew that I had learned of this offer, he explained, "How could I, as a pastor of this Schöndorf flock, desert my congregation and move to the BRD. None of my parishioners is permitted to emigrate. Can you imagine the impact that my deserting my post would have on people who have been very faithful to me?" What Pastor Urban did not reveal to me, but what was known to his friends, was the fact that his refusal to accept the offer to emigrate caused estrangement in his marriage. His wife, placing priority on the future of their son and daughter, insisted that the family should seize the opportunity to emigrate, especially since the children, because they were not members of the Free German Youth, would not be admitted to any university. Despite excellent grades in their secondary school, both Gabriel and Annette Urban were not admitted to a university education. The stress in the Urban marriage was difficult to conceal. Because he could not attend the university, Gabriel, who desired to study medicine, became apprenticed in one of the trades. Annette acquired a position working with handicapped children in an institution some distance from Weimar. When she was able to visit her parents, she noticed the estrangement between them. Depressed by her daily contact with and care for severely handicapped children and distraught about the relationship between her mother and father, one evening in her room, Annette opened the gas burner. In a note, she requested that her parents be reconciled.

Each time I return to Weimar, I make my way to the graves of my friends—Frau Giese, Dorothea Schirow, Mayor and Mrs. Luitpold Steidle, and Pastor Urban, who is buried in the grave with his daughter, Annette, 1960-1980. A white stone in the form of a cross with the X (chi) and P (rho), the first letters in the Greek spelling of Christ, and the words from John 3:16 mark the site.

As I did each summer, I returned to Niepokalanow in the summer of 1993 and 1994 in order to continue to prepare the Saint Maximilian biography with Brother Jerome and the other brothers who could contribute their remembrances to the story. In the autumn of 1994, Brother Jerome returned to the US for a second six-week visit. Once again, I had Brother Jerome speak to students at West Chester University. Once again, we were invited to speak to the congregation at the West Chester Saints Simon and Jude Roman Catholic Church. Once again, after the early Saturday evening service, we stood in the narthex of the church where the parishioners could greet Brother Jerome. A very attractive woman, about fifty years of age, embraced Brother Jerome. Standing before him, she asked, "Do you recognize me, Brother Jerome?" When I translated the question, Brother Jerome looked perplexed. He had seen hundreds of people during his first visit to the United States. Then the woman said, "I'm the woman you visited in 1992 in the Chester County Hospital. I'm Margaret Murphy." This was the woman who had been given only a short time to live by her physicians. The cancer had gone into remission; she recovered her health. She was able to return to her family and to her employment. "It was after your visit and prayer vigil at my bedside that I began to recover," she said. Mrs. Murphy did not die of cancer in 1992, but on September 2, 2003, more than two years after Brother's Jerome's death. This story concerning Brother Jerome and Mrs. Margaret Murphy was published in Rycerz Niepokalanej under the title: "The Ecumenical Friar."

During Brother Jerome's second visit to the United States, hearing that Brother Jerome, secretary to Saint Maximilian, was in the Philadelphia area, the retired Archbishop of the Philadelphia Archdiocese from 1961 to 1988, John Cardinal Krol, invited us to lunch in the archdiocesan headquarters in Philadelphia. From the Cardinal's table on the top floor of the tall building, we had a panoramic view of Philadelphia. I knew that the Cardinal had Polish ancestry, but that he had been born in the United States. The Cardinal's ability to speak and to understand the Polish language was limited and frequently the conversation had to be conducted in three languages, Polish, English and German. When the Cardinal had difficulty with the Polish communication, I translated the Cardinal's words from English to German for Brother Jerome and then translated Brother Jerome's reply from German to English for the Cardinal. Although his rational faculty was very sharp, Cardinal Krol at that time was in feeble physical health and had to be in a wheel chair. I noted that both the Cardinal and the friar were about the same age. On the drive back to West Chester, I asked Brother Jerome, "Brother, how do explain that you and the Cardinal are about the same age (Cardinal Krol, born October 26, 1910; Brother Jerome, born January 26, 1912), but he is plagued by physical infirmities and your health seems so robust? Brother Jerome answered, "It's quite simple." I replied, "It's not so simple for me." Brother Jerome, with a twinkle in his eye, solved the riddle: "He's a cardinal archbishop. I'm a Franciscan friar." John Cardinal Krol died on March 3, 1996 and was buried in the crypt of the Cathedral of Saints Peter and Paul in Philadelphia.

Having published my biography of Pastor Paul Schneider in 1995, I was honored to receive this letter from Mrs. Margarete Schneider on November 15. She wrote to me from Liederbach, Germany,

> Since yesterday, I have held your work in my hand, and I am moved by your feeling for our life, especially in the Nazi era.
>
> Since my English is not so good and I would not be able to read the book with complete understanding, Evmarie (daughter of Pastor and Mrs. Schneider) reads it to me and she will continue to read it to me after our trip to Mühlheim to celebrate Ilse's 75th birthday. We leave on November 18/19 and return in time for my eye surgery on November 28 in Frankfurt.
>
> Last Sunday Evmarie and Hans picked me up (in Dickenschied) with sack and pack. It always is somewhat stressful to gather together what one will need for 5 or 6 months, but now I feel at home here also.
>
> I wish to present your book to my children as a Christmas present. Can you please send me ten copies per normal post with the bill? My bank will then transfer the sum. Please send the bank account number. Pastor Maurer requests an autographed copy. I will inform my nephew, Paul. I will send one of my books to the Reverend Ross.
>
> Poor fellow—how much work invested; how many years of research!! I can imagine the effort and commitment. May God bless you and fill you with His spirit and make you happy despite the Anfechtung (assaults) and weariness which can overcome you —my dear man—when you have completed the great service which you have rendered to the Christian world by making Paul's witness known and comprehensible. May a renewal and strengthening of faith bless us. I am convinced that a new work and a new witness awaits you. But, now, for a time, pause and recuperate.
>
> With grateful greetings,
> Margarete Schneider

I also received letters that winter from two of Frau Schneider's children, Evmarie Vorster and Karl Adolf Schneider as well as from her nephew, Paul Dieterich, Superintendent of the Lutheran Church in Schwäbish-Hall. Each was pleased with the biography.

In March 1996, I received a telephone call from Director of Ecumenical Affairs at the Holocaust Museum in Washington, D.C. The lady told me that an ecumenical conference was planned at the museum for early April. She said that someone had called her attention to my Pastor Paul Schneider biography, *The Buchenwald Apostle: A Christian Martyr in Nazi Germany: A Sourcebook on the German Church Struggle*, published in 1995. The director wanted me to attend the conference and to read excerpts from the biography. I replied that I would be happy to attend the conference and, if she permitted, I had a suggestion. "Of course," she replied, "what is the suggestion?" I answered, "A son of Pastor and Mrs. Schneider, Paul Hermann, resides in California, and in the first half of April he and his wife will be visiting in our region. I believe that it would be most appropriate and impressive to have Paul Hermann read the excerpts." Enthusiastically, the director replied, "That's a wonderful suggestion, Professor Foster. How can I contact Paul Hermann Schneider?" I provided Paul Hermann's telephone number. "On second thought," the director said, "it probably would be more persuasive if you called Paul Hermann and invited him on my behalf." I made the call.

At first, Paul Hermann was reluctant to accept the invitation. "I'm not a public speaker," he said. "But Hermann (Paul Hermann usually is addressed with his second name)," I responded, "think of the opportunity to make your father's witness known to a large audience, and imagine the impact on the audience by the son's reading of the martyr's words." Finally, Paul Hermann agreed to accept the invitation. I selected the passages that were to be read and we agreed to meet at the museum on the day of the conference.

The director had prepared a very impressive program. Leading Catholic, Jewish and Protestant religious leaders presented challenging ideas. The spacious auditorium was filled to capacity. After each presentation, there was brief and polite applause. Finally, as the last speaker on the program, Paul Hermann took his place at the podium.

Not accustomed, as were the other speakers, to addressing large audiences, Paul Hermann was nervous, but after a short introduction of himself as the third of six children born to Pastor and Mrs. Schneider, his birthday being Saturday, December 6, 1930, he proceeded with deep emotion to read excerpts from his father's sermons and letters. Listening to the son read the words of his martyred father was a deeply moving experience. At the conclusion of the readings, the entire audience rose to its feet and applauded loud and long. There was an electricity in the air, an empathetic mood, and there were many tear-filled eyes. It was as if we wished to honor the father in the son.

Paul Hermann and his wife, Gundela, then traveled to West Chester where we were joined by Karl Adolf Schneider (Paul Hermann's younger brother) and his wife Ursula. On April 14, 1996, an ecumenical Memorial Service dedicated to the victims of Nazi brutality (1933-1945) was held at the Westminster Presbyterian Church. The Reverend Dr. Robert Young welcomed the congregation that filled the large sanctuary. The Westminster choir contributed to the service with exceptional musical and choral selections. Poems composed by children in the Nazi death camps were read by junior high school pupils. I presented a brief homily on three victims, one Jewish (Rozza Robota), one Roman Catholic (Saint Maximilian Maria Kolbe) and one Protestant (Pastor Paul Schneider). There was a reception, and lively conversations followed the memorial service. The Schneiders were hosted by families in the West Chester area. After visits to Philadelphia and Longwood Gardens, they departed for home.

In the course of the research conducted by Brother Jerome and me, I came across information concerning the founding of the Franciscan mission at Nagasaki in April 1930 and the subsequent building of the monastery, Mugensai no Sono in the spring of 1931. Brother Jerome told me that Brother Sergiusz (1907-2010) and Brother Gregory (1902-2003) had been summoned to Nagasaki in 1931. Brother Roman (1914-2014) had been called to Japan in 1934. Brother Jerome said that these three friars would be able to supply me with information concerning Saint Maximilian's tenure in Japan, 1930 to 1936. In September 1999, sixty-eight years after having arrived in Nagasaki, Brother Gregory returned to Niepokalanow. Brother Sergiusz, after having marked his 103rd birthday on July 14, 2010, died in Japan on December 16, 2010.

In March 1999, I flew from Philadelphia to Nagasaki. I had been in correspondence with Brother Sergiusz and with Mrs. Yukiko Matsuda for about one year. Yukiko had translated Brother Sergiusz's memoirs from Japanese into English and had sent me a copy. I accepted the invitation to visit Mugensai no Sono and to have ample opportunity to interview Brother Sergiusz, Brother Gregory and Brother Roman, and to become familiar with the monastery, built on a slope of Mount Hikosan. When I published the Saint Maximilian biography, *Mary's Knight: The Mission and Martyrdom of Saint Maksymilian Maria Kolbe*, in 2002, the Japanese chapter turned out to be the longest one.

One of the more impressive sights at Mugensai no Sono is the view from the monastery's "Lourdes." After climbing many steps up the side of the mountain, one comes to a plateau. At one end of the plateau, ranging skyward, is a rock face out of which a grotto has been hewn. In a recessed alcove and under the protection of a massive rock formation, stands a figure of the Virgin Mary. At the opposite side of the plateau, there is a clear view of the Ohato Port and the city of Nagasaki, a few miles distant. The many severe difficulties that confronted the Franciscans in general and Saint Maximilian in particular in Japan can be discerned from Saint Maximilian's letters, written during his residence in Nagasaki, 1930 to 1936.

My ten-day residence in Nagasaki afforded me daily contact with and instruction from my Franciscan hosts and especially from Yukiko, who guided me about Nagasaki and related the fascinating history of the city to me. Yukiko guided me through the museum dedicated to the victims of the atomic bomb attack on August 9, 1945. The exhibits provoked a somber and disturbing pathos in me. The attack killed 36,000 people, mostly civilians, and exposed thousands to radiation poison that would cause their death in the ensuing years. The beautiful

Mugensai no Sono - Nagasaki, Japan, March 1999

Catholic Cathedral in the center of Nagasaki was completely destroyed. Only the large clock, falling from its elevation, was intact, its hands pointing for all subsequent generations to note the time of the explosion—12:00 noon. Brother Francis, the Mugensai no Sono librarian and archivist, related his personal experience to me,

I was a child working in an underground munitions factory. At the sound of the explosion—not knowing the danger from radiation—we children hurried toward our respective homes. When I arrived at the location of my home, there were only deep ashes, no house and no sign of life. Frantically, I called for my widowed mother (my father had been killed in military action), but I received no answer. I searched the ashes.

Finally, I found a metal hair brooch that my mother wore. It was twisted out of shape. After hours of futile calls and searching, I joined a column of survivors headed for Mugensai no Sono. The monastery, situated on the slope of Mount Hikosan outside of the city, had not been destroyed. The Franciscans adopted me and I ultimately became a Franciscan friar.

Later, the world learned that in the August 6 attack on Hiroshima, 78,150 people were killed, 13,939 were missing and 9,284 were severely injured. Here in Nagasaki, 36,000 were killed and 40,000 were injured—many of whom subsequently died of radiation burns. I was moved by Brother Francis' account. The reaction of Carl Friedrich von Weizsäcker on hearing of the atomic attacks was sobering: "What the Americans have done is terrible. I consider it insanity."

Before my departure from Nagasaki, Yukiko invited Brother Sergiusz, Brother Roman and me to dinner in her home not far from the friary. Yukiko's gracious and generous hospitality and the friendly reception that I enjoyed at Mugensai no Sono made my visit to Nagasaki a most rewarding and informative experience. Yukiko and I continue to keep in touch with each other.

In 1999, in collaboration with Pia-Monika Nittke and her daughter, Elisabeth Heinemann, I published a volume of selected poems from the more than one hundred poems accumulated in my filing cabinet. While residing with my group in the Hospiz, I had met Monika. At that time, she was the piano accompanist for a baritone. Pianist and singer presented concerts in the Weimar Castle courtyard. During the concert series, Monika also had accommodations in the Hospiz. She invited me to visit her family. We remained in correspondence, and some years later, I accepted her invitation. Pia-Monika Nittke resides in Magdeburg and was, before her retirement, concert pianist in the Magdeburg Theater. Elisabeth Heinemann is a prize-winning photographer. *Poetic Allegories* contains 26 poems, each accompanied by a stunning photo by Elisabeth Heinemann. Each poem also is translated into the German language by Pia-Monika Nittke and, in addition, she transposed 6 of the poems into a musical score. These poems, set to music, were sung several times in the Magdeburg Theater by Roland Fenes, a well-known baritone.

Following persistently our routine of working together each summer at Niepokalanow, Brother Jerome and I completed the manuscript in July 2001. My Pastor Paul Schneider biography, "The Buchenwald Apostle," had been published in a German language edition in that same year. I had given Brother Jerome a copy of the book. He was very impressed with Pastor Schneider's bravery and faith. In a May 7, 2000 homily, presented in the Roman Colosseum, Pope John Paul II drew attention to Christian martyrs of the twentieth century. In referring to the twentieth-century Protestant witnesses to the Christian faith, the Pope named, as representative, Pastor Paul Schneider. Brother Jerome suggested that we send a copy of the German edition of the "The Buchenwald Apostle" to Pope John Paul II. "I'll write an accompanying letter in the Polish language," Brother Jerome said. At Niepokalanow, we received the following letter from the Vatican, dated July 6, 2001:

> Very Honorable Professor Foster,
>
> I gladly acknowledge reception of your esteemed letter of June 16, 2001 and of the book with your personal dedication.
>
> The Holy Father is indebted in sincere gratitude to you for your expression of concord.
>
> May your Paul Schneider biography point Christians in the 21st century onto the path of unity.
>
> Pope John Paul II happily includes your future endeavors and designs in his prayers and petitions for you, Frau Otterpohl, (the translator of the German language edition) and all who are near to you, the support of the Holy Spirit.
>
> > With best wishes
> > Monsignor Pedro Lopez Quintana

Brother Jerome and I read and re-read the letter several times. I shall never forget that mid-July evening in 2001 when I jubilantly announced to Brother Jerome that we had completed our manuscript. With red wine with which I kept Brother Jerome supplied, we toasted the fulfillment of our goal. Some years earlier, Brother Jerome told me that his physician had recommended that each evening before retiring, he drink a glass of red wine. Of course, Brother Jerome could not request the Niepokalanow Guardian to supply him with red wine when Niepokalanow is a tobacco- and alcohol- free friary. Therefore, during my summer residences at Niepokalanow, I purchased a supply of red wine for Brother Jerome, a supply that would serve him for a long time even after my return to the US. To justify the red wine indulgence for Brother Jerome, we invoked the rationale that Brothers Zeno, Hilary, Zygmund and Seweryn employed in March of 1930 on the transit through the Red Sea when a sand storm caused Father Maximilian respiratory problems: "Please Father drink some wine which we concealed in our backpack. In this severe case, you may regard the wine as medicine." Finally, Maximilian was persuaded. As Brother Jerome's eyes caressed the manuscript, he said, "This is my last work on earth. Now I can go to heaven." I replied, "Not yet, Brother Jerome. I want you to see the book when it is published." Brother Jerome answered, "I'll not be able to remain long enough to see the book, but I know what's in the manuscript and it's the best biography of our saint. I thank God that He permitted me to remain on earth to help you until our work was completed." Suffering from congestive heart failure, Brother Jerome was taken to a Warsaw hospital. Just before I had to depart to return to the US, I visited him. He was in good spirits and, after having received a pacemaker, seemed to have improved. As I would later learn, Brother Jerome was transferred to the Niepokalanow friary infirmary where, at 6:00 a.m. on Saturday, August 4, 2001, he departed this life.

Friends in Poznan and Teresin telephoned me to announce Brother Jerome's death. Because I was visiting my sister, Betty, who was seriously ill at her home in Lewes, Delaware, I did not receive the news of Brother Jerome's death until late Sunday evening when I checked the calls on my answering service. Because the funeral was scheduled for Tuesday, 11:00 a.m. on August 7, there was no possibility for me to attend. The airlines were booked and the one connection that I would have been able to reserve could not get me to Warsaw before Tuesday afternoon. I called my Polish friends and requested that they purchase flowers for me. My friends in Poznan, Maria Lewicka and her mother, Ursula Wachowska, as well as the Jarzabowski family in Teresin, represented me at Brother Jerome's funeral. I reflected on the timing of my meeting and working with Brother Jerome and the interviews that I was able to conduct with other friars to whom Brother Jerome introduced me—friars who had personally known and had worked with Saint Maximilian, and also the interviews that I conducted with Prince Jan Maria Drucki Lubecki and Franciszek Gajowniczek. The interview with Prince Jan Maria Drucki Lubecki took place at Niepokalanow in July 1990, just three weeks before the prince died. The interview with Franciszek Gajowniczek took place in West Chester in December 1990, five years before Franciszek Gajowniczek died on March 13, 1995. In 1999, I visited Brother Sergiusz Pęsiek and Brother Roman Kwiecien in Nagasaki. It was in the decade of the 1990s that the interviews with the Niepokalanow residents took place—each summer rehearsing with each friar and priest what earlier had been told to me, adding whatever information came to mind as the friars recalled from memory their close association with Saint Maximilian. Brother Juwentyn Maria Mlodozeniec was the first of my friar witnesses to die, on Sunday, July 27, 1997. Brother Pelagiusz Maria Poplawski died on Monday, December 18, 2000. Brother Jerome died on Saturday, August 4, 2001. Brother Grzegorz Maria Siry died on October 6, 2003. Brother Felicissimus Maria Sztyk died on March 21, 2005. Father Jerzy Domanski, who had suffered a stroke in 2002 that incapacitated him, died on Tuesday, August 28, 2007; Brother Ivo Maria Achtelik died on April 15, 2008. Brother Sergiusz Maria Pęsiek died in Japan on December 18, 2010 at 103 years of age. Brother Roman Maria Kwiecien, also in Japan, is 98 years old as of 2012. In brief, had I not met Brother Jerome when I did and interviewed his fellow Franciscans when I did, I could not have written the Saint Maximilian biography. This biography, so dependent upon the testimony of those who knew and worked with Saint Maximilian, and for whom I served as scribe, could not be written today. When the first English language edition of the book was published in the autumn of 2002, three of the key witnesses already had died.

After the manuscript was completed in July 2001, I began to seek a publisher in the US. I called several Catholic presses. The editors were interested in the biography, but they wanted a manuscript of no more than 450 pages. The manuscript that Brother Jerome and I had prepared was over 700 pages. When I mentioned to Brother Jerome in July 2001 that we might have to abridge the manuscript to find a publisher, he looked very sad and said, "Please don't do that. You would have to delete so many stories and anecdotes." I promised Brother Jerome that I would not abridge our work even if I had to publish the manuscript at my own expense, which I did. *Mary's Knight, The Mission and Martyrdom of Saint Maksymilian Maria Kolbe* was published by the West Chester University Press in the autumn of 2002.

In the summer of 2002, before returning to the US from Germany and Poland, I had visited Frau Margarete Schneider who resided with her daughter, Eva Marie Vorster, in Liederbach, near Frankfurt am Main. Frau Schneider was confined to bed and received nursing care. During my visit, Frau Schneider recognized me and responded with a smile when I showed her photos of my grandchildren. Frau Schneider went to her heavenly reward on December 27, 2002. I returned to Dickenschied for her funeral on January 4, 2003. January 4 was a bitter cold winter day. Strong winds drove snow showers across the cemetery campus. Because of the strong winds, I had to anchor firmly in the semi-frozen earth the wreath that the US members of the Pastor Paul Schneider Association had provided. As Frau Schneider's coffin was lowered into the grave next to her husband's burial site, we bade a fond farewell to this most extraordinary Christian witness. Margarete Schneider (1904-2002) had lived out her confirmation verse that her Father, Pastor Karl Dieterich had given his daughter, "Ye are the light of the world. A city that is set on a hill cannot be hid." (Matthew 5:14).

I reflected on the many hours, days and weeks Frau Schneider and I had spent together preparing the text of *The Buchenwald Apostle*, and I was very grateful that I had been privileged to serve as scribe in providing a permanent witness to Pastor Paul Schneider's courage and conviction in opposing Nazi tyranny. It struck me that two of the people who had made such an impact on my life shared, though in different years, the same birthday; Saint Maximilian Maria Kolbe, January 8, 1894, and Margarete Dieterich Schneider, January 8, 1904. Two other individuals who played a major role in my life, the Polish Franciscan friar, Brother Jerome Maria Wierzba and the French Protestant pastor, Aimé Bonifas, also shared the same birthday date in January, albeit not in the same year—Brother Jerome, January 26, 1912; Pastor Bonifas, January 26, 1920.

In July 2004, I participated in and was a speaker at the annual Pastor Paul Schneider Association Convention in Weimar. I also participated in the memorial service at Buchenwald marking the 65th anniversary of the martyrdom of Pastor Paul Schneider. While visiting friends in Poznan in late July 2004, one of my hostesses, Mrs. Ursula Wachowska, (deceased January 10, 2007) mother of my former student, Maria Lewicka, suggested to me that I should interview Lech Wałęsa. I laughed and said, "Yes I will call him on the phone and request an interview." "No," Mrs. Wachowska said, "I'll call him and make arrangements for you to interview him."

Mrs. Wachowska and her deceased husband, Eugene, had been Solidarity leaders in Poznan and were on intimate terms with Lech Wałęsa. Mrs. Wachowska dialed the number. Wałęsa's secretary answered. Mrs. Wachowska said, "This is Ursula Wachowska; please have Lech call me at his earliest convenience." One hour later the telephone rang. It was Lech Wałęsa. Mrs. Wachowska said, "Lech, we have a guest from the United States, a professor of history. I would like very much if you could welcome him for an interview concerning our Solidarity Movement." Then Mrs. Wachowska said, "July 30 at 11:00 a.m. in your Danzig office. Thank you, Lech. Our guest will come at that time."

And so it occurred that I was able to spend one hour with Lech Wałęsa in his office. His son translated for us. He explained to me that the Solidarity Movement gained great impetus by Pope John Paul II's visit to Poland in June 1979. He said, "After that papal visit and the Pope's encouragement, 'Don't be afraid,' membership in Solidarity increased by leaps and bounds, and finally the Communist government had to negotiate with us and to recognize our independent union. Up until our union's independence, the Communist Party had sought to divide our membership by offering crumbs from the state's abundant table. However, we remained united in our demand for full independence, for we had learned by bitter experience that a fragmented solution is no solution. Ultimately, it was Pope John Paul II, a son of Poland, who was the architect of our union's and of our nation's liberation."

In August 2004, through friends in Augustow, Poland, I made contact with Mrs. Marianna Popieluszko, the mother of Father Jerzy Popieluszko (1947-1984). We were invited to visit her in her Okopy village home not far from Augustow. Father Popieluszko had been a chaplain in the Solidarity Movement. His bold, spiritual leadership inspired the thousands who attended worship in his church, Saint Stanisław Kostka (1550-1568), named after the Jesuit Novice, and located in the Zoliborz section of Warsaw. Father Popieluszko was a large thorn in the side of the Polish Communist regime. Thousands attended the Masses he celebrated for the Polish Nation. His solidarity with the workers and his great reverence for Saint Maximilian Maria Kolbe, who had preached and demonstrated by his martyrdom at Auschwitz that spiritual freedom was possible in the midst of physical enslavement, made Father Popieluszko an intolerable dissident to the tyrannical Communist dictatorship. Several attempts to assassinate him had failed. Father Popieluszko's escape from one attempt on his life was considered by his congregation to be miraculous. Late at night, seated in his study in the parish house, just opposite his church, Father Popieluszko was reading. The would-be assassins, outside in the cover of darkness, seeing the priest in his chair, prepared to throw a bomb through the window. Just at that moment, however, Father Popieluszko decided that he would brew himself a cup of tea. He rose from his chair and went into the kitchen that was located next to his study. There was the sound of breaking glass. The bomb exploded in his study. The wall separating study from kitchen saved his life.

Finally, on October 19, 1984, he was abducted, tortured and murdered and his body was thrown into the Vistula River reservoir near Włocławek. The body was recovered on October 30, and the murderers, Captain Grzegorz Piotrowski, Leszek Pekala, Waldemar Chmielewski and Colonel Adam Petruszka, apprehended. They were members of the Polish Secret Police. Later, the assassins were released as part of an amnesty. On November 3, 1984, Father Popieluszko was buried in the courtyard of his church. The streets of suburban Warsaw could not contain the thousands of people (estimated at 250,000) who attended the funeral. When it became known that agents of the Polish Communist government had murdered a beloved and popular priest, and that the corpse bore marks of brutal torture, the Polish people were enraged and the Polish Communist Party lost all creditability. Father Popieluszko's murder marked the beginning of the end of the Communist control of Poland.

Today there is a museum housed in the Saint Stanisław Kostka Church. The exhibits depict the history of Solidarity and the ministry and martyrdom of Father Jerzy Popieluszko. In the summer of 2004, Mr. Karandyszowski (Barbara Wachowska Karandyszowska's father-in-law) drove me along the route from Bydgoszcz to Warsaw that Father Popieluszko was traveling on the night in which he was abducted. We stopped at the place on the Vistula River Reservoir near Włocławek where Father Popieluszko's body had been recovered. Earlier in the summer, Mrs. Popieluszko had told my hosts and me about Father Popieluszko's youth, his desire to be a priest and the discrimination to which he was subjected as an inducted recruit in the Polish army because of his desire to study for the priesthood. As a child, he was anxious to serve in the church in Suchowola, the city where church and school were located. Walking from his village of Okopy the 8 kilometers to church and school, winter and summer, did not diminish his zeal for piety and learning. Mrs. Marianna Popieluszko, through my Augustow hosts, who translated for me, then described the terrible shock and grief that overwhelmed her family at the news of Father Popieluszko's murder. The photos of the grieving parents at the bier of their dead son, against a background of teeming thousands of mourners, gripped with deepest empathy all who saw those photos. At the time of this 2004 interview, Mr. Popieluszko was deceased. Across from her old farmhouse residence on the only road through the Okopy village, in which house she and her husband had reared their children, Mrs. Marianna Popieluszko, in a small garden, had a memorial prayer station erected in memory of her son. There, before a framed photograph of Father Popieluszko, pilgrims may pause for prayer and to meditate on the sacrifice of this young priest—a martyr who had died in the quest for the liberation of his beloved homeland. In solemn reflection, we took our leave from Mrs. Marianna Popieluszko, the still grieving mother, and from the shrine in memory of her son in the little garden opposite her Okopy village home.

On the Feast of Corpus Christi, June 6, 2010, Father Jerzy Popieluszko was beatified by the Roman Catholic Church. As of June 2010, seventeen million people had visited his grave. There are more than eighty streets and squares in Poland named after the martyred priest. Hundreds of statues and memorial plaques have been unveiled, and more than eighteen hundred schools, clubs, charities and groups have been named after him.

During the visits to Niepokalanow, and, in some years, allowing for two visits in the same year, (the visits to the friary in March 2009 and again in November 2009, marking my 26th trip to the monastery), I made many friends and acquaintances. In the summer of 2004, while walking with a group of my countrymen for whom I was a guide, from the friary to Lasek (small woods), a retreat area for Niepokalanow friars and priests, I met a young woman, Katarzyna Pniak. I had not walked the one kilometer to Lasek in several years and at the intersection of two streets where I should have led my group left into the intersecting street, I continued on to the next intersection. At that point, I realized that I had made a mistake, and I retraced my steps, my countrymen following me like little goslings behind the mother goose, to the proper intersection. Just as we arrived at the intersection, a young woman with two children was crossing the street. She heard us speaking the English language and she inquired in the English language concerning our US homeland. "Where's your home? Why are you here? How do you like Poland?" We continued our conversation until we reached the Lasek chapel. I told the young woman about my Saint Maximilian Maria Kolbe biography that had been published in 2002. I also told her that I was looking for a person to translate the biography into the Polish language. "That's a project in which I would be interested," she said. "I'm not a professional translator, but I would very much like to see a copy of the English language text." We made a date for the next morning when she would meet me at the Niepokalanow guesthouse at which time and place I could show her a copy of the biography. Kasia (familiar for Katarzyna) registered surprise at the great size of the volume. I lent Kasia a copy of the book for her perusal and consideration. A few days later, she came to the guesthouse where I resided with my group and informed me that she would like to undertake the translation of the biography into the Polish language. Kasia said, "Out of great esteem for

Saint Maximilian, I wish to make the research, which you and Brother Jerome have conducted, known to my countrymen."

I sensed Kasia's great devotion to Saint Maximilian and I was convinced that she was The Chosen One to translate the biography. If I had not erred in going to Lasek, my group and I would have been ten minutes ahead of Kasia and her children. My error caused me to retrace my steps and to arrive at the intersection exactly at that moment when Kasia also arrived. It was as if our meeting was providential. At any rate, Kasia undertook the task and three years later Rycerz Maryi appeared in the Polish language. After seeing the English language edition of Mary's Knight, Father Marek Iwanski, director of the Niepokalanow Press, expressed interest in publishing Kasia's Polish language translation of the biography. Father Iwanski and Kasia agreed on a contract. Kasia and I kept in frequent contact with each other via email and telephone. When she needed a more complete explanation of the English text, I provided it. By consulting with friends who have an admirable command of the Polish language, we gave diligence to polishing the text. Aniela Czendlik, Lidia Bregula, Ursula Wachowska and her daughters, Maria Lewicka and Barbara Karandyszowska made helpful suggestions to improve the text. The Polish language manuscript also was read by some of the priests and friars at Niepokalanow.

In the summer of 2004, I was interviewed by Doug Keck on the Eternal Word Television Network (EWTN) program, Book Mark, the Roman Catholic network established by Mother Angelica in Alabama. For a period of thirty minutes, Director Keck presented questions concerning my research on and publication of Mary's Knight. Later, in sending me DVD copies of the interview, Director Keck wrote, "This is one of our better interviews."

On Thursday, June 21, 2007, I presented the Professor Albert Schweitzer letters, which Frau Giese had entrusted to me in October 1967, to Dr. Bettina Stier, director of the Albert Schweitzer Memorial Museum on the Kegelplatz in Weimar. On Friday, June 22, the Weimar newspapers published a photo of Dr. Stier and me before a statue of Dr. Schweitzer as I presented the letters.

The press reported,

> I heartily thank you for your precious and interesting gift. Here everything goes well, and the clinic never ceases to expand," Albert Schweitzer once wrote to the Weimar nurse, Elsbeth Giese. Frau Giese, who resided on the Ackerwand, entrusted to Professor Foster, shortly before her death in 1967, her correspondence with Dr. Schweitzer and his chief assistant, Mathilde Kottmann in Lambarene. The letters are informative and reveal that Mathilde Kottmann visited Frau Giese in Weimar. Yesterday Professor Foster presented the letters from Lambarene to the Albert Schweitzer Committee, assured that they now have found a secure home."

The Weimar Albert Schweitzer Museum is located not far from the Ilm Bridge and the bench where I first met Frau Giese, and only a short walk from where she resided. Before traveling to Weimar, I visited friends, Hermann and Rosi Hützen, in Freiburg, Germany. We made a day's excursion into Alsace and visited the Albert Schweitzer Museum in Günsbach. I presented a copy of these two Lambarene letters to the Günsbach museum.

In June 2007, the Polish language edition of Rycerz Maryi was published at Niepokalanow. Because I had traveled to Germany on June 10, I did not receive the email sent to my home computer announcing the publication of Rycerz Maryi. As I sat in the office of Father Iwanski on Monday, July 9, 2007, he went to the corner of the room and returned with a copy of the recently published biography. Because Father Iwanski earlier had written to me that the book might not become available until after the August vacation period, I was amazed to see the handsome, hardback volume that he handed to me. Just before I departed Niepokalanow, the Guardian, Father Stanislaw Piętka, requested me to autograph a copy of the biography that he planned to give to a bishop who was coming to the friary for a visit. I autographed the book. That afternoon, the Guardian was showing the bishop around the friary compound. The Guardian saw me walking toward the archives and he called to me, "Professor!" I went to see what he wanted. The Guardian introduced me to the bishop, whereupon the bishop hugged me and planted a firm kiss on my left cheek and then on my right cheek, all the time repeating the words "bardzo dziękuje. (Thank you very much).

In the same summer of 2007, I met Sister Antonella Di Piazza, who led a group of youthful Italian pilgrims to Niepokalanow. Sister Antonella requested me to speak to her group concerning the Saint Maximilian Kolbe biography that had just appeared in the Polish language. Sister Antonella invited Jim, Erik, Mark (my small group of three) and me to visit the Franciscan Retreat Center that she administered in Harmęze, near Auschwitz. With Brother Joseph as chauffeur and Beate Lang as interpreter, my group and I were driven on our tour of southern Poland in a Niepokalanow van. The highlight of our journey to Harmęze was our visit to the Auschwitz starvation bunker in which Father Kolbe died on August 14, 1941. In October 2007, I returned to Niepokalanow to participate in the ceremonies marking the 25th anniversary of Saint Maximilian's canonization. Sister Antonella Di Piazza came to the ceremonies as did Father Timothy Alkire from Lafayette, Indiana.

In March 2009, I was invited to participate in the annual Saint Maximilian Maria Kolbe Seminar convoked at Harmęze near Auschwitz. I presented a lecture based on themes in my Saint Maximilian Kolbe biography. Mrs. Lidia Bregula and Mrs. Irma Szott translated my remarks. At this seminar, I also met again Mrs. Aniela Czendlik who had provided great help preparing the Polish edition of Mary's Knight, Rycerz Maryi. In the summer of 2006, Aniela had traveled the great distance from her home in Cieszyn to Niepokalanow for this purpose. In October 2009, I was invited to return to Harmęze to participate in an Ecumenical Symposium. With the consent of Sister Antonella Di Piazza, the administrator of the Harmęze Kolbe Retreat Center, I invited Karl Adolf Schneider to present a lecture on his father, the Reverend Paul Schneider. I presented a lecture on Saint Maximilian. Karl Adolf was received with great hospitality. His lecture was very well received and I am convinced that, for the first time, a large Polish audience heard the Pastor Paul Schneider story. I presented a lecture on ecumenical aspects in the thought of Saint Maximilian. Mrs. Irma Szott translated for me. Mrs. Szott is a member of the Militia Immaculatae and frequently writes articles on religious topics. I found her to be an excellent collaborator.

In the summer of 2009, I once again resided for a period at Niepokalanow. I also made trips to Harmęze and visited many friends in Ozarow, Teresin and Poznan. It was during this sojourn at Niepokalanow that Sister Antonella Di Piazza, acting as agent for the Italian publisher, Edizioni Dell' Immacolata, offered me a contract for the publication of my Saint Maximilian Maria Kolbe biography in the Italian language. Early in 2010, the Italian publisher sent me a sample of the book jacket and a chapter of the book in the Italian translation. On Sunday, December 19, 2010, at the West Chester University Commencement, I received the award of "Emeritus" designation. In March 2011, the Edizioni Dell' Immacolata published my Maximilian Maria Kolbe biography in an Italian language edition: San Massimiliano Maria Kolbe: La Missione e il martirio.

Final Thoughts

In writing these memoirs, I pursued the prescription practiced by Emily Dickinson:

> The thought behind I strove to join
> unto the thought before,
> But sequence raveled out of reach
> like balls upon a floor.

As one looks back over one's life, one can reflect on the various paths that were available at the beginning of the pilgrimage. One path only, however, could be selected. In his novel, "Jolly Corner," Henry James entertains these thoughts with such expressions as: "Footfalls echo in the memory down the passage we did not take towards the doors we never opened." Thus, at the end of our life's journey, we cannot suppress our disquieting preoccupation with the thoughts of: "What might have been," "what if," "if only." There were broader paths, well traveled and well populated, which many in my life's entourage, no doubt, would have preferred I had taken. But that adventurous spirit, which inspired me as a child to build an incline to escape the confines of the backyard and thus gain access to the wider world, also dictated the choice of "the path less traveled by (Robert Frost), and that has made all the difference."

As my earthly pilgrimage draws to a close, another observation of Emily Dickinson impresses itself on my mind.

> Not what we did shall be the test
> When act and will are done,
> But what our Lord infers we would—
> Had we diviner been.

POSTSCRIPT

In November 2009, doctors diagnosed Claude with lymphoma. He received chemotherapy and continued to work when he felt strong enough. Two years later, he travelled to Europe in Summer 2011 where he visited old friends in Freiburg, Hattingen, Weimar, Berlin, and Saint Maximilian Kolbe's monastery in Niepokalanow.

Claude with Hermann Hützen in Freiburg, Germany, 2011

In late spring 2012, Claude received an invitation to speak about Saint Maximilian Kolbe in Italy. Due to family obligations, he could not attend. We decided to videotape his presentation with images and to send it to his friends in Italy. We did the videotaping at West Chester University on August 31, 2012.
https://www.youtube.com/watch?v=Yg-DYgTPo-o

Claude died exactly two weeks later.

Claude often commented on the connections that he made in Europe as well as how he connected American friends with European friends. I have friends in Germany and Poland because of Claude. When Claude retired from West Chester University in 2008, I began teaching some of the courses that he had taught. He often shared his memoirs with me as he was writing them. As he neared what he thought was the end of the memoirs, I offered to read them aloud with him. I read aloud, slowly, and he listened to what he had written. When he realized that his cancer might not allow him to finalize his memoirs, he asked me to see to their publication. He had decided on two types of volumes – one for family and friends that was comprehensive and a condensed volume for students. One week before Claude died, we were still working on condensing the memoirs. In 2014, I had West Chester University Press publish *Memoirs of an American in the Communist East Bloc*, sending copies to Claude's family members and friends in both the United States and in Europe. Claude tasked me with finishing what he could not and I have been proud to do so.

Brenda Gaydosh, 2019

CPSIA information can be obtained
at www.ICGtesting.com
Printed in the USA
LVHW082047080720
660121LV00004B/75

9 781948 210096